This book focuses on musical writings in the daily and periodical press in France during the nineteenth century. It covers the criticism of a wide range of Western music, from *c.* 1580 to 1880, explaining how composers such as Bach and Beethoven secured a permanent place in the repertory. In particular, Dr Ellis considers the music journalism of the *Revue et Gazette musicale de Paris*, the single most important specialist periodical of the mid nineteenth century, explaining how French music criticism was influenced by aesthetic and philosophical movements.

Dr Ellis analyses the process of canon formation, the development of French musicology and the increasing sensitivity of critics to questions of performance practice. Chapters on new music examine the conflict, inevitable in publishers' journals, between commercial interest and aesthetic integrity.

Music criticism in nineteenth-century France

Music criticism in nineteenth-century France

La Revue et Gazette musicale de Paris, 1834–80

Katharine Ellis

Royal Holloway
University of London

CAMBRIDGE
UNIVERSITY PRESS

Published by the Press Syndicate of the University of Cambridge
The Pitt Building, Trumpington Street, Cambridge CB2 1RP
40 West 20th Street, New York, NY 10011–4211, USA
10 Stamford Road, Oakleigh, Melbourne 3166, Australia

First published 1995

Printed in Great Britain at the University Press, Cambridge

A catalogue record for this book is available from the British Library

Library of Congress cataloguing in publication data

Ellis, Katharine.
Music criticism in nineteenth-century France: La revue et
gazette musicale de Paris / Katharine Ellis.
    p.   cm.
Includes bibliographical references and index.
ISBN 0 521 45443 3 (hardback)
1. Music – France – 19th century – History and criticism. 2. Music
criticism – France – 19th century. 3. Music – France – 19th century –
Philosophy and aesthetics. I. Gazette musicale de Paris.
II. Revue et gazette musicale de Paris.
ML270.4.E45   1995
780′.944′09034–dc20   94–35618   CIP   MN

ISBN 0 521 45443 3 hardback

CE

For my mother, with love

Contents

Acknowledgements

By their help, support, advice and criticism, many people have contributed to this book. Among those involved with its earlier incarnation as a doctoral thesis, John Warrack deserves particular thanks for unfailingly supportive supervision. I should also like to thank Bojan Bujić, whose interest in aesthetics and criticism sparked my own. Other scholars generously shared their ideas and their work: Elizabeth Bartlet, Peter Bloom, Matthias Brzoska, David Cairns, David Charlton, James Day, Donald Gíslason, D. Kern Holoman, Hugh Macdonald and Jim Samson kindly responded to requests for information, sometimes making available much of their own research. Other scholars' contributions arose from informal discussions: Nigel Bowles, Cyril Ehrlich, Liz Francis and Vincent Wright all helped sharpen the book's analytical focus. I am most grateful to my two anonymous readers for their incisive comments; they will doubtless recognise their influence.

Thanks are due to staff at the Bodleian Library's Music Reading Room and the Library of the Faculty of Music, University of Oxford. The former spent much time tracking down errant volumes of the *Gazette*, the latter allowed me extended access to materials. In Paris, the Archives nationales staff deserve special thanks for arranging for me to work at the Centre des archives contemporaines, Fontainebleau, during its Easter closed period in 1990. I should also like to acknowledge the Comte de Paris, M. Yann Uguen and M. Rémy Corpechot, who gave authorisations to consult restricted archival documents.

This project could not have been undertaken without the financial assistance of several funding bodies and academic institutions. I should like to thank the British Academy, University College, Oxford, the Faculty of Music, University of Oxford, St Anne's College, Oxford, and the Open University, all of which provided generous financial support. In addition, the moral and intellectual support of colleagues, particularly those at St Anne's College and the Open University, has benefited me greatly.

Penny Souster and Julia Harding at Cambridge University Press have shown unfailing patience and goodwill; my sincere thanks go to them. Finally, for his encouragement, criticism and endless supply of tea beside the word processor, Nigel Bowles has earned more thanks than I can give.

Charlbury
February 1995

Abbreviations

AN	Archives nationales, Paris
BN	Bibliothèque nationale, Paris
CAM	*La Correspondance des amateurs musiciens*
FM	*La France musicale*
GM	*Gazette musicale de Paris*
JD	*Journal des débats*
JE	*Journal de l'Empire*
JM	*Journal de musique* (1876–82)
MM	*Le Monde musical*
QSP	*Les Quatre saisons du Parnasse*
RGM	*Revue et Gazette musicale de Paris*
RM	*Revue musicale* (1827–35 and 1839)
TP	*Les Tablettes de Polymnie*

Introduction

This book is a history of musical culture in nineteenth-century Paris as revealed by some of its most prominent music critics. As such it has three interrelated aspects: a study of music criticism *per se*, a reception history of composers whose music was regularly performed in nineteenth-century Paris, and a study of the philosophical ideas which permeated musical thought and which are implicit in critical judgements of the period. Its cultural milieu is primarily that of the literate (and, in addition, musically literate) élite – the readership addressed in the pages of the *Revue et Gazette musicale de Paris*. It can, therefore, represent no more than a thin slice of history. Yet within this slice lie the foundations of many twentieth-century assumptions about Western art music, its conventions and the relative merits of its composers. The *Revue et Gazette musicale de Paris*, founded by the publisher Maurice Schlesinger in 1834 as the *Gazette musicale* and bought, along with his publishing house, by Louis Brandus in 1846, was the most important and influential music journal in France until its closure at the end of December 1880.[1]

[1] Maurice Schlesinger (1797–1871), Louis Brandus (1816–87). In November 1835 Schlesinger took over the *Revue musicale* of François-Joseph Fétis (1784–1871). The merger resulted in the new (and ungrammatical) title *La Revue et Gazette musicale de Paris*, though contemporaries, including Fétis himself, almost universally persisted in referring to it simply as the *Gazette*. The journal's readership was small by the standards of daily newspapers: in 1836, official figures from the Administration de l'Enregistrement et des Domaines set the print run of the *Journal des débats* (the most popular daily paper that year) at an average of 10,008 per day; by contrast, the government-run *Moniteur universel* had an average daily print run of 2,417; the *Gazette* and *Le Ménestrel* averaged 600 copies per issue (AN, Paris, BB[17] A 99/14). This latter figure is extrapolated from the government figures, which give hypothetical daily *tirage* figures for all periodicals. Figures for 1846 from the same source show that *Le Siècle*, the then most popular daily paper, printed 41,500 copies daily in February of that year (the *Journal des débats*, now much less popular, printed only 9,821 per day); *La France musicale*, a weekly rival to the *Gazette*, was by far the most popular music journal with 1,662 copies per issue for the same month; the *Gazette* printed 875 copies, *Le Monde musical* 765 copies and *Le Ménestrel*, 500 (AN, Paris, BB[17] A 145/1). These figures do not necessarily reflect the number of readers. By paying a token entry fee, members of the public could read the latest issues of newspapers and periodicals in a *cabinet de lecture*, of which Paris saw nearly 500 established between 1815 and 1830; such reading rooms were still thriving in

As a document of nearly half a century of musical thought it is unsurpassed; only *Le Ménestrel*, produced by the Heugel publishing house, equalled it in breadth. From the 1860s the two journals, both published weekly, vied with each other in quality and scope; after the *Gazette*'s closure, *Le Ménestrel* took its place as France's most prestigious music journal.

In its forty-seven years, the *Gazette* accepted contributions from over 130 writers, many of whom became regular columnists.[2] Their work spanned all aspects of French musical life: opera and concert reviews, the mainstay of the journal, were supplemented with regular historical essays (encompassing music as early as the Medieval period), source studies, composer biographies and articles on music theory, acoustics, organology and topical subjects. Other contributions, some in the form of short stories, focused directly on philosophical debates or on the relationship of music to other arts. The journal's correspondence section provided a forum for debate among readers, and a news section featured reports from foreign correspondents. Space permitting, the journal advertised its publisher's music and accepted advertisements from other businesses.

Specialist music periodicals such as the *Gazette* or *Le Ménestrel* reached a limited audience. Yet, unlike newspapers and many less prestigious periodicals, they were not viewed as a disposable source of information, either by their producers or their consumers. Annual indexes of the *Gazette* and detailed annual tables of contents in *Le Ménestrel* indicate their character as publications to be collected and consulted. That contributors frequently referred to articles printed in earlier issues of the *Gazette* illustrates its status, even in its own time, as an important source of opinion and information on musical culture, both historical and contemporary. This book's purpose is to explain the significance of the journal's criticism for our understanding of musical culture and thought in nineteenth-century France. The *Gazette*'s scope was considerably wider than can be adequately conveyed here. The decision to concentrate on its criticism, rather than to treat the entire span of its interests in a more general manner, draws the focus away from historiography (and, indeed, a history of the journal itself) and

the 1880s, though they were at their height in the middle of the century. Some *cabinets* offered lending facilities; many were also bookshops. For a detailed study of *cabinets de lecture* during the Restoration, see Françoise Parent-Lardeur, *Lire à Paris au temps de Balzac. Les cabinets de lecture à Paris: 1815–1830* (Paris, 1981). Newspapers and periodicals were also available in cafés, restaurants and reading circles; in 1856, the *Gazette* printed a list of 88 public places in which readers would have access to a copy (*RGM* XXIII/19: 11 May 1856, 155).

[2] See Appendix 1.

towards a reception history of particular composers and genres. However, the journal's critics, their opinions, and the ramifications of those opinions, remain central.

Depending on the writer concerned, criticism in nineteenth-century France was capable of degenerating into personal spite and polemic (whether against composers or performers) or aspiring to educate public taste. The use of numerous contributors to cover a wide range of subject matter has important implications both for the character of the *Gazette* itself and for indicating an appropriate strategy with which to interpret that character. The *Gazette*'s directors had to balance two opposing forces: the wish for the journal to be a forum for musical discussion, in order to give it credibility as a serious and objective intellectual enterprise; and the need for solidarity of critical approach, particularly in the service of house composers such as Meyerbeer and Halévy, for whose works the *Gazette* was a vehicle. To what extent such solidarity was imposed upon contributors by an editorial board, the chief editor, or the publishing-house director, will be impossible to establish as long as the Schlesinger archive is closed to researchers. However, glimpses of editorial authority can be caught in occasional footnoted disclaimers to a contributor's work, or gleaned from the silences of critics who are named as contributors but whose known views on specific composers conflict with those of the journal. Such concerns are less important in interpreting the work of critics who discussed music written before the death of Schubert. Some of the *Gazette*'s most important critical work concerned music whose reputation had to be made in retrospect: by supporting the work of specialist performers of Classical and earlier music and printing defences of composers from different epochs, the journal encouraged the public to free itself from a thirst for accessible novelty. In this respect the *Gazette* proved itself a worthy successor to its original rival, the *Revue musicale*, and was instrumental in the campaign to establish an aesthetic of reception which would allow works actively to outlive their creator. Although Maurice Schlesinger published Beethoven's music, the journal's early saturation with impassioned articles promoting the understanding of his genius was not mere advertisement, but an expression of artistic allegiance and an employment of the discipline of music criticism for educative (and evangelistic) purposes to ensure the posterity of certain works. Processes of canon formation are thus revealed through the writings of the *Gazette*'s critics.

The musical canon has two dimensions: firstly, the practical dimension of performance and repertoire; secondly, that of a governing aesthetic by which the value of specific items of repertoire may be judged. The rise of the musical canon was intimately linked with that of public concerts and their middle-class audiences in the later eighteenth century; its rise also depended upon a fundamental change in philosophical ideas about the nature and potential of music – in particular, autonomous music. Judged by the yardstick of *mimesis* for much of the eighteenth century, autonomous music fared badly in comparison with other, clearly representational, arts, the character and effect of whose imitation of nature was more readily comprehended. The first writers to argue that music's goal was not the imitation of nature were a (still) obscure pamphletist – Boyé – and Michel Paul Gui de Chabanon,[3] writing in 1779 and 1785 respectively. Despite his rejection of *mimesis*, Boyé, however, did little to advance music's cause. His rather mocking contribution to musical aesthetics placed dance music at the top of the hierarchy of musical genres by virtue of its 'effet', which exceeded that of other genres.[4] By allying music's appeal to the ear with that of perfume, fireworks or a banquet to their respective senses, and denying it any appeal to the imagination, he placed it squarely among life's pleasurable luxuries.[5] Summing up his argument, he noted that recitative – the kind of music most susceptible to expression – was also the most boring, and that although music might on occasion be memorable, it could never be 'pittoresque'.[6] Chabanon, writing six years later, argued that music was indeed an expressive art, but restricted its potential in this regard to four broad musical characters, each defined by melody independently of harmony – the tender, the gracious, the gay, and the lively, strong and loud.[7] Such attempts to liberate music from the imitation principle were far-reaching in the long term; however, having dismissed the idea of *mimesis*, neither Boyé nor Chabanon filled the lacuna with a theory of expression which went beyond establishing that music's function was simply to please the ear. Their work gave it no loftier rationale than an 'art décoratif'. As such, music could inspire neither reflection nor respect and was, implicitly, denied the status enjoyed by other arts, such as painting, whose historical traditions were both publicly accessible and a source of national cultural pride. A comparison of two Revolutionary institutions founded in the 1790s illustrates the disjunction between the status of the visual arts and that of music in the eyes of the French State at the end of the eighteenth century.

---

[3] See Boyé (first name(s) unknown), *L'Expression musicale mise au rang des chimères* (Paris and Amsterdam, 1779), and Michel Paul Gui de Chabanon, *De la musique considérée en elle-même et dans ses rapports avec la parole, les langues, la poésie et le théâtre* (Paris, 1785).

[4] Boyé, *L'Expression*, 28.

[5] *Ibid.*, 24.

[6] *Ibid.*, 39–40.

[7] Chabanon, *De la musique*, 145.

In the summer of 1793, after forty years of complaints (not least from Diderot) that the royal art collections were kept hidden from the people, the Louvre palace was opened to the public; two years later the Paris Conservatoire was officially founded (it had existed on an informal basis since 1790). The Conservatoire's establishment in 1795 might have been expected to signal a realignment of music in parallel with its sister arts; however, with its roots in the Revolution's need for military music for public festivals and in its first official incarnation as the Ecole de Musique de la Garde Nationale (1792), the new institution served only to reinforce the predominant image of music as a contemporary art lacking an historical dimension of any importance. The Louvre collection, full of historical treasures (later enriched by Napoleon), was matched in status only by the most prestigious opera houses – the Opéra and Opéra-Comique – whose repertoires contained few historical works, and for whose personnel the Conservatoire provided a training which included no historical study. An art which appealed only to the senses was exceptionally vulnerable to changes in taste; of necessity, its producers discarded outmoded styles in a continuing search for novelty. The legacy of late eighteenth-century philosophies of music in France was to leave music as the last of the fine arts to be perceived as having a heritage worthy of preservation or revival – the result being a musical culture based largely on contemporary ephemera, particularly in opera.

For music to be freed from a paradigm in which it was merely decorative and ephemeral, two conditions were essential: firstly, the belief that its character was emotive or morally grounded (rather than merely sensual); secondly, that music perceived as beautiful in its own time continued to be so. In France, the first of these battles was largely won by the beginning of the nineteenth century, coinciding (significantly) with the French discovery of, and increasing fascination for, Mozart. The second condition, upon which the existence of a musical canon depended equally, required an historical perspective which could assess the beauty of a work by the standards of its original system of production, pass retrospective judgement, and adopt it as contemporary culture. A work's 'contemporaneity' – defined by its public acceptance as repertoire – was essential to its status as canonic, but its canonicity was argued and defended by practitioners of two new disciplines: musicology and music criticism.[8] In the absence of the term 'canon', the words 'classic', 'model' and 'masterpiece' were, throughout the nineteenth century, conferred upon music which had achieved, or was deemed worthy of achieving,

---

[8] See Joseph Kerman, 'A Few Canonic Variations', *Critical Inquiry* 10 (September 1983), 112, and William Weber, 'The Eighteenth-Century Origins of the Musical Canon', *Journal of the Royal Musical Association* 114/1 (1989), 6.

canonic status. Such terminology was derived from that of other arts, whose masterpieces (and their right to be claimed as masterpieces) the French had recognised long before.

Professional and public reappraisal of early works and public debates about the merits of new repertoire distinguish ideas of canon in nineteenth-century France from long-standing respect for tradition, a feature of the reception of music in academia (the use of 'models' for teaching purposes) and in the liturgy. The value of historical teaching models lay not in their right to be part of a living tradition, but in their exemplary status as representatives of past styles; they were, therefore, not necessarily a part of contemporary culture. Tradition, so important in conferring status on sacred works, had no place in the formation of a canon, which consistently demanded the (re-)appraisal of sacred works by secular standards. As late as 1869 the première of Rossini's *Petite messe solennelle* took place not in a church, but in the Théâtre Italien; *Messiah* and the *St Matthew Passion* became canonic in France only in the 1870s, after repeated concert performances given under the direction of Charles Lamoureux. The process could also work in reverse: in 1846 the critic **Maurice Bourges**[9] recognised the canonic status of Mozart's Requiem whilst decrying it as a convincing piece of sacred music. Exclusive domains such as the Church were, therefore, not those of the canon, which was essentially a secular (or a secularising) phenomenon involving performers, critics/musicologists and the public as arbiters. Moreover, the element of public debate was distinct from that of the pamphleteering supporters of Gluck or Piccinni because the object was not current dominance, but posterity.

In nineteenth-century France, the overtly secular nature of canon formation reached to the heart of mercantile Paris. The ever-present tensions between commercialism and aesthetic judgement in the music publishers' periodical press (which began in the 1830s) are well illustrated by the reception of contemporary composers, particularly those who worked in the potentially lucrative genres of opera and piano music. Once dead, a composer was more likely to be accorded a considered judgement untainted by commercial interest: the critical and public reception of Beethoven in France shows the process from wary acceptance to lionising. Historical figures present the process of canon formation in a third light: in music composed before around 1780, the relationship between traditions of respect, current repertoire and musicological study is complex, and provides the aesthetic foundation for the emergence of the canon itself. The latter part of this book concentrates on the *Gazette*'s reception of music in these three broad

[9] Persons marked in bold appear in Appendix 2.

chronological categories, and explains the motivation behind biased appreciations of certain composers.

The founding of the *Gazette musicale* was part of a sudden expansion of the musical press in the 1830s, triggered in part by the success and example of Fétis's *Revue*, which first appeared in 1827. Earlier attempts to set up a specialist musical press were sporadic and mostly short-lived (though no less important from the historian's point of view). With the criticism of **Julien-Louis Geoffroy** (who reviewed opera as part of his theatre criticism for the *Journal des débats*), reviews in early nineteenth-century music journals formed the basis from which professionals such as Castil-Blaze (1784–1857), F.-J. Fétis and Berlioz developed music criticism into an educative discipline which was to guide public opinion. In order to understand the character and importance of the *Gazette*, the nature of its ancestry and milieu requires explanation.

1 Crosscurrents in early nineteenth-century criticism

The first three decades of the nineteenth century saw music criticism change from a discipline dominated by literary critics to one presided over by trained musicians addressing their readers in technical language; in the fourth decade, Romanticism's penchant for a fusion of the arts brought writers back into the music critic's domain, producing some of the most imaginative and original criticism of the entire century. This book's first two chapters focus on newspapers and periodicals in which important critical traditions (of both message and medium) were established and modified. They do not offer a comprehensive survey of critical opinion up to 1834; rather, they address philosophical and practical issues in early music criticism, provide a set of reference points by which to assess the *Gazette*'s importance, and illuminate the reception of particular composers and schools of composition. Chapter 1 concentrates on four sources of criticism: Julien-Louis Geoffroy's column in the *Journal des débats*, 1800–14, the *Correspondance des amateurs musiciens*, 1802–5, the *Tablettes de Polymnie*, 1810–11, and Castil-Blaze's criticism for the *Journal des débats*, 1820–32.

Julien-Louis Geoffroy

It is one of the paradoxes of the history of music criticism in France that the discipline should have gained its first major impetus through the work of a literary critic who 'insisted on talking about music for his entire career, despite understanding hardly a single note of it'.[1] Before Julien-Louis Geoffroy's appointment as theatre critic at the *Journal des débats* early in 1800, music criticism had, indeed, appeared in daily newspapers, specialist journals such as the short-lived *Sentiment d'un harmonophile* of 1756 or the sporadic and ill-fated *Journal de musique* (1770–1, 1773–4, 1777), or in general philosophical and cultural journals

---

[1] 's'est obstiné toute sa carrière à parler de musique sans en connaître à peu près une seule note', Jean Mongrédien: *La Musique en France des Lumières au Romantisme (1789–1830)* (Paris, 1986), 201.

such as *La Décade* (1794–1807).[2] Yet it fell short of the critical mass necessary to arouse public interest to the extent of creating public demand. By contrast, Geoffroy, whose theatre *feuilleton* appeared regularly from February 1800 until February 1814, was able to create and sustain the interest of the paper's readers.[3] Geoffroy wrote about every aspect of theatrical life in Paris, from Classical drama at the Académie française to the humblest vaudeville show. The vast majority of his articles concerned spoken theatre, and it was from a literary, and musically conservative, standpoint that he approached the criticism of opera. He judged libretti as plays (rather than as texts for musical setting) and frequently emphasised the need for the music to take a secondary role in the partnership, since if it drew too much attention to itself it could only weaken the force of the drama. In a late review of *Iphigénie en Tauride* he stated this idea at its starkest: 'Music enfeebles and degrades every genre to which it is joined: a grand opera is no more a tragedy than an opéra-comique is a comedy' (*JE* 10 Jul. 1812, 2).[4]

Geoffroy was a dilettante who, in the course of writing about a subject of which he knew very little, adopted a breadth of focus which embraced many of the musical issues of his time, and prefigured more.[5] Unable to write knowledgeably about music itself, he concentrated on larger philosophical questions concerning its nature and importance. He viewed music as among the 'arts décoratifs', occupying a modest place characteristic in eighteenth-century thought: slightly higher than dance in a hierarchy presided over by poetry. His favourite means of condemning music was to refer to it as a mere distraction, judged not by the soul, but only by the ear.[6] It was the most fickle of the arts, the longevity of

---

[2] The extent and utility of such eighteenth-century sources has only recently been explored systematically with reference to particular composers. See David Charlton, 'Cherubini: A Critical Anthology, 1788–1801', *Research Chronicle*, 26 (1993), 95–127, and Belinda Cannone, *La Réception des opéras de Mozart dans la presse parisienne (1793–1829)* (Paris, 1991). A general study is provided in Shelagh Aitken, 'Music and the Popular Press: Music Criticism in Paris during the First Empire' (unpublished PhD dissertation, Northwestern University, 1987).

[3] From 16 July 1805 / 27 messidor an 13 to 31 March 1814 the *Journal des débats* was retitled the *Journal de l'Empire*; thereafter it reverted to its previous title.

[4] 'La musique affoiblit et dégrade tous les genres auxquels on la marie: un grand opéra n'est plus une tragédie qu'un opéra comique n'est une comédie' (*JE* 10 Jul. 1812, 2). Archaic forms and orthographical idiosyncrasies have been preserved in all quotations.

[5] I use 'dilettante' in the pejorative sense, though Geoffroy would have welcomed the appellation as indicating that he belonged to that category of listeners whose intuitive understanding of music was unhampered by technical knowledge and whom he thus considered to be uniquely qualified for the task of judging music objectively and usefully. Cf. his comments in *JD* 23 messidor an 10 / 12 Jul. 1802, 3), quoted in Aitken, 'Music and the Popular Press', 130.

[6] Review of Rousseau's *Le Devin du village* (*JD* 16 thermidor an 11 / 4 Aug. 1803).

specific works dictated by changes in fashion and their composers quick to respond stylistically to the vagaries of public taste. Music was also, along with dance, an art which could easily be manipulated by the State in the service of a showcase genre, that of grand opera.[7] Thus he saw music and the majority of its composers as lacking the dignity of artistic autonomy. Few composers roused Geoffroy to genuine enthusiasm – there is an air of disparagement in much of his work[8] – but composers who did were often those in whom he could detect artistic conviction adhered to despite opposition.[9]

Geoffroy's inspiration as a writer on music was Rousseau, to whose Italophile aesthetic of the 'natural' and the 'simple' he referred frequently in operatic reviews (especially those of opéra-comique), and whose writings he was apt to quote.[10] Yet his beliefs that Italian opera had sold its dramatic soul to melody and that the French style sacrificed melody to both drama and text prompted him to seek operatic salvation in composers in whom he could detect a balance between extremes of national style – the very qualities which he found in Rousseau's Le Devin du village:

It is the mid-way between Italian and French music: the melodic style is simple, natural and uncomplicated; the harmony well-suited to the melody; the balance between the words and the music is perfect. (JD 16 thermidor an 11/4 Aug. 1803, 2)[11]

It was on the basis that Mozart represented a retreat from the 'false brilliance' (JD 4 fructidor an 9/22 Aug. 1801, 4)[12] of the Italian style that Geoffroy was able to participate in the almost unanimous delight that greeted Les Mystères d'Isis, adapted from Die Zauberflöte and given at

---

[7] Review of Grétry's La Caravane du Caire (JD 6 fructidor an 10/24 Oct. 1802).
[8] This is particularly true of his reviews of Grétry, whom he regarded as a very good second-rate composer distressingly prone to over-ambition. See, for example, his review of La Caravane du Caire (JD 6 fructidor an 10/24 Oct. 1802).
[9] The roots of this attitude lie in Geoffroy's experience as a Royalist in exile from Paris. His outspoken Parisian writings resulted in persecution by other journalists; throughout his later career he was extremely sensitive to cases of artistic persecution, identifying with the victim. This partly explains his adulation of Sacchini, who is portrayed as a hero and neglected genius, and (despite his antipathy to his music) his respect for Gluck. See his reviews of Gluck's Armide (JD 12 messidor an 10/1 Jul. 1802) and Sacchini's Arvire et Evelina (JE 29 Jan. 1811).
[10] His review of Pergolesi's Stabat mater (JD 20 germinal an 12/10 Apr. 1804) quotes extensively from Rousseau's Lettre sur la musique française as corroboration of his opinion.
[11] 'C'est le moyen terme entre la musique italienne et la musique française: la mélodie est simple, naturelle et facile; l'harmonie bien mariée avec la mélodie; l'accord est parfait entre les paroles et la musique' (JD 16 thermidor an 11/4 Aug. 1803, 2).
[12] 'de faux brillians' (JD 4 fructidor an 9/22 Aug. 1801, 4).

the Opéra in 1801.[13] Geoffroy wholeheartedly welcomed the work and saw it as symbolic of opera's regeneration by a German who knew the proper relationship between melody and accompaniment. However, Geoffroy helped set in motion the French canonisation of a composer whose music generally surpassed the limits of his musical taste. In 1805, among the critics of *Don Juan* in the daily press Geoffroy alone held out against Mozart's dramatic music; applying the same criteria as in 1801, he found the opera too complicated and Germanic, and (predictably) attributed its success to a passing fashion aimed at the composer's deification (*JE* 19–20 Sep 1805). When, by the time of the production of *Don Giovanni* at the Théâtre de l'Impératrice in 1811, the Mozart fashion had still not passed, Geoffroy hardened his position of 1805 and became increasingly sarcastic, his opinion even further removed from that of his contemporaries.[14]

A second candidate for the regeneration of opera in Geoffroy's eyes was Sacchini, who represented a synthesis of Gluck's dramatic power and Piccinni's lyricism:

There came a man of genius superior to that of Gluck and Piccinni: for a long time he studied the ground; he observed that Gluck was too French, Piccinni too Italian; that the former was too concerned with the drama at the expense of the music, and that the latter, giving everything to the music, neglected the drama. After a few attempts at striking a good balance between the two genres, Sacchini found the middle way in *Œdipe à Colonne*. He resolved the problem which consists in allying the dramatic interest with the musical effect; in reconciling the delights of the spirit and the heart with the pleasure of the senses. He gave Europe a new spectacle, in letting her watch a touching tragedy clothed in delicious melody. (*JD* 10 brumaire an 13/1 Nov. 1804, 3)[15]

In his review of *Œdipe à Colonne*, Geoffroy distinguishes between 'the delights of the spirit' (afforded by the drama) and 'the pleasure of the senses' (the domain of music). This is consistent with his general theory

---

13 For studies of the early reception of *Les Mystères d'Isis*, see Cannone, *La Réception*, 53–72 and 149–97, and Jean Mongrédien, '*Les Mystères d'Isis* (1801) and Reflections on Mozart from the Parisian Press at the Beginning of the Nineteenth Century', *Music in the Classic Period. Essays in Honor of Barry S. Brook*, ed. Allan W. Atlas (New York, 1985), 195–211.

14 See especially his review of 15 October 1811, quoted in Cannone, *La Réception*, 306–8.

15 'Un homme vint ensuite avec un génie supérieur à celui de Gluck et de Piccini; il étudia long-temps le terrain; il observa que Gluck étoit trop français, Piccini trop italien; que le premier s'occupait trop de la scène au préjudice de la musique, et que le second donnant tout à la musique, oublioit trop la scène. Après quelques essais pour former un heureux accord entre les deux genres, Sacchini rencontra le juste milieu dans *Œdipe à Colonne*. Il résolut le problème qui consiste à joindre l'intérêt dramatique avec l'effet musical; à concilier les jouissances de l'esprit et du cœur avec le plaisir des sens: il donna un spectacle nouveau à l'Europe, en lui faisant voir une tragédie touchante, revêtue d'une mélodie délicieuse' (*JD* 10 brumaire an 13 / 1 Nov. 1804, 3).

of the function of music as a purveyor of lower, purely sensual, pleasures. Geoffroy supported the arguments, first promulgated by Boyé and Chabanon, against music as *mimesis*,[16] but usually set limits on the strength of passion which music was capable of reflecting truthfully. His wish for the heights of dramatic tension to be 'clothed in delicious melody' rather than in Gluck's expressive declamation was judged adversely by an unsigned writer for *Les Quatre saisons du Parnasse*, after Geoffroy complained in a review of *Iphigénie en Aulide* that the climaxes of Clytemnestra's rôle reached beyond music into animal cries, thereby sacrificing beauty to realism (*JE* 17 thermidor an 13/5 Aug. 1805, 3). The *Quatre saisons* critic argued that it was music's task to reflect the states of the soul and that in extreme circumstances the principle of musical beauty should be abandoned in the name of drama:

From where, then, does the anonymous writer wish the musician to take the bases of his art, if it is not in the relation of sounds with the soul? Does he want music to be merely an insignificant song whose only goal is to amuse the ear for a while? I consent to this only if music is not called an art, and that it is given, at most, the title of trade. (unsigned, *QSP* Automne 1805, 291–2)[17]

This was exactly the place Geoffroy assigned to music, at least in theory. His moments of inconsistency, however, pushed him closer to Romantic theories of music's high status among the arts than he would have wished to recognise. At its extreme, Geoffroy's love of Sacchini's music threatened to undermine his entire philosophy of the arts. Of the end of Arvire's Act II aria in *Arvire et Evelina* he wrote: '[it] is wrenchingly expressive. It is in such pieces that music rises to the level of poetry'. (*JE* 29 Jan. 1811, 1)[18]

The natural corollary of Geoffroy's predominant view of music, combined with his notion that the public and the State virtually conspired to maintain the status of music as fashion, would have been for him to argue that music intrinsically lacked the potential for longevity and canonicity. However, Geoffroy's attitude to early music suggests otherwise, and his defence of Pergolesi's *La serva padrona* as 'a classic'

---

[16] See Geoffroy's reviews of Haydn's *The Seasons*, in which he explicitly states that music's strength is in expressing emotion rather than depicting nature (*JD* 27 germinal an 10/17 Apr. 1802, 2, and *JE* 19 Apr. 1811, 4).

[17] 'Où l'anonyme veut-il donc que le musicien prenne les bases de son art, si ce n'est pas dans le rapport des sons avec l'ame? veut-il que la musique ne soit qu'un ramage insignifiant qui n'a d'autre but que d'amuser un instant l'oreille? j'y consens, pourvu qu'elle ne s'appelle point un art, et qu'on lui donne tout au plus le titre de métier' (unsigned, *QSP* Automne 1805, 291–2). *Les Quatre saisons du Parnasse* (1805–9) was a quarterly arts journal which contained occasional opera reviews.

[18] 'est d'une expression déchirante. C'est dans de pareils morceaux que la musique s'élève à la hauteur de la poésie' (*JE* 29 Jan. 1811, 1).

and 'a model of taste, of naturalness, of melody and expression ... a yardstick for all composers working in the comic genre', speaks of an entirely different aesthetic (*JD* 19 frimaire an 10/11 Dec. 1801, 2),[19] as do his complaints that early music, by the use of inferior casts and low-budget productions, was unjustly neglected in performance.[20] Geoffroy's attitude arose partly from pique, since with the exception of Le Sueur, his favoured composers all belonged to previous generations. Yet his arguments are not those of a prejudiced reactionary; moreover, they often prefigure debates which did not arise with force until a generation later. In a review of Pergolesi's *Stabat mater* he penetrated to the very heart of the problem of resurrecting early music:

One of the main reasons why we now leave older works in profound oblivion is that it is impossible to grasp and communicate the spirit of these masterpieces. (*JD* 20 germinal an 12/10 Apr. 1804, 2)[21]

He made a similar point in a later review of Egidio Duni's *La Fée Urgèle* (1765), indicating that the performance of such works demanded a degree of effort which few were willing to bestow upon them:

The music of *La Fée Urgèle* is charming and contributed greatly to its success; but it is now very difficult to preserve, in singing it, the spirit and the taste in which it was composed: it is easier to disparage this music than to perform it well. (*JE* 18 Nov. 1807, 3)[22]

Geoffroy thus implies two things: first, that it would be beneficial for certain works to be respected and kept in the repertory, and second, that the maintaining of older performance traditions is a precondition for the future success of early music. In such discussions of the work of Duni and Pergolesi he is talking not only about repertoire, but, with words such as 'classic', 'model' and 'masterpiece', about canon. Though Geoffroy claimed to subscribe to a particular aesthetic of dramatic and choral music, in practice, his taste was the final arbiter; his importance as

---

19 'un ouvrage classique ... un modèle de goût, de naturel, de mélodie et d'expression ... la règle de tous les compositeurs qui travaillent dans le genre comique' (review of Paisiello *La serva padrona*, *JD* 19 frimaire an 10/11 Dec. 1801, 2). The review consistently compares Paisiello's version unfavourably with that of Pergolesi.

20 Review of Rousseau's *Le Devin du village* (*JD* 16 thermidor, an 11/4 Aug. 1803). Here, Geoffroy argued against the prevailing contemporaneity of operatic culture in France, and lamented the absence of support (among public and performers alike) for early music.

21 'Une des causes principales de l'oubli profond où on laisse aujourd'hui les anciennes compositions musicales, c'est l'impossibilité de saisir et de rendre l'esprit de ces chefs-d'œuvre' (*JD* 20 germinal an 12/10 Apr. 1804, 2).

22 'La musique de la *Fée Urgèle* est charmante, et contribua beaucoup à son succès; mais il est aujourd'hui très difficile de conserver, en la chantant, l'esprit et le goût dans lequel elle a été composée: il est plus aisé de dédaigner cette musique que de la bien exécuter' (*JE* 18 Nov. 1807, 3).

a music critic lies in the fact that his few objects of enthusiasm were justified by an appeal to arguments which were to become dominant later in the century.

With writings such as these, Geoffroy reached a readership of around 10,000 subscribers – far more than a specialised journal could hope to attract. Nevertheless, two specialist publications made major contributions to music criticism during Geoffroy's reign in the daily press, and place his opinions in perspective. The first, the *Correspondance des amateurs musiciens*, was produced between 1802 and 1805 by *citoyen* **Cocatrix**. A lacuna in the musical press from 1805 was eventually filled in 1810–11 by the *Tablettes de Polymnie*, edited by the singing teacher and composer Alexis de Garaudé (1779–1852) and Giuseppe Maria Cambini (1746–1825), his former composition teacher. Of the two publications, the latter has generated more attention, largely due to its tone (by turns intemperate and dogmatic) and De Garaudé's celebrated judgement of Beethoven as 'containing doves and crocodiles together' (*TP* II/20: 20 Mar. 1811, 311).[23] The former publication, despite its title's implications of non-professional status, was the more serious, and, of its type, relatively successful.[24]

La Correspondance des amateurs musiciens

Whilst Geoffroy wrote little criticism of autonomous music (giving every impression that he lacked strategies with which to approach it), Cocatrix's prospectus of 1802 embraced all aspects of musical life in Paris. First, he proposed a series of organological studies accompanied by critiques of the various tutors and methods available for each instrument treated; second, he proposed regular reviews of sheet music suitable for amateur players, with a numerical system for grading their difficulty; third, he promised occasionally to print pieces of music suitable for domestic use. Among the supplementary goals of the journal he included the provision of advertising space for instruments for sale, tuition, and orchestral vacancies. Seventh and last among his supplementary goals was the reviewing of opera and concert performances. During the journal's first year Cocatrix kept largely to his self-imposed brief; by its second, the journal was becoming oriented more towards concert reviews and historical articles on selected (mostly eighteenth-century)

[23] 'renfermer ensemble des colombes et des crocodilles' (*TP* II/20: 20 Mar. 1811, 311).
[24] The *Correspondance* began with twice-weekly publication; early in its second year, the editor promised a third edition each week once the subscription rate had reached 500 (II/8: 18 Jan. 1804/27 nivôse an 12), col. 41. The third edition each week never materialised; nevertheless, Cocatrix's proposal suggests that his number of subscribers made such a proposal a serious possibility.

composers. Opera received scant attention until the journal's final year, 1805.

The journal's reviews ranged widely, in that they were concerned not only with aesthetic issues but also with aspects of performance style. They centred around three orchestral concert societies: the student concerts (*exercices*) at the Conservatoire, the Concerts des Amateurs at the rue Cléry, and the Concerts Grenelle.[25] Reviews of the Concerts Cléry and the Concerts Grenelle (the latter often signed 'P.P.') were written by different contributors but show significant points of contact.[26] Of these, the two most important concern Haydn's supremacy as a symphonist, and the exceptional reverence accorded Mozart. Since many of the Cléry orchestra were former members of the disbanded Loge Olympique orchestra it is no surprise to find them adjudged as unrivalled in their performances of Haydn. The reviewer for the Concerts Cléry generally took little notice of the music itself; by contrast, in his reviews of the Concerts Grenelle, 'P.P.' emphasised the particular merits of Haydn's music and the unique responsibility which its greatness laid at the door of its performers:

I am of the opinion that the performance of Haydn's symphonies is not a vain orchestral amusement; that works so profoundly conceived need to be felt and expressed with a degree of energy equal to that which gave birth to them. (*CAM* II/1: 1 Jan. 1804 / 10 nivôse an 12, col. 5)[27]

The tone of this response to Symphony no. 103 is one of respect; 'P.P.' attempts to refute a commonly held view of instrumental music, and to give it a higher aesthetic value. The key phrase is his reference to 'vain orchestral amusement', which is aimed at those critics, such as Geoffroy and Cambini, who resisted the notion that untexted music could amount to more than an idle distraction. The following month, Cambini wrote a (rare) article for the *Correspondance*. Its opening section set out his view of instrumental music:

When music does not excite or calm the passions, it should at least hold our attention, to console us and distract us from melancholy and sombre ideas, engendered all too often by the vicissitudes and irritations of public life. Instrumental music, deprived of poetry's aid, seems destined to reach only the latter goal. But to reach this far, it must be well composed and well performed.

---

[25] The three concert societies are discussed in Boris Schwarz, *French Instrumental Music between the Revolutions (1789–1830)* (New York, 1987), 21–34.

[26] The likeliest identity for 'P.P.' is Pierre Porro, whose signed writings for the *Tablettes de Polymnie* share many of the characteristics of 'P.P.''s reviews for the *Correspondance*.

[27] 'je me persuade que l'exécution des symphonies de Haydn n'est pas un vain amusement d'orchestre; que des ouvrages si profondément conçus ont besoin d'être sentis et exprimés avec le même degré d'énergie qui les enfanta' (*CAM* II/1: 1 Jan. 1804 / 10 nivôse an 12, col. 5).

Haydn's symphonies are proof of my argument; nobody has heard them without experiencing some kind of fairly strong emotion to make him forget his moral suffering. (*CAM* II/18: 29 Feb. 1804/9 ventôse an 12, col. 137)[28]

In opposition to Cambini's view of instrumental music as a panacea, the journal's regular writers embraced the idea of autonomous music as containing expressive potential, and argued for it to be perceived as having a higher goal than that implied by an aesthetic of music as the imitation of nature or as a merely sensual pleasure. This is implicit in the journal's response to Haydn, but emerges explicitly in an article signed 'L.F.' entitled 'Sur l'expression musicale'.[29] The importance of this article lies not so much in the quality of its argument (which is weak) as in its character as an apologia for autonomous and texted music as expressive media. In the third and final instalment, the writer attempted to find a place for music outside the theory of imitation to which he felt all the fine arts were still unreasonably made to submit. His discussion of vocal music gave music and poetry distinct rôles. Of poetry, he stated:

Essentially, what it expresses through words is ideas; moreover it details images and recounts feelings. Only music expresses the lively affections of the soul. (*CAM* II/63: 4 Aug. 1804/16 thermidor an 12, col. 501)[30]

Such a separation of the appropriate realms of music and poetry is of great significance as a precursor of Romantic, and specifically, German Romantic, thought on music's expressive potential in French music criticism. After refusing to judge music as a failure by the standards of *mimesis*, the author posits an alternative theory in which music and text enjoy a complementary relationship, with the elaboration of details of meaning left to poetry and the expression of pure emotion to the realm of music. The writer talks of words 'recounting' ('raconter') feelings, but music 'expressing' ('exprimer') emotions. Music can thus be judged on its own terms, its unspecificity of meaning no longer viewed as an impediment to elevated status as an art form. 'L.F.' thus dismisses ideas

---

[28] 'Lorsque la musique n'excite ou ne calme pas les passions, elle doit au moins captiver assez notre attention, pour nous consoler et nous distraire des idées mélancoliques et sombres, trop souvent engendrées par les vicissitudes et les contrariétés qu'on éprouve dans la vie sociale. La musique instrumentale, privée du secours de la poésie, paroît destinée à n'atteindre que ce dernier but. Mais pour y parvenir, il faut qu'elle soit bien composée et bien exécutée; les symphonies d'Haydn sont une preuve de ce que j'avance; personne ne les a entendues sans éprouver une espèce d'émotion assez forte pour lui faire oublier ses souffrances morales' (*CAM* II/18: 29 Feb. 1804/9 ventôse an 12, col. 137).

[29] *CAM* II/59–63: 21 Jul. 1804/2 thermidor an 12 – 4 Aug. 1804/16 thermidor an 12. The identity of 'L.F.' is unknown.

[30] 'Ce qu'elle exprime par des mots, ce sont essentiellement des idées; du reste elle détaille des images et raconte des sentimens. La musique seule exprime les vives affections de l'âme' (*CAM* II/63: 4 Aug. 1804/16 thermidor an 12, col. 501).

of music as either materialist (the depiction/imitation of *mimesis*) or sensationalist (appealing only to the senses), and prepares the ground for later critics, such as Fétis, to argue the idealist case for music in France.

'P.P.''s reviews of Haydn employed different tactics to convince the *Correspondance*'s readers of the value of his instrumental music. He conferred on Haydn the status of genius. For him, the symphonies merited attention on three grounds: their construction, their ability to stimulate the imagination, and (in consequence) the importance of doing them justice in performance. 'P.P.''s appeal to the imagination is of considerable importance, since it offers new possibilities for the criticism of autonomous music, and raises its status in the artistic hierarchy. In an extraordinarily advanced critique of the 'London' Symphony, he gave his imagination free rein in a portrait of the opening Adagio, which conjured up images of:

unfortunates who seem to beg the gods for clemency; at last their wailings touch them, and the brilliant Allegro, in the major, which follows, like an angel of consolation, changes this scene of pain and sadness into a merry festival. (*CAM* II/13: 11 Feb. 1804/21 pluviôse an 12, col. 98)[31]

'P.P.' remarked that the Andante was a little too Romantic in style, but still found it grand and sublime. His stance is thus Janus-like, for his response to the symphony presages an important characteristic of Romantic criticism in its belief in the utility of a direct appeal to the emotions and its attempt to communicate the expressive force of the music with a narrative structure running parallel to that perceived in sound. The strategy, which is both novel and adventurous, aims to broaden the minds of a readership accustomed to regarding autonomous music as devoid of meaning and therefore inferior to texted music. 'P.P.' invests the symphony with meaning by supplying a narrative suggested to him by the music itself and by which it may be followed by the listener. By giving the music a drama of its own he implicitly sets it on a par with texted music.[32] In the coming decades, the impetus of E.T.A. Hoffmann's aesthetic of autonomous music as the most Romantic of the arts, and the example of his criticism, would provide the springboard for German and French critics (Schumann and Berlioz in particular) to develop 'creative

---

[31] 'des malheureux qui semblent implorer la clémence des dieux; leurs gémissemens les touchent enfin, et le brillant allégro, majeur, qui suit, comme un ange de consolation, change cette scène de douleurs et de peines en une fête riante' (*CAM* II/13: 11 Feb. 1804/21 pluviôse an 12, col. 98).

[32] This interpretation of the 'narrative' criticism of autonomous music has been propounded by Katherine Kolb Reeve. See 'Rhetoric and Reason in French Music Criticism of the 1830s', in *Music in Paris in the Eighteen-Thirties*, ed. Peter Bloom (Stuyvesant, 1987), 543. However, Reeve sees narrative critiques of autonomous music as a phenomenon of 1830s Romanticism, whereas its roots lie considerably earlier.

criticism', in which the emotional ebb and flow of music's utterances was re-created in narrative prose. 'P.P.''s response to Haydn marks the beginnings of one of the characteristic traditions of nineteenth-century criticism, its proximity to those traditions clarified by a comparison with Berlioz's critique of the Allegretto (which he invariably referred to as the Andante) of Beethoven's Seventh Symphony in 1838:

incompatible rhythms grate painfully against each other; these are tears, sobs, supplications; it is the expression of limitless grief and overwhelming suffering. . . But a glimmer of hope has just appeared: to these agonising accents there succeeds a vaporous melody, pure, simple, soft, sad and resigned, *like patience smiling at grief.* Only the basses continue their inexorable rhythm beneath this rainbow of melody. (*RGM* V/6: 11 Feb. 1838, 65)[33]

Berlioz's running commentary to a less extreme change of mood is more analytical than 'P.P.''s, but shares its use of narrative and metaphorical prose.

A narrative thread was not 'P.P.''s only weapon against the arguments of such as Cambini. An unsigned review of the 'Military' Symphony (for which 'P.P.' indicates authorship ten days later) provides an apologia for the intrinsic merit of Haydn's style. This symphony

needs to be heard, listened to, thought about several times before it can be judged in a considered manner. He is a master so profound, this Haydn, that stones turn to diamonds in his hands. Beware; his motifs will, at first, seem ordinary, familiar, maybe even outworn. You are mistaken; the creating genius who prepares them, and the purified taste which directs them, will soon prove to you that you are hearing them for the first time. He is a Proteus, truly a magician. (unsigned, *CAM* II/2: 4 Jan. 1804 / 13 nivôse an 12, col. 13)[34]

In exhorting the public to listen carefully to Haydn's music and to study it carefully before judging it, 'P.P.' again prefigures arguments of the later nineteenth century by which composers perceived as difficult were defended on the grounds that the finest music did not give up its secrets immediately. His view, however, is not that Haydn's music is difficult, but that its complexity is concealed by its accessibility. As such, he proposes

[33] 'des rythmes inconciliables s'agitent péniblement les uns contre les autres; ce sont des pleurs, des sanglots, des supplications; c'est l'expression d'une douleur sans bornes, d'une souffrance dévorante. . . Mais une lueur d'espoir vient de naître: à ces accents déchirants succède une vaporeuse mélodie, pure, simple, douce, triste et résignée *comme la patience souriant à la douleur.* Les basses seuls continuent leur inexorable rythme sous cet arc-en-ciel mélodieux' (*RGM* V/6: 11 Feb. 1838, 65).

[34] 'a besoin d'être entendue, écoutée, méditée plusieurs fois avant d'en porter un jugement motivé. C'est un maître si profond, cet Haydn, qu'avec lui les pierres se changent en diamans. Prenez-y garde; ses motifs paroîtront d'abord ordinaires, connus, usés peut-être. Erreur; le génie créateur qui les prépare, et le goût épuré qui les conduit, vous prouveront bientôt que vous les entendez pour la première fois. C'est un Prothée, un véritable magicien' (unsigned, *CAM* II/2: 4 Jan. 1804 / 13 nivôse an 12, col. 13).

an aesthetic of genius concealing art, a notion which gained considerable impetus in the writings of François-Joseph Fétis twenty years later.

By 1805, repetition of a small number of Haydn's symphonies each season threatened to petrify the repertoire; in the *Correspondance* the sense of stagnation was emphasised by the reviewer noting that in the season's six performances not a single symphony by Mozart had been played at the Concerts des Amateurs.[35] That this should have been considered important is indicative of Mozart's spectacular rise to prominence, initiated in 1793 with a production of *Figaro* at the Opéra, but given its major momentum by the adaptation of *Die Zauberflöte* which appeared as *Les Mystères d'Isis* in 1801. Despite the excitement caused by *Les Mystères*, it was not in the sphere of dramatic music that Mozart seems first to have achieved status equal to that of Haydn as a symphonist, but in that of sacred music. In the *Correspondance*, Mozart's Requiem was the subject of an unsigned essay of 1804 which attempted explicitly to educate the journal's readers.[36] Unique for its time both in its intention and in its multi-instalment analysis of a single work, the essay was presented as a music review of the full score published by Breitkopf and Härtel. Copies were advertised as being available for purchase at the journal's office, and indeed the article's detail was such that for any conscientious reader a copy was almost essential, particularly given the absence of music examples in the text. The article was prepared in advance and published to coincide with the French première by performers from the Conservatoire under Cherubini in December 1804.[37] From the outset, there is no attempt to conceal a sense of evangelism; the Requiem is among those distinguished works which 'broaden the domain of the art and deserve to pass into posterity'(*CAM* II/89: 3 Nov. 1804 / 12 brumaire an 13, col. 708).[38] Analysis of the score is presented as a legitimate activity which separates those who view music as 'a frivolous amusement' (*ibid.*, col. 709)[39] from those whose interest is serious. The descriptive analysis which follows is aimed exclusively at a literate and technically informed readership.

Further evidence of Mozart's status is occasioned in 1805 by the first Paris production of *Don Giovanni*, adapted by **Christian Kalkbrenner** and given in French at the Opéra with its leading tenor, **Lainez**, in the title rôle.[40] It is unfortunate indeed that the *Correspondance* ceased publica-

---

[35] Unsigned, *CAM* III/13: 30 Mar. 1805 / 9 germinal an 13, col. 100.
[36] Unsigned, 'Analyse', *CAM* II/89–98: 3 Nov. 1804 / 12 brumaire an 13 – 29 Dec. 1804 / 8 nivôse an 13.
[37] *CAM* II/89: 3 Nov. 1804 / 12 brumaire an 13, col. 708.
[38] 'aggrandissent le domaine de l'art, et méritent de passer à la postérité' (*ibid.*).
[39] 'un amusement frivole' (*ibid.*, col. 709).
[40] For a detailed discussion of this production, see Aitken, 'Music and the Popular Press', 216–81. Reviews in leading journals are printed in Cannone, *La Réception*, 211–67.

tion before the first night of this production, since the author of a preview took the unusual step of condemning the project on the grounds that Mozart's score would be mutilated. The complete notice runs as follows:

> Paris. Ever since *Don Juan* was announced at the Opéra, music lovers who know the score of this work have been wondering which actor will take the part of Don Juan; they will doubtless be surprised to learn that this rôle, written for a baritone, will be *sung* by M. Lainez. Moreover, the fears which we demonstrated regarding the manner in which Mozart's masterpiece will be rendered, have been given further cause; the principal rôle will undoubtedly be mutilated, the arias will probably be transposed, certain notes which are too low for the singer will be taken out and substituted with others, or if there is no change the vocal line will be inaudible, which will certainly be the first time that M. Lainez has not made himself heard. Thus it is that we make the finest works fail; *quod Deus omen avertat.* (unsigned, *CAM* III/6: 9 Feb. 1805 / 20 pluviôse an 13, col. 46–7)[41]

Such concerns were new among French critics. Although the adaptation of *Les Mystères* in 1801 had drawn adverse comment, this was largely confined to Germans who knew the original and were anxious to disabuse the French.[42] By 1805 Mozart's status was vastly enhanced and his work better known; as part of the process of canonisation, with such status came respect for his works as he conceived them. The ensuing tension between preserving the integrity of a canonic foreign composer's artwork and bowing to the demands of French theatrical tradition, dogged Francophone productions of Mozart, Gluck and Weber for the entire century.

The *Correspondance*'s openness to German music extended to Beethoven, though his music featured only rarely in the journal. An unsigned music review of the Violin Sonatas Op. 30 is the journal's only

---

[41] '*Paris.* Depuis que *Dom-Juan* est annoncée à l'Opéra, les amateurs, qui connoissent la partition de cet ouvrage, se demandent quel est l'acteur qui fera le personnage de Dom-Juan; ils seront sans doute étonnés d'apprendre que ce rôle, qui est écrit pour une basse-taille, sera *chanté* par M. Lainez. Aussi, les craintes que nous avons manifestées sur la manière dont le chef-d'œuvre de Mozart seroit rendu, ont un motif de plus; le rôle principal sera sans doute mutilé, les airs seront probablement transposés, on ôtera telle ou telle note qui se trouvera trop grave pour le chanteur, pour lui en substituer un autre, ou si on ne la change pas, on n'entendra plus le chant, et ce seroit assurément la première fois que M. Lainez ne se feroit pas entendre. C'est ainsi qu'on fait tomber les meilleures ouvrages; *quod Deus omen avertat*' (unsigned, *CAM* III/6: 9 Feb. 1805/20 pluviôse an 13, col. 46–7). The italics for 'chanté' are original, a sarcastic reference to the problem of 'hurlement' at the Opéra, where the auditorium was so large and the orchestral writing for new operas so prominent that singers were forced to project beyond what many critics deemed acceptable. Castil-Blaze complained of a similar phenomenon as late as 1821 in the *Journal des débats*. See Donald G. Gíslason, 'Castil-Blaze, *De l'opéra en France* and the Feuilletons of the *Journal des Débats* (1820–1832)' (unpublished PhD dissertation, University of British Columbia, 1992), 182–3.

[42] See Mongrédien, '*Les Mystères*', 204–7.

article devoted exclusively to his music (*CAM* II/46: 6 Jun. 1804/17 prairial an 12). The reviewer, who actually reviews only the A major Sonata of the set, is disappointed – not because he finds the music too complex, but because it lacks the elevation and originality of other, unspecified works. In all three sonatas the reviewer detects 'only rarely this original and sublime composer whose name they bear' (*ibid., col.* 364).[43] The reviewer's conclusion is unusual; the process by which he reaches it is even more so, since his premise is that Beethoven's artistic and creative superiority over mere critics is such that an adverse judgement on his music should be offered with considerable trepidation. Defined thus, the critic's primary function is not to judge from above, but to strive, from a humbler position, to understand the products of genius. It is significant that the first composer to inspire such thoughts on the nature of the critic's position was Beethoven.[44]

Les Tablettes de Polymnie

On its closure in April 1805 the *Correspondance* had no rival or successor. The publication at the beginning of 1810 of the *Tablettes de Polymnie* was the next attempt at a specialist journal – this time, of an Italophile persuasion.[45] The major weakness of De Garaudé and Cambini's criticism was its unthinking partiality; in the pages of the *Tablettes*, Italian operatic ideals of transparency and simplicity were espoused to the exclusion of all else. Both Spontini (viewed as French) and Méhul received their most bruising reviews here, whilst any composer who dared to use counterpoint or Germanic richnesses of harmony risked being outlawed entirely. Of the attacks on Spontini and Méhul, the journal's reviews of *La Vestale* and *Joseph* in 1810 were particularly savage, the latter provoking Gossec's celebrated letter to the editors demanding to be taken off the journal's list of subscribers (though he kept the offending issue of the journal as a curiosity).[46] Several tactics

---

43 'très-rarement ce compositeur original et sublime dont elles portent le nom' (*CAM* II/46: 6 Jun. 1804/17 prairial an 12, col. 364).

44 Along with the *Correspondance des amateurs musiciens, La Décade* contains important early Beethoven criticism which helps counter the argument, proposed by James Johnson in 'Beethoven and the Birth of Romantic Musical Experience in France', *Nineteenth-Century Music* XV/1 (Summer 1991), 23–35, that Beethoven was received adversely in France in the first decade of the nineteenth century. See also Schwarz, *French Instrumental Music*, 30–1.

45 Ten numbers appeared monthly from January 1810; thereafter the journal appeared twice monthly.

46 The letter is quoted in Arthur Pougin, 'Notes sur la presse musicale en France', *L'Encyclopédie de la musique et dictionnaire du Conservatoire*, ed. Lavignac and De la Laurencie. 11 vols. (Paris, 1920–31), pt II, vol. 6, 3846.

recur: each composer is chastised for writing orchestral parts which cover the voice, or which are in themselves too complicated; vocal lines which lack the clarity of regular phrasing and singable contours are highlighted and their distance from Italian models discussed; thirdly, harmonic originality, which is perceived principally as a German phenomenon, is stamped upon and denounced in technical language. So it is that the critic 'C***' (probably Cambini) accuses Spontini of using a 'strange Beethovenian modulation' at the words 'la Vierge impure est bannie à jamais' in the Act I Vestal hymn of Spontini's opera (*TP* I/[6]: Jun. 1810, 12).[47] The editors of the *Tablettes* regarded Beethoven as the ultimate pernicious influence in matters of harmony; he was to the Italian camp of 1810 what Wagner became to the conservative camp of the 1850s. An aside in a review by 'A.M.' of Méhul's Fourth Symphony (played at a Conservatoire *exercice*) made clear the unpleasant implications of his contact with the new German style:[48]

The surprising success of Beethoven's compositions is a dangerous example for the art of music. The contagion of Teutonic harmony seems to be gaining ground in the modern school of composition which is forming at the Conservatoire. (*TP* I/[3]: Mar. 1810, 9)[49]

In 1810, Méhul's *Joseph* was awarded the Institut's prestigious decennial prize for the best opéra-comique, and a celebratory performance was duly arranged at the Théâtre Feydeau. In the notorious *Tablettes* review, which Pougin attributed to Cambini,[50] Méhul became the victim of a multi-pronged attack which illustrated most of the journal's enduring hobbyhorses. First came the accusation of scholasticism in the form of an overture which sacrificed the evocation of local colour to motivic interest; 'Thus the listener is disoriented; he thought he was in the fields of Chaldea or Memphis, but finds himself at the Conservatoire!' (*TP* I/[7]: Jul. 1810, 5)[51] Secondly, in the ensemble for Jacob's sons in Act I, Cambini found harmonic progressions not sanctioned by the Italian school. Thirdly, he drew attention to the unwonted prominence of the orchestra in the main body of the opera. The orchestral detail accompanying Benjamin's *couplets* in Act II provoked a suggestion of how the passage could be reworked

47   'étrange modulation à la Béthowen' (*TP* I/[6]: Jun. 1810, 12).
48   The identity of 'A.M.' is unknown. He was the least polemic of the critics who regularly reviewed for the *Tablettes*.
49   'L'étonnant succès des compositions de Bethoowen [sic] est d'un exemple dangereux pour l'art musical. La contagion d'une harmonie tudesque semble gagner l'école moderne de composition qui se forme au Conservatoire' (*TP* I/[3]: Mar. 1810, 9).
50   Pougin: 'Notes', 3846.
51   'Alors, l'auditeur est dépaysé; il pensoit être dans les champs de la Chaldée ou de Memphis, il se retrouve au Conservatoire!' (*TP* I/[7]: Jul. 1810, 5).

according to Italian principles, leaving the voice unencumbered by motivic interest in the strings (*ibid.*, 8). Fourthly, Cambini claimed that much of the libretto was set to dramatically inappropriate or, at best, dramatically all-purpose, music – what he termed '[musique] de facture'. Above all, Cambini aimed to demonstrate that the music was written to a system of composition iniquitous to opera. The word 'système' was used to refer both to Méhul's supposed technique of making the orchestra the principal character (*ibid.*, 7), and to those passages which he thought formed a mismatch with the action. The entire review was gratuitously barbed, though not, unfortunately for Méhul, without flashes of wit. The single traditionally French operatic ideal to which the writers of the journal subscribed, hinted at by Cambini in his review of *Joseph*, was that of dramatic appropriateness in the music. To the extent that this was perceived as absent in *Joseph* it appeared abundant in the work of Cherubini, who was seen to ally it with an equally appropriate division of labour between the voices and the orchestra; the unsigned review of *Les Deux journées* published in August 1810 forms a photographic positive to the negative of the Méhul review, complimenting Cherubini in almost sycophantic tone but saying very little about the music itself. The journal's reception of Cherubini reveals how, with the exception of Spontini, its bias extended as much towards Italian musicians as to Italian music. Although Cherubini was Méhul's colleague at the Conservatoire, in the *Tablettes* he was presented as sharing none of Méhul's learned stylistic features, and was conveniently dissociated from all criticisms of composition teaching at the Conservatoire.

It is a measure of their security as canonic figures that Haydn and Mozart were the only composers to receive critical attention which nearly transcended polemics of national style in the *Tablettes*. Among operatic composers, only Mozart merited hints that his work attained the level of 'masterpiece'. In November 1810, when the Opera Buffa mounted *Figaro*, the journal responded positively. The unsigned author (whose style and outlook have much in common with 'A.M.') gave not a descriptive analysis of the work but a critique of the performance and an appreciation of Mozart's position in French musical life. Gone are the petty sarcasms and the factional polemics of reviews of newer operas, whether Italian or French. The author leaves the reader to infer that the quality of this music is, by contrast, uncontentious. At the outset he refers to it as a 'chef d'œuvre'; later, when he discusses the Countess's second aria, which had been borrowed from Mayr, his choice of words is revealing: 'This latter aria is the only foreign [piece] which they dared to introduce into Mozart's domains' (*TP* I/11: 5 Nov.

1810, 168).[52] From this it might be expected that the author would hold Mozart up as a model to be emulated by those working in the French tradition. Instead, he argued that those who attempted such emulation of Mozart did so at their peril.

Mozart is (after Haydn) pre-eminent among all the great composers; but the richnesses of his school are so many seductive snares for whoever might wish to imitate him without possessing his genius. (*ibid.*, [169])[53]

To members of the Italian camp, Mozart was thus *sui generis*; admired, but viewed as too original to be a reliable model. The author cited above presented much of the new French operatic style as a misguided attempt to naturalise Mozart, resulting in overburdened orchestration and lack of dramatic appropriateness.

The journal's writers also held Mozart in high regard as an orchestral composer, though he was not spared their animus against what they saw as contrapuntal virtuosity for its own sake. Complaining about the fugue in the finale of the 'Jupiter', the critic 'A.M.', who was responsible for most concert reviews in the journal, began a tradition which lasted well into the latter half of the century. Here, though, the main thrust of his complaint is that the sheer complexity of the music prevents the ordinary listener from comprehending it immediately:

The four-subject fugue which ends this symphony is understood by only a very small minority of connoisseurs; however, the public, which wants to pass itself off as such, applauds all the more frantically for understanding absolutely nothing. (*TP* I/[5]: May 1810, 13)[54]

The perception that an audience responds to a work on cue rather than by making an independent judgement says much for Mozart's position and finds an analogue in the reception of Beethoven later in the century.[55] The

---

52 'Ce dernier air est le seul étranger qu'on ait ôsé introduire dans les domaines de *Mozart*' (unsigned, *TP* (I/11: 5 Nov. 1810), 168. The aria in question was 'Sento mancarmi l'anima'.

53 '*Mozart* est (après *Haydn*) le premier de tous les grands compositeurs; mais les richesses de son école sont autant de piéges séducteurs pour quiconque voudra l'imiter sans avoir son génie' (*ibid.*, [169]).

54 'La fugue à quatre sujets qui termine cette symphonie, n'est comprise que par un très-petit nombre de connaisseurs; mais le public, qui veut passer pour tel, l'applaudit avec autant plus de fureur qu'il n'y conçoit absolument rien' (*TP* I/[5]: May 1810, 13).

55 Fétis recounts with some relish that when Liszt, **Batta** and **Urhan** performed piano trios by Pixis and Beethoven in the reverse order to that advertised, the audience responded rapturously to the former thinking it was the latter (*RGM* XVI/50: 16 Dec 1849, 391). Charles Hallé's recollection of the incident (which happened in 1837) erroneously gives the newer work as being by Mayseder, not Pixis. Charles and Marie Hallé, *Life and Letters of Charles Hallé. Being an Autobiography (1819–1860) with Correspondence and Diaries* (London, 1896), 39. Berlioz, who reviewed the concert and also dwelt upon the audience's ignorant snobbery, affirms that the Trio was by Pixis (*RGM* IV/8: 19 Feb. 1837, 63).

same critic had made similar comments in March 1810 regarding Méhul's Fourth Symphony, arguing that music needed effects of light and shade in the manner of painting. A consistently detailed and contrapuntal texture had little to recommend it, since it was, he said, tiring without giving any pleasure (*TP* I/[5]: Mar. 1810, 8).[56] The latter criticism was levelled in exactly the same way at Mozart's 'Jupiter'. It is notable that the *Tablettes* contains few of the proto-Romantic, narrative critiques of instrumental music found in the *Correspondance* of five years earlier. Instead, untexted music is described wholly in terms of its texture, instrumentation and melodic outline, with general comments on its quality.

At the end of the journal's lifetime, Mozart received an article of deification from 'P.P.' (Pierre Porro) in a short, anecdotal biography which reinforced many of the ideas which characterised Mozart criticism in the first half of the century (*TP* II/32–33: 20 Sep. – 5 Oct. 1811). In particular, Porro gave further impetus to the legend of Mozart's fluency of inspiration, a myth which affected the criticism of Wagner and Berlioz as late as the 1870s:

Not once did he go near the piano in his moments of inspiration. On picking up his pen he wrote with a rapidity which, at first sight, might have seemed precipitate. The whole piece, as he had conceived, pondered, and matured it, played in his head, as he said himself, while he threw the notes onto the paper. (*TP* II/33: 5 Oct. 1811, 516)[57]

Such facility, speed and the perceived absence of a need for revision or working-out on paper became touchstones for the definition of genius; an aesthetic of the true genius composing works 'd'un seul jet' – in a single moment of inspiration – reflected badly on those in whose work the element of painstaking labour was apparent. The facility of genius (as opposed to talent) enabled art to conceal art.

The *Tablettes'* criticism, like that of the *Correspondance* and that of Geoffroy, both documents audience reaction and attempts to shape it.

---

[56] In fact, Méhul's Fourth Symphony contains more dialogue and imitation than strict counterpoint, and certainly has nothing to compare with the finale of K551.

[57] 'Jamais il n'approchait du clavecin dans ses momens d'inspiration. Dès qu'il avait saisi sa plume, il écrivait avec une rapidité qui, au premier aspect, eut pu ressembler à de la précipitation. Le morceau tout entier, tel qu'il l'avait conçu, médité et mûri, s'exécutait dans sa tête, comme il le disait lui-même, pendant qu'il jettait les notes sur le papier' (*TP* II/33: 5 Oct. 1811, 516). Porro's article also contains the celebrated episode of the Requiem's commissioning. Such anecdotes were first made popular in France by Ch. Fr. Cramer's *Anecdotes sur Mozart. Traduites de l'allemand* (Paris, 1801).

The similarity of style and approach between this article and that of 'P. Porro' on Gluck's *Armide* (*TP* II/26–7: 20 Jun. – 5 Jul. 1811, 404–26) makes the attribution of articles signed 'P.P.' in the *Tablettes* less problematic than that of their counterparts in the *Correspondance*, which contains no such signed article.

Wittingly or not, the comments of critics revealed their own aesthetic premises and those of their intended readership. So it was that 'A.M.' poked fun at Geoffroy's predilection for older Italian music (and at the music itself) when the Conservatoire bowed to pressure from the *Journal de l'Empire* and performed Paisiello's overture to *La frascatana* (1774). According to the writer, the performance was desultory and the piece suffered from being placed at the end of a concert which included one of Haydn's best symphonies and an overture by Winter:

Placed at the end of the concert and after the rich harmony of Haydn's symphony and Winter's overture, it could only seem feeble and antiquated in colour; the students sniggered as they played it, and the public left shrugging its shoulders. (*TP* I/[4]: Apr. 1810, 13)[58]

By allying himself both with the performers (who were, by now, of near-professional quality, with Habeneck at their head) and the audience, the critic could be instrumental in consolidating a commonly held view of early music as inevitably *passé*. By contrast, it was in the critic's power to effect change by occupying aesthetically higher ground than the performers he reviewed, thus pressurising them to submit to his authority. When the Conservatoire orchestra substituted a well-known andante for the adagio from an unnamed Haydn symphony in B-flat, 'A.M.' was annoyed enough to make a point of principle:

They allowed themselves, for some unknown reason, to substitute for the adagio a different, very familiar andante. These changes are rarely successful and never replace that totality of ideas whose vast picture the composer wanted to draw. (*TP* I/[6]: Jun. 1810, 4)[59]

In the *Tablettes*, the critic 'A.M.' was unusual in referring, albeit cursorily, to the larger philosophical questions surrounding the music he reviewed. Here, Haydn is treated as a composer whose works should be kept intact simply because that was how he conceived them. Such comments are important because they reveal that concern for the integrity of a canonic composer's work was not restricted to journals, such as the *Correspondance* and, later, the *Gazette*, which allied themselves with German musical traditions. Most reviews in the *Tablettes*, however, were less considered. With the exception of an astonishing

---

[58] 'Placée à la fin du Concert et après la riche harmonie de la symphonie d'Haydn et de l'ouverture de Winter, elle devait nécessairement paraître d'un coloris antique et mesquin; les élèves l'exécutaient en ricannant, et le public est sorti en haussant les épaules' (*TP* I/[4]: Apr. 1810, 13).

[59] 'On s'était permis, je ne sais pourquoi, de substituer à l'*adagio* un autre *andante* très-connu. Ces changemens sont rarement heureux et ne remplacent jamais cet ensemble d'idées dont le compositeur a voulu tracer un vaste tableau' (*TP* I/[6]: Jun. 1810, 4).

essay by Pierre Porro on Gluck's *Armide* in 1811,[60] opera reviews were reduced to the level of an age-old battle between national styles. Such bias and lack of complexity inevitably makes for predictable reading, and indeed the *Tablettes* do not represent French music criticism at its spirited best.

Castil-Blaze

On the closure of the *Tablettes* on 5 October 1811 there was another lacuna in the specialist musical press, this time lasting until the historian-critic François-Joseph Fétis founded and ran, virtually single-handedly, the famous *Revue musicale* (1827–1835). Meanwhile, music criticism as a discipline for musicians (rather than literary dilettantes) gained considerable headway in the work of François-Henri-Joseph Blaze (*dit* Castil-Blaze), a former lawyer who wrote the musical *feuilleton* in the *Journal des débats* from 1820 until 1832. It is with Castil-Blaze's arrival in Paris and his first 'Chronique musicale' of 7 December 1820 that French music criticism took a decisive turn towards professional status.[61] This most vilified of critics and composer-arrangers is a central and under-rated figure in the history of French music criticism. Despise him as he did, Hector Berlioz (Castil-Blaze's successor at the *Journal des débats*) learnt much from his work. However, seen from the perspective of the entire first half of the nineteenth century, Castil-Blaze was less a bringer of overnight change than a transitional figure whose work brought together the progressive strands of earlier criticism and added new layers. This interpretation is at odds with Castil-Blaze's own estimation both of his goals and of his achievement.

Castil-Blaze sought to institute a musicians' music criticism in place of the literary music criticism practised by dilettantes who, he felt, judged music by irrelevant standards which invariably worked to the detriment of the music under discussion. The literary approach was particularly

---

[60] *TP* II/26–7: 20 Jun.–5 Jul. 1811, 404–26. This two-instalment essay constitutes a eulogy – a 'critique admirative' – of *Armide*, and contrasts sharply with an earlier review of *Orfeo* by a different contributor, which is both ambivalent and evasive ('O.O.', review of *Orfeo*, *TP* II/20: 20 Mar. 1811, 311–14).

[61] Gíslason, 'Castil-Blaze', 57–8. Moreover, Gíslason notes that such professional criticism appeared not in a 'marginal publication', but in a prestigious daily paper with the second highest circulation in Paris, and that it appeared not in a primitive form, but 'in a fully-formed state' (*ibid.*). I take the strength of Gíslason's position to be conditioned in part by his concentration on the ancestral line from Geoffroy to Castil-Blaze as providing a representative selection of music criticism in Paris during the first two decades of the nineteenth century. Though he acknowledges that the specialist papers concurrent with the *Journal des débats* widened the range of subjects covered in music criticism, he rejects them as material for analysis on account of their small readership (*ibid.*, 25).

apparent in the case of Geoffroy's conception of opera as a play with music. Castil-Blaze countered it with a coherent aesthetic of opera as a genre in its own right, containing its own dynamic tensions between words and music. Having swept away the literary idea of opera as a mixed genre he was free to re-create it on his terms. The result was his book *De l'opéra en France* (1820), which gave music pride of place in the music–text partnership and redefined the role of the libretto accordingly:

> The relationship of libretto to music proposed by Castil-Blaze was that of intention to realization, and it is meant to replace the previous relationship of realization to ornament.[62]

The natural corollary of a view of operatic music shaped, in the first instance, by the libretto, is that a weak libretto cannot be redeemed by the composer, since if the music responds to the text (as good dramatic music should), it will inevitably, to use Gíslason's term, 'realize' its flaws. This was exactly the argument which Castil-Blaze used to defend Hérold's *L'Auteur mort et vivant* in 1820. Noting that censorious critics had blamed the composer for a lack of invention and melody, he produced his counter-argument:

> I shall not reproach M. Hérold for this; he has done what will always be done when one works on a graceful, light, but trivial poem which has little musical potential, lacks images, lacks definite colour, which offers no situation which might inspire, no developments, no tensions. The musician follows his guide, and if he succeeds, like him, in being amiable and light, he has accomplished his task. (*JD* 30 Dec. 1820, 3)[63]

Such arguments bring us very close indeed to Berlioz's image of dramatic music, and find an echo both in his 'admirative' articles on Gluck[64] and in his diplomatic reviews of Meyerbeer. That Berlioz can say the following of Act II of *Les Huguenots* and simultaneously register his ambivalence regarding the composer's music shows how, by 1836, Castil-Blaze's paradigm had been institutionalised to the extent of providing a plausible cover for the expression of disparagement:

---

[62] *Ibid.*, 92. In fact, there were some pointed objections to the literary view of opera promulgated by Geoffroy. In 1804 an unsigned reviewer for the *Correspondance* noted that: 'It is in the spirit of this journal, when reviewing operas, to consider them in terms of their music much more than in terms of the poem' ('Il est dans l'esprit de ce journal, en rendant compte des opéras, de les considérer sous le rapport de la musique bien plus que sous celui du poëme') (*CAM* II/18: 29 Feb. 1804 / 9 ventôse an 12, col. 140).

[63] 'Nous n'adresserons pas ce reproche à M. Hérold; il a fait ce que l'on fera toujours quand on travaillera sur un poëme gracieux, léger, mais futile, peu propre à la musique, sans images, sans couleur prononcée, ne présentant aucune situation qui puisse s'inspirer, point de développemens, point d'efforts. Le musicien suit son guide, et s'il parvient à être aimable et léger comme lui, sa tâche est remplie' (*JD* 30 Dec. 1820, 3). Quoted in Gíslason: 'Castil-Blaze', 100.

[64] Discussed below, in Chapter 4.

To my mind, Act II has been judged very severely and very badly. Its level of interest is nowhere near as high as that of the rest of the work; but is this the musician's fault? Could he do other than compose gracious cantilenas, cavatinas with roulades, and calm, soft choruses for verses which speak only of *pleasant gardens, verdant springs, melodious sounds, of loving torrents, of folly, coquetry,* and *of refrains of love repeated in echoes all around*? I think not; and indeed, it took no less than a man of superior ability to draw as much out of them. (*JD* 10 Nov. 1836, 1–2)[65]

Yet Castil-Blaze's musical taste was too Italianate to embrace the full consequences of his theory of dramatic music. Like Geoffroy, he saw highly dramatic music as acceptable only within the limits of an overarching idea of musical beauty. This aesthetic, which he also applied to the rôle of the performer, explains one of the major differences between Castil-Blaze's and Berlioz's approach to musical expression: the former believed in the ascendancy of beauty, the latter in the ascendancy of dramatic truth. An example from works based on *Romeo and Juliet* serves to point up the difference. In the course of an appreciation of Giuditta Pasta in September 1822, Castil-Blaze touched on the dénouement of Zingarelli's *Romeo e Giulietta*:

Does not Romeo, devoured by the poison, share his anguish with the spectators, [but] does his singing cease to be ornamented and true? He tears the heart-strings, but he flatters the ear: it is a triumph of art. Music should always be music; the feeling for beauty should be present even in the expression of the most horrible pain. (*JD* 10 Sep. 1822, 3)[66]

By contrast, when Berlioz wrote *Roméo et Juliette* in 1839 his interpretation of this very scene, noted for its sense of graphic representation and purely orchestral drama, was perceived as gratuitously realistic.[67]

Unlike Geoffroy, who wrote on little but opera, Castil-Blaze reviewed

---

[65] 'Le second acte a été jugé très sevèrement, et fort mal à mon avis. L'intérêt n'en est pas à beaucoup près aussi grand que celui du reste de la pièce; mais la faute en est-elle au musicien? Et celui-ci pouvait-il faire autre chose que de gracieuses cantilènes, des cavatines à roulades et des chœurs calmes et doux, sur des vers qui ne parlent que de *rians jardins, de vertes fontaines, de sons mélodieux, de flots amoureux, de folie, de coquetterie,* et *de refrains d'amour* que *répètent les échoes d'alentour*? nous ne le croyons pas; et certes, il fallait rien moins qu'un homme supérieur pour s'en tirer aussi bien' (*JD* 10 Nov. 1836, 1–2).

[66] 'Roméo, dévoré par le poison, ne fait-il pas partager ses angoisses aux spectateurs, son chant cesse-t-il d'être orné et d'être vrai? Il déchire le cœur, mais il flatte l'oreille: c'est le triomphe de l'art. Il faut que la musique soit toujours la musique, il faut que le sentiment du beau se trouve jusque dans l'expression de la douleur la plus horrible' (*JD* 10 Sep. 1822, 3). Quoted in Gíslason, 'Castil-Blaze', 190. Castil-Blaze's theory of ornamentation as a rhetorical device which allowed singers to participate in the compositional process would also, in due course, be anathema to his successor. For a discussion of this question, see Gíslason: 'Castil-Blaze', 187–96.

[67] *Roméo et Juliette*'s reception in the *Gazette* is discussed in Chapter 11.

concerts, Conservatoire competitions, instrument methods, treatises and other educational publications, new music and new editions of early music.[68] With few exceptions, throughout these reviews the predominant considerations are those of the practical musician. So it is that in a review of the Paris publisher Carli's edition of Marcello's *Psaumes* [motets], Castil-Blaze spent more time discussing the problems of producing a suitable realisation of the figured bass than discussing the qualities of the music itself (*JD* 11 Mar. 1822, 1–2). In a review of Beethoven's *Christ on the Mount of Olives*, his attention was directed primarily to the weakness of the translation as a text to be sung, as distinct from its strength as a literary translation (*JD* 14 Mar. 1822, 2). His one criticism of the 'Cum sancto spiritu' fugue in Cherubini's Mass for Three Voices, the Kyrie and Gloria of which formed part of the Société des Concerts du Conservatoire's opening concert in March 1828, was that such intricate music was unsuited to the vast acoustic of Reims cathedral, for which it was originally written (*JD* 19 Mar. 1828, 2–3). He acknowledged that writing a fugue at this point in the Mass was traditional; however, in his mind tradition was subordinate to gaining maximum effect with the simplest means. His practical approach extended to minute details of orchestration in those works he knew particularly well; most of a review of the overture to *Der Freischütz* (*Robin des bois*) at the Société des Concerts concentrated on a specific problem of indistinct writing in the timpani part (*JD* 7 Apr. 1830, 1). To an extent, Berlioz also adopted the technique of selecting details, usually of harmony or orchestration, for analysis; however, such mini-analyses were, in the case of works he admired, surrounded by prose of an imaginative richness to which Castil-Blaze never aspired and of an interpretive depth which he never achieved.

Already in Castil-Blaze's writing we see a trinity of Austro-German domination in autonomous music. His reviews of the Conservatoire concerts and the Concerts Spirituels, hitherto neglected by scholars, reveal much about perceptions of Haydn, Mozart and Beethoven in the 1820s. As hinted earlier, Haydn's symphonies were, in the first decade of the nineteenth century, already in danger of being taken for granted. For Castil-Blaze in 1822 they represented fine examples of old music; yet, after defending the 'Drum Roll' by an appeal to the aesthetic of universal beauty, he inadvertently alighted upon a problem which was to characterise Haydn reception for most of the century:

The concerts are always opened with these old Haydn symphonies, most of which are nearly 60 years old, proving to us, nevertheless, that well composed music

[68] For a comprehensive list, see Gíslason, 'Castil-Blaze', 87–8.

which was beautiful 50 years ago is still beautiful now. The monotony of their perfection tires no-one. (*JD* 14 Mar. 1822, 4)[69]

In just over a decade, the monotony of their perfection would threaten to impair their status. Castil-Blaze left his readers in no doubt as to the status of certain of Mozart's works: in 1824, he noted that the Requiem 'produced its usual effect' (*JD* 1 Dec. 1824, 3),[70] as though to elaborate on that effect and its causes was to state the obvious. Two years later, he noted that Mozart's K550 'enchanted the entire audience' (*JD* 14 Mar. 1822, 4).[71] He, too, was transported by the complexity of Mozart's symphonic style; one of his first reviews, at the end of 1820, included a quasi-analysis of the overture to *Die Zauberflöte* which concentrated on Mozart's skill in defeating the harmonic expectations of his (educated) listeners. Two comments in particular are important for their proximity to those of his fellow critic and exact contemporary, François-Joseph Fétis.[72] Both relate to the modernity of Mozart's harmonic style: 'When one possesses works of this power, it is permissible to believe that the limits of the art are fixed ... It seemed as though all harmony's resources had been exhausted in the course of this piece' (*JD* 30 Dec. 1820, 1–2).[73] Yet when faced with music which appeared to transcend that of Mozart – particularly the Beethoven symphonies at the Société des Concerts – he redefined his horizons, welcomed the new revolution in musical style, and, in his first Société des Concerts review, chided the French for taking over twenty years to perform the 'Eroica' (*JD* 19 Mar. 1828, 1). By contrast, Fétis judged Beethoven by a fixed set of principles which did not admit some of the composer's more original achievements.[74] After a second hearing of the 'Eroica', Castil-Blaze detected some over-development in the first movement and some obscurity of form in the finale. Such comments would, in the *Revue musicale*, have preceded a negative judgement; Castil-Blaze turned such 'weaknesses' into virtues:

[69] 'On commence toujours les concerts par ces vieilles symphonies de Haydn, dont la plupart comptent près de soixante hivers, et nous prouvent néanmoins que la musique bien faite, et qui a été belle il y a cinquante ans l'est encore de nos jours. La monotonie de leur perfection ne fatigue personne' (*JD* 14 Mar. 1822, 4).

[70] 'a produit son effet ordinaire' (*JD* 1 Dec. 1824, 3).

[71] 'a ravi tout l'auditoire' (*JD* 14 Mar. 1822, 4).

[72] Discussed in Chapter 2.

[73] 'Lorsque l'on possède des morceaux de cette force, il est permis de croire que les bornes de l'art sont fixées ... Il sembloit que toutes les ressources de l'harmonie avoient été épuisées dans le courant de ce morceau' (*JD* 30 Dec. 1820, 1–2).

[74] For a full discussion of Fétis's Beethoven criticism, see Peter Bloom, 'François-Joseph Fétis and the *Revue musicale* (1827–1835)' (unpublished PhD dissertation, University of Pennsylvania, 1972), 92–207.

There are some over-extended developments in the first movement; the finale above all shows some indecision of form, and from time to time clouds obscure the horizon. But if this obscurity adds brilliance to the bright lightning flashes, to the explosion of the thunder, then it must be regarded as a gift from the magician who has made every effort to enchant us. (*JD* 29 Mar. 1828, 1)[75]

In one of his few passages of metaphorical prose, Castil-Blaze showed his predisposition to argue in favour of Beethoven's originality of form, using elemental imagery which was to become commonplace among Romantic critics.

Above all, Castil-Blaze was concerned with the realities of the business of composition and performance. His criticism, much of which has to do with specific aspects of performance, is imbued with a pragmatist's sense of the present, rather than an idealist's eye to the future. As Gíslason points out, Castil-Blaze had more influence on music criticism than he did on opera (or, indeed, on autonomous music).[76] By the time of his departure from the *Journal des débats* in 1832, his technique of criticism, in comparison with that of Fétis, appears insular and restricted. In what can be seen as a natural wish to counteract the lack of focus displayed by literary critics writing about music, his music criticism is so professional and practical as to be isolationist. This may be partly due to his rather Classical idea of music as craft rather than art. Nevertheless, at a time when Parisian artists and thinkers were wrestling with the new political and philosophical ideas presented in literary Romanticism and in the thought of Saint-Simon, Auguste Comte and Victor Cousin,[77] Castil-Blaze appears to have had little interest in the wider rôle of music in society, and to have neither envisioned nor feared change. Knowledge of the intellectual turmoil around him lends a sense of false security to the neatness, clarity and consistency of his criticism. The alternative, embodied in the work of François-Joseph Fétis and discussed in the next chapter, was to engage with new ideas and to bring them to bear on a wide range of musical genres. The resulting criticism was more dogmatic, less consistent, and extremely influential.

---

[75] 'On peut trouver dans le premier morceau quelques développemens trop étendus; le finale surtout offre de l'indécision dans son plan, et des nuages viennent de temps en temps obscurcir l'horizon. Mais si cette obscurité sert à donner plus d'éclat à la lueur des éclairs, à l'explosion du tonnerre, on doit la regarder comme un bienfait du magicien qui a pris soin de nous enchanter' (*JD* 29 Mar. 1828, 1).

[76] Gíslason: 'Castil-Blaze', 197.

[77] Henri, Comte de Saint-Simon (1760–1825): French socialist philosopher. The philosophers Auguste Comte (1798–1857) and Victor Cousin (1792–1867) are discussed in Chapter 2.

2 The rise of the specialist press from 1827

A philosopher of music history: F.-J. Fétis

Despite their seemingly Classical outlook and their exact contemporaneity, Castil-Blaze and Fétis were critics of very different kinds. Fétis, by far the more intellectual and ambitious as a critic, was, by his death in 1871, the undisputed *doyen* of music journalism in France – despite residing in Brussels from 1833 onwards.[1] The impact of his thought on French critics working in virtually every branch of the discipline has yet to be appreciated fully, and merits a study in itself. The *Revue musicale*, which Fétis produced almost single-handedly from 1827 to 1833, and direction of which was passed to his son until its close in 1835, is a supremely important cultural document of the years preceding and inaugurating the July Monarchy.[2] It is important not only because of the range of subject matter about which Fétis wrote with authority (though not without pedantry), but also because many of the ideas contained within his criticism represent the application to music of important cultural and philosophical notions of the 1820s. The sheer force and originality of Fétis's arguments, combined with the length of his career, ensured that his ideas, born of the heady intellectual atmosphere of the Sorbonne during the Restoration, outlived him. The history of the *Revue musicale* and its criticism has been treated in detail elsewhere;[3] the

---

[1] Fétis took up the directorship of the newly founded Brussels Conservatoire in 1833.

[2] The *Revue musicale* was not Fétis's first attempt at producing a music periodical. For information on his *Journal de musique* (Jan.–Feb. 1804) see Bloom, 'François-Joseph Fétis', 21–4.

[3] The most important work on Fétis the critic is Bloom's thesis, parts of which were published as separate articles; see below, n. 6. A summary of the argument of the thesis is presented in 'A Review of Fétis's Revue musicale', *Music in Paris in the Eighteen-Thirties*, ed. Peter Bloom (Stuyvesant, 1987). The only biography is that of Robert Wangermée: *F.-J. Fétis, musicologue et compositeur. Contribution à l'étude du goût musical au XIXe siècle*. Académie Royale de Belgique. Classe des Beaux-arts. Mémoires, t. VI, fasc. 4 (Brussels, 1951). The *Revue musicale* has been fully indexed in the *Répertoire internationale de la presse musicale* (*RIPM*) series.

philosophical context of Fétis's thought has received less attention.[4] This section presents Fétis's philosophy of music in the light of German idealist aesthetics and the dominant French philosophies of Victor Cousin and, to a lesser extent, Auguste Comte. It thus provides a reference point for later discussions of Fétis's writings in the *Gazette*.

Fétis's aim in setting up the *Revue musicale* was primarily didactic. His journal included articles on all aspects of music and musical life. Rudiments and theory, music reviews, descriptive analyses of selected pieces, concert and opera reviews, historical articles, composer biographies and articles on instruments and orchestration were all grist to his mill, making the *Revue musicale* the most wide-ranging specialist periodical to date. In each kind of article, the views Fétis wished to promulgate were eminently detectable, both in his prose and in his choice of material for inclusion; it was not by chance that the opening article of the journal's first regular issue was a discussion of Mozart's Requiem.[5] For Fétis, Mozart represented the summit and the limit of musical art; everything either led towards him or was indicative of post-Mozartian decadence. However, to ally Fétis squarely with the Classicists in a Classical–Romantic debate, because of his love of Mozart, his hostility to Berlioz and his ambivalence towards Beethoven's output after 1804, would be misleading. Fétis's wholehearted support for Meyerbeer militates against such an interpretation of his musical taste and his aesthetic of music, as does the nascent Romanticism of much of his criticism.[6] Fétis's love of Renaissance and Baroque music (Bach in particular) is evident throughout the *Revue musicale*'s pages, not least in reviews of his own 'concerts historiques', which helped establish his reputation as one of the first champions of early music in France. He did for historical musicology what Castil-Blaze did for opera criticism: he helped give it the status of a professional activity. To do so he had to overcome several obstacles, outlined earlier, which hampered the acceptance of early music, whether as repertoire or as a subject worthy of academic study. Yet, as the previous chapter has shown, there was indeed an incipient debate about canon and posterity emerging in the

---

[4] The German roots of Fétis's philosophy of music have been summarised and interpreted in Rosalie Schellhous, 'Fétis's Tonality as a Metaphysical Principle: Hypothesis for a New Science', *Music Theory Spectrum* XIII/2 (Fall, 1991), 219–40. However, Schellhous's argument elevates German influences at the expense of French.

[5] *RM* I [13] Feb. 1827, 26–30.

[6] For discussion of Fétis's criticism of Beethoven, Berlioz and Meyerbeer, see Peter Bloom, 'Critical reaction to Beethoven in France: F. J. Fétis', *Revue belge de musicologie* XXVI–XXVII (1972–3), 67–83; 'Berlioz and the Critic: La Damnation de Fétis', *Studies in Musicology in Honor of Otto E. Albrecht*, ed. J. W. Hill (Kassel, etc.), 1980), 240–65; and 'Friends and Admirers: Meyerbeer and Fétis', *Revue belge de musicologie*, XXXII–XXXIII (1978–9), 174–87.

early nineteenth-century press; it was Fétis who first placed such debates on a firm philosophical footing. Much of Fétis's philosophy of music derives ultimately from the German transcendental idealists, as indicated in a letter of 1838 to the Paris publisher Troupenas in which he listed specific works by Kant, Fichte and Schelling as primary influences on his philosophy of music.[7] Despite the inclusion of a French translation of Schelling's critique of Cousin in Fétis's list, among French philosophers, Cousin was a major formative influence.[8]

Cousin was, essentially, a German-oriented historian of philosophy who criticised and reinterpreted the work of others. His central original achievement, which led to his becoming 'the academic Pope of the July Monarchy',[9] was to develop the (conservative) official philosophy of Louis-Philippe's reign: eclecticism. His theory held that the key to a sound philosophy lay in a synthesis of what was good and true in the philosophies of previous ages.[10] Rather than reject all that preceded him and posit his philosophy as its replacement, he argued that the past should be regarded as a source of truth and renewal. His relativism allowed him to claim that each era had produced a philosophy appropriate for its time, and that the value of past errors lay in their proximity to the truth.[11] By rigorous observation (which he compared with that of the physical sciences), Cousin taught that such incomplete truths could be identified and used in a higher, eclectic, synthesis.[12] The result was intended to avoid extremes; it was a *juste milieu*, or 'middle path'. Cousin's philosophy of history contained two levels: the real and the true. The historian traced external events – the real; the philosopher of history analysed such events and penetrated to the (purposive) truth behind them.[13] Cousin's notion of the two levels derives from the transcendental idealist principle of nature and art as teleological systems in which each individual species or artwork is a manifestation of an overarching, purposive, principle.[14] For Cousin,

7 Schellhous, 'Fétis's *Tonality*', 222 and nn. 13–14.
8 Fétis's library contains two different translations of Schelling's work: the *Jugement de M. Schelling sur la philosophie de M. Cousin*, trans. J. Willm (Paris and Strasbourg, 1835), and a translation by Paul Grimblot accompanying that of the *Système de l'idéalisme transcendental* (Paris, 1842).
9 Alan B. Spitzer, *The French Generation of 1820*, 79.
10 Cousin, *Fragmens philosophiques* (Paris, 1826), vii.
11 Cousin, *Fragmens*, vi–viii.
12 Cousin, *Fragmens*, xlviii.
13 Cousin, *Fragmens*, 199–200.
14 The teleological principle in art receives its strongest expression in Schelling. See Schelling, *System des transzendentalen Idealismus in Schellings Werke*, ed. Manfred Schröter, 12 vols. (Munich, 1927–54), II, 607–11.

Knowing only the truth is impossible, since one arrives at the truth only by way of the real; knowing only the real amounts to little, since the real is just the manifestation of the true.[15]

The implications of eclecticism and a teleological approach to history for music and musicology were apparent to Fétis. Cousin's approach provided philosophical justification for the study and performance of early music, and a model for contemporary composers. At worst, early music was appropriate for its time; at best, it contained features of permanent value. Fétis's belief in the musical beauty of the past was such that he wanted to construct future composition (at least in part) as a re-interpretation of the finest that earlier styles had to offer. Of his contemporaries, Meyerbeer provided the best example of a composer adept at moulding different styles into a new, coherent whole. Fétis himself put eclecticism into practice in his compositions and, on a more theoretical level, in the *Méthode des méthodes de piano*, written with Ignaz Moscheles in 1840. Part of the preface reads as a paraphrase of Cousin:

To sum up everything good which has been produced to date, in each case to supply the opinions and the principles of the most celebrated masters, to make a reasoned analysis of them and to apply them with discernment; this is now the only way to produce a work which is of universal utility; this is the only way of replacing prejudice with reason.[16]

Fétis's theory of harmony applied transcendental idealist and eclectic ideas to changes in musical style from modality to the breakdown of tonality. For him, beauty – the ideal – was the 'truth' in music; changes in musical style accounted only for the 'real'. What distinguishes his criticism fundamentally from that of Castil-Blaze, is that Castil-Blaze, like Cousin's historian, concerned himself with the external realities of music, and that, by contrast, Fétis searched for the ideal, of which such external realities were but isolated manifestations. Thus Fétis was not just a critic, or even just an historian, but a philosopher of music history. Nowhere is his philosophy more evident, though it is not trouble-free, than in his theory of harmony. Fétis's theories of both harmonic and metrical practice were first presented in his 'Cours de la philosophie

[15] 'Connaître le vrai tout seul est impossible, puisqu'on ne peut arriver au vrai qu'en passant par le réel; connaître le réel seul est peu de chose, le réel n'étant que la manifestation du vrai.' Cousin, *Fragmens*, 200.

[16] 'Résumer tout ce qui a été produit de bon jusqu'à ce jour; donner sur chaque chose les opinions et les principes des chefs d'école les plus célèbres; en faire une analyse raisonnée et les appliquer avec discernement, telle est pour l'époque actuelle la seule manière de faire un ouvrage qui soit d'utilité universelle; tel est le seul moyen de mettre la raison à la place des préjugés.' François-Joseph Fétis and Ignaz Moscheles, *Méthode des méthodes de piano* (Paris, [1840]), 4.

musicale' of 1832, third-person summaries of which he published in the *Revue musicale*.[17] His theory of harmony outlined a process in four stages: the *ordre unitonique*, which comprised all modal music; the *ordre transitonique*, initiated by Monteverdi through the 'invention' or 'discovery' (Fétis uses both words) of the dominant seventh and the process of modulation; the *ordre pluritonique*, for which he gives no starting date, but in which greater freedom of modulation is possible through the use of enharmony and substitution within chords;[18] finally, the *ordre omnitonique*, which allowed unprecedented freedom of resolution for any given note. Fétis was aware of the prophetic nature of the *ordre omnitonique* concept, which he had included in a harmony treatise as early as 1815, only to have the work rejected as outlandish by the Institut.[19] The freedom of chromatic resolution within the *ordre omnitonique* prefigured the breakdown of tonality itself; Fétis was adamant that it represented the end of music's potential:

> M. Fétis predicts the moment when the ear will have become so familiar with the multiplicity of these resolutions of a single note, that the end result of this *ordre omnitonique* will be the total destruction, in certain cases, of the scale, and the beginnings of an acoustic division of the musical scale into twelve equal semitones, on account of the equality of attractions. (*RM* VI/25: 21 Jul. 1832, 198)[20]

By positing a termination point for processes through which the Idea of music can be manifested, Fétis implicitly rejects a teleological principle.[21] Moreover, by stressing the increased possibilities of each stage, he implies that his principle is evolutionary. As such, it has much in common with the work of the positivist philosopher Auguste Comte, whose ideas about the progress of civilisation were fundamentally opposed to those of Cousin and the German idealists. From 1826, Comte presented a series of semi-private lectures which proposed a theory of civilisation in three evolutionary stages: the religious, the metaphysical and the positive.[22] The third stage of this linear progression was the only

---

17 *RM* VI/17–25: 26 May – 21 Jul. 1832.
18 In later writings he placed Mozart at the head of this development. For a detailed critique of Fétis's theory of harmony as expounded in the *Esquisse de l'histoire de l'harmonie* of 1840 and the *Traité d'harmonie* of 1844, see Mary I. Arlin, 'Fétis' Contribution to Practical and Historical Music Theory', *Revue belge de musicologie* XXVI–XXVII (1972–3), 106–15.
19 *RM* VI/24: 14 Jul. 1832, 186.
20 'M. Fétis prevoit le moment où l'oreille aura acquis une telle habitude de la multiplicité de ces résolutions d'une note, que le résultat de cet ordre omnitonique sera l'anéantissement total de la gamme dans certains cas, et l'origine d'une division acoustique de l'échelle musicale en douze demi-tons égaux, à cause de l'égalité des tendances' (*RM* VI/25: 21 Jul. 1832, 198).
21 Schellhous, 'Fétis's *Tonality*', 239–40.
22 Comte's ideas were published in the *Cours de philosophie positive* of 1830–42.

one in which humanity was freed from the shackles of religion and superstition – an atheistic, scientific age whose principles would be based on rigorously defined empirical truths. Like Cousin, Comte placed his philosophy on a quasi-scientific basis which would undoubtedly have appealed to Fétis's love of factual precision and methodological rigour. Moreover, the idea of civilisation progressing was (at least in part) compatible with Fétis's belief that music embodied features of both art and science. Fétis rejected Comte's atheism and its consequent denial of a spiritual element in art. However, he accepted some of Comte's theories of biological predestiny in his ethnomusicological work,[23] and was, despite himself, always attracted to his theory of the progress of civilisation.

In the 1832 lecture series, Fétis outlined his philosophy of musical development:

Having established that there are sciences, such as geometry, whose first principles, once constructed, remain the same for ever because they result from evident truths; that there are others such as physics and chemistry some parts of which can be improved through observations made on better foundations and a more rational language without having to rework their theory from scratch, the professor stated that music cannot be categorised with any of these sciences because it is at once a science and an art, because from time to time the art undergoes transformations which give the science very different directions from those it had taken previously, and lastly because the instinct which presides over these transformations of the art creates phenomena which bear so little relation to those previously known that it becomes necessary to begin the science again as soon as the relevant transformations have been accomplished. Such are the causes, said M. Fétis, which have hitherto affected the science of music, and which have meant that this science, in its current form, is so different from that of the Middle Ages; it has accomplished not only progress, but has undergone transformations. (*RM* VI/18: 2 Jun. 1832, 139–40)[24]

---

[23] Schellhous, 'Fétis's *Tonality*', 235.

[24] 'Après avoir établi qu'il est des sciences, comme la géometrie, dont les premières élémens se forment tels qu'ils doivent être à jamais, parce qu'ils resultent de vérités évidentes; qu'il en est d'autres, comme la physique et la chimie, dont on peut perfectionner quelques parties par des observations mieux établies et un langage plus rationnel, sans être obligé d'en refaire toute la théorie, le professeur a dit que la musique ne peut être assimilée à aucune de ces sciences parce qu'elle est à la fois un art et une science, parce que l'art subit de temps en temps des transformations qui impriment à la science des directions très différentes de celles qu'elle avait prises d'abord, et enfin parce que l'instinct qui préside à ces transformations de l'art crée des phénomènes si peu analogues à ceux qu'on connaissait antérieurement qu'il devient nécessaire de recommencer la science aussitôt que les transformations dont il s'agit sont accomplies. Telles sont les causes, a dit M. Fétis, qui ont jusqu'ici agi sur la science musicale, et qui ont fait que cette science, telle qu'elle est aujourd'hui, est si différente de ce qu'elle était dans le moyen-âge; car ce ne sont pas seulement des progrès qu'elle a faits, ce sont des transformations qu'elle a subies (*RM* VI/18: 2 Jun. 1832, 139–40).

In the closing formula of the above quotation, Fétis refers not to any element of progress within music's essence, but exclusively to the progress and transformation of its phenomenal reality – that part of it which is susceptible to scientific observation and from which generalisations of theory can be made. He thus gives a view of Western music history as a compartmentalised series of different states of the art each requiring, *ex post facto*, its own scientific justification and explanation.[25] Progress occurs, but only within each stylistic compartment. The art as a whole does not progress in linear fashion, and Comtian ideas of progress are, seemingly, rejected.[26] Such arguments gave rise to Fétis's most important formulations: that the external trappings of music may change but that its essence – the ideal – remains constant; and that detectable external changes do not constitute progress in the scientific sense. The relation of these notions to Cousin's two levels of truth – the transient and the intemporal – and Kant and Schelling's teleological theories, is apparent.

Moreover, unlike Comte, who was proposing a new model for society, Fétis denied that the *ordre omnitonique* should prevail over its antecedents in new compositions. Instead, at the last moment he revealed his theory of harmony as eclectic:

However, it would be erroneous, he said, to suppose that by the future necessity of using the *ordre omnitonique* frequently, the other orders of tonality will not be used: God forbid that it should be so! Each of the orders has its advantages, its own qualities which we must be careful not to renounce, for this would be to impoverish the art on the one hand while enriching it on the other. The mixture of the four orders, each one employed appropriately, will be the final stage of tonal perfection; this perfection will be rooted in appropriateness and variety simultaneously. (*RM* VI/25: 21 Jul. 1832, 198)[27]

Fétis's conclusion can be explained not only by his eclecticism, but by his musical taste. An examination of the relationship between his theory's implications and the reality of its practice reveals significant disjunctions.

[25] The nature of music as a series of different arts is expressed in its most cogent form in the *Resumé philosophique de l'histoire de la musique*, which was published in Volume I of the first edition of the *Biographie universelle des musiciens* in 1833. The relevant passage is quoted and translated in Robert Nichols, 'Fétis' Theories of Tonalité and the Aesthetics of Music', *Revue belge de musicologie* XXVI–XXVII (1972–3), 119.

[26] Schellhous accepts Fétis's formulation as a rejection of Comte's idea of progress. See 'Fétis's *Tonality*', 231–2. In Fétis's criticism, however, the distinction between the two types of 'progress' is often unclear.

[27] 'On serait cependant dans l'erreur, dit-il, si l'on croyait que par la nécessité future de l'emploi fréquent de l'ordre omnitonique, on ne fera plus usage des autres ordres de tonalités: à Dieu ne plaise qu'il en soit ainsi! Chacun de ces ordres a ses avantages, ses qualités auxquels il faut bien se garder de renoncer, car ce serait appauvrir l'art d'un côté pendant qu'on l'enrichirait de l'autre. Le mélange des quatre ordres, chacun d'eux étant employé à propos, sera le dernier terme de la perfection tonale; cette perfection sera fondée à la fois sur la convenance et la variété (*RM* VI/25: 21 Jul. 1832, 198).

As Fétis explained in the final instalment of the series, the *ordre omnitonique* could take three forms: the use of a long unison as a bridge between keys; the use of melodic lines with affinities to more than one key; the use of chromatic alteration. Of these techniques, the first two are surprisingly commonplace for such a prophetic *ordre*. The impression that the *ordre omnitonique* was rooted in established practice is reinforced by Fétis's illustrations, taken from the introduction to the first movement of Beethoven's Fourth Symphony, an unspecified Haydn slow movement and *Guillaume Tell*. However, for the third category Fétis was obliged to fabricate examples, there being none in the repertory. It was here, in his examples of the resolution of a single note in sixteen different ways, that the prophetic nature of the *ordre omnitonique* lay; yet it was exactly this modulatory freedom from which Fétis advised composers to draw back. That part of him which saw music as science had opened up possibilities of development (in the Comtian sense) which his artistic taste could not countenance in practice; he retreated into a *juste milieu* within which his favoured composer – who initiated the *ordre pluritonique* and strayed only rarely into the realms of the *ordre omnitonique* – was Mozart. Using the harmony treatise of 1844 as her major primary source, Rosalie Schellhous argues that Fétis was unaware that in positing that 'the end of musical history has arrived ... his teleology annihilates itself'.[28] Yet his retreat into the *juste milieu* indicates exactly this realisation, confirmed throughout his career in the split between the implications of his theories and his critical practice. Moreover, a similar process takes place in Fétis's theory of rhythmic innovation.

In addition to setting out his theory of harmony, Fétis's 1832 series of lectures discussed the history of notation and rudiments of rhythm. Prominent in his discussions of rhythm was the theory of 'carrure', in which each antecedent phrase was to be answered by a consequent phrase of equal length. For Fétis, such symmetry had the status of a natural law, though even symmetry had its limits of acceptability; he declared that although pairs of three-bar phrases were perfectly acceptable, divisions into and multiples of five were incomprehensible to the human ear. Fétis's invocation of the law of 'carrure' throughout his long career hindered his appreciation of attempts at compositional modernity. Yet when he wrote on rhythm and metre for the *Gazette* in 1852, his ideas on the future possibilities for rhythm approached the complexity of those he had seen in 1815 for harmony (*RGM* XIX/35–52: 29 Aug. – 26 Dec. 1852); his theory of 'carrure' however, remained constant, thus

---

[28] Schellhous, 'Fétis's *Tonality*', 239–40.

ensuring that acceptable rhythmic innovation retained the allure of antecedent and consequent phrase structure.

Although Fétis could never be considered a Romantic himself, his aesthetic of composition was influenced largely by the ideas of the German idealists and Romantics – in particular, Schelling and Hoffmann. Much of their thought also found its way (in aphoristic and simplified form) into Cousin's lecture series of 1818, which was published in various forms in the 1830s and 1840s, and formed the basis of *Du vrai, du beau et du bien* of 1853.[29] Fétis's aesthetic was infinitely more subtle than Cousin's, though Lectures XIV–XVI of the 1818 series show the extent of their common ground. In his account of genius, Cousin followed Schelling's notion that such exceptional people were not generally completely in control of their creativity, but were impelled by external necessity to take a particular course.[30] True genius displayed two defining characteristics: a lively need to produce, and the power of creative production. Artists who displayed the first characteristic but lacked the second were explicitly dubbed 'false geniuses':

for the need [to create] without the power is just an affliction which simulates, but is not, genius. Essentially, genius is, above all, the power to make, to invent, to create. Taste is content to observe and admire. False genius, ardent and impotent imagination, consumes itself in sterile reveries and produces nothing, or nothing of greatness. Only genius has the virtue of converting conception into creation.[31]

Cousin's formulation is an expanded and intensified version of Schelling's analysis of genius in 1800.[32] In 1828, Cousin expanded the idea still further in his lecture on 'grands hommes': such men, who comprised statesmen and military officers as well as artists, were 'instruments of destiny' who realised that their greatness lay not in their individuality but in their knowledge that they were vehicles for the expression of widely felt ideas which lesser men were unable to articulate.[33] Fétis's concept of

---

[29] Cousin, *Cours de l'histoire de la philosophie moderne. Nouvelle édition, revue et corrigée*, 5 vols. (Paris, 1846), II, 171–4 (1818, Leçon XIV), and Cousin, *Cours de philosophie. Introduction à la philosophie* (Paris, 1828), Leçon X, 15–26 (each lecture is paginated separately). Fétis's library contains the 1841 edition of the 1828–9 lectures and the 1846 set mentioned above, in addition to several of Cousin's shorter works (including editions of the *Fragmens philosophiques*) and translations.

[30] Cousin, *Cours de l'histoire* (1818 [1846]), II, 172–3. Schelling had put forward this idea in his *System des transzendentalen Idealismus* of 1800. See *Schellings Werke*, II, 616–18.

[31] 'car le besoin sans la puissance n'est qu'une maladie qui simule le génie, mais qui n'est pas lui. Le génie, c'est surtout, c'est essentiellement la puissance de faire, d'inventer, de créer. Le goût se contente d'observer et d'admirer. Le faux génie, l'imagination ardente et impuissante, se consume en rêves stériles et ne produit rien ou rien de grand. Le génie seul a la vertu de convertir ses conceptions en créations.' Cousin, *Cours de l'histoire* (1818 [1846]), II, 173.

[32] *Schellings Werke*, II, 618.

[33] 'les instrumens du destin'. Cousin, *Cours de philosophie* (1828), Leçon X, 17.

genius was taken both from the picture of the 'grand homme' which Cousin presented in the 1828 lecture series, and from the German idealist notion of the creative artist as participating in a teleological process. The logical corollary of Cousin's position – that a 'grand homme' was a man of, rather than ahead of, his time – represents a departure from Schelling's formulation, and helps to explain Fétis's resistance to the avant-garde of Romanticism.[34] Moreover, just as Cousin taught that moments of crisis produced their own saviours, so Fétis believed that at points of musical crisis the right composer would appear, ready and qualified to respond to music's new needs. Success was a defining characteristic of 'great men', whether artists, thinkers or warriors, the idea of an unsuccessful chosen vehicle being a contradiction in terms. When, in 1835 and 1852–4 respectively, Fétis came to judge Berlioz and Wagner as 'false geniuses', he did so in terms of precisely this aesthetic.[35] Moreover, using Cousin's dictum of 1828 that great men emerged through historical necessity (rather than of their own volition), and that if history did not require a great man to transform and lead, no such man would appear, Fétis denounced self-styled genius and an overt commitment to reform among avant-garde composers on the grounds that such reform was not part of musico-historical predestiny.[36] Moreover, those who theorised about their work failed the test of genius because they claimed to understand their motivation and their intended direction; Schelling had stated explicitly that genius was, to an extent, uncomprehending of the larger destiny within which it operated.[37]

A tendency to formalism and idealism characterises Cousin's philosophy of music. Like Schelling, Cousin believed that 'art's single goal is beauty. If it strays from this, art abandons its own self.'[38] Such ideal beauty contained an element of the infinite; music's semantic vagueness, unmatched by any other art, afforded the listener unparalleled freedom of imagination and interpretation.[39] In his elevation of autonomous music, Cousin may have been influenced by E. T. A. Hoffmann, in whose

[34] See Cousin, *Cours de philosophie* (1828), Leçon X, 19.

[35] See Fétis's review of the *Symphonie fantastique*, *RM* IXme année/5: 1 Feb. 1835, 33–35, and his essays of 1852–4 on Wagner, discussed below in Chapter 10. Fétis's review of the *Fantastique* has been translated in full by Edward T. Cone in the Norton Critical Score of the work (New York, 1971), 215–20. Fétis's review of the *Fantastique* and *Lélio* in the *Revue musicale* of 15 December 1832 set the pattern for later articles.

[36] See Cousin, *Cours de philosophie* (1828), Leçon X, 15. Before Berlioz's personal attack on Fétis in *Le Retour à la vie*, the critic had welcomed Berlioz's work by the application of identical aesthetic standards. For a discussion of their relationship, see Bloom, 'Berlioz and the Critic', 240–65.

[37] *Schellings Werke*, II, 617.

[38] 'Le seul objet de l'art est le beau. L'art s'abandonne lui-même, dès qu'il s'en écarte.' Cousin, *Cours de l'histoire* (1846 [1818]), II, 193.

[39] Cousin, *Cours de l'histoire* (1846 [1818]), II, 197–9.

writings it was raised to unprecedented status because of its indeterminate, yet powerfully emotional, significance.[40] However, Cousin's conception of autonomous music was limited in comparison with Hoffmann's; moreover, his wish for a *juste milieu* prompted him to view the extreme vagueness of autonomous music as, in part, a disadvantage. Since it could combine an appeal to the imagination with semantic precision, poetry stood at the head of Cousin's artistic hierarchy.[41] Cousin was singularly ill-equipped to discuss music knowledgeably. Whilst he and Fétis shared opinions on music's representational potential and on the value of keeping the arts separate, Cousin is as unlikely a primary source for Fétis's aesthetic of formalism as Hoffmann is a likely one. Fétis's denunciation of Berlioz in 1835 illustrates the proximity of his view to that of Hoffmann. Discussing the utility of the *Fantastique*'s programme, he writes:

I have already observed on several occasions that programmes such as this stem from the narrowest possible conception of music's purpose; for the sole reason that this art has such power over our feelings is that it is essentially vague and indeterminate. (*RM* IXme année/5: 1 Feb. 1835, 34)[42]

The roots of Fétis's antipathy to programme music lie in his perception that it constituted a regression to older ideas of imitation. The arguments of Schelling, Hoffmann and other German Romantics had enhanced the status of autonomous music, whose emancipation was, in Fétis's view, jeopardised by new attempts to tie it to other arts. As late as 1829, in his review of the French première of the 'Pastoral' symphony, he still felt the need to rehearse the arguments against music as an imitative art (*RM* V/ [8]: [Mar.] 1829, 173–6). Despite the new definition of imitation provided in Berlioz's essay 'De l'imitation musicale' (*RGM* IV/1–2: 1–8 Jan. 1837), Fétis's definition of music – an art of the emotions whose aim was ideal beauty – remained irreconcilable with such attempts to broaden music's semantic potential. Here, Cousin's frequent analyses of the eighteenth-century philosophies of sensationalism (promoted by Locke and extended by Condillac), his fear of a return to pure secular empiricism (represented by Comte's positivism), and his abhorrence of the tenets of materialism, inform Fétis's intransigent attitude.[43] As a Christian

---

40   The opening of Hoffmann's review of Beethoven's Fifth Symphony, published in the Leipzig *Allgemeine musikalische Zeitung* of 4–11 July 1810, contains the most explicit exposition of Hoffmann's new world of autonomous music.

41   Cousin, *Cours de l'histoire* (1846 [1818]), II, 201–3.

42   'J'ai déjà fait remarquer plusieurs fois que de tels programmes sont puisés dans l'idée la plus rétrécie qu'on puisse se faire de la destination de la musique; car cet art n'agit avec tant de puissance sur notre sensibilité que parce qu'il est vague et indéterminé dans ses conditions' (*RM* IXme année/5: 1 Feb. 1835, 34).

43   John Locke (1632–1704): English empirical philosopher; Etienne Bonnot de Condillac (1715–80): French sensationalist philosopher.

philosopher, Cousin repeatedly exposed the weaknesses of Condillac's philosophy of sensationalism, and, in his 1829 lectures, noted that because of its concentration on purely physical response, 'the philosophy of sensation necessarily ends up at materialism'.[44] Whereas idealism and eclecticism attempted to explain the nature of the higher (the true) by means of the lower (the real), materialism held that the lower was an explanation only of itself, with no higher ideal. The perceived sensationalism and materialism of programme music's representational intent meant that it flouted every one of Cousin's aesthetic principles regarding music: firstly, it emphasised descriptive truth, rather than the ideal, and thus, at the extreme, ceased to be music (the tendency of Romantics to portray scenes of horror or ugliness compounded this problem); secondly, its specificity of meaning denied the listener the freedom of interpretation Cousin so prized. In music, materialism could manifest itself in several ways: in the perceived supremacy of compositional systems over inspiration in a composer's output; in the use of graphically realistic effects in dramatic and programme music; in the perceived supremacy of orchestral colour over formal or expressive considerations in a composer's work. Fétis's belief that ideal beauty, as opposed to truth, was the goal of music, led him to reject utterly all that pertained to materialism. His conviction formed the backdrop for much of his criticism of Berlioz and Wagner, and posed serious problems for Berlioz's apologists.

When he came to write about specific composers or works, Fétis was unable to practise all that he preached. Tensions between what his theories allowed and what his musical taste sanctioned were exposed, enabling the historian of criticism to examine the opposing forces which shaped the practice of his eclectic vision. Fétis never entirely escaped Comtian notions of progress in music. His emphasis upon the development of harmony as a major evaluative criterion had the unfortunate consequence of reducing the music of the *ordre unitonique*, in particular, to a status inferior to that of later categories. His frequent references to modal music as harmonically incomplete militated against his allegiance in principle to idealist theories of art as the realisation, in different forms, of a constant Idea, since he denied such music the potential for beauty which he attributed to more developed styles. The theory that 'art, in its essentials, does not progress, and its products are imperishable' proved illusory (*RGM* XVII/22: 2 Jun. 1850, 181).[45] However, Fétis's increasing

---

[44] 'la philosophie de la sensation aboutit donc nécessairement au matérialisme.' Cousin, *Cours de l'histoire de la philosophie. Cours de 1829. Histoire de la philosophie du XVIIIe siècle* (Paris, 1829), 144.

[45] 'l'art, en ce qu'il a d'essentiel, ne progresse donc pas, et ses œuvres sont impérissables' (*RGM* XVII/22: 2 Jun. 1850, 181).

disenchantment with avant-garde contemporary music strengthened his belief in the need for eclecticism as its antidote, and prompted his rejection of Comtian theories of progress. The resulting view of history was one in which Mozart stood as the peak of two centuries of achievement flanked by decadence on the one hand and music based on an incomplete harmonic system (i.e. before 1600) on the other.

When the *Gazette musicale* took over the *Revue musicale* in November 1835, Schlesinger welcomed both Fétis and his son Edouard onto the staff. Fétis *père* thus moved from having control of a journal's ethos (even when his son directed it from 1833–5) to being one of over a dozen contributors, many of whom held views diametrically opposed to his own. However, before discussing the nature of Fétis's position among the *Gazette*'s staff, it is important to assess the character and influence of journals founded before the takeover – rivals of both the *Revue* and the *Gazette*.

New music journals in 1833

Several papers, of which only one posed any intellectual threat, appeared in late 1833 and early 1834 to disturb the monopoly of the Fétis family. One of them, *Le Ménestrel*, became the longest-running and most prestigious weekly journal of them all, closing finally in 1940. Its first issue, on 1 December 1833, contained little which augured such status. Dominated by the *romance* which took the centre spread (i.e. fully half) of a four-page publication, the space for enlightened discussion was small – much smaller than in the *Tablettes* or the *Correspondance*. But enlightened discussion was not (yet) a primary aim of *Le Ménestrel*, whose mission was not didactic. Instead, it aimed to tempt the purchasers of Heugel's music with samples from his collections of salon pieces, and to provide an urbane readership with news items concerning Parisian musical life, with brief and innocuous reviews of major premières. The journal is an early example of a new phenomenon in the world of music criticism – the publishing-house journal. It is debatable whether the specialist music periodical *per se* would have flourished to such an extent had publishing houses not set up their own journals, each advertising its own music and making explicit its artistic allegiance. The appearance of several papers in the 1830s created a market for publications to suit an extremely diverse readership: Maurice Schlesinger, whose composers included Meyerbeer, Berlioz and Beethoven, set up the *Gazette musicale* in January 1834; the Escudier brothers, who specialised in Italian music, published *La France musicale* from December 1837; Romagnesi, primarily a publisher of *romances*, was publishing *L'Abeille musicale* as early as January 1828. With the financial backing of a larger business, journals stood a better chance of survival, even if they ran at a loss, since their importance as an advertising outlet and a source of public attention encouraged publishers, except *in extremis*, to subsidise them.[46]

In the short term, the advent of commercially secure publishers' journals caused the closure of smaller, independent papers. G. d'Egrefeuille, who published *Le Dilettante* – a journal in the Fétisian mould but including brief columns on art and fashion – saw the impending arrival of the Schlesinger publication as direct competition, and surrendered just three days after the *Gazette*'s first issue and three months after his own:[47]

There seemed to be a lacuna in the periodical press three months ago. Among all the publications appearing at that time, music had only one truly specialised journal ... The *Gazette musicale*, which M. Schlesinger, one of the most distinguished music publishers in Paris, is bringing out from 5th January, opens with significant means of success; we shall not undertake to begin a struggle with it. (*Le Dilettante* II/2: 8 Jan. 1834, 1)[48]

D'Egrefeuille may have sold his journal to Schlesinger: his final editorial offered his subscribers copies of the *Gazette* until the end of their term.[49]

However, the new-found financial stability of outlets for criticism had its dangers. It would indeed be surprising to find the criticism of a house journal reflecting few of the strengths of its parent company; nevertheless, commercial interest imperilled critical impartiality. In some papers, such as *La France musicale*, the quality of criticism suffered from insistence upon maintaining the party line: in May 1845 the Escudier brothers secured simultaneous publication rights with Ricordi of Milan for forthcoming operas by Verdi. The publishing house had always been as pro-Italian as Schlesinger's was pro-German, but the coup of 1845 set its criticism in stone to the extent that it forced other papers, notably the *Gazette*, to draw up equally intransigent battle lines. At the margins, such debates between publishers' journals were less about maintaining profits than about the esteem which a particular living composer merited. As such, they form part of the larger debate about canon and posterity. Far from deserving to be jettisoned as unreliable or biased, the *parti pris*

---

[46] See Appendix 4 for information regarding the Brandus brothers' willingness to subsidise the *Gazette* from publishing-house funds.

[47] Nothing is known of D'Egrefeuille's identity or career.

[48] 'Une lacune semblait exister il y [a] trois mois dans la presse périodique. Entre toutes les publications de cette époque, la musique ne comptait qu'un seul organe vraiment spécial ... La *Gazette musicale*, que publie, à compter du 5 janvier, M. Schlesinger, l'un des éditeurs les plus distingués de Paris, débute avec de grands moyens de succès: nous n'entreprendrons pas d'établir de lutte avec elle' (*Le Dilettante* II/2: 8 Jan. 1834, 1).

[49] The handing over of subscribers is confirmed in the *Gazette* (*GM* I/4: 26 Jan. 1834, 27). *Le Pianiste* mocked the 'marriage' (*Le Pianiste* Année I/4: 6 Jan. 1834, 49).

reviews of a house journal are invaluable as an extension of the acting principles of the publishing house itself.

In addition to the first significant house journal, 1833 saw an early sign of fragmentation within specialist music journalism. **Chaulieu's** *Le Pianiste* lasted two years, appearing from November 1833 to October 1835, abandoning its specialist character at the end of the first year in a futile and (as its editors eventually acknowledged) misguided attempt to increase its readership.[50] The main editors of *Le Pianiste* – **J. Delacour** and Charles Martin (*dit* Chaulieu) – attempted none of the philosophical argument of the *Revue musicale*. Their journal was didactic in a practical sense, printing detailed technical analyses of new pieces whilst also inculcating a sense of decorous taste in its young (and probably predominantly female) readership. Critical sections of the journal provide early sources of opinion on the music of Chopin and Schumann in Paris, and indicate the ambivalence with which music of the Romantics was received among writers whose god of the piano was Clementi and who supported wholeheartedly the salon music – *airs variés* and *variations brillantes* – composed by, among others, Henri Herz, Franz Hünten, Johann Pixis and Friedrich Kalkbrenner. Chopin's originality was viewed with a mixture of admiration and fear. An unsigned review of the Rondo Op. 16 and the Four Mazurkas Op. 17 alighted on the problems posed by Chopin's harmonic practice, and though explicitly supportive of the works in question, ended with the almost Fétisian warning that: 'It is but one step from originality to the bizarre' (*Le Pianiste* Année I, 110)[51] An earlier review of the Three Nocturnes Op. 15 concentrated on the near-unplayability of such technically and harmonically original works, and pleaded with Chopin to bring his talent within reach of the fingers of lesser mortals.[52] By contrast, Schumann attracted nothing but sarcastic polemics; the journal's unsigned critics considered his work both unplayable and impenetrable.[53] The extreme stance of *Le Pianiste*'s writers on contemporary piano music was doubtless influenced by the *Gazette musicale*'s opposing view.[54] Given the prominence of articles on piano music in the *Gazette*'s opening numbers, Chaulieu and

[50] *Le Pianiste* Année II/24: 20 Oct. 1835, 187–88. The journal appeared monthly in its first year and twice monthly in its second. Unfortunately, the copy used for the Minkoff reprint (Geneva, 1972) lacked the prospectus and several music supplements. The latter are often essential to an understanding of the analyses presented in the main body of the text. Complete original copies can be found in the Bibliothèque nationale, Paris, and the Bodleian Library, Oxford.

[51] 'Il n'y a qu'un pas de l'originalité à la bizarrerie' (*Le Pianiste* Année I, 110).

[52] *Le Pianiste* Année I, 79.

[53] See especially a copiously illustrated review of the Impromptus Op. 5 (*Le Pianiste* Année I, 89).

[54] See below, Chapter 7.

Delacour's decision to widen *Le Pianiste*'s field of vision may also have been a response to such competition.

La Gazette musicale de Paris

Schlesinger's intention was to produce a journal whose criticism departed from current modes and which would, specifically, provide an antidote to the professorial aridity of the *Revue musicale*. A Prussian whose family already ran a prestigious music publishing house in Berlin, Maurice (Moritz) Schlesinger founded the Paris publishing house in 1821 and directed it until 1846, when he sold the business to Louis Brandus. With their various business partners, Louis and Gemmy Brandus (1823–73) oversaw the journal until its closure in 1880.[55] Excepting a lacuna of thirteen months during the Franco-Prussian War and an experiment with twice-weekly publication from the end of 1838 to April 1841, the *Gazette* appeared weekly from 5 January 1834 to 31 December 1880.[56] Its readership comprised composers, artists and amateurs, as did its line-up of contributors, of whom around twenty were regular writers at any one time.[57] In its lifetime the journal received regular contributions from over one hundred named writers. Despite their number and their variety, these writers between them produced a journal which, for most of its career, possessed a coherent, dominant aesthetic code. That code did not, however, remain stable. The rest of this book examines how and why changes of critical allegiance arose.

When the *Gazette musicale* printed its first issue on 5 January 1834, its dominant character was that of German Romanticism. An introductory editorial by Schlesinger attacked Fétis and hinted at an ensuing war on the meaningless virtuosity of fashionable piano music, but said nothing of the broader beliefs of his journal. However, the new direction in which Schlesinger wished to take music criticism could scarcely have been stated more openly than through the subject and genre of the piece following his editorial: rather than print an historical article (as Fétis had done on Mozart) or an opera review, he commissioned the popular writer Jules Janin to write a short, Hoffmannesque, story on Beethoven.

[55] After the sale of the business Schlesinger kept control of 25 per cent of the shares in the journal. See Devriès and Lesure, *Dictionnaire des éditeurs de musique français*, 2 vols. (Geneva, 1979–88), II, 389. Some of the Brandus direction of the *Gazette* was done at arm's length; the brothers employed various directors and showed little of the personal interest which Schlesinger had constantly displayed. The most celebrated portrait of Schlesinger is that by Gustave Flaubert, who used him as a model for Jacques Arnoux in *L'Education sentimentale* of 1869.

[56] For details of the exceptional period, see Appendix 4.

[57] They were generally listed either on the front page of each issue or as part of the index for each year.

Set in Vienna in 1819, the story portrayed Beethoven as a social outcast, alienated and misunderstood.[58] The result, as literature, was 'mediocre and vulgar';[59] as a journalistic ploy it was both arresting and timely;[60] as a means of explaining the journal's artistic credo without preaching to its readership it was ideal.[61] A string of specially commissioned stories by authors including Sand, Janin, Dumas, Balzac, Wagner and Berlioz, followed in the years up to Schlesinger's sale of the business.[62] Schlesinger was not the first to include a series of *contes fantastiques* in a music periodical: in the winter of 1830–1, Fétis had printed several of Hoffmann's own musical *Tales* in translations which conform to neither of the complete editions available.[63] However, these stories were included as items of interest, rather than constituting an artistic credo – they jar with the predominant tone of the material which surrounds them. Many of the *Gazette*'s stories were evidently inspired by Hoffmann's work; Janin's second contribution was a portrait of the composer-critic himself.[64] Allegiance to Hoffmann brought with it a substantial amount of intellectual baggage concerning the nature of the artist, of criticism and of the artist's place in society. As such it gave Schlesinger and his writers a framework of ideals within which to work, and a ready-made genre in which these ideals could be presented. Both the message and the means were new to music criticism in France, and Schlesinger made the most of their novelty to give the journal's first years a Romantic lustre in which the content of his *contes fantastiques* informed all other criticism, whether music reviews or historical articles.

---

[58] 'Le Dîner de Beethoven' (*GM* I/1–2: 5–12 Jan. 1834). A letter from Schlesinger to A. B. Marx, dated 27 February 1859 (and included in Schindler's biography of Beethoven), describes the story's scenario almost exactly, but is presented as Schlesinger's personal recollection of a meeting with Beethoven. It is thus highly likely that Janin's image of Beethoven was supplied by the *Gazette*'s director. The letter is translated in O. Sonneck, *Beethoven: Impressions by his Contemporaries* (New York, 1967), 112–13.

[59] 'médiocre et vulgaire'. Pierre Citron, 'Autour de Gambara II. "Gambara", Struntz et Beethoven', *Année balzacienne* (1967), 169.

[60] Though only just; in 1833–4 the French craze for Hoffmann began to die down. See the history of Hoffmann's reception in Elizabeth Teichmann, *La Fortune d'Hoffmann en France* (Geneva and Paris, 1961).

[61] A selection of Hoffmann's *Tales* first appeared from 14 June 1829 in the *Revue de Paris*, translated by Loève-Veimars. Complete editions of the *Tales* were available from 1830 in two translations: *Œuvres complètes*, 19 vols., trans. Loève-Veimars (Paris, 1830–2), and *Œuvres complètes de E. T. A. Hoffmann, trad. M. Théodore Toussenel et l'auteur des romans de Veit-Wéber*, 12 vols. (Paris, 1830).

[62] See Appendix 3, which lists literary pieces in Schlesinger's *Gazette*.

[63] Those published were: 'L'Archet de Baron de B***', 'Le Chevalier Gluck', 'Kreisleriana', 'Don Juan', 'Biographie de Kreisler (fragment)' and 'L'Ennemi de la musique'. Fétis also published Hoffmann's essay on Beethoven's instrumental music.

[64] Jules Janin, 'Hoffman' (*GM* I/13–14: 30 Mar. – 6 Apr. 1834). Janin frequently misspells Hoffmann's name.

A major by-product of the allegiance to Hoffmann was the active reversal of the idea, promulgated by Castil-Blaze and continued by Fétis, that professional criticism was the surest means of introducing musical ideas to the public. Instead, Schlesinger created an alliance between music and literature which emphasised the fusion of the arts and put into practice an idea attributed to Hoffmann by Janin: that critics should be artistically creative themselves, and that creativity in a different field was a lesser impediment to judging an artist's work than a purely theoretical relationship, however intimate, with the art in question. This is the most important message of Janin's 'Hoffman', the latter part of which presents a distorted and expanded translation from Hoffmann's 'Casual Reflections on the Appearance of this Journal', a late and little-known essay dating from 1820 (*GM* I/13–14: 30 Mar. – 6 Apr. 1834).[65] The casting of such a judgement within a piece of creative prose was, of course, the ultimate justification of Janin's endeavour.

The journal's idea of the rôle of criticism stemmed from Hoffmann's vision of the artist as a man apart, living on a superior plane to that of the common herd and often suffering the indignity of incomprehension at the hands of philistines who disparaged him in part for his lowly status as a servant. Hoffmann's theories of artistic nobility and of the musical genius as an undervalued figure struggling against traditional social hierarchies found a partial corollary in French socialist philosophies of the 1830s in which the artist had recently been raised to priestly status: Fourierism and Saint-Simonism. The ideal of genius as a vessel through which change worked is conspicuous in the *Gazette* only by its absence. Liszt's famous articles on the artist's position in society, inspired by Lamennais (*GM* II/18–41: 3 May – 11 Oct. 1835), provided a complement to discussions which were already in readers' minds from their indirect exposition in Hoffmannesque *contes*. However, truly utopian ideas of the artist's integrated rôle in society never gained the ascendant in Schlesinger's *contes*, which prized too highly the pre-eminence of alienated genius. The journal's acceptance of utopian ideas was selective, winnowing out Fourier's emphasis on the ennobling and pacifying of the community through harmonious, pleasing music, but leaving music as highest of the arts with the artist as a figurehead. The status of the art was enhanced, but so was the élitism, alienation and egotistical individualism of its creators.

The theme of alienated genius, ubiquitous in Schlesinger's *contes*,

[65] The essay is translated in E. T. A. Hoffmann, *E. T. A. Hoffmann's Musical Writings: Kreisleriana, The Poet and the Composer, Music Criticism*, trans. Martyn Clarke, ed. David Charlton (Cambridge, 1989), 423–31. It first appeared in the *Allgemeine Zeitung für Musik und Literatur* (9–16 Oct. 1820).

forms the main focus of Balzac's 'Gambara' and Janin's 'Le Dîner de Beethoven', and returns at the climax of Wagner's 'Une visite à Beethoven'.[66] The composer Gambara presents the argument at its most explicit:

We are victims ... of our own superiority. My music is beautiful, but when music passes from sensation to idea, it can have only people of genius as listeners, because they alone have the power to develop it. My misfortune comes from having heard the concerts of angels and having believed that men could understand them. (*RGM* IV/34: 20 Aug. 1837, 381)[67]

Gambara's idea of opera was indeed ahead of its time: Balzac describes his trilogy *Mahomet* as a history of humanity which owes more to drama than to opera and contains themes which recur throughout the work, gathering symbolic associations as they proceed. Moreover, Gambara's contempt for professional librettists has led him to write his own text. The prefiguring of Wagner's practice is uncanny. The fact that Balzac was nearly musically illiterate and may not have been responsible for (or indeed have believed in) many of the ideas contained in 'Gambara' is largely irrelevant to the question addressed here; from the point of view of the journal's image, the story, bullied out of a celebrated writer by a determined music publisher with a mission, is more important as Schlesinger's creation than as Balzac's.[68]

The consistent portrayal of genius as aloof and comprehended by only a select few inevitably set up a paradigm of élitism from which neither the journal's stories nor its criticism escaped during the Schlesinger years. Janin was the most ardent supporter of a quasi-religious distinction between initiates and the crowd, with its attendant restrictions on the flow of information from the former to the latter. Such a paradigm inevitably ran counter to the journal's educational intent, but reinforced the notion of a commitment to originality and to modern music. Beethoven's presence at the centre of such discussions is significant – the prominent placing of Janin's 'Le Dîner de Beethoven' as the journal's

---

[66] Balzac, *RGM* IV/30–34: 23 Jul. – 20 Aug. 1837; Janin, *GM* I/1–2: 5–12 Jan. 1834; Wagner, *RGM* VII/65–9: 19 Nov. – 3 Dec. 1840).

[67] 'Nous sommes victimes ... de notre propre supériorité. Ma musique est belle, mais quand la musique passe de la sensation à l'idée, elle ne peut avoir que des gens de génie pour auditeurs, car eux seuls ont la puissance de la développer. Mon malheur vient d'avoir écouté les concerts des anges et d'avoir cru que les hommes pourraient les comprendre' (*RGM* IV/34: 20 Aug. 1837, 381).

[68] For discussions of the genesis and content of 'Gambara', see Jean-Pierre Barricelli, 'Autour de Gambara I: Balzac et Meyerbeer', *Année balzacienne* (1967), 157–63; Bloom, 'François-Joseph Fétis', 102–9; Matthias Brzoska, ' "Mahomet" et "Robert-le-Diable": l'esthétique musicale dans "Gambara" ', *Année balzacienne* (1983), 51–78; Citron, 'Autour de Gambara II'; and Maurice Regard, 'Balzac est-il l'auteur de "Gambara"?', *Revue d'histoire littéraire de la France* LIII (1953), 496–507.

first article made the identity of its flagship composer clear from the outset (as Fétis had done with Mozart). More than any journal before or after, the *Gazette* promoted Beethoven's cause, having first transformed him into a Romantic hero; attempts to ensure the posterity of his music rested as much on the image presented through literature as that presented in reviews of his music. Contemporary composers who were to benefit from being judged in a Hoffmannesque light included Berlioz and the self-consciously alienated Chopin. By contrast, in the 1830s Liszt was not included in this category, partly because his music was too squarely in the virtuoso style and partly because his popularity was excessive. Much to Liszt's frustration, Schlesinger welcomed articles and reviews from him but consistently refused to advertise his compositions.[69]

During the 1840s the enthusiasm and energy required to continue the tradition of musical discussion through literature gradually waned. The *contes fantastiques* of the 1840s by Wagner and Berlioz, and George Sand's 'Carl', are nearly isolated examples of Schlesinger's original editorial policy, and represent some of the last examples of the *conte fantastique* genre. As popular literary taste for *romans feuilletons* increased, so Schlesinger and Louis Brandus commissioned lighter, serialised fiction from contributors such as Edouard Monnais. Such pieces are indistinguishable in quality or content from their counterparts in non-specialist magazines. Yet by 1846 Schlesinger had, through his *contes*, developed a philosophical context for the weekly criticism of contemporary music in his journal – an artistic credo which rejected the perceived vulgarity of Paris salon society. The engagement of celebrated and rising literary and musical stars served to strengthen the case argued in Janin's 'Hoffman' that art should be discussed only by those whose relation to it was creative, a situation which was mostly true of the *Gazette* whilst under Schlesinger's directorship, but which ceased to be so under Brandus, by which time the Romantic image of the journal had weakened (as indeed had the force of Romanticism itself). Yet in so mixing musical discussion and literature, Schlesinger offered his public a unique approach to the appreciation and understanding of central issues of the time, in an experiment which was never imitated successfully. Whatever their literary merits, the *contes* and *nouvelles* of Schlesinger's *Gazette* are a rich source of Romantic artistic thought and a testament to the originality and resourcefulness of his directorship.

Aside from, and overshadowed by, the Romantic glow of the *contes*, Schlesinger's early *Gazette* also contained material which smacked of the

---

[69] See Jacqueline Bellas, 'La Tumultueuse amitié de Franz Liszt et de Maurice Schlesinger', *Littératures* XII (Nov. 1965), Annales publiés trimestriellement par la Faculté des lettres et des sciences humaines de Toulouse. Nouvelle série, t. I, fasc. III, 7–20.

juste milieu. A natural extension of the publishing-house rights over the works of Meyerbeer and, to a lesser extent, Halévy, this trait became more apparent after the loudly heralded arrival of Fétis *père* as a contributor to his journal's erstwhile rival.[70] In his account of manifestations of eclecticism in French culture of the 1830s, Albert Boime sees the potential for musical eclecticism solely in texted music and points to the mixed genre works of Berlioz and Félicien David as examples of the resulting *juste milieu*.[71] However, in music the phrase *juste milieu* became common in criticism of exactly the repertoire which Boime outlaws – autonomous music – on account of a simplification of Cousin's vision. The most prestigious composer of instrumental music on Schlesinger's books was Georges Onslow, a specialist in chamber music whose output was both popular (within necessarily restricted circles) and respected. A rare Frenchman writing autonomous music in the Viennese tradition, his music was neither Romantic nor Classical in style, but post-Beethovenian in the sense of following the path of the middle period works and steering clear of the problems of idiom and form posed by, in particular, the late quartets. **François Stoepel**'s biographical sketch of 11 May 1834 represented the first major assessment of a living composer's output in the pages of the *Gazette*, even though the logical counterpart to the *contes fantastiques* would surely have been Berlioz. In his article, Stoepel complimented Onslow on his modesty of stylistic ambition – specifically, for:

never having wanted to try to elevate himself (as Beethoven did) above this form, to which an entire century has, so to speak, devoted itself, in the string quartet genre. (*GM* I/19: 11 May 1834, 153)[72]

Though Stoepel never rooted his thoughts in philosophical ideas as Fétis did, and although his response to Romanticism was far more open than this opinion might imply, his stance here is Fétisian: he wants to see chamber music 'stop' at middle-period Beethoven and explore new possibilities within recognisable formal schemes. At its least sophisticated, this stance, which the journal also extended to orchestral music, represented merely a reworking of the Classical–Romantic debate, though the outcome was often referred to in Cousinian terms as a *juste milieu*.

[70] The hyperbole of the welcoming editorial written by Liszt can be seen as an atonement for the harshness of Schlesinger's attack on the *Revue musicale* in his opening issue of 5 January 1834. Cf. *RGM* III/1: 3 Jan. 1836, 5.

[71] Albert Boime, *Thomas Couture and the Eclectic Vision* (New Haven and London, 1980), 20.

[72] 'n'avoir jamais voulu tenter de s'élever à l'example de Beethoven, au-dessus de cette forme qu'a consacrée, pour ainsi dire, tout un siècle pour le genre du quatuor (*GM* I/19: 11 May 1834, 153).

Fétis's influence on the journal strengthened considerably after the Brandus takeover of the publishing house and the *Gazette* in 1846. Neither brother was a hothead in the manner of Schlesinger; neither had Schlesinger's Romantic vision. Moreover, relations between the Branduses and Fétis were warmer than the latter's relationship with Schlesinger, which was tainted by the past and not improved by the publisher's chronic unwillingness to pay contributors for their work. Most of Fétis's contributions to the journal were extended abstract articles which tackled issues concerned with the development of musical style, the reasons underlying current decadence and the possibilities for finding a way out of the morass. Even articles devoted to a particular composer, such as the famous attacks on Wagner in 1852–4, contained a significant proportion of aesthetic discussion. Whatever their critical allegiance, other contributors were forced to take notice of Fétis's articles. Those who shared his point of view found a ready-made set of artistic tenets which could be plundered at will; those who did not had the more difficult task of marshalling counter-arguments. Composers such as Schumann, Liszt and Wagner, who might have benefited in the 1850s from a theoretical framework for criticism which was dependent upon German Romanticism and which bent French utopianism to its own ends, stood little chance of favour once these tenets had been overturned. Fétis's views on art as serving society's needs may well have been influenced by Fourier and Saint-Simon;[73] however, Cousin's transformation theory, by which genius was merely a vehicle through which change worked under its own momentum, was probably more influential, resulting in a condemnation of Romanticism and the 'music of the future' as arrogant individualism, particularly when composers theorised about their work. A new tendency to approach criticism through biography only reinforced this effect, often denying the artist special understanding for morally questionable conduct. Though Cousin's idea of the 'grand homme' specifically stated that the sordid details of such men's personal lives should not be allowed to prejudice any estimation of their greatness, Fétis followed Cousin's lead only when it was expedient. Wagner, a defender of the artist's exemption from traditional moral codes, became his most famous victim. By contrast, the reputations of the main beneficiaries of the *Gazette*'s initial credo – Beethoven, Berlioz and Chopin – outlived the theories which had helped to enhance them.

Fétis's influence was not, however, restricted to contemporary music. On the contrary, his rejection of the notion that music was either a passing fashion, or an art in linear progression, was instrumental in

---

[73] See Jane Fulcher, 'Le Socialisme utopique et la critique musicale en France sous le second Empire', *Revue internationale de musique française* V/14 (Jun. 1984), 67–8.

changing attitudes towards early music and extending ideas of canon to music which antedated Gluck. The tensions in his theories of early music and the journal's criticism of music before c. 1750 form the subject of the next chapter.

3   Early music

Schlesinger's original distancing of the *Gazette*'s tenor from that of the *Revue* meant that his journal tended to neglect early music in favour of the living repertory. In the months leading to the merger, one of the journal's staff had referred scathingly to Fétis's unsuccessful series of 'concerts historiques' as an 'abortive musical speculation' (unsigned II/16: 19 Apr. 1835, 139).[1] However, once Fétis was on board, Schlesinger was too shrewd not to change tack and utilise fully the talents of the most distinguished Francophone critic-historian of the time. Thus, instead of attacking Fétis's endeavours, in April 1836 he acknowledged that the journal had hitherto neglected the discussion of early music. He proposed to set up a forum for discussion:

The *Retrospective Review* which the director of the *Gazette musicale* plans to start this year, will, as far as possible, attempt to compensate for that institution so dreamed-of and clamoured for to no avail by the friends of the art, in which the fine products of the centuries would be played each year in such a way as to present the great musicians of past centuries with the utmost fidelity, or, rather, *exhibit* them, as are exhibited Raphael, Corrége, Titian, Rubens and Rembrandt at the Louvre. (III/14: 3 Apr. 1836, 106)[2]

Schlesinger's motivation was educational, based on premises with which the eclectic Fétis would have agreed: that artistic progress would be stunted unless great works of the past were studied and appreciated, and that the riches of past epochs were 'equal to those we have just conquered' (*ibid.*).[3] The journal's support for the study and performance of early music depended largely upon adherence to the ideals of universal beauty and

[1] 'spéculation musicale manquée' (unsigned, *GM* II/16: 19 Apr. 1835, 139).
[2] 'La *Revue rétrospective* que le directeur de la *Gazette musicale* se propose de commencer cette année, tendra donc à suppléer, autant que possible, à cette institution tant de fois rêvée et si inutilement réclamée par les amis de l'art, dans laquelle les belles productions de toutes les époques devraient être exécutées chaque année, de manière à ce que les grands musiciens des siècles passés fussent reproduits avec la fidélité la plus scrupuleuse, ou, pour mieux dire, *exposés* comme le sont au Louvre Raphael, Corrége, Titien, Rubens et Rembrandt' (*RGM* III/14: 3 Apr. 1836, 106).
[3] 'égales à celles qu'on vient de conquérir...' (*ibid.*).

historical value transmitted by Fétis. Moreover, these ideals achieved longevity in the journal due to Fétis's lifelong aesthetic consistency and the extent of his influence on the journal's other writers, whether historian-critics or not. The *Gazette*'s coverage of issues in early music ranged widely, from debates in 'archéologie musicale' – the study of Medieval manuscripts – to those concerning editing and performance practice. Such debates took as a fundamental premise the value of early music, both as a subject worthy of historical study and as a source of performing repertoire. This chapter examines the attitudes of the *Gazette*'s critics to musicology *per se* and to the nature of early music performance in Parisian concert life.

The case for musicology

When the *Gazette* began publication, Fétis's was almost a lone voice campaigning for the public performance of Renaissance and Baroque music. In the eyes of many, securing the regular performance of such music was dependent upon promoting an understanding of its time and place within the continuum of music history; justifying musicology's relevance as a discipline was, therefore, the precondition both of intellectual advance and the popular dissemination of an unfamiliar repertory.[4] The natural consequence of a wish to bring early music into the public domain was a need to educate performers, to which end the journal printed articles until the mid century advocating the teaching of music history in Conservatoires. Using arguments of impeccable Fétisian pedigree, **Louis Fanart** and Maurice Bourges argued the case for an appreciation of early music on the grounds of universal beauty.[5] For Fanart, the alternative was too awful to contemplate:

everything is beautiful, everything is ugly, according to each person's fancy, following the passions or the fashion of the day. So let us no longer state that the arts are marked out with the seal of immortality, but speak of them as children's toys which give us pleasure today and which we shall break in smithereens tomorrow! (*RGM* XII/44: 2 Nov. 1845, 359)[6]

The crux of Fanart's article is that, since artists in other fields respect the products of the past, musicians should do the same, and that such respect

[4] The *Gazette*'s first apologist for musicology was Bottée de Toulmon (1797–1850) (*RGM* III/9: 28 Feb. 1836).

[5] L.-S. Fanart: 'De la necessité d'étudier la musique dans son histoire' (*RGM* XII/43–4: 26 Oct. – 2 Nov. 1845); and Maurice Bourges: 'De l'histoire de la musique appliquée à l'enseignement' (*RGM* XVII/41: 13 Oct. 1850).

[6] 'tout est beau, tout est laid, selon la caprice de chacun, suivant les passions ou la mode du jour. Alors ne disons plus que les arts sont marqués au front du sceau de l'immortalité, mais disons que ce sont des jouets d'enfants qui font aujourd'hui notre bonheur et que nous briserons demain en morceaux!' (*RGM* XII/44: 2 Nov. 1845, 359).

can be achieved only through an understanding of the changes in musical style through the ages. As in Fétis's work, there is an implicit tension between what Fanart mentions as 'first musical attempts' (*ibid.*, 358)[7] and his claim that there is no such thing as progress in music. Likewise from Fétis comes his comment that the notion of progress in the arts has come about because of an erroneous and misleading equation of music with the sciences, where progress towards perfection is more clearly evident. By contrast, he posits that:

The art changes, but it remains stationary, because its principle [the ideal] remains intact; the emotions which it produces have varied neither in nature nor in intensity, [and] only the secondary forms have undergone modification. (*ibid.*, 359)[8]

Fanart's intellectual ancestry is apparent. His distinction between music's primary and secondary elements recalls Cousin's distinction between temporally specific (superficial) truth and universal truth, an axiom itself taken from Hegel and Schelling and readily applied to musical style by Fétis as the cornerstone of his aesthetic of music history. That Fanart should paraphrase Fétis's ideas of the 1820s so closely a generation later is evidence not of reaction, but of the strength of his influence. The intellectual proximity of the two men can be illustrated by comparing Fanart's ideas on art, science and the theory of transformation with those contained in an article of 1850 by Fétis, in which the historian reiterated his theory of musical transformation in explicit contrast to scientific progress.

The object of science is reality; that of art, is the ideal. This simple distinction suffices to demonstrate that the art cannot progress, and that its products cannot perish. (*RGM* XVII/22: 2 Jun. 1850, 181)[9]

Fanart's belief in a universal beauty rendering the music of one era accessible to music lovers of another led him to condemn contemporary musicians for judging music 'not according to the constituent laws of beauty, but according to their ingrained habits' (*RGM* XII/43: 26 Oct. 1845, 350).[10] In 1850, Maurice Bourges laid part of the blame on the Paris Conservatoire, which neglected to train its musicians in their musical

---

[7] 'premiers essais musicaux' (*ibid.*, 358).

[8] 'l'art se modifie, mais il reste stationnaire, car son principe [l'idéal] est demeuré intact, les émotions qu'il produit n'ont varié ni dans leur intensité ni dans leur nature, les formes secondaires seules ont subi quelques modifications' (*ibid.*, 359).

[9] 'Dans la science, l'objet est le réel; dans l'art, c'est l'idéal. Cette simple distinction suffit pour faire comprendre que l'art ne peut progresser, et que ses produits ne peuvent périr' (*RGM* XVII/22: 2 Jun. 1850, 181).

[10] 'non d'après les lois constitutives du beau, mais d'après les habitudes qu'ils ont contractées' (*RGM* XII/43: 26 Oct. 1845, 350).

heritage. Such training would have enabled them to 'appreciate, in the broad lines and the principal elements of history, the secret, but indissoluble, link which unites the past with the present' (*RGM* XVII/41: 13 Oct. 1850, 342).[11] Instead, it fostered, whether deliberately or through negligence, the fallacy that only contemporary music was of artistic worth. Whilst Bourges's wish was not fulfilled until 1872 when Auguste Barbereau became the first tutor in music history at the Conservatoire,[12] revolution came about much earlier in the world of performance, and the *Gazette*'s critics concentrated upon educating future audiences.

In 1837, François Benoist defended Philippe Musard's inclusion of extracts from *Alexander's Feast* and *Messiah* in a Concert Spirituel despite the fact that they were badly received:

Why restrict ourselves exclusively to listening to modern compositions? Why restrain thus and confine the art within narrow and impoverished limits, instead of considering it from a more elevated point of view by studying the composers who were the pride of centuries past? (*RGM* IV/13: 26 Mar. 1837, 104)[13]

Fétis's reasons for reviving early music were often concerned more with moulding music's future: a review of a concert of historical piano music given in London by Ignaz Moscheles noted that the performance of early music would form 'the point of departure for a doctrine of eclecticism which will soon prevail' (*RGM* V/6: 11 Feb. 1838, 62).[14] In a rare discussion of music before Gluck, Berlioz blamed the public for the lamentable state of early music's reputation:

we are the ones who become old, it is our sensibility which is dulled, it is our imagination which fades; but the power and the vital warmth of the music remain undiminished; on the contrary, they increase day by day. (*RGM* VII/5: 16 Jan. 1840, 38)[15]

However, in the ensuing review of Baroque music performed at the Conservatoire, Berlioz was less enthusiastic when faced with individual

---

[11] 'saisir dans les grandes lignes et les principaux aspects de l'histoire le lien secret, mais indissoluble, qui unit le passé au présent' (*RGM* XVII/41: 13 Oct. 1850, 342).

[12] Danièle Pistone, *La Musique en France de la Révolution à 1900* (Paris, 1979), 37. Barbereau was nominated in the autumn of 1871 and began teaching early the following year.

[13] 'Pourquoi, en effet, se borner exclusivement à l'audition des compositions modernes? pourquoi restreindre ainsi et resserrer l'art dans d'étroites et mesquines limites, au lieu de le considérer d'un point de vue plus élevé, en étudiant les compositeurs qui furent l'honneur des siècles précédents?' (*RGM* IV/13: 26 Mar. 1837, 104). François Benoist (1794–1878): organist and composer. He taught at the Paris Conservatoire for over fifty years. Philippe Musard (1792–1852): composer and conductor of dance music.

[14] 'le point de départ d'une doctrine d'éclectisme qui réglera plus tard les jugements concernant les œuvres d'art' (*RGM* V/6: 11 Feb. 1838, 62).

[15] 'c'est nous qui vieillissons, c'est notre sensibilité qui s'émousse, c'est notre imagination qui s'éteint; mais la force et la chaleur vitale de la musique ne diminuent point, au contraire, elles augmentent de jour en jour' (*RGM* VII/5: 16 Jan. 1840, 38).

pieces; in his introduction he inadvertently revealed a paradox in the popularity of early music which was long in being overcome – its novelty value: 'At last we have had something new!' (*ibid.*, 37).[16] Whilst Berlioz's outburst has to be seen in the overall context of his Conservatoire reviewing, which, from around 1838, repeatedly complained of stagnant and predictable programming,[17] the harmonic novelty of early music, particularly that of the Renaissance, captured the attention of the limited public which had access to it, to the point that even as late as 1873 a choral piece by Cavalieri was characterised purely by its quaint harmonic practice:

Harmonic progressions which would nowadays be considered anti-tonal, in any case far bolder than the use of the dissonance which dates only from this period and which remained unknown to this composer, give this chorus a strange savour. (unsigned, *RGM* XL/17: 27 Apr. 1873, 133)[18]

Throughout the *Gazette* and in the fabric of concert life for the half-century up to 1880, attitudes towards early music fractured at the music of *c.* 1600: Renaissance music was considered unsuitable for regular performance, but Baroque music, especially in its more monumental guises of Passion and oratorio, eventually achieved considerable success with a large public once the ground had been prepared through smaller genres and the performance of excerpts. Although Renaissance music was accepted in small doses primarily as a curiosity, more strenuous efforts of understanding were encouraged for music which bore a manifestly greater resemblance to contemporary tradition. The author (almost certainly **Charles Bannelier**) of the review of Cavalieri quoted earlier, follows Fétis's theory that Monteverdi invented tonality via the discovery of the dominant seventh chord (to which he alludes), thereby producing the *ordre transitonique.*[19] Despite his wish not to advocate progress in music, Fétis's concentration on a tonal revolution brought about specifically by Monteverdi inevitably cast the composer's predecessors and unreconstructed contemporaries in an inferior light; in the

[16] 'Enfin nous avons eu du nouveau!' (*ibid.*, 37). This paradox had been identified as early as 1803 by Geoffroy, who approved of a patchwork oratorio called *Saul* on the grounds that Pergolesi, Porpora and other contemporaries 'would now be newer than our most modern composers, whose politenesses are already exhausted' ('seroient aujourd'hui plus nouveaux que nos compositeurs les plus modernes, dont les gentillesses sont déjà épuisées') (*JD* 18 germinal an 11 / 8 Apr. 1803, 4).

[17] See below, p. 105.

[18] 'De successions harmoniques qui seraient considérées aujourd'hui comme antitonales, bien plus hardies en tout cas que l'emploi de la dissonance [sic] qui date seulement de cette époque et qui est resté étranger à ce compositeur, donnent une saveur étrange à ce chœur' (unsigned, *RGM* XL/17: 27 Apr. 1873, 133).

[19] For a discussion of this attribution, see Appendix 5. Unsigned articles attributed to Bannelier are marked '?Bannelier'.

journal, Fétis repeatedly revealed the tensions between his musical taste and his philosophical allegiances, and between his philosophical allegiances themselves.

In 1861 Aristide and Louise Farrenc published the first volume of a monumental anthology containing a large proportion of Renaissance, Baroque and pre-Classical keyboard music of which much had not previously appeared in print.[20] Entitled *Le Trésor des pianistes*, it was an attempt to bring together the finest European keyboard music from the English virginalists to Chopin. With the exception of the new collected editions, few publications of the nineteenth century can have been conceived with such canonic intent. Fétis was intimately involved in the project, even lending the Farrencs some of his own manuscripts for inclusion.[21] This did not prevent him from contributing an extensive and laudatory review of each volume as it appeared, though he did devote most of each review to analyses of the pieces within each volume. Volume six, which Fétis reviewed in November 1864, contained unlikely bedfellows: the English virginalists, W. F. Bach, C. P. E. Bach and Beethoven. Fétis's comments on Byrd, Bull and Gibbons demonstrate the longevity of his attempt to reconcile the intellectual legacies of Comte and Cousin:

The monuments of the art of the past are of two kinds: either they belong to the complete art, that is, music possessing all the elements of modern tonality, harmony, melodic forms and rhythm which make up the works of the eighteenth and nineteenth centuries; or they belong to the period when artists, still yoked to the laws of ancient tonality, nevertheless by instinct made efforts to penetrate the domain of a new tonality whose basic precepts were unknown to them ... This is not, however, to say that this music holds no interest for us. (*RGM* XXXI/48: 27 Nov. 1864, 379)[22]

He also noted with dismay that the novelty of works in the 'incomplete' category often ensured them a better reception in his 'concerts historiques' than their more developed neighbours. Fétis cannot conceal the

---

[20] Aristide Farrenc (1794–65): Flautist, composer, writer and music publisher, with a particular interest in early music. Collaborated closely on the second edition of Fétis's *Biographie universelle*. Louise Farrenc (*née* Dumont) (1804–75): respected composer of orchestral and chamber music, pianist and piano teacher at the Conservatoire.

[21] A letter from Aristide Farrenc thanking Fétis for practical and moral support was published by the *Gazette* (*RGM* XXXI/8: 21 Feb. 1864, 60).

[22] 'Les monuments de l'art rétrospectif sont de deux sortes: ou ils appartiennent à l'art complet, c'est-à-dire à la musique en possession de tous les éléments de tonalité moderne, d'harmonie, de formes mélodiques et de rhythme qui constituent les œuvres du XVIIIe et du XIXe siècle; ou ils sont dans les conditions de l'époque où les artistes, encore soumis aux lois de la tonalité ancienne, faisaient cependant, par instinct, des efforts pour entrer dans le domaine d'une tonalité nouvelle dont la base leur était inconnue ... Ce n'est pas à dire pourtant que cette musique soit pour nous dénué d'intérêt' (*RGM* XXXI/48: 27 Nov. 1864, 379).

tension between the theory of transformation and his musical taste, which tells him that tonal music is more advanced than modal music. When he writes of the clearer cadences and melodic line, and the purer harmony of John Bull's work as opposed to that of Byrd or the renegade Gibbons (*ibid.*, 379–80) – his preferences are fully exposed. Whilst he would never have dismissed the music of Adam de la Halle as containing 'harmonic faults', as Castil-Blaze did (*RGM* III/26: 26 Jun. 1836, 213),[23] with no consideration for contemporary artistic standards, he could not view as fully expressive music which lacked the sophisticated power of modulation. Since his definition of music rested on the question of expression, he had no option but to consign that composed before 1600 to an inferior order.

This division was tacitly sustained both in the pages of the *Gazette* and in concert life. The *Gazette*'s coverage of Renaissance music was almost entirely restricted to purely historical studies which might even emphasise the unsuitability of such music for performance. Indeed, from the middle of the century, it was a sign of musicology's growing stature as a discipline that the life and work of secondary or unperformed (and unperformable) figures could be discussed at length with impunity. The liveliest manifestation of historical activity in the *Gazette* concerned Medieval music, the study of which was fuelled by the discovery of various manuscripts – among them those of Montpellier and St Gall – whose dating and provenance provoked heated debate. Although in the middle of the century most articles still constituted passionate defences of the worth of particular figures, early signs of confidence in the value of musicology for its own sake can be seen in **Maurice Germa**'s introductions to his articles on the history of specific genres (written in the late 1850s and 1860s), in many of which his stated aim is simply to fill lacunae in musicological knowledge. Conversely, musicological activity which might tarnish the reputation of revered figures was discouraged. Fétis was dismayed that Mozart's early symphonies had been unearthed: 'It is regrettable that an indiscreet zeal has brought them out of the oblivion where, for the sake of the artist's glory, they should have remained' (*RGM* XIV/19: 9 May 1847, 155).[24] Once a composer had been elevated to canonic status, the preservation of an infallible image was of paramount importance to exponents of the 'great man' theory, and resulted in the curious phenomenon whereby detailed historical articles concentrated on lesser figures.

In the years following the Franco-Prussian War, the practice of

---

[23]   'des fautes contre l'harmonie' (*RGM* III/26: 26 Jun. 1836, 213).
[24]   'Il est fâcheux qu'un zèle indiscret les ait tirées de l'oubli où elles auraient dû rester pour la gloire de l'artiste' (*RGM* XIV/19: 9 May 1847, 155).

musicology achieved the status of an accepted professional activity analogous to the critical and historical branches of the other fine arts.[25] The new confidence of musicologists is revealed by their studies of composers whose main service to music was to place the achievement of genius in perspective. In his study of Handel's precursors (*RGM* XLII/ 4–7: 24 Jan. – 14 Feb. 1875), Octave Fouque defined the musicologist's duty as being to study and analyse the works of secondary composers and the disciples of genius in order to cast light on the work of great composers.[26] His aim was not to convince a sceptical world of the artistic worth of an unjustly neglected figure, but to demonstrate the historical importance of a group of isolated composers. He can thus maintain an emotional detachment from his subject matter. Whether, as an historian, he likes or esteems the work of Purcell or Gibbons, is largely irrelevant, even in the context of an apologia for the musicality of the English. Fouque manages to illustrate the sophistication of their musical culture whilst remaining tepid in his evaluation of the composers of the Golden Age. He dismisses Thomas Morley's contribution to *The Triumphs of Oriana* as 'desperately feeble' (*RGM* XLII/4: 24 Jan. 1875, 27),[27] and finds Purcell's harmony 'incorrect' at times (*RGM* XLII/6: 7 Feb. 1875, 50). Yet he neither questions the validity of his subject nor fails to emphasise the historical importance of the English choral tradition as an influence on Handel. A similar trait is apparent in **Ernest David**'s study of Monteverdi (*RGM* XLI/2–7: 11 Jan. – 15 Feb. 1874), in which, after providing a detailed biography and evaluation of the importance of the composer, the author admits:

Nowadays the music of this master, a source of delight for his contemporaries, would doubtless give us little pleasure. In two centuries the art has undergone transformations such that our ears would find the harmonies and innovations which provoked such violent quarrels feeble indeed. Whatever one's opinion, the memory of the man who rendered such important services to his art should not be forgotten. (*RGM* XLI/7: 15 Feb. 1874, 51)[28]

Three years later, Gustave Chouquet wrote an article on the English madrigalists (*RGM* XLIV/19–20: 13–20 May 1877) which reinforced the separation between musicology and performance:

[25] Such recognition was symbolised by Barbereau's appointment at the Conservatoire.
[26] (Pierre-)Octave Fouque (1844–83): salon/operetta composer and historian-critic.
[27] 'de la dernière faiblesse' (*RGM* XLII/4: 24 Jan. 1875, 27).
[28] 'Aujourd'hui la musique de ce maître, source de délices pour ses contemporains, nous plairait sans doute médiocrement. L'art, depuis deux siècles, a subi des transformations telles que nos oreilles trouveraient bien maigres les combinaisons et les innovations qui soulevèrent de si violentes querelles. Quoi qu'il en soit, la mémoire de l'homme qui a rendu à son art des services aussi importantes, ne doit pas être oubliée' (*RGM* XLI/7: 15 Feb. 1874, 51).

madrigalian music no longer responds to the predominant tendencies of our time; it belonged to a period of religious faith, of simple beliefs, of calm and ordered life, and we are going through a period of torment, where art necessarily reflects our agitations, our struggles, our doubts and our cries of desperation. (*RGM* XLIV/20: 20 May 1877, 156)[29]

The underlying premise of the quotations above – particularly Chouquet's – is that early music must satisfy the demands of nineteenth-century taste if it is to be acceptable as current repertoire. Such an extreme position may well be a by-product of the drive towards securing musicology's newly won status; it was not a widely held view in the journal except among concert/opera critics with little sense of history. On the contrary, those historically minded contributors who were also active concert reviewers, such as Maurice Bourges or Charles Bannelier, were anxious to promote an understanding of changing musical style among critics and listeners; they called repeatedly for an end to the demand that early music should respond to and survive judgement by the terms of a nineteenth-century musical aesthetic. Bourges maintained that every work of art was conditioned by its cultural environment and that an artwork could be appreciated whether or not one agreed with or shared in the aesthetic which helped produce it. Reviewing an anthology of sixteenth-century Franco-Netherlandish music, he emphasised the need to view all artistic productions in historical perspective. His opinion is important for its sensitivity and influence:

if one were minded to judge the beauties of this music according to the constituent laws of our own, that which I am showering with praise and eulogies here would undoubtedly appear scholastic, heavy, and shapeless to prejudiced eyes. It is in transporting oneself back to the spirit of their epoch, in penetrating the artistic conditions of their century that one must judge these early masters. It is essential to speak their language and to see the worker at his task with only the tools available to him. (*RGM* XVI/5: 4 Feb. 1849, 39)[30]

Bourges's historical imagination provides a constructive strategy for judging the merits of specific examples of early music. Not unlike

---

[29]   'la musique madrigalesque ne répond plus aux tendances qui prédominent de nos jours: elle convenait à une époque de foi religieuse, de croyances naïves, de vie calme et régulière, et nous traversons une période tourmentée, où l'art nécessairement se ressent de nos agitations, de nos luttes, de nos doutes et de nos cris désespérés' (*RGM* XLIV/20: 20 May 1877, 156). (Adolphe-)Gustave Chouquet (1819–86): music historian; twice winner of the Prix Bordin.

[30]   'si on s'avisait de vouloir juger des beautés de cette musique d'après les qualités constitutives de la nôtre, ce que nous entourons ici d'estime et d'éloge paraîtrait sûrement scolastique, pesant, informe à des yeux prévenus. C'est en se reportant à l'esprit de leur époque, en se pénétrant des conditions de l'art dans leur siècle, qu'il faut juger ces anciens maîtres. Il est indispensable de parler leur langue et de voir l'ouvrier à l'œuvre avec les seuls outils qu'il lui fût donné de manier' (*RGM* XVI/5: 4 Feb. 1849, 39).

Cousin's vision of eclecticism in its wish to uncover the best of the past, it also reflects Bourges's anxiety to give historical study in the wake of Thierry, Guizot, Quinet and Michelet a significance and justification nobler than mere 'curiosity and retrospective fantasy' (*RGM* XIII/9: 1 Mar. 1846, 68).[31] However, Bourges's idea of beauty is historically informed rather than universal. His premise is identical to that of David, Chouquet and Fouque, but his conclusion is diametrically opposed; instead of asking the music to be other than of its own time, Bourges demands that both the critic and the amateur listener alter their perspectives. Bourges was not alone in suggesting that historically informed listening was the best way to approach the unfamiliar repertories of early music. In an article on Allegri's *Miserere*, Fromental Halévy warned that on entering the Sistine Chapel it was essential to 'leave at the door all our memories of modern music, forget all the strong emotions with which the masters of our art have filled our souls, and hear Allegri's music with the virgin ears of the listeners of two hundred years ago' (*RGM* XX/14: 3 Apr. 1853, 115).[32] Within the journal, the combination of historical articles and reviews of early music performances could only help readers to achieve this objective.

However, to claim that all approaches to early music were rooted in philosophical arguments or a thirst for musicological discovery would be misrepresenting the journal. Two long-serving contributors – the violinist, playwright and composer, Henri Blanchard (1787–1858) and the civil servant **Edouard Monnais** – were respectively ambivalent and prejudiced, though the latter's splenetic expressions of distaste are not without interest. Monnais was belligerently antipathetic to the performance of Baroque music, which constituted most early music heard in Paris between 1830 and 1880 and about which he was almost entirely ignorant. Primarily a contributor of opera reviews and journalistic articles, he was rarely called upon to write on early music; when he did so it was invariably with sarcasm:

We must admit that this kind of composition is quite devoid of charm and is of only archaeological interest. It was good of M. Pasdeloup to show us a specimen, but we do not think he will do it often. Call it classic music if you will, but it will

[31] 'curiosité et fantaisie rétrospective' (*RGM* XIII/9: 1 Mar. 1846, 68). Bourges's comment, in a review of a Conservatoire concert, was an attempt to combat the idea of music antedating 1600 as mere novelty. François Guizot (1787–1874), Jules Michelet (1798–1874), Edgar Quinet (1803–75), and Augustin Thierry (1795–1856) were among France's most prominent nineteenth-century historians and reformers.

[32] 'laisser à la porte tous nos souvenirs de musique moderne, oublier toutes les fortes émotions dont les maîtres de l'art ont rempli nos âmes, et entendre la musique d'Allegri avec les oreilles vierges des auditeurs d'il y a deux cents ans' (*RGM* XX/14: 3 Apr. 1853, 115).

never be popular music. The performance was perfect, and it required nothing less to safeguard a few passages eminently capable of exciting a little modern-day hilarity. (*RGM* XXX/47: 22 Nov. 1863, 370)[33]

In this estimation of Bach's orchestral Suite no. 3 in D BWV 1068, Monnais comes close to positing canon (classic music) and repertoire (popular music) as mutually exclusive categories. The use of the term 'archaeological' is also barbed, since by the middle of the nineteenth century the term 'archéologie musicale' was a standard descriptive category in the journal for articles dealing with pre-Renaissance music. In 1848, Maurice Bourges had argued that, in the interests of unearthing the country's musical heritage, state aid should be made available to scholars engaged in such 'archaeological' work (*RGM* XV/51: 17 Dec. 1848, 391–2). By contrast, for Monnais, early music of all kinds could be justified only as a retreat from the decadence of the 'music of the future'. In 1866 he pitted the success of the 1861 revival of Gluck's *Alceste* against the failure of *Tannhäuser* (*RGM* XXXIII/41: 14 Oct. 1866, 321), yet he also argued in the other direction, complaining that a resurgence of interest in the past was stifling opportunities for young composers and that it presented an obstacle to originality.[34] Of the *Gazette*'s other regular critics, only Blanchard showed ambivalence towards the increasing popularity of early music, noting a 'rétrospectivomanie' among chamber music lovers who could accept what was to him the inevitable anticlimax of a Boccherini quintet after one by Beethoven (*RGM* XVIII/9: 2 Mar. 1851, 68). In 1857, he complained of Louise Farrenc's programming an evening dominated by seventeenth- and eighteenth-century keyboard music, implying that one could have too much of a good thing (*RGM* XXIV/49: 6 Dec. 1857, 394). Yet he admitted the importance of the work of **Charles Lebouc** and the singer Paulin in their historical concerts (*RGM* XXII/11: 18 Mar. 1855, 83),[35] and, though not entirely consistently, urged early music's acceptance on its own terms and disapproved of its 'modernisation' by means of reorchestration, ornamentation or virtuoso performance style. In

---

[33] 'Avouons que ce genre de composition est tout à fait dépourvu de charme et n'offre qu'un intérêt purement archéologique. M. Pasdeloup a bien fait d'en donner un spécimen, mais nous ne pensons pas qu'il y revienne souvent. C'est, si l'on veut, de la musique classique, mais ce ne sera jamais de la musique populaire. L'exécution en a été parfaite, et il ne fallait pas moins pour sauver quelques passages bien capables d'exciter un peu l'hilarité moderne' (*RGM* XXX/47: 22 Nov. 1863, 370). Monnais puns on the title of the concert series founded and conducted by Jules Pasdeloup (1819–87) – the highly successful Concerts Populaires de Musique Classique (1861–84, 1886–7).

[34] See below, p. 200.

[35] Louis-Joseph Lespinasse, *dit* Paulin (1814–67), made his début as a tenor at the Paris Opéra in 1845. Little else is known about him.

demanding fidelity from operatic producers as early as 1841,[36] Blanchard
placed himself among those, such as Maurice Bourges, **Adolphe Botte**
and Charles Bannelier, who applied Berliozian ideals of the integrity of
the composer's thought to early music, and whose insistence upon the
application of appropriate performance styles marks them as among the
first campaigners for authenticity in interpretation (though not in the use
of original instruments).

Performance practice

The problems of performing music whose tradition had been broken
were more keenly felt than has hitherto been supposed. Such recognition
was implicit in Halévy's article on Allegri's *Miserere* (*RGM* XX/14: 3
Apr. 1853), where he commented (erroneously) that the manuscript was
so jealously guarded by the Vatican authorities that copying it was
prohibited, a measure with which he stated his full agreement. His
reasons are significant: even an accurate copy of the manuscript could
not transmit the tradition of the Vatican choir; therefore, in the absence
of the composer to ensure fidelity to his original conception, it was better
for the piece to be performed only where the interpretation's authenticity
could be guaranteed (*ibid.*, 115). The argument's destructive implications
for the performance of early music should not be allowed to overshadow
Halévy's main point, which was to demonstrate that a score is only the
skeleton of a work, containing notation often insufficiently precise to
guarantee the accurate replication of performance style. As Fétis noted
of his own 'concerts historiques', the difficulties inherent in music of an
unfamiliar style meant that: 'the performance never matched what I had
in mind, and unfortunately I could not hope for better' (*RGM* V/6: 11
Feb. 1838, 62).[37] Such problems of interpretation implied the need for
specialist performers, a need which, though supplied by a small core of
devoted musicians among whom **Delsarte**, Beaulieu,[38] Lebouc and
Paulin were prominent, was still evident in the 1870s, and indicated that
although early music had won a segment of the public, its performance
techniques were not common currency. The reception of a fine work
could be jeopardised by insensitive or inadequate performance. Even
Monnais realised that, especially in vocal music, 'for early music
concerts ... the choice of artists is a delicate matter ... it will always be

---

[36] The *Gazette's* response to the Opéra-Comique's 1841 revival of Grétry's *Richard Cœur-de-Lion* is discussed below.

[37] 'l'exécution n'a jamais répondu à mes vues, et malheureusement je n'en pouvais espérer de meilleure' (*RGM* V/6: 11 Feb. 1838, 62).

[38] Marie-Désiré Beaulieu [Martin-Beaulieu] (1791–1863): composer and author. Famous for promoting Baroque choral music in the provinces and, later, in Paris.

difficult to find performers knowledgeable enough to give a fine interpretation of works which are no longer of our time' (*RGM* XXVII/ 20: 13 May 1860, 177).[39] His opinion was corroborated by Adolphe Botte later in the year (*RGM* XXVII/48: 25 Nov. 1860, 406).

In instrumental music the situation was healthier due to the work of pianists such as **Louise Mattmann**, **Charlotte Tardieu de Malleville** (*née* D'Arpentigny de Malleville) and **Wilhelmine Szarvády** (*née* Clauss), who included Baroque works in their programmes and adjusted their playing style accordingly. This was particularly true of Szarvády, to whom Botte paid tribute in 1860 as a pioneering force in the public acceptance of Baroque keyboard music as a component of instrumental recitals (*RGM* XXVII/8: 19 Feb. 1860, 58). The question of the use of the piano as opposed to the harpsichord rarely arose; the journal's critics concentrated on the style of playing, the essential nature of a 'jeu lié' in contrapuntal music, and the importance of clarity of touch, minimal use of pedal, and consistency of tempo.[40] Problems of authentic fingering and ornamentation were left to historians such as Adrien de Lafage (1805–62). In reviews of Aristide and Louise Farrenc's *Le Trésor des pianistes*, the nearest Fétis came to championing the use of the harpsichord was prompted by the staccato nature of Scarlatti's music: 'it has often caused me to miss the harpsichord, for which it was composed' (*RGM* XXIX/47: 23 Nov. 1862, 380).[41] An article by Lafage stands almost in isolation in the journal as an examination of historical performance practice *per se*.[42] 'Du doigté, de l'enseignement et du caractère des instruments à clavier au XVIIe siècle' (*RGM* XXII/49–52; 9–30 Dec. 1855) seems to have been written expressly to illustrate the differences in performing style between the seventeenth and nineteenth centuries, taking as its starting point Saint-Lambert's treatise of 1702. Lafage's attitude towards playing music of the period with original fingerings is much less dogmatic than his view on ornamentation; he feels that modern fingering techniques have superseded those of the seventeenth century: 'While entering perfectly into the spirit of these old compositions, we can of course perform them according to our own

---

[39] 'pour des concerts d'un genre rétrospectif ... le choix des artistes est une affaire délicate, ... on aura toujours peine à en trouver d'assez instruits pour bien interpréter des œuvres qui ne sont plus de notre temps' (*RGM* XXVII/20: 13 May 1860, 177).

[40] See for example, Fétis, *RGM* XXVIII/37: 15 Sep. 1861, 291.

[41] 'elle m'a souvent fait regretter le clavecin, pour qui elle a été faite' (*RGM* XXIX/47: 23 Nov. 1862, 380).

[42] The only comparable article concerns the implications of chiavette in sixteenth-century vocal music (Prince de la Moskowa: 'De l'exécution de l'ancienne musique vocale', *RGM* XVIII/3: 19 Jan. 1851). Lafage's article was inspired by Michel de Saint-Lambert's treatise, *Les Principes du clavecin, contenant une explication exacte de tout ce qui concerne la tablature et le clavier* (Paris, 1702).

traditions without their losing anything in the process' (*RGM* XXII/49: 9 Dec. 1855, 383).[43] However, on the subject of ornaments in the works of François Couperin (the most significant aspect of Saint-Lambert's treatise), his view is stricter:

The indication of these ornaments demanded specific signs which now cause problems for those who wish to perform the music of the old French masters as they did themselves. (*RGM* XXII/52: 30 Dec. 1855, 410)[44]

His article implies not only that performance of early French keyboard music was widespread enough to warrant such discussion, but that it was accepted that players would want to approach it in an authentic spirit.

A sense of resignation pervades critical reaction to the replacement of obsolete instruments with nineteenth-century equivalents. However, censure of other means of modernisation is nearly unanimous throughout the *Gazette*'s history; indeed it is exactly this sense of outrage at the adulteration of works (either through arrangement or in performance) which sets the journal apart from its less historically sensitive rivals. Such feeling might result in the direct censure of respected figures, as in the case of Adolphe Adam, whose reorchestration of Grétry's *Richard Cœur-de-Lion* for revival at the Opéra-Comique was roundly condemned both by an unidentified critic signing himself 'T.L.N.' and by Henri Blanchard.[45] Their arguments brought together the needs of historians and the public. In an unusually sensitive comment more redolent of Bourges, Blanchard complained that: 'To touch up the works of a man of genius or talent is to wish this man no longer of his time' (*RGM* VIII/49: 5 Sep. 1841, 404);[46] more cynically, 'T.L.N.' saw its motivation as commercial:

Besides its absolute merit, every work of art has an historical merit which can be established only by comparing it with works which preceded and succeeded it. How can one establish such points of comparison if one changes the work through arbitrary modifications? We shall be told that there are too few connoisseurs, and that we must court the masses. What a fine notion! commercial

---

43 'Tout en entrant parfaitement dans l'esprit de ces vieilles compositions, nous pouvons fort bien les exécuter d'après nos principes sans qu'elles aient rien à y perdre' (*RGM* XXII/49; 9 Dec. 1855, 383).

44 'L'indication de ces agréments exigeait des signes particuliers qui aujourd'hui embarrassent ceux qui veulent exécuter la musique des anciens maîtres français telle qu'ils le [sic] faisaient eux-mêmes' (*RGM* XXII/52: 30 Dec. 1855, 410).

45 'T.L.N.', 'Quelques mots sur la reprise prochaine de Richard Cœur-de-Lion [sic]' (*RGM* VIII/36: 5 [6] Jun. 1841). Henri Blanchard, 'Du respect pour les grands maîtres' (*RGM* VIII/49: 5 Sep. 1841) and the review itself (*RGM* VIII/53: 3 Oct. 1841).

46 'Retoucher les ouvrages d'un homme de génie ou de talent, c'est vouloir que cet homme ne soit plus de son époque' (*RGM* VIII/49: 5 Sep. 1841, 404).

success is all that matters; this is how art is sacrificed to the interests of business. (*RGM* VIII/36: 5 [6] Jun. 1841, 296)[47]

A fine line separated legitimate alterations (aimed at courting popularity for neglected works) from mutilation. In 1854, Fétis went so far as to say that the addition of modern-style dynamics, 'is not only permissible, but that it is now the only way to save from obscurity precious monuments of the art worthy of being preserved for discriminating posterity' (*RGM* XXI/37: 10 Sep. 1854, 295).[48] In some cases, such as the use of Mozart's instrumentation for *Messiah*, compromises were accepted.[49] However, Mozart's version was not unanimously deemed an improvement on the original: as early as 1840, the publisher Antonin Aulagnier (1800–92) lamented his omission of Handel's characteristic high trumpet parts, although he agreed that Mozart's additions to the woodwind section 'give a new lease of life to Handel's rather meagre orchestra' (*RGM* VII/37: 24 May 1840, 312).[50]

When Lamoureux followed *Messiah* with a revival of the *St Matthew Passion*, he again presented a cut version, 'due as much to the dimensions of the work as to dealing with a public which it was most important not to tire first time around' (?Bannelier, *RGM* XLI/14: 5 Apr. 1874, 108).[51] Neither Fouque nor Bannelier, the main critics who covered the Baroque choral revival in Paris for the *Gazette*, criticised this policy. Fouque, however, questioned Lamoureux's choice of omissions in *Messiah*, in particular 'the soprano aria in E which begins Part III, an admirably expressive number and which is perhaps preferable to some of those

[47] 'Toute œuvre d'art, à côté de son mérite absolu, a un mérite historique, qui ne peut s'établir qu'en la comparant avec les productions qui l'ont précédée et qui l'ont suivie. Comment établir ces points de comparaison, si vous changez cette œuvre en y apportant des modifications arbitraires? On nous répondra que les connaisseurs sont très peu nombreux, et qu'il faut briguer de la masse. A la bonne heure! on veut des succès d'argent; et voilà comment l'art est sacrifié aux intérêts de l'industrie' (*RGM* VIII/36: 5 [6] Jun. 1841, 296). The production was a runaway success, with 236 performances between 1841 and 1847. See David Charlton, *Grétry and the Growth of Opéra-Comique* (Cambridge, 1986), 251.

[48] 'est non-seulement permise, mais qu'elle est aujourd'hui le seul moyen de sauver de l'oubli de precieux monuments de l'art, dignes d'être conservés pour la postérité intelligente' (*RGM* XXI/37: 10 Sep. 1854, 295). Fétis's comment arises as part of a discussion of Haydn's symphonies for the Loge Olympique, but is equally applicable to earlier styles.

[49] Using Mozart's wind parts was a well-established tradition, though no near-complete performance of *Messiah* was given in Paris until Charles Lamoureux's monumental achievement of six performances in close succession from 19 December 1873.

[50] 'donnent une nouvelle vie à l'orchestre un peu maigre de Haendel' (*RGM* VII/37: 24 May 1840, 312).

[51] 'tant à cause de la dimension de l'œuvre que pour ménager un public qu'il importait extrêmement de ne pas fatiguer tout d'abord...' (?Bannelier, *RGM* XLI/14: 5 Apr. 1874, 108).

which were performed' (*RGM* XL/52: 28 Dec. 1873, 414).[52] Lamoureux must have been particularly concerned about the initial reception of the Bach, omitting sufficient numbers to leave time for some excerpts from *Messiah* with which to round off the concert. However, Bannelier assured his readers that Lamoureux was not a man to 'stop in midstream' (?Bannelier, *RGM* XLI/14: 5 Apr. 1874, 108).[53] The policy of tempting the public with incomplete versions of giant works and sweetening the pill with better-known items was ingrained in Parisian concert life, and characterised not only the introduction of early music to large audiences, but also that of Haydn, Beethoven, Berlioz, Wagner and Schumann. Whether the practice was condoned or not depended largely on the audacity of the enterprise and the organic unity and status of the work in question. Hence, Bannelier accepted Lamoureux's cut version of the *St Matthew Passion* in 1874 but complained about Edouard Colonne's cutting of the finale of the 'Rhenish' Symphony (?Bannelier, *RGM* XLII/ 9: 28 Feb. 1875, 69) on the grounds that it destroyed the work's unity.

With instrumental recitals and chamber concerts the problem was less one of mutilation than of unsympathetic performance style. Around the mid-1850s, performances of music from both the Baroque and Classical periods began to attract adverse comment, particularly from Henri Blanchard and his successor, Adolphe Botte. The reasons for such a change are clear: increasing numbers of virtuoso-composers were becoming interpreters of solo and chamber works by other composers, past and contemporary. Their interest in early music tended to stem not from a wish to promote the music itself, but to vary the musical style of vehicles for technical display. Detecting the use of respected works as means rather than ends, the *Gazette*'s critics were unanimous in their condemnation on the grounds of disrespect for the integrity of the artwork. In 1855, alongside some of Liszt's Wagner transcriptions and a series of showpieces, Alfred Jaëll (1832–82) programmed a Bach fugue in C:

which he wound up towards the end in the manner of a modern fantasy, to give the public what is known as the crack of the whip or the signal for applause, an acknowledgement which can do nothing to enhance Sebastian Bach's reputation, but which doubtless gave M. Jaëll pleasure. (Blanchard, *RGM* XXII/11: 18 Mar. 1855, 84)[54]

---

[52] 'l'air de soprano en *mi* majeur par lequel débute la troisième partie, page d'une admirable expression, et qui est peut-être préférable à quelques-unes de celles qui ont été exécutées' (*RGM* XL/52: 28 Dec. 1873, 414). The aria in question is the now indispensable 'I know that my redeemer liveth'.

[53] 's'arrêter à mi-chemin' (?Bannelier, *RGM* XLI/14: 5 Apr. 1874, 108).

[54] 'qu'il a jouée en la chauffant vers la fin, comme on fait d'une fantaisie moderne, pour donner au public ce qu'on appelle le coup de fouet ou le signal des applaudissements, suffrages qui ne peuvent rien ajouter à la réputation de Sébastien Bach, mais qui ont sans doute fait plaisir à M. Jaëll' (Blanchard, *RGM* XXII/11: 18 Mar. 1855, 84).

As late as 1875, Bannelier accused the cellist Karl Davidov (1838–89) of a similar tendency to alter his interpretation to suit public taste. Earlier in the season he had chided him for using portamento in an arrangement of the Air from Bach's orchestral Suite no. 3 in D (?Bannelier, *RGM* XLII/6: 7 Feb. 1875, 46); in a later article he strengthened the accusation of playing to the gallery. Davidov had repeated his programme of the previous week, except that, taking into account the audience's preferences, he had replaced his own concerto with the Bach Air:

This single change sufficed to rally the support of the whole audience, which showered warm appreciation on the virtuoso. He played this piece with delicate expression, but weakening the tone of his instrument a little too much, and, as we have already mentioned, using too much portamento in order to win over an audience always easily charmed by such affectations of style, which have no place in any serious work, and least of all in those of Bach. (?Bannelier, *RGM* XLII/10: 7 Mar. 1875, 77)[55]

Three things are significant here: not only that Davidov's style of playing was commented upon in such detail, but also that the Air had already become an early music 'pop'; by playing it in preference to his own concerto, Davidoff reversed the traditional image of the virtuoso-composer, with which Paris audiences had been familiar for over half a century. Moreover, Bannelier's response reveals the cleavage between works which were not deemed to suffer from such interpretive freedom, and canonic works which merited greater respect.

The treatment of dynamic variation in the face of minimal guidance in scores was the main problem facing nineteenth-century interpreters both of Renaissance and Baroque music. Fétis theorised at length in essays of 1854, 1859 and 1864, which discussed the history of expression and dynamic markings.[56] Of the *Gazette*'s writers, he was among the least rigorous in the quest for an appropriate performance style, and these essays show him at his most contradictory, often abandoning all thought of the empirical evidence which he demanded of others for speculative claims. His theory, as set out in the 1854 essay, was that dynamics ('nuances') were an accessory to the composer's thought (albeit an accessory which increased in importance from Mozart's time onwards)

55 'Ce simple changement a suffi pour rallier les suffrages de tout l'auditoire, qui a décerné de chaleureux bravos au virtuose. Il a joué ce morceau avec une expression délicate, mais en amoindrissant un peu trop le son de l'instrument et, comme nous l'avons déjà dit, en usant trop des *portamenti* pour gagner les suffrages d'auditeurs toujours faciles à charmer par ces mièvreries de style, qui ne conviennent à aucune œuvre sérieuse, et moins qu'à toute autre à celles de Bach' (?Bannelier, *RGM* XLII/10: 7 Mar. 1875, 77).

56 F.-J. Fétis: 'De l'expression en musique par les nuances d'intensité des sons' (*RGM* XXI/ 29–37: 16 Jul. – 10 Sep. 1854); 'De l'expression en musique' (*RGM* XXVI/14–26: 3 Apr. – 26 Jun. 1859); 'De la sonorité dans la musique d'orchestre, comme élément de variété, de coloris et d'expression' (unfinished, *RGM* XXXI/27–30: 3–24 Jul. 1864).

and were the domain not of knowledge and the intellect, but of feeling and sensibility; 'From this comes the fact that the dynamic shading of instrumental music is a matter of choice, and that the same melody can be accentuated in various ways, and always ring true' (*RGM* XXI/33: 13 Aug. 1854, 261).[57] In applying his aesthetic of expressivity – his very definition of what constituted music – to works of all eras, he justified the addition of dynamics to early music without reservation, asking: 'Are we to believe that in these times, already long past, passionate expression was banned from an art which cannot exist without it?' (*ibid.*).[58] Since nuance was an accessory, the integrity of the music itself was deemed to remain intact. The implication of this position is that Fétis would support the addition of 'modernising' dynamics to a piece if doing so enhanced the chances of an unjustly neglected work gaining public acceptance.[59] However, this definition also meant that nuance became subject to the vagaries of taste; in practice, Fétis could not defend his preference by any more rigorous principle.[60]

A more rigorous attitude is apparent in a late review by Bannelier of Buxtehude and Bach organ music. Applying the same editorial scruples as are shown in an extended (signed) review of Beethoven editions (*RGM* XLIII/46–53: 12 Nov. – 31 Dec. 1876), he refused to commit himself on an appropriate performance style on the grounds of insufficient evidence: 'until trustworthy documents reveal either Bach's own thoughts on this subject, or the tradition of his playing, we shall treat the question as one of taste, and refrain from taking sides' (?Bannelier, *RGM* XLVI/23: 8 Jun. 1879, 190).[61]

Editing

Increasingly, as the *Gazette*'s critics responded to and campaigned for new initiatives in the performance of early music, the problem of producing both scholarly and working editions came to the fore. In his

---

57 'De là vient que le coloris de la pensée instrumentale est facultatif, et que la même mélodie peut être accentuée de diverses manières, et frapper toujours juste' (*RGM* XXI/ 33: 13 Aug. 1854, 261).

58 'Devons-nous croire que dans ces temps déjà loin de nous l'expression passionnée était bannie d'un art qui n'existe que par elle?' (*ibid.*).

59 Later in the 1854 article he argued exactly this with reference to Haydn's symphonies for the Loge Olympique (*RGM* XXI/37: 10 Sep. 1854, 295). See above, note 48.

60 The same was true of those critics who complained at the seemingly indiscriminate use of blunt alternations of piano and forte in Renaissance vocal music at the Conservatoire (?Bannelier, *RGM* XLVI/51: 21 Dec. 1879, 415) or those, such as Mathieu de Monter, who advocated the use of smooth gradations of dynamic in Palestrinian-style pieces (*RGM* XXXV/16: 19 Apr. 1868, 124).

61 'jusqu'à ce que des documents certains nous révèlent soit la pensée même de Bach à cet égard, soit la tradition de son jeu, nous considérerons la question comme affaire de goût, et ne prendrons point parti' (?Bannelier, *RGM* XLVI/23: 8 Jun. 1879, 190).

review of the Franco-Netherlandish anthology cited earlier, Maurice Bourges was aware of the problems facing any editor. He was anxious to establish that the editor's choice of works was indeed representative of the repertoire, provided a critical account of each volume's contents and discussed the merits of the editorial procedures employed. In the 1870s, continuing publication of collected works by past composers heightened the need for enlightened editorial procedure. With no need to justify the importance of such a project on the grounds of music's aesthetic quality, as Fétis felt impelled to do when reviewing the first volumes of the *Bach-Gesellschaft* (*RGM* XX/14–19: 3 Apr. – 8 May 1853), attention shifted to editorial standards. Bannelier's signed review of a new edition of Gluck's two 'Iphigénie' operas (*RGM* XLI/26: 28 Jun. 1874) concentrated on the editors' findings regarding the genesis of the works, and provided evidence of an increasing interest in manuscripts as sources of information regarding the composer's method, revisions and borrowings. By the 1870s it was expected that an editor should reveal both sources and method in detail and discuss all problems incurred, so that the reader would be fully informed as to the more crucial decisions. **H. Lavoix** *fils* was insistent on this point, concentrating on the supreme importance of the introductory preface. His review of editions of Lully's *Bellérophon*, Rameau's *Dardanus* and Grétry's *La Caravane de Caire* in the series *Chefs-d'œuvre classiques de l'Opéra français* (*RGM* XLVII/39: 26 Sep. 1880) focused not on the pieces themselves, but on a comparison of the editorial practice of Théodore de Lajarte (1826–90), **Charles Poisot** and François Auguste Gevaert (1818–1909). Poisot, editor of *Dardanus*, was reprimanded for failing in his duty to the public, providing an inadequate preface which enthused about the work and its potential for revival at the Opéra to the detriment of factual detail. The age of Romantic, effusive, justifications for early music had ceded to a more analytical age. As a corrective measure, Lavoix discussed the differences between the 1739 and 1744 versions of *Dardanus*, and stressed that an edition of a work such as this should constitute a definitive version suitable for all types of user and giving an exhaustive analysis of the sources.

M. Poisot, who, it must be admitted, has had the good idea of publishing the variants of the two revivals, has not indicated his sources in sufficient detail. It is unlikely that *Dardanus* will ever be revived at the Opéra; but in the event of an historian wanting to study Rameau's work in depth, M. Poisot's edition would provide only an incomplete guide. (*RGM* XLVII/39: 26 Feb. 1880, 306)[62]

[62]   'M. Poisot, qui a eu, il faut le reconnaître, l'heureuse idée de publier les variantes des deux reprises, n'a pas indiqué suffisamment ses sources. Il est peu probable que *Dardanus* soit jamais repris à l'Opéra; mais, dans le cas possible où un historien voudrait étudier à fond l'œuvre de Rameau, le travail de M. Poisot ne serait pour lui qu'un guide incomplet' (*RGM* XLVII/39: 26 Feb. 1880, 306).

Lavoix's view thus reinforces the idea of musicology as an end in itself, and of the value of the publication and dissemination of historical music regardless of its potential for subsequent public performance.

From the years when Fétis became an ally, the *Gazette* developed and maintained an attitude of encouragement towards early music, providing a forum for the discussion of theoretical questions and taking an active interest in performances of important works. Indeed, after around 1860, when historical articles unmotivated by performances of specific works (written in profusion by **Emile Mathieu de Monter**, Maurice Germa (writing as Cristal), Ernest David and H. Lavoix *fils*) were supplemented by regular and sometimes extended concert reviews of early music, a shift took place in the journal's balance. Originally dedicated to the Romantic ideal and the challenge of avant-garde music from which other journals, particularly the *Revue musicale*, shied away, the *Gazette* moved further towards the prevailing historical focus of its erstwhile rival. Its treatment of the issues surrounding early music had four discernible but not entirely distinct aspects: first, the worth of musicology was justified on grounds of a teleological and/or an eclectic view of music history; second, the journal printed enthusiastic articles which described specific works; third, performers engaged in the difficult task of reconstructing such repertoire were encouraged; and fourth, their interpretations were reviewed in detail, particularly if they appeared unusual or wayward.

When untainted by commercial interest, nineteenth-century music criticism was primarily an educative discipline; once a work was perceived to have been understood by the public, detailed explanations of its workings dwindled to brief comments. Unless a work was unfamiliar, the end result of this process was a concert-reviewing style which concentrated on the act of re-creation rather than that of creation. In the *Gazette,* an identical progression in the nature of writings on early music indicates the increasing acceptance of such repertoire in Parisian musical life: early music, having entered the domain of musicology, proceeded to that of music criticism and, finally, to that of concert reviewing. However, only music dating from around 1600 onwards reached the third stage of acceptance; that of the earlier periods continued to provide subject matter primarily for historians. A separation between musicology and criticism can thus be seen taking place, beginning in the early 1850s. With the exception of the specialist journals dealing with sacred music, the *Gazette* was the only Parisian journal of the mid nineteenth century to give significant emphasis to early music; reaction to its corporate views both on the repertoire itself and on appropriate ways of performing it is thus difficult to gauge. Fétis's relativism and Monnais's scepticism excepted, the very modernity of the

Gazette's 'authentic' approach may, paradoxically, have made it seem reactionary and inflexible to contemporary readers. This would only have been compounded by the journal's retreat from modernism in its later years; by 1880 it may indeed have been perceived as putting into operation Fétis's disillusioned cry in a review of Farrenc's *Trésor*: 'Today it is with a profound feeling of sadness that I am forced to state ... that, for art, the beautiful and the great belong solely to the past' (*RGM* XXVII/37: 15 Sep. 1861, 289).[63]

When discussing music of the Classical era, the journal's critics applied the same demand for fidelity to the composer's intention as for early music. The difficulties of achieving such fidelity, though less acute due to an almost unbroken tradition in the case of seminal works by Mozart and Haydn, were highlighted by the implications of the new concept of interpretation indicated in Fétis's article of 1854, though they were incipient even in the 1830s. It is to these issues, and to the centrality of the Viennese classics to the musical canon in nineteenth-century France, that I shall now turn.

---

[63] 'Aujourd'hui, c'est avec un profond sentiment de tristesse que je suis forcé de déclarer ... que, pour l'art, le beau et le grand ne sont que dans le passé' (*RGM* XXVII/37: 15 Sep. 1861, 289).

4   The Austro-German tradition I: The reception of Gluck, Haydn and Mozart

Introduction

Questions of canon lie behind much of the historical and musicological discussion analysed in the previous chapter; however, such questions are more consistently apparent in connection with music from Gluck onwards. In French musical life and criticism, the music of the years around 1780 marks a watershed in the early nineteenth-century perception of a musical canon: Haydn was popularly viewed as the father of modern music, whilst Gluck was the earliest operatic composer acceptable to critics (but not, until the late 1850s, the musical public) for performance on a regular basis. The term 'canon' was never used in the *Gazette*; instead, canonic status was indicated by references to 'la musique classique' and 'les grands maîtres'. In France, traditions in liturgical music and the example of Lully provide exceptions to the general contemporaneity of musical experience in the eighteenth century;[1] however, the formation of a canon centring around the Viennese classics is essentially a product of the nineteenth. This chapter charts and explains the journal's response to music comprising the traditional core of the Austro-German canon (Haydn, Mozart, Beethoven) and its peripheries (including Gluck and Mendelssohn). The *Gazette* was unusual in its breadth of coverage regarding issues in performance and editorial practice. Most of the writing on these subjects occurred in reviews, and was therefore reactive rather than proactive; its character as a response to contemporary practice illustrates how arguments for authenticity within a continuous tradition arose as a protest against interpretive innovation. Moreover, it illustrates the inextricable link between arguments for authenticity and the nature of the canon, since, as with Bannelier's and Botte's complaints of Karl Davidov and Alfred Jaëll respectively,[2] only canonic repertoire elicited such impassioned defences of the *status quo*.

---

[1] This is argued by William Weber in 'La Musique ancienne in the Waning of the Ancien Régime', *Journal of Modern History* LVI/1 (March 1984), 58–88.
[2] See Chapter 3.

Five critics are of particular importance in the *Gazette*'s criticism of the Germanic tradition after 1780: Berlioz (Conservatoire concerts reviewer until 1843), Henri Blanchard (concerts reviewer from 1849 to his death in December 1858), Maurice Bourges (occasional Conservatoire concerts reviewer and champion of Weber and Mendelssohn), Adolphe Botte (concerts reviewer after Blanchard's death) and Charles Bannelier (concerts reviewer from 1865 and general editor in the years before the journal's closure).[3] All were important for their contribution to the *Gazette*'s changing image over its forty-seven-year publication span. This chapter is thus concerned not only with the repertoire under discussion, but with developing and explaining the nature of each critic's work.

Despite the journal's lifelong commitment to chamber music, in its first decade, emphasis in concert reviews fell inexorably on the Conservatoire series for three reasons. Firstly, the re-institution of a Conservatoire concert series on 9 March 1828 under Habeneck had represented the founding of a temple for the worship of Beethoven's symphonies and, to a lesser extent, his other orchestral works. The nature of the Société des Concerts' artistic allegiance fitted perfectly with the *Gazette*'s own Romantic image of Beethoven as portrayed in its opening numbers. Secondly, Fétis had interpreted Habeneck's return as symbolising a revitalisation of the entire concert life of Europe;[4] as Fétis's rival (at least initially), the *Gazette* was obliged to indicate its serious artistic intent by giving the Société equal coverage. Thirdly, Berlioz's reviews from 1836 until the close of the 1842 season (when he begged to be relieved of his post) eclipsed, in both column space and quality, the efforts of the *Gazette*'s lesser critics writing on other concerts.

Once Berlioz had left his post as Conservatoire concert reviewer, Schlesinger was left with a considerable gap to fill. At first, Berlioz was replaced by Maurice Bourges; in 1844 Stephen Heller took over, only to hand the job back to Bourges in 1845. In 1849 Berlioz made a guest appearance, but by this stage critical interest in the Conservatoire series was waning rapidly, and after 1850 it received coverage only when unusual repertoire was performed. As the critic and composer Léon Kreutzer observed in 1853, explaining the *Gazette*'s lack of regular reviews over the previous three years:

for twenty-seven years, the Society has possessed an admirable repertoire in which the symphonies of Beethoven occupy pride of place. The public never tires

---

[3] For a defence of the attribution of unsigned concert reviews to Bannelier, see Appendix 5.

[4] *RM* 1ʳᵉ série, III/3 ([Mar] 1828), 145–49.

of listening to them; but criticism has a more difficult mission: it exhausts itself eulogising the same works each year. (*RGM* XX/13: 27 Mar. 1853, 106)[5]

Kreutzer's attitude indicates a number of modes of thought regarding criticism's nature and uses. It presupposes the educational value of criticism through journalism, in that once an audience is familiar with a piece of quality music and can appreciate it unaided, the critic's work is accomplished; it demonstrates the limitations of contemporary musical commentary (by the 1850s it was widely held that the last word had been said on a variety of works, particularly those of Mozart and Beethoven); and it places criticism's focus on the work rather than on its interpretation. Throughout its career, the journal's criticism displayed the first two characteristics. However, there is abundant evidence that in the 1850s attitudes were changing concerning the third, where the prospect of a performing tradition under threat forced critics to take a stance on the proper relationship between the performer, the composer, and the printed text.

In respect of the *Gazette*'s criticism of eighteenth- and early nineteenth-century music, the years 1849 to 1858 belong essentially to Henri Blanchard, particularly because of his conversion to late Beethoven, which took place through his concert reviews (themselves a testament to his perseverance and documents of revelation). Fétis noted that, 'Towards the end of his life, his critical capacity had weakened considerably'.[6] However, given Fétis's lifelong dislike and distrust of the late works and of those who worshipped them – 'the sheep-like public which judges an artwork's merit only by the label on the packet' (*RGM* XVI/50: 16 Dec. 1849, 391)[7] – his estimation of Blanchard's failing discernment and the latter's very public conversion may not be unrelated. Moreover, it is clear from Blanchard's responses to works other than the late quartets that his critical style matured and that his musical taste became more adventurous in the wake of the inclusion in chamber programmes of works from a variety of historical epochs. The sudden proliferation of concerts in the 1850s inevitably had repercussions on the detail of his reviews, which lacked the technical minutiae of Berlioz's

---

[5] 'la Société, depuis vingt-sept ans, possède un répertoire admirable où les symphonies de Beethoven occupent le premier rang. Le public ne saurait se lasser de les écouter; mais la critique a une mission plus difficile: elle s'épuise en faisant chaque année l'éloge des mêmes œuvres' (*RGM* XX/13: 27 Mar. 1853, 106). Léon Kreutzer (1817–68): nephew of the violinist and composer Rodolphe.

[6] 'Vers la fin de sa vie, son talent de critique s'était beaucoup affaibli'. François-Joseph Fétis, *Biographie universelle des musiciens et bibliographie générale de la musique*, 2nd edn (Paris, 1860–5) I, 435.

[7] 'le peuple moutonnier qui ne juge du mérite d'une œuvre d'art que sur l'étiquette du sac' (*RGM* XVI/50: 16 Dec. 1849, 391).

Conservatoire reports. However, his generally aphoristic style threw lengthy accounts of a particular work into sharp relief.

With a couple of Beethovenian exceptions, the years from Blanchard's death in 1858 to the closure of the journal consolidated the status of much eighteenth- and early nineteenth-century music. Although performances and reviews of contemporary and specifically French instrumental music increased markedly after the Franco-Prussian War of 1870–1, there developed simultaneously a strong sense of repertoire – a growing corpus of works which had survived the ravages of time and fashion and which remained unaffected by the anti-Germanism of the war's aftermath. Despite the continued development of concert life in Paris, enforced selectivity was the net result of such expansion. In 1863, **Gustave Héquet** (writing as Léon Durocher) pointed out that if complaints regarding the repetitious and conservative nature of the Société des Concerts's programming policy bore fruit, the outcome could only be the substitution of the 'novel' (whether early or contemporary music) for established works. He feared a weakening of standard works' status if the Conservatoire did not extend its concert season to accommodate an ever-expanding repertoire (*RGM* XXX/8: 22 Feb. 1863, 60).

Gluck

Most of the journal's discussion of Gluck is concentrated in its first decade – when Berlioz's involvement was at its closest.[8] Successful revivals in the 1850s and 1860s notwithstanding, although Gluck was held in high respect it would be difficult to argue that he was ever canonic during the nineteenth century. However, that the question arises at all is due almost entirely to Berlioz, whose fervent early writings for the *Gazette* presented the composer as a Romantic hero. His celebrations of Gluck enabled him both to define his own ancestry as a composer and to attempt a redefinition of Gluck's relevance to nineteenth-century audiences.[9] Much of Berlioz's reviewing was allied to performances of extracts from Gluck's French operas in the Conservatoire series,[10] but

[8] The other articles with major sections on Gluck are, F.-J. Fétis: 'Mozart. Ses œuvres – son influence sur l'art et les artistes' (*RGM* VI/47–60: 15 Sep. – 17 Nov. 1839; 'J. d'O......' (Joseph d'Ortigue): 'Représentation de retraite d'Ad. Nourrit. *Armide* – *Les Huguenots* – Mlle Taglioni – la Cérémonie' (*RGM* IV/15: 9 Apr. 1837); 'C.': 'Opéra allemand de Londres. *L'Euryanthe*, de Weber; *la Jessonda*, de Spohr; *l'Iphigénie en Tauride*, de Gluck' (*RGM* VII/47: 2 Aug. 1840); Richard Wagner: 'De l'ouverture' (*RGM* VIII/3–5: 10–17 Jan. 1841).

[9] In Germany, Gluck and Romanticism had already been linked in Hoffmann's *Ritter Gluck*. Moreover, this story was the first of Hoffmann's *Tales* to be published in French (*Revue de Paris*, 14 Jun. 1829), translated by Loève-Veimars.

[10] Some of this material was used later in *A travers chants*.

his main work on Gluck appears in two lengthy articles of 1834 which contain much of his scholarly investigation into the relation of the French operas to his Italian ones.[11] Berlioz's opinion of a composer's merit can be gauged in part by his readiness to conduct musicological investigations on that composer's behalf. During this period only three composers received such attention: Beethoven, Mozart and Gluck.[12]

The first of Berlioz's Gluck essays shows the extent to which he identified with the composer whose scores he had so avidly devoured in the Conservatoire library. Genuinely informative about Gluck, it tells us even more about Berlioz himself. The identification of one genius with another can be seen in Berlioz's admiration for Gluck's audacity in writing *Iphigénie en Aulide* without any guarantee of performance (*GM* I/ 23: 8 Jun. 1834, 181). Comparison with the *Symphonie fantastique*'s genesis is invited implicitly; Schlesinger's readers might also have noted the connection with other uncommissioned Romantic manifestos, including Hugo's *Hernani*. Through anecdote, Gluck emerges as an indomitable force prone to public outbursts of indignation in the name of art, triumphing in *feuilleton* fights and inspiring acts of homage from the young Mozart and Méhul. Analysing the music, Berlioz emphasises points of contact between Gluck's work and his own – specifically Gluck's dramatic use of the orchestra and his commitment to dramatic realism. The two come together in an anecdote relating to a rehearsal of *Iphigénie en Tauride*: the composer is portrayed assuring the turbulent violas in Orestes' aria 'Le calme rentre dans mon cœur' that they are indeed playing the right notes, since: '*He is lying, he has killed his mother!*' (*ibid.*, 184).[13] In his later article on the opera, Berlioz referred again to the passage, which was one of his favourites, as 'this magnificent misinterpretation' (*GM* I/49: 7 Dec. 1834, 390).[14] The subordination of formal correctness to dramatic truth was an ideal to which Berlioz subscribed throughout his life; it is, therefore, unsurprising to find him praising Gluck for displaying similar priorities. The absence of a closing ritornello in 'Ah, je l'ai toujours présent' (*Il Telemaco*) destroyed the symmetry of the aria. However, after the emotional tension of its final, fragmented cries, Berlioz felt that a closing ritornello could add nothing

---

[11] 'Gluck' (*GM* I/22–3: 1–8 Jun. 1834) and '*Iphigénie en Tauride*' (*GM* I/45–9: 9 Nov. – 7 Dec. 1834).

[12] However, Berlioz's musicological interest in Mozart in preference to Weber, for instance, is surprising, particularly since his subject matter is Lachnith's *Les Mystères d'Isis* (*RGM* VI/5: 3 Feb. 1839). No such discussions of *Robin des bois* or *La Forêt de Senart* appeared.

[13] '*Il ment, il a tué sa mère!*' (*GM* I/23: 8 Jun. 1834, 184).

[14] 'ce magnifique contre-sens' (*GM* I/49: 7 Dec. 1834, 390).

to the overall effect. The flouting of formal balance was to be supported, not condemned (*GM* I/22: 1 Jun. 1834, 174).

Only one of the *Gazette*'s critics dissented from Berlioz's position of admiring (but not uncritical) champion. Fétis's dedication to Mozart led him to underplay the significance of his predecessor (*RGM* VI/49: 29 Sep. 1839, 388). Ironically, the opera which Fétis used in this essay to illustrate Mozart's rejection of Gluck's style – *Idomeneo* – was that which on its performance at the Conservatoire in 1836 immediately elicited eulogistic comparisons with Gluck from Berlioz, for whom such a lofty comparison was the ultimate compliment to Mozart:

in these two works, the stylistic similarity of the two masters is such that it is quite impossible to detect an individual trait which might differentiate them. (*RGM* III/5: 31 Jan. 1836, 39)[15]

Much of Berlioz's enthusiasm for Mozart's dramatic music was predicated on his admiration for Gluck. He saw extensive Gluckian influences on *Don Giovanni* and drew particular attention to the priests' and Sarastro's music in *Die Zauberflöte*, claiming to love this opera above all other Mozart because it contained 'all this poetry of great temples, great men and the great gods of antiquity' (*RGM* VII/17: 27 Feb. 1840, 136).[16]

By contrast with Fétis, Berlioz's fervour was shared by both Wagner (*RGM* VIII/3–5: 10–17 Jan. 1841)[17] and Maurice Bourges, who replaced Berlioz as Conservatoire reviewer in 1843. Yet despite frequent and critically acclaimed performances of operatic extracts at the Conservatoire, audience response to Gluck in the first half of the century remained too cool to guarantee the success of a full staging of one of his works at the Opéra. On the retirement of the tenor Adolphe Nourrit (1802–39), whose career had been launched by the rôle of Renaud, and who was acknowledged as the only worthy interpreter of Gluck at the time, Joseph d'Ortigue despaired of a Gluck revival in Paris (*RGM* IV/15: 9 Apr. 1837, 124). Both he and Berlioz understood that the minimum condition for a successful revival was a series of fully staged productions; the very nature of the operas as dramatic meant that individual scenes lost most of their impact when taken out of context and sung as concert

---

[15] 'la ressemblance du style des deux maîtres est telle dans ces deux ouvrages qu'il est vraiment impossible de retrouver le trait individuel qui pourrait les faire distinguer' (*RGM* III/5: 31 Jan. 1836, 39).

[16] 'toute cette poésie des grands temples, des grands hommes et des grands dieux de l'antiquité' (*RGM* VII/17: 27 Feb. 1840, 136).

[17] For a discussion of Wagner's essay 'De l'ouverture', which lauds Gluck's overture to *Iphigénie en Aulide*, see Thomas S. Grey, 'Wagner, the Overture, and the Aesthetics of Musical Form', *Nineteenth-Century Music* XII/1 (Summer 1988), 3–22.

pieces. Ironically, as Berlioz often lamented, the prominence given to Gluck at the Conservatoire concerts worked against him.

With Berlioz's demise as a regular contributor in the late 1840s, the *Gazette* printed few apologias for the work of Gluck as an essential part of current musical life. Indeed, while his worth was never questioned, he moved steadily into the ranks of 'la musique rétrospective' and was championed as such by singers such as François Delsarte, whose speciality was introducing early vocal music to the Paris public along the lines of a 'concert historique' (but without the historical lecture with which Fétis had customarily introduced the music), and Pauline Viardot, whose interpretation of *Orphée* in 1859, specially prepared for her by Berlioz, was a major success at the enterprising Théâtre-Lyrique.[18] That *Orphée* was not staged at the Opéra and that the Opéra waited for the outcome of the Théâtre-Lyrique's production before putting on *Alceste* in 1861 is significant. At the Conservatoire, a limited selection of excerpts, mostly choruses, was regularly performed, and two items from *Armide* and *Iphigénie en Tauride* respectively achieved enough popularity to be included in C.-V. Alkan's piano album *Souvenir des concerts du Conservatoire*, a collection published by Brandus in 1849. Thus, Gluck did not decline into oblivion by the middle of the century: he was respected as a master of the past but in spite of successful revivals of his operas, his music always remained on the fringes of the repertoire.

Haydn and Mozart

By the 1830s, opinion on Haydn as a symphonist was divided between public acceptance and critical misgivings among Romantics. Berlioz's Haydn criticism is the inverse of his criticism of Gluck and his unwillingness to engage with the music shows at every turn. Sometimes he gave no indication of which symphony was played at the Conservatoire; at others he was unsure of the number (*RGM* VI/5: 3 Feb. 1839, 35); needing to recover his composure after the Scythian chorus from *Iphigénie en Tauride*, he even admitted to having left the hall in order to avoid listening to one (*RGM* VI/11: 17 Mar. 1839, 86). His tone was invariably one of disparagement unless he detected something unusual in the form or instrumentation of a particular movement. He detested the Haydnesque Minuet as opposed to the Beethovenian Scherzo, and on similar grounds of triviality objected to the vital, lighthearted nature of his finales. Haydn did not fulfil Romantic criteria, lacking the element of

---

[18] The nature of Berlioz's version is meticulously documented in Joël-Marie Fauquet, 'Berlioz's Version of Gluck's *Orphée*', *Berlioz Studies*, ed. Peter Bloom (Cambridge, 1992), 189–253.

struggle inherent in Beethoven and falling short of Gluck's emotional power.

> Nowadays we are no longer content with *music alone*; in any substantial work we seek a poetic idea, a more or less dramatic feeling ... there is nothing of the kind in the work of *The Creation*'s illustrious composer. His symphony consists merely of an ingenious working of gentle melodies which are *relatively happy, relatively sad, relatively slow*, or *relatively lively*, never warming to passion and with a calm which rises neither to contemplation nor reverie. (attrib. Berlioz, *RGM* II/8: 22 Feb. 1835, 66)[19]

The use of feline images following a non-review (which depicted the calm flow of the music as a day of contented domesticity) merely served to remove Haydn further from the Romantic model:

> The orchestra understood perfectly the style and allure of this gentle composition; it drew in its claws, it mewed softly, it lapped its milk with charming grace, its tawny eyes only half-open ... The public was entranced. (*RGM* VIII/29: 18 Apr. 1841, 225)[20]

There is no hint that Haydn was received badly at the Conservatoire during this period; indeed, Berlioz would often express dismay at the audience's preference of Haydn rather than Beethoven (e.g. *RGM* VI/9: 3 Mar. 1839, 70), suggesting that its members were not responding to treatment, since Habeneck's programming policy aimed to convert a small segment of the Parisian public to Beethoven's music. At times Berlioz felt the public had not comprehended its fortnightly dose: in 1837, he lamented that a portion of the audience regarded Beethoven's music as 'passé', despite continued incomprehension (*RGM* IV/4: 22 Jan. 1837, 30). Only in 1842, in one of his final Conservatoire reviews, did he state that the audience had reacted to the first movement of the Fifth Symphony in a fully comprehending manner (*RGM* IX/11: 13 Mar. 1842, 103), although the finale of the Ninth still confounded them. To a public still grappling with Beethoven, Haydn's order and refinement was a source of relaxation and relief, and may indeed have been intended as a palliative. In 1843,

---

[19] 'Nous ne nous contentons plus aujourd'hui de *musique seulement*, nous cherchons dans toute production de quelque étendue, une pensée poétique, un sentiment plus ou moins dramatique ... il n'y a rien de pareil dans l'œuvre de l'illustre auteur de la création [sic]. Sa symphonie ne consiste qu'en un tissu ingénieux de douces mélodies *un peu gaies, un peu tristes, un peu lentes* ou *un peu animées*, ne s'échauffant jamais jusqu'à la passion et dont le calme ne s'élève jamais non plus jusqu'à la contemplation où [sic] la rêverie [sic]' (attrib. Berlioz, *RGM* II/8: 22 Feb. 1835, 66). For a defence of this attribution and that of other articles attributed to Berlioz, see Kerry Murphy, *Hector Berlioz and the Development of French Music Criticism* (Ann Arbor, 1988), 75–87.

[20] 'L'orchestre a parfaitement compris le style et les allures de cette douce composition; il a fait patte de velours, il a miaulé à voix basse, il a bu du lait avec une grâce charmante, sans ouvrir tout grands ses yeux fauves ... Le public a été enchanté (*RGM* VIII/29: 18 Apr. 1841, 225).

Bourges reported that the adagio of a symphony in E-flat provoked 'infinite pleasure' (*RGM* X/6: 5 Feb. 1843, 47),[21] and Berlioz stated that the andante in G from what he called Symphony no. 80 spread an 'effect of calm pleasure and well-being' among the audience (*RGM* VI/5: 3 Feb. 1839, 35).[22] With the advent of Bourges as Conservatoire reviewer in 1843, Haydn was partly rehabilitated in the *Gazette*, although Bourges, too, found that his music prized formal perfection over expression, and was well aware of the stylistic gulf between his symphonies and those of Beethoven.

In the mid-century, public opinion regarding Haydn remained stable but critical reaction continued to divide between modernism and traditionalism/eclecticism. During these years his music, although limited almost exclusively to late symphonies and a few quartets, enjoyed as much popularity as ever, regularly requiring encores. Isolated quartet movements were still used, much to the chagrin of Maurice Bourges and Léon Kreutzer, as a vehicle for virtuoso displays of ensemble by the first violins of both the Conservatoire orchestra and the Société Sainte-Cécile (1849–56), founded and conducted by the violinist François Seghers (1801–81). In 1844, Heller reported that the variation movement of a symphony in G (probably no. 100) had been 'showered with frenetic applause', and praised its qualities as a 'spirited and pleasant conversation' (*RGM* XI/3: 21 Jan. 1844, 22).[23] The adjectives 'fraîche' and 'jeune' were consistently applied in critiques of the symphonies, but between 1844 and 1858 no work of Haydn's received detailed treatment, giving the impression that such an approach was deemed unnecessary.

The two sides of the critical division are conveniently represented by two uncannily symmetrical Conservatoire concert reviews written in successive years by Bourges and Berlioz. The first, that of Bourges in 1848, emphasised the character of Haydn's music as the reflection of an enviable degree of domestic order and emotional containment, music which had attained formal perfection: 'drawn with such precision, set out with such art and directness, the relationship of detail to the whole so finely proportioned, truly complete in its own way (*RGM* XV/7: 13 Feb. 1848, 52).[24] This last phrase holds the key to Bourges's viewpoint and differentiates it from that of Berlioz. As a critic with an interest in music history, the criteria which Bourges applied to value judgements did not concern contemporary relevance but quality within the idiom in which a

---

[21] 'un plaisir infini' (*RGM* X/6: 5 Feb. 1843, 47).

[22] 'effet de plaisir calme et de bien-être' (*RGM* VI/5: 3 Feb. 1839, 35).

[23] 'couvert d'applaudissements frénétiques ... causerie spirituelle et aimable' (*RGM* XI/3: 21 Jan. 1844, 22).

[24] 'dessinée avec tant de précision, disposée avec tant d'art et de rectitude, si bien proportionnée dans le rapport des détails et de l'ensemble, vraiment complète en sa manière' (*RGM* XV/7: 13 Feb. 1848, 52).

work was composed. Hence he was able to compare Haydn's symphonies with those of Beethoven without denigrating them, yet admitting that they responded to an outdated aesthetic:

> One listens to Haydn's music without turmoil, without agitation, but with a sweet and contained pleasure, a smile of satisfaction on the lips ... It requires neither tiring listening, nor efforts of the imagination, nor nervous torment; one could listen to it for a long time without becoming bored. (*ibid.*)[25]

His closing plea was for more performances of the works of a composer who was of universal value (*ibid.*).

By contrast, Berlioz remained unwilling to accept Haydn's music except by the standard of a nineteenth-century aesthetic; his comparison of what was billed at the Conservatoire as Symphony no. 51 in G and Beethoven's First, played at the same concert, is illuminating for its closeness of observation to that of Bourges, combined with its diametrically opposite conclusion. In contrast to most other *Gazette* critics, Berlioz argued here for Beethoven's First to be accepted as more than derivative *juvenilia*. This was an attitude which Berlioz had himself displayed in 1836 and, more specifically, in the essay of 1838. Reversing his opinion resulted in the denigration of Haydn's style:

> it is impossible to misunderstand the enormous distance which separates Beethoven's First Symphony from Haydn's 51st. On one side we find exhilaration, hot-bloodedness, strength, the sparkling look of youth and a certain *virtuosity* in the use of the orchestra; on the other, we see tranquillity, wisdom, the calm of ripe old age – a little too ripe – and a restrained instrumental practice, comparable to the playing of the early harpsichordists. Beethoven's symphony is proud, elegant; it walks purposefully, head high; it commands attention. Haydn's is humbler; it comes forward modestly; its look is respectful; it hardly dares raise its voice; it creeps around; it resigns itself in advance to passing unnoticed, and is full of gratitude to the honourable listeners who wish to hear it. (*RGM* XVI/5: 4 Feb. 1849, 35)[26]

[25] 'La musique d'Haydn s'écoute sans trouble, sans agitation, mais avec un plaisir doux et contenu, le sourire de satisfaction aux lèvres ... Elle ne demande ni fatigue d'ouïe, ni efforts d'imagination, ni tortures nerveuses; on l'entendrait longtemps sans se lasser' (*ibid.*).

[26] 'il est impossible de méconnaître la distance énorme qui sépare la première symphonie de Beethoven de la 51ᵉ de Haydn. On trouve d'une part l'allégresse, le sang chaud, la force, le brillant regard de la jeunesse et une certaine *virtuosité* dans la manière d'employer l'orchestre; de l'autre, on reconnaît la tranquillité, la sagesse, le calme de l'âge mûr, un peu trop mûr, et une pratique réservée des ressources instrumentales, comparable au jeu des anciens clavecinistes. La symphonie de Beethoven est fière, élégante; elle marche droit, la tête haute; elle commande l'attention. Celle de Haydn est plus humble; elle s'avance modestement; son regard est respectueux; elle ose à peine élever la voix; elle s'insinue; elle est d'avance résignée à passer inaperçue et pleine de reconnaissance pour les honnêtes auditeurs qui voudront bien l'écouter' (*RGM* XVI/5: 4 Feb. 1849, 35).

As a final insult, he brands Haydn's work 'table music' (*ibid.*),[27] a remark which he justifies by reference to the original conditions of its composition. Thus, Haydn's tolerance of servitude is held against him and the containment of his music ridiculed. In voicing this opinion, Berlioz, in one of his final concert reviews, stood well apart from his colleagues on the *Gazette*, for whom the lasting appeal of Haydn's music became increasingly apparent. There was never any doubt that this music, which in the words of Blanchard 'will always be in fashion' (*RGM* XXI/6: 5 Feb. 1854, 42),[28] would remain an essential component of the repertoire, and only a cello concerto, a work with a strong Baroque flavour, received the pejorative epithet 'antiquated'[29] from Blanchard in 1857 (*RGM* XXIV/15: 12 Apr. 1857, 123). However, there are also indications that, alongside widespread acceptance of Haydn's continuing place in the repertoire, there was both complacency and an unwillingness to look beyond his stylistic accessibility in search of inner complexities. Already in 1857 Blanchard observed that the Dancla Quartet played Haydn's Quartet no. 66 'as an introduction' (*RGM* XXIV/9: 1 Mar. 1857, 68);[30] moreover, it is notable that his approach when considering Beethoven is markedly more analytical than when discussing Haydn, to the point that he mentions sophisticated metrical irregularities and harmonic twists in relation to the former but not the latter.

The two areas in which Haydn's music faced uniformly adverse criticism from the *Gazette*'s writers concerned his dramatic and sacred works. The former were virtually unknown in Paris, and in his extended study of 1849 'De l'opéra en Europe', Léon Kreutzer merely stated that Haydn's dramatic works were overshadowed by those of Mozart (*RGM* XVI/31: 5 Aug. 1849, 241); they were excluded both from the canon and the repertoire. His sacred music, alongside that of Mozart and Rossini, was attacked by both Kreutzer and Bourges as being essentially secular music with sacred texts.[31] Although the purely musical quality of Haydn's sacred works was never in doubt, and those parts of *The Creation* which received performances enjoyed increasing popularity with the public, the aesthetic which it was felt to represent was constantly berated by Bourges and Kreutzer. Instead, they favoured the religious expression of Mendelssohn and Beethoven respectively, each of whom

---

27 'de la musique de la table' (*ibid.*).
28 'sera toujours de mode' (*RGM* XXI/6: 5 Feb. 1854, 42).
29 'vieillot' (*RGM* XXIV/15: 12 Apr. 1857, 123).
30 'pour préface' (*RGM* XXIV/9: 1 Mar. 1857, 68).
31 For a discussion of the background to this view and its promulgation by Joseph d'Ortigue in the 1830s see Dorothy Veinus Hagan, 'French Musical Criticism between the Revolutions (1830–48)' (unpublished PhD dissertation, University of Illinois, 1965), 41–67.

was championed on the grounds that his music represented a return to and renewal of the true means of the expression of devotion through music as manifested in the work of J. S. Bach. In 1844, Bourges hailed the complete performance of *The Creation* as an historic event, previewing it the week before its performance at the Opéra under Habeneck (*RGM* XI/43: 27 Oct. 1844). Significantly however, despite commenting on the distance between its repute and its familiarity in Paris, he provided no detailed description of the work.[32] That the expression of religious sentiment should prevail over stylistic convention in sacred music emerged as the main aesthetic criterion imposed by Kreutzer, Bourges and Berlioz alike. In addition they all disapproved of the composition of sacred music in an overtly secular style. Even 'le divin Mozart' had to submit to this demand, with the result that immensely popular works such as the motet *Sancti et justi* (attrib. Mozart) or the fugal movements of the Requiem attracted critical disdain, a circumstance which mirrored the double-edged reception of Haydn's *The Creation*. A typical response to the problem occurs in Bourges's review of the third Conservatoire concert of 1846, in which the *Ave verum corpus* and *Sancti et justi* were performed as a pair. The former was 'that incomparable piece, sweet emanation of religious sentiment (*RGM* XIII/7: 15 Feb. 1846, 53).[33] The latter, however:

conceived from start to finish in fugal style, is the dry and rigid type of purely scholastic form, deprived of inspiration and relevance ... As workmanship, it is noteworthy; but in terms of religious music, it is absolute nonsense. (*ibid.*)[34]

Of the movements of the Requiem, only the Lacrymosa responded fully to Bourges's expectations of a sacred work, the Dies irae, Rex tremendae and Confutatis lacking religious feeling. In order to strengthen his case, in 1847 Bourges compared the Requiem's musical spirit and its reputation with that of the Agnus dei from the C minor Requiem by Cherubini, whose very name conjured up ideas of an 'halo of learning' (*RGM* XIV/16: 18 Apr. 1847, 132).[35] Contrary to their composers' respective reputations, the Cherubini appeared to Bourges as far superior in its ability to inspire religious thought, particularly in the moving decrescendo and sustained pianissimo at its close. By contrast, extracts from Mozart's Requiem only emphasised its irreligiosity:

[32] By contrast, he wrote an extensive and evangelising introduction to Mendelssohn's *St Paul* in 1846–7 (*RGM* XIII/35–XIV/2: 30 Aug. 1846 – 10 Jan. 1847).

[33] 'incomparable morceau, suave émanation du sentiment religieux' (*RGM* XIII/7: 15 Feb. 1846, 53).

[34] 'conçu d'un bout à l'autre en style fugué, est le type sec et roide de la forme simplement scolastique, dépourvue d'inspiration et d'à-propos ... Comme travail, c'est très remarquable; mais en matière de musique religieuse, c'est tout bonnement un contre-sens' (*ibid.*).

[35] 'auréole scientifique' (*RGM* XIV/16: 18 Apr. 1847, 132).

The reputation of Mozart's Requiem as a classic always pales when the work is performed in church. One can detect only too easily the almost total absence of sacred spirit. Here, faith is obscured by learning. (*ibid.*)[36]

Here, Bourges comes close to attempting to exclude the Requiem from the canon; however, his distinction between the work's secular reputation and its quality as a sacred work only highlights the secular nature of canon formation. Ultimately, the Requiem's status was completely unthreatened by charges of irreligiosity, since its place in the canon was dependent more upon secular considerations (in particular, the Romantic allure of its commissioning) than sacred ones.

The immense difference between the reception of Haydn and that of Mozart in early nineteenth-century Paris centred on their perceived ability to express emotion. Whilst Haydn's reputation rested on his symphonic output (despite the French affection for parts of *The Creation* and Baillot's introducing the public to his chamber music), that of Mozart rested largely on his dramatic music, and in particular on *Don Giovanni*, in which Fétis detected the beginnings of Romanticism in music: 'this music ... created, fifty-two years ago, the genre which was later called *Romantic*, and ... its style is quite different from that of Mozart's other dramatic works' (*RGM* VI/60: 17 Nov. 1839, 475).[37] The essay from which this quotation is taken was the primary discussion of Mozart's work in Schlesinger's *Gazette*.[38] Reflecting the general French view of Mozart's importance, it concentrated on the dramatic music, which was used to illustrate Fétis's estimation of Mozart as a revolutionary and an ideal. Of the operas, Fétis talked most about the least known of Mozart's mature works – *Idomeneo* – specifically so that, having explained its revolutionary nature, he could demonstrate how the later works continued in the same vein. Fétis's insistence on judging composers primarily according to the complexity of their harmonic language had already, in his view of music history, spotlighted Monteverdi to the detriment of his contemporaries. In this essay he did the same with Mozart's operas, evoking Victor Cousin's theory of transfor-

---

[36] 'La réputation classique du *Requiem* de Mozart pâlit toujours lorsque l'œuvre est exécutée à l'église même. On y reconnaît trop l'absence presque totale de l'esprit sacré. L'école y masque la foi' (*ibid.*).

[37] 'cette musique ... créa, il y a cinquante-deux ans, le genre qu'on a appelé lors *romantique*, et ... son style est absolument différent de celui des autres ouvrages dramatiques de Mozart' (*RGM* VI/60: 17 Nov. 1839, 475).

[38] *RGM* VI/47–60: 15 Sep. – 17 Nov. 1839. This contribution was a response to a spectacularly foolish article in *La France musicale* by Jules Maurel: '*Les noces de Figaro et le Barbier de Séville*' (*FM* II/51–61: 25 Aug. – 3 Nov. 1839). That Fétis was incensed by Maurel's insults to Mozart is clear; he had printed the first instalment of his defence within a month of Maurel's first attack.

mation to make an enormous harmonic leap from the works of Jommelli
and the Italian school to those of Mozart, bypassing Gluck altogether:

> Placed in an order of facts and ideas whose consequences their genius developed,
> these artists [the Italian school] had not arrived at one of these epochs where the
> need for transformation makes itself felt, and during which the right man is never
> lacking, as M. Cousin quite rightly remarked in his Philosophy Lectures of 1828.
> (*RGM* VI/49: 29 Sep. 1839, 387)[39]

Later, Fétis expressly denied that Gluck had had any influence on
Mozart, and sidelined his achievement:

> If Mozart borrowed nothing from the new style of declamation, it is because it
> was not the new art, which was entirely his own conception and whose
> manifestation awaited only a favourable opportunity. Thus, when he proceeded,
> two years later, to invent a new music in *Idomeneo*, all the music of Italy,
> Germany and France vanished before him, to be substituted by an immense
> creation, that of contemporary music. (*ibid.*, 388)[40]

Thus he attributed to Mozart the creation of a new and universal musical
language. Here again, though Fétis explicitly evokes Cousin, his image of
Mozart sweeping aside the music of three nations and positing a superior
model is anything but eclectic, suggesting a greater adherence to
Comtian theories of progress. Harmonically, what Fétis saw in Mozart
was the *ordre pluritonique* spiced with the *ordre omnitonique* – a fully
developed modulatory procedure with the occasional use of an expanded
tonality. In the coda of the overture to *Idomeneo*, with its cycle of
drooping modulations and its pedals, he detected 'an entirely new
musical world' (*ibid.*).[41] Most important in Mozart's new harmonic style
was, 'the feeling of the *unexpected*, which did not exist before' (*ibid.*).[42]
To Fétis, the wider range of harmonic possibilities represented an
immense increase in the flexibility of music. However, he deplored the
exploitation of 'l'inattendu' as an end in itself, and composers such as
Schumann and Wagner, who made great use of it, were later condemned
for confusing ends with means. This was not the only point at which
Fétis detected in Mozart's style a compositional technique which would,

---

[39]   'Placés dans un ordre de faits et d'idées dont leur génie a développé les conséquences, ces
    artistes [the Italian school] n'étaient point arrivés à une de ces époques où la nécessité de
    transformation se fait sentir, et dans lesquelles l'homme nécessaire ne manque jamais,
    ainsi que l'a très bien remarqué M. Cousin dans son cours de philosophie de 1828'
    (*RGM* VI/49: 29 Sep. 1839, 387).

[40]   'Si Mozart n'emprunta rien à la nouvelle déclamation musicale, c'est qu'elle n'était point
    l'art nouveau qu'il concevait tout entier et dont la manifestation n'attendait qu'une
    occasion favorable. Lors donc qu'il alla deux ans après inventer une autre musique dans
    l'Idoménée, toute la musique de l'Italie, de l'Allemagne et de la France s'anéantit devant
    lui pour faire place à une immense création, celle de la musique actuelle' (*ibid.*, 388).

[41]   'tout un monde musical nouveau' (*ibid.*).

[42]   'la sensation de l'*inattendu*, qui n'existait pas auparavant' (*ibid.*).

ultimately, contribute to the breakdown of tonality at the end of the century. In answer to Jules Maurel's complaints that Mozart's phrases were too short, he answered:

Very few composers have been able to avoid this defect [short phrases] via the art of suspensions which delay and bring about a desire for the concluding cadence. At their head we must put Scarlatti at the end of the seventeenth century, and Mozart around a century later. (*RGM* VI/51: 13 Oct. 1839, 402)[43]

Fétis's terminology suggests a Wagnerian context, though his examples, including Cherubino's 'Non so più', indicate that his reference is to the use of successive half closes or interrupted cadences acting as bridges between melodic units, rather than tonally ambiguous and highly chromatic suspensions. Characteristically, Fétis accompanied a theoretical standpoint implying modernism with an example which revealed the opposite.

Parisian exposure to Mozart's orchestral music at this time was restricted to his mature symphonies, of which the most popular by far was K550. Its perceived melancholy and passion contributed to its reputation, though Berlioz recalls Schumann in referring to it as 'this model of delicacy and naïvety' (*RGM* III/10: 6 Mar. 1836, 79).[44] Critics never regarded the symphonies as Mozart's finest work: in a mode of reception unchanged from the beginning of the century, the finale to the 'Jupiter' K551 was seen as too cool and scholastic, whilst Berlioz was true to his nature in dismissing the Haydnesque finale of no. 39 in E-flat K543 as 'truly unworthy of such a master' (*RGM* IX/7: 13 Feb. 1842, 61).[45] Later in the century, criticism of Mozart as over-scholastic extended beyond the symphonies to the quartets, and audience reaction to the symphonies became tepid. The difference in critical and audience reaction to the symphonies of Mozart in comparison with those of Haydn is marked: Mozart, it seems, was rarely encored, and the 'Jupiter' Symphony rarely played without calling forth accusations of meaningless scholasticism, a charge which was, by the middle of the century, extended even to K550. Despite its expressivity, for Blanchard the Symphony in G minor contained 'a little too much *strict imitation* (*RGM* XIX/8: 22 Feb. 1852, 58).[46] Blanchard particularly disliked Mozart's virtuoso approach to counterpoint; he berated the Quartet in D major K499 as 'skill,

---

[43] 'Un très petit nombre de compositeurs a su éviter ce défaut [short phrases] par l'art des suspensions qui reculent et font désirer la cadence finale. A la tête de ceux-ci, il faut placer Scarlatti à la fin du dix-septième siècle, et Mozart environ cent ans plus tard' (*RGM* VI/51: 13 Oct. 1839, 402).

[44] 'ce modèle de finesse et de naïveté' (*RGM* III/10: 6 Mar. 1836, 79).

[45] 'vraiment indigne d'un tel maître' (*RGM* IX/7: 13 Feb. 1842, 61).

[46] 'un peu trop cependant l'*imitation obstinée*' (*RGM* XIX/8: 22 Feb. 1852, 58).

harmonic calculation, incessant *imitation*, the merest hint of melody, and nothing more' (*RGM* XXV/4: 24 Jan. 1858, 27).[47] Moreover, in 1850 the usually eclectic Maurice Bourges complained that although the crafts-manship of the 'Eighth' Symphony (K551), especially its finale, was particularly elegant and learned, 'What a shame that the melodic tints of the two final movements have lost a little of their freshness, and that certain formulae, certain ideas now appear old-fashioned!' (*RGM* XVII/5: 3 Feb. 1850, 37).[48]

With the expansion of orchestral concert repertoire in the second half of the century, the space allotted to the 'grands maîtres' became restricted. As Gustave Héquet had predicted in 1863, the increasing interest in historical music and the efforts of conductors such as Pasdeloup to introduce the work of contemporary or controversial composers to a sometimes unwilling public led to the paring down of the standard repertoire. Haydn and Mozart in particular were represented by a few quintessential works. Haydn's Symphonies nos. 85 ('La Reine'), 100 ('Military') and 94 ('Surprise') were overexposed at the expense of the remainder of his output; at the Conservatoire, no. 85 came to perform the function of emergency standby previously reserved for certain movements of the Beethoven Septet. However, there is evidence to suggest that the restriction of the Classical repertoire was also due in large measure to public apathy (which was reinforced in the *Gazette*). When, in 1880, Ernest Deldevez (1817–97) ventured to introduce two movements from an unfamiliar Haydn symphony (no. 86), he received no encouragement:

It would certainly be an abuse of language to say that these two pieces have enriched the repertoire of the Society, since they are rather dreary, the Largo especially, despite its subtitle 'Capriccio'; the frosty reception among the audience should not tempt M. Deldevez to congratulate himself on his find. (?Bannelier, *RGM* XLVII/50: 12 Dec. 1880, 398)[49]

In 1876 Bannelier was less disparaging about Symphony no. 95 (?Banne-lier, *RGM* XLIII/10: 5 Mar. 1876, 76), but the general impression given in the *Gazette* after Adolphe Botte ceased to contribute concert reviews in 1863/64 is that the perceived similarity of spirit among the symphonies,

---

47   'de la science, du calcul harmonique, d'incessantes *imitations*, de la mélodie à fort petite dose, et voilà tout' (*RGM* XXV/4: 24 Jan. 1858, 27). Identified in Joël-Marie Fauquet, *Les Sociétés de musique de chambre à Paris de la Restauration à 1870* (Paris, 1986), 385.

48   'Quel dommage que les couleurs mélodiques des deux derniers morceaux aient un peu perdu de leur fraîcheur, et que certaines formules, certains traits paraissent maintenant vieillis!' (*RGM* XVII/5: 3 Feb. 1850, 37).

49   'Ce serait, certes, un abus de langage de dire que ces deux morceaux viennent enrichir le répertoire de la Société, car ils sont assez pâles, le largo surtout, malgré son sous-titre "capriccio"; l'accueil glacial qu'on leur a fait ne doit pas encourager M. Deldevez à se féliciter de sa trouvaille' (?Bannelier, *RGM* XLVII/50: 12 Dec. 1880, 398).

combined with their predictable quality, worked against them to the extent that they ceased to arouse any critical curiosity. Héquet, in a rare review of instrumental music in 1863, summed up the situation:

With Haydn, the stock – as our bankers would say – is considerable, but one does not have a problem of choice. One has only to pick at random. One is sure to lay a hand on an object of value. (*RGM* XXX/13: 29 Mar. 1863, 99)[50]

In the second half of the century, the lot of Mozart's orchestral music was no better, and was again condoned by the *Gazette*'s critics. The divide between the reception and the performance frequency of his dramatic, as against his orchestral, music, widened considerably, with an important increase of interest in operas other than *Don Giovanni* (in particular, a series of productions at the Théâtre-Lyrique from 1858) which left his symphonic works entirely in the shade. The choice of acceptable symphonies did not reduce appreciably, but attempts to widen the field were not welcomed by audiences at the Concerts Populaires or the Conservatoire. The set menu became K543, K550 and, at a pinch, K551. Of these, the Minuets of the first two were immeasurably more popular than any movement of K551, and were regularly played alone or encored during the performance of the whole work. The audience of Pasdeloup's Concerts Populaires was particularly intransigent on the subject of suitable Mozart repertoire – so much so that after a performance of the 'Haffner' Serenade K248b, Bannelier noted with some surprise that: 'The public seemed to depart from the coldness with which it usually receives the symphonic works – save one or two – of the composer of *Don Giovanni*' (?Bannelier, *RGM* XXXIX/51: 22 Dec. 1872, 406).[51] After a performance of K543 where the Minuet was encored, he noted that this symphony was 'one of only three of his to which this public will willingly listen' (?Bannelier, *RGM* XLI/46: 18 Nov. 1877, 366).[52] The Conservatoire audience was no better disposed towards unfamiliar Mozart symphonies: in 1879 Deldevez attempted to introduce it to another symphony in C major, probably no. 34, only to find it indifferently received. The public's attitude was ingrained (?Bannelier, *RGM* XLVI/51: 21 Dec. 1879, 415).[53]

[50] 'Avec Haydn, le *stock* – comme disent nos boursiers – est considérable, mais on ne connaît pas l'embarras du choix. On n'a qu'à prendre au hasard. On est toujours sûr de mettre la main sur un objet de prix' (*RGM* XXX/13: 29 Mar. 1863, 99).

[51] 'Le public a semblé se départir de la froideur avec laquelle il accueille les œuvres symphoniques – sauf une ou deux – de l'auteur de *Don Juan*' (?Bannelier, *RGM* XXXIX/51: 22 Dec. 1872, 406).

[52] 'l'une des trois seules du maître que ce même public entend volontiers' (?Bannelier, *RGM* XLI/46: 18 Nov. 1877, 366).

[53] As Kerman points out, the growth of the canon in Europe was non-linear: 'While Beethoven always stayed at dead center, Haydn and much of Mozart dropped or at least faded out, to be reinstated later' (Kerman, 'A Few Canonic Variations', 114).

Issues in performance practice

The idea that by the middle of the nineteenth century Mozart's late orchestral and chamber music was finally entering the realms of the canonic 'rétrospective' is reinforced by the comments of various critics on the performance styles used by singers and instrumentalists. Increasingly, one becomes aware of a dichotomy between new ideas on interpretation emanating from performers, particularly virtuosi who entered the hallowed field of chamber music, and the views of older critics who saw the dissolution of a performing tradition occurring before their very eyes. With the exception of Fétis, whose essay on dynamics, nuance and expression (*RGM* XXI/29–37: 16 Jul. – 10 Sep. 1854) argued essentially that the end justified the means, general feeling among the contributors of the *Gazette* held that early music, including that of the later eighteenth century, should not have its classic purity defiled by the imposition upon it of new interpretive traditions. The strength with which this opinion was expressed depended on the extent to which an interpretation was perceived as wayward, but also increased in the case of particularly hallowed works. A minority of the journal's critics encouraged the monumentalisation of works of the Classical period, but their views were countered early in the *Gazette*'s lifetime. Berlioz initiated a tradition which remained constant up to the journal's closure in 1880, whereby stylistic fidelity was demanded of performers. In 1836 he complained that a Haydn symphony in E-flat had been played without delicacy and finesse by the Conservatoire orchestra. Everywhere he found 'too much coarseness of articulation, and an exaggerated energy in forte passages in the strings'. Perhaps, he mused:

being accustomed to the vehement and fiery outbursts of Beethoven and Weber may have contributed somewhat to turning the orchestra away from the vastly different method which it should have followed here. (*RGM* III/7: 14 Feb. 1836, 54)[54]

A major catalyst for increased sensitivity to the interpretation of the classics by the middle of the century was a new generation of pianists including Charlotte Tardieu de Malleville, Wilhelmine Szarvády, Louise Mattmann and **Aglaé Massart** (*née* Masson), who spearheaded a campaign for chamber concerts which contained music of the highest quality from a variety of epochs. Each pianist had her distinctive bias – Szarvády was the most eclectic, playing everything from Bach to

[54] 'trop de rudesse dans l'attaque, et une exagération de vigueur pour les forte … l'habitude du style véhément et des fougueuses apostrophes de Beethoven et de Weber, n'est-elle pas sans avoir contribué un peu à détourner l'orchestre de la méthode si différente qu'il aurait dû suivre en cette circonstance' (*RGM* III/7: 14 Feb. 1836, 54).

Schumann and, in the 1870s, Brahms, while Tardieu de Malleville was more renowned for her performances of Mozart and his predecessors. All were recognised as having the ability to perform whatever music they chose in the appropriate style. With reference to Mozart, this entailed purity of sound, clean execution and a generally anti-virtuoso attitude to the music. William Weber sees the same phenomenon differently:

A new generation of virtuosos, most prominently Henri Vieuxtemps, Joseph Joachim, and Anton Rubinstein, began playing the concertos of Mozart and Beethoven (as Liszt had done), and their performances became feature attractions.[55]

In France these names were merely the tip of an iceberg. Moreover, with the exception of Joachim, such virtuosi were viewed as dangerous in their attitude to the classics, whose reputations had already been established through the less spectacular and considerably more faithful work of chamber musicians.

That clarity and a certain understatement were the major characteristics of the style of the four pianists who formed the keyboard backbone of several chamber music series is repeated many times in the pages of the *Gazette*, almost as a welcome break from the displays of showmanship of virtuoso pianists. The impression is strengthened by their essential character as chamber musicians. The occasions on which Tardieu de Malleville, Mattmann, Massart and Szarvády played Classical concertos with orchestral accompaniment in Paris were rare. Yet they often performed solo and multiple keyboard concertos by Mozart and Bach in a chamber context with only a string quintet and single wind for accompaniment.[56] For Heller, Mattmann's performance of Beethoven's Piano Concerto in C minor (her own choice) at the Société des Concerts was so straightforward as to raise an important question regarding the performer's relation to the work. Heller felt she had abdicated her responsibility as an artist.

Admittedly, she interpreted it in her own way, and in this way there was neither great profundity nor great warmth, in a word, nothing surprising. But since she did not want to comment on the work (as a great artist ought), she naturally avoided the danger of misinterpretation; she confined herself to playing the

[55] William Weber, 'The Rise of the Classical Repertory in Nineteenth-Century Orchestral Concerts', in *The Orchestra: Origins and Transformations*, ed. Joan Peyser (New York, 1986), 372.

[56] Chamber violinists such as Alard and Maurin were of the same self-effacing nature in comparison with Wieniawski and Vieuxtemps. In 1849, when Alard played one of the Beethoven *Romanzen* at the Société des Concerts, Berlioz paid fitting tribute to his artistic integrity and humility (*RGM* XVI/14: 8 Apr. 1849, 106).

concerto faithfully, loyally, letting the work speak for itself. (*RGM* XI/7: 18 Feb. 1844, 53)[57]

When Mattmann played the Fourth Piano Concerto the following season she received a very different reception from Maurice Bourges, for whom the unintrusive nature of her approach was its very strength: 'The clear, limpid, fluent playing, the simple and true expression, so admired by connoisseurs, earned her something of a triumph' (*RGM* XII/17: 27 Apr. 1845, 132).[58] Blanchard's comments on Tardieu de Malleville's playing in 1853 illustrate the new problem of style which he felt was presented to any potential performer of eighteenth-century music.

There is in the correct and polished playing of this charming virtuoso something which smacks a little too much of the particle which separates her two names; she plays Handel and Mozart nobly, as it seems their music was played in the eighteenth century. Nowadays, we interpret it, to use current jargon, in the sense of interpreting a foreign language. (*RGM* XX/9: 27 Feb. 1853, 76)[59]

Blanchard sees the problem of interpretation much in the manner of Stephen Heller on Mattmann: he takes Tardieu de Malleville's reluctance to impose her personality on the music as a resignation of artistic responsibility. However, his point about interpretation can be read two ways: Tardieu de Malleville declines to 'interpret' by projecting her ideas onto the music, but, by Blanchard's own admission, she 'interprets' the foreign languages of Handel and Mozart in the sense of seeming to convey their original meaning to a nineteenth-century audience.

In his essay on dynamics, Fétis wrote one of the *Gazette*'s few articles devoted to problems of interpretation. His view on the rôle of the interpreter lay midway between that of Bourges and Heller, setting up a creative tension between the integrity of a work's intrinsic character and a degree of poetic licence for the performer, 'in accordance with the composer's intention' (*RGM* XXI/37: 10 Sep. 1854, 294).[60] The spirit,

[57] 'Elle l'a interprétée à sa manière, il est vrai, et dans cette manière il n'y avait ni grande profondeur ni grande chaleur, en un mot rien de surprenant. Mais comme elle ne voulait nullement commenter l'œuvre (ainsi que doit le faire un grand artiste), elle s'est naturellement préservée du danger de tomber dans le faux; elle s'est bornée à jouer le concerto fidèlement, loyalement, en laissant agir l'œuvre elle-même' (*RGM* XI/7: 18 Feb. 1844, 53).

[58] 'Le jeu clair, limpide, facile, l'expression simple et vraie, l'exécution aussi riche que précise de la jeune pianiste, si fort estimée des connaisseurs, lui ont valu ce qu'on peut appeler un triomphe' (*RGM* XII/17: 27 Apr. 1845, 132).

[59] 'Il y a dans le jeu correct et poli de cette charmante virtuose quelque chose se ressentant un peu trop de la particule qui sépare ses deux noms; elle joue noblement Handel et Mozart, comme il semble qu'on exécutait leur musique au XVIIIe siècle. De nos jours, on l'interprète, pour nous servir du mot à la mode, comme si l'on disait interpréter une langue étrangère' (*RGM* XX/9: 27 Feb. 1853, 76).

[60] 'suivant la volonté du compositeur' (*RGM* XXI/37: 10 Sep. 1854, 294).

not the letter, is important, as Fétis's copious examples of alternative interpretations of the Andante cantabile theme of the 'Dissonance' Quartet K465, and the opening of K421 in D minor, demonstrate. Yet, as so often, Fétisian theory and practice do not coincide. He claims that:

Perhaps the objection will be made that if one restricted oneself to rendering precisely the dynamics indicated, the talent of performance would be restricted to achieving fidelity in the rendition, and that the personality of a great talent would be annihilated: but this would be wrong. Superior talent manifests itself in the smallest details. (*ibid.*)[61]

However, his own versions of Mozart's phrases contain more than 'les moindres choses', sometimes even overriding the few, important markings (such as the *subito piano* in bar 7 of the first movement of the Quartet in D minor K421), which were the composer's intention, by the substitution of graded dynamics. His theory that dynamics do not constitute the essence of the music enables him to talk of the nuances which, though unindicated, are 'implicitly inherent' (*ibid.*)[62] in the chamber music of Boccherini, the absence of specific markings being taken to indicate that the performer has freedom of choice; 'dynamic shading is dependent absolutely on the wish of the composer, when it is indicated, or the performer, if the absence of markings leaves to the latter the liberty of his or her own feeling' (*RGM* XXI/34: 20 Aug. 1854, 271).[63] Though he clings to the principle that one should 'distinguish in the performance the historical period of the work which one is interpreting' (*RGM* XXI/37: 10 Sep. 1854, 294),[64] his argument finally dissolves into judgements of taste. In one instalment, Fétis deplores the addition, ostensibly to bring it up to date, of modern dynamics to Handel's *Messiah*; in the penultimate instalment he argues that the only way to save Haydn's symphonies for the Loge Olympique from oblivion is to do just this.[65] The implication is that *Messiah* had a high profile even though it was not (yet) popular in France, whilst in Fétis's eyes the acceptance of unfamiliar Haydn symphonies into the repertoire was a necessary precondition for their elevation to similar status. As an historian, Fétis was perfectly capable of defending the value of older works which had

---

61 'Peut-être fera-t-on cette objection, que si l'on se bornait à rendre avec exactitude les nuances d'intensité indiquées, le talent d'exécution se bornerait à la fidélité du rendu, et que la personnalité d'un grand talent serait annihilée: ce serait une erreur, le talent supérieur se manifeste dans les moindres choses' (*ibid.*).

62 'implicitement inhérentes' (*ibid.*).

63 'le coloris est absolument dépendant de la volonté du compositeur, lorsqu'il l'indique, ou de l'exécutant, si l'absence de signes laisse à celui-ci la liberté de son sentiment' (*RGM* XXI/34: 20 Aug. 1854, 271).

64 'distinguer dans l'exécution l'époque à laquelle appartient l'ouvrage qu'on interprète' (*RGM* XXI/37: 10 Sep. 1854, 294).

65 See above, Chapter 3, n. 48.

dropped out of the repertory; moreover, his eclecticism enabled him to value them for their worth in their own time, rather than for their worth as relevant in a century to which they did not belong. His entire self-justification as a musicologist was built upon this ideal. Ironically, his wish for certain works to be retained or reinstated in the repertoire overrode the implications of his eclectic approach, and it was left to the *Gazette*'s other critics to argue the case for authentic performance according to eclectic principles.

Although the term 'nuancer' was in use throughout the nineteenth century, once Fétis's article had appeared it became something of a catchword in the *Gazette*; the manner in which works were 'nuancé' in performance gained in importance in concert reviews. A pivotal year in this respect was the 1857/58 season, in which the number of virtuosi participating in chamber concerts increased, to the detriment, in the opinion of many of the *Gazette*'s critics, of the overall standard of interpretation. Suddenly there appeared widespread complaints that hallowed performance traditions were being flouted. The commonest concerned choice of tempo, which became excessively contrasted between slow and fast movements, and inconsistency within each tempo. One of the first soloists to be criticised thus was the pianist Anton Rubinstein, whose performance of an unnamed concert piece by Weber was, in Edouard Monnais's opinion, far too fast. Moreover, Monnais suspected that Rubinstein had persuaded Henryk Wieniawski to do likewise with all but the variation movement of the 'Kreutzer' Sonata. Writing as Smith, he objected to the alteration of the piece's character by such a decision, and wryly pointed out: 'When Beethoven wrote his sonata and Weber his concert piece, neither the railways nor the electric telegraph was in use, and today's virtuosi should make sure they don't forget it' (*RGM* XXV/17: 25 Apr. 1858, 134).[66] A fortnight later, Blanchard complained similarly with reference to Rubinstein's playing of Bach and Mendelssohn (*RGM* XXV/19: 9 May 1858, 155).

However, the strongest censure of a virtuoso came from Blanchard's successor, Adolphe Botte, in one of his first reviews for the journal. Not only had Henri Vieuxtemps been indulgently slow in the first movement of Mozart's Quartet in G K387, but:

what is even more serious, it was played with certain affectations of style, certain alterations in note values, in the overall tempo, which produce the best effect in fantasy pieces but which in Mozart's direct and limpid music, whilst allowing the virtuoso to shine, can deprive the piece of an element of cleanness, unity of

[66] 'Lorsque Beethoven écrivait sa sonate et Weber son morceau de concert, ni les chemins de fer, ni le télégraphe éléctrique n'étaient encore en usage, il faut que les virtuoses de nos jours se gardent bien de l'oublier' (*RGM* XXV/17: 25 Apr. 1858, 134).

rhythm, and the four-squareness which everyone recognises and consequently wishes to find there. We appreciate how difficult it is for great artists like Vieuxtemps to strip away the soloist and to refrain from bringing to classic music the charming indulgences of style so justly applauded in modern music. But in the long run it would be worthy of Vieuxtemps, who is an authority among violinists and among true musicians, to show an example of the severity of style which the interpretation of Mozart demands. (*RGM* XXV/48: 28 Nov. 1858, 395)[67]

In the coming decade, Botte paid close attention to changing performance styles in Classical music, and never wavered from this viewpoint. Thus, whilst the *Gazette*'s critics were not entirely united on the question of appropriate performance styles for the music of the Classical era, they were acutely aware that the purity of a performing tradition was gradually being lost; in many cases, their misgivings were strongly expressed. The dividing line between music which was in danger of becoming contaminated by the new style of playing, and that for which the latter style was appropriate, is of prime importance in establishing the extent to which Classical works were viewed as part of the repertoire of contemporary music. In 1857, an author signing himself 'X.' chided **Deloffre**, conductor at the Théâtre-Lyrique, for a wilful alteration of tempo in the overture to *Oberon* (*RGM* XXIV/9: 1 Mar. 1857, 67), but such a complaint with reference to Weber was rare, and a more representative line of demarcation would be drawn between first- and second-period Beethoven. This is borne out in Berlioz's reviews of Beethoven's symphonies, and in those of Blanchard on his chamber music.

During the *Gazette*'s first decade the modernity of Mozart's style was never doubted by critics or the public. Only in the realm of the symphony was he felt to have fallen short, particularly by Berlioz, whose dedication to Beethoven led him to underestimate the inner drive of Mozart's late symphonies, just as his love of Gluck coloured his view of Mozart's operas. For Fétis, Mozart represented the model of perfection – he was at once the revolutionary agent for and the refiner of a musical language whose ideal proportions were, he felt, already being distorted in the

[67] 'ce qui est plus sérieux encore, il a été dit avec certaines mignardises de style, certaines altérations dans la valeur des notes, dans le mouvement général, qui produisent le meilleur effet dans la fantaisie, mais qui, dans la musique si franche et si limpide de Mozart, peuvent, tout en faisant briller le virtuose, enlever au morceau quelque chose de la netteté, de l'unité du rhythme, et des allures carrées que chacun lui connaît, et que, par conséquent, chacun veut y retrouver. Nous le savons, il est bien difficile aux grands artistes comme Vieuxtemps de dépouiller, pour ainsi dire, le soliste et de ne pas porter dans la musique classique les charmantes mollesses de style si justement applaudies dans la musique moderne. Mais enfin il serait digne de Vieuxtemps, qui fait autorité parmi les violonistes et parmi les vrais musiciens, de donner l'exemple de la sévérité de style que demande l'interprétation de Mozart' (*RGM* XXV/48: 28 Nov. 1858, 395).

music of Beethoven. Although universally regarded as the father of modern music and praised among musicians such as Berlioz, Fétis and Bourges for the formal perfection and delicate craftsmanship of his work, Haydn paled in comparison with Mozart, and still more, with Beethoven, on the question of expressivity. His place in the canon was always secure, but was, by the 1870s, retained largely out of respect alone, rather than a fusion of respect and enthusiasm.

5 The Austro-German tradition II: The reception of Beethoven

Introduction

In the reception of Haydn and Mozart, public and critical responses coincided significantly, even when their final evaluations differed; with the music of Beethoven the rôle of criticism was not to reflect (or deflect) public opinion but to inform and educate it. The *Gazette*'s Beethoven criticism took a wide variety of forms, including descriptive analysis, literary portrayals and Romantic accounts of Pauline conversions to his music. Diverse as these approaches were, they shared a wish to mould public appreciation in favour of some of the most difficult music it had yet known. In comparison with Gluck, Mozart or Haydn, the number of articles on Beethoven which are independent of a performance is considerably larger, particularly if one includes Berlioz's Conservatoire reviews of 1838, which contained scant information about each programme, presenting instead an analytical survey of all nine symphonies. The *Gazette* offered its readers an extended justification of Beethoven from different perspectives, each providing a different way into the music. Its attitude was apparent from the outset; the composer's Romantic image as explored in Janin's 'Le Dîner de Beethoven' (*GM* I/1–2: 5–12 Jan. 1834) was continued throughout its first decade. Such Romantic effusions may explain why, despite being welcomed as a member of the editorial staff in 1836, Fétis *père* contributed little of substance on Beethoven in the journal's entire lifetime. His views, as revealed in his own *Revue musicale*, were both too ambivalent and too professorial for Schlesinger. The strength of Berlioz's voice in the 1830s and early 1840s meant that Beethoven was staunchly defended against both the unbelievers and the agnostics. By the mid 1840s, cleavages between followers of Fétis and those of Berlioz were becoming more apparent, and Beethoven's late music became a particular focus of debate. In the journal's final fifteen years, the Beethoven criticism of Charles Bannelier provided a *juste milieu* between the Romantic tone of the early years and the extreme conservatism represented by the work of Edouard Monnais and Adolphe Botte.

Germanic images of Beethoven

One of the first elements of Beethoven's music to be stressed in the journal was its relation to the character of religious experience. Whilst the music itself inspired appreciative listeners with a quasi-religious fervour, its performance context at the Conservatoire was alluded to by means of religious images: the concert hall became a 'temple' and its performers, 'the faithful' (Berlioz, *GM* I/17: 27 Apr. 1834, 133).[1] Such an attitude was not new: Castil-Blaze had referred to the Salle des Menus-Plaisirs as a temple newly re-opened to harmony in his review of the opening concert in 1828 (*JD* 19 Mar. 1828, 4), and, six years earlier, had spoken of the 'religious terror' instilled by the introduction to *Christ on the Mount of Olives* (*JD* 14 Mar. 1822, 2). François Stoepel, who wrote several articles on Beethoven for the *Gazette* between its foundation and his death at the end of 1836, was the first of the *Gazette*'s critics to use religious imagery in the discussion of Beethoven's music. In his opening Conservatoire review he revealed his expectations of a worthy performance of the Fifth Symphony by quoting his own response to the Conservatoire's playing five years earlier:

Not once did I feel my heart shaken by this kind of religious terror, by these elevated images which, in the first movement, should produce such powerful emotion in the soul, by the deeply profound character of the adagio [Andante con moto] which has always seemed to me to be a heavenly prayer addressed by angels to the divine creator. (*GM* I/5: 2 Feb. 1834, 41)[2]

The tendency to interpret Beethoven in religious terms was reinforced in Stoepel's next contribution, 'Beethoven et sa musique' (*GM* I/6: 9 Feb. 1834), a personal and, in its prose style, Schumannesque confession of the revelation to him of Beethoven's genius. The revelation itself, which Stoepel combined with a critique of a Beethoven symphony, is the most Schumannesque part of the article. Taking the form of an extended dream sequence, it progresses from images of fear, supernatural distortion and darkness to those of natural beauty, fulfilment and purity of light. Hopelessly banal by literary standards, the device was nevertheless the

---

[1] 'fidèles' (*GM* I/17: 27 Apr. 1834, 133).
[2] 'Je n'ai pas un seul instant senti mon cœur ébranlé par cette espèce de terreur religieuse, par ces images élevées qui, dans le premier morceau, doivent procurer à l'âme une émotion si puissante, par cet accent si profond de l'adagio [Andante con moto] qui m'a toujours paru une prière céleste adressée par des anges au divin créateur' (*GM* I/5: 2 Feb. 1834, 41).

ideal means of presenting Beethoven as a Romantic hero capable of converting his greatest detractors; furthermore, it was a fitting pendant to Janin's *conte*, 'Le Dîner de Beethoven', which had appeared the previous month. Stoepel also deliberately stressed his earlier, negative, opinion as a prelude to the conversion sequence, thus allowing a more emphatic rejection both of his original stance, and that of current unbelievers:

It was in vain that I searched in him for naturalness, simplicity, pleasant ideas, order, symmetry, melody, everything, in fact, which I found so attractive in Haydn, as in Mozart, and which to me seemed alone to constitute a composer's true merit. In Beethoven I saw nothing but labour, constraint, the bizarre, a collection of contradictory ideas; piles of harmonic agglomerations thrown together as if by chance, and swimming, so to speak, against the tide. (*GM* I/6: 9 Feb. 1834, 43)[3]

His point, ultimately, is that one cannot judge the works of one period by those of another: whereas he had previously complained that Beethoven always broke the rules of composition, he now admitted; 'He created his own rules' (*ibid.*, 45).[4]

Given Schlesinger's status as a Prussian expatriate, it is unsurprising to find contributions on Beethoven by other German or Prussian critics, including Ludwig Rellstab (1799–1860) and A. B. Marx (1795–1866). The three instalments of Rellstab's 'Beethoven. Tableau des souvenirs de ma vie' (*RGM* VII/48–51: 9–30 Aug. 1840) present the most Fétisian interpretation of Beethoven in the early years of the journal, particularly with regard to the late works. As opposed to Stoepel's Romantic view of the essential qualities of good music, Rellstab's opinions were firmly rooted in the values of Classicism.

Nobody who saw Beethoven at this time could escape the conviction that his last works are somehow impregnated with this dark cloud of sullen sadness, of bitter melancholy, even chagrin. Because of their origin, therefore, these works may be less beautiful, less free, in some respects even cause us a painful discomfort, because they are unhealthy, and it is health which gives a work of art its ultimate value. (*RGM* VII/51: 30 Aug. 1840, 441)[5]

---

[3] 'C'était en vain que je cherchais en lui le naturel, la simplicité, des pensées aimables, l'ordre, la symétrie, la mélodie, tout enfin, tout ce qui me plaisait si fort dans Haydn, comme dans Mozart, et me semblait seul constituer le vrai mérite du compositeur. Dans Beethoven, je ne voyais rien que de la recherche, de la contrainte, de la bizarrerie, un assemblage d'idées contradictoires; des débris de masses harmoniques jetés comme au hasard, et nageant, pour ainsi dire, contre le courant' (*GM* I/6: 9 Feb. 1834, 43).

[4] 'C'est lui-même qui a créé ses règles' (*ibid.*, 45).

[5] 'Quiconque a vu Beethoven à cette époque ne pourra jamais perdre la conviction que ses derniers ouvrages sont comme imprégnés de ce sombre nuage de maussade tristesse, d'amère mélancholie, sinon de chagrin. Ces productions peuvent donc, en raison de cette origine, être moins belles, moins libres, nous causer même, à certains égards, une gêne pénible, parce que la santé leur manque, qui donne à une œuvre d'art sa valeur complète' (*RGM* VII/51: 30 Aug. 1840, 441).

He thus equates physical health with the health of the genius, a line of reasoning which was repeatedly used to condemn both late Beethoven and late Schumann. For Rellstab, the late works appeared as the 'ruins of this young beauty and of the masculine sublimity of his genius' (*ibid.*, 440).[6] Such an attitude was virtually forced upon him by his own dislike of Germany's new music, particularly that of Schumann, in whom he saw the worst, unhealthy, elements of late Beethoven being treated as virtues:

Unfortunately, in artistic theories and recent works we have seen the consecration of this inversion. We can interpret this only one way: these *successors* and these sycophants have never understood Beethoven's real grandeur. (*ibid.*, 442)[7]

Such sentiments were to find French echoes in the writings of Fétis-influenced critics from the early 1850s. Yet Rellstab revered the early and middle-period repertoire, in which he found the real Beethovenian genius at work.

A. B. Marx's contribution of 1834 (*RGM* I/51: 21 Dec.) produced as Romantic an image of Beethoven as did Stoepel's. As in the later biography of 1859, the elevation of Beethoven's status took place at the expense of Haydn and especially Mozart, a tradition carried on in the *Gazette* by Berlioz. Unlike Berlioz, however, Marx concentrated his discussion on the chamber music. Despite the perfection of the Ninth Symphony, the genres in which he felt Beethoven was strongest were the piano sonata and the string quartet (*ibid.*, 407). The importance of these genres lay in their being private music divorced from constraints of ceremony or public taste; Marx saw them as representing the composer's genius in its purest and least compromised form. Beethoven's isolation from his public is turned into a saving grace, and the spectre of Janin's alienated genius rises once more.

Berlioz on Beethoven

Berlioz dominates the first decade of the *Gazette*'s Beethoven reviewing. The essays on the symphonies (1837–8) were later incorporated, with minor changes, into *A travers chants*, and constitute the most important

---

[6] 'ruines de cette beauté juvenile et de la mâle sublimité de son génie' (*ibid.*, 440). Given these comments, Robin Wallace's claim that in Rellstab's collected writings 'one looks in vain ... for a hint of adverse criticism toward Beethoven', is unconvincing. Robin Wallace, *Beethoven's Critics. Aesthetic Dilemmas and Resolutions during the Composer's Lifetime* (Cambridge, 1986), 68.

[7] 'Malheureusement nous avons vu dans des théories artistiques et des productions récentes la consécration de cet intervertissement. Nous n'y voyons qu'une chose, c'est que ces *successeurs* et ces thuriféraires de Beethoven n'ont jamais compris sa véritable grandeur' (*RGM* VII/51: 30 Aug. 1840, 442).

aspect of his work on Beethoven for the journal.[8] However, it is important not to view them in isolation, even though Berlioz's earlier reviews sometimes merely present widely dispersed snatches of his later ideas. These essays must be seen in the context of the overall pattern of Berlioz's Conservatoire reviewing for the *Gazette*, which falls into four distinct stages. Unequivocally enthusiastic at first, from 1837 he worries about the Conservatoire's stagnant programming and the sincerity of the public's admiration of Beethoven; sometimes public opinion was divided, as after the performance of the Ninth in 1837, when one half of the hall applauded wildly while the other remained unmoved (*RGM* IV/6: 5 Feb. 1837, 51); earlier the same year, Berlioz lamented that some members of the Conservatoire audience would apparently be happier hearing a Musard galop for the fiftieth time than a Beethoven symphony for the tenth (*RGM* IV/4: 22 Jan. 1837, 30). The third phase, heralded by Berlioz's analysis of the 'Eroica' in 1837, includes his essays of 1838 on the symphonies. After 1838, his reviews become shorter and repetitious. He confesses himself unable to say more about Beethoven's symphonies, criticises the Conservatoire's stagnation, and frequently discusses the background to particular pieces. In 1841, Berlioz was virtually begging in print to be relieved of the job of Conservatoire reviewer, at last feeling 'at the end of my tribulations' (*RGM* VIII/30: 25 Apr. 1841, 235),[9] only to find that he was again saddled with covering the 1842 season. His most important and considered criticism is thus contained in the years up to and including 1838, when the glow of the Conservatoire, that 'Wonderful institution!! noble monument erected to the art, to protect and conserve its existence' (*GM* I/17: 27 Apr. 1834, 133),[10] was still bright.

In the early *Gazette* reviews, which had to combine comments on a variety of different works, restricted column space made the absence of an overarching idea almost inevitable. Berlioz's comments, however, revealed his interest in specific aspects of Beethoven, in particular his instrumentation and the emancipation of his symphonic style from those of Haydn and Mozart, especially in the first two symphonies. Habeneck neglected the First Symphony between 1834 and 1844, but the Second was frequently performed. In 1834, Berlioz stated that, although there

[8] Berlioz did not restrict himself to reviewing symphonic concerts – there are short reviews of chamber music, including the Quartet in C-sharp minor Op. 131 (*RGM* III/8: 21 Feb. 1836), and the 'Archduke' Trio Op. 97 played by Liszt, Batta and Urhan (*RGM* IV/6: 5 Feb. 1837), at which he was so moved that he claimed he would exchange it for the most beautiful of the symphonies. But these reviews contain no technical information, and give the impression that Berlioz felt too awed by the chamber music and too inexperienced in the genre to make well-founded judgements.

[9] 'à bout de mes tribulations' (*RGM* VIII/30: 25 Apr. 1841, 235).

[10] 'Belle institution!! noble monument élevé à l'art pour en conserver et protéger l'existence' (*GM* I/17: 27 Apr. 1834, 133).

was no need to make allowances for the Second, it was nevertheless unmistakably Mozartian, albeit 'already vastly expanded' (*ibid.*, 134).[11] He reinforced the connection with Classicism by alighting on a passage in the Scherzo which was always linked in his mind with a similar passage in Haydn's Symphony no. 102, where a tiny three-note motif was handed between the violin sections.[12] The finale, however, was more like real Beethoven, specifically because of its 'diverting, most *unpredictable* caprices' (*GM* I/17: 27 Apr. 1834, 134).[13] In 1836, this opinion was strengthened by the programming of K550 and the Second Symphony in the same concert, which invited a comparison of the two. In his wish to elevate Beethoven, Berlioz (like Marx) disparaged Mozart; but his disparagement makes all the more conspicuous his wish to drag the Second Symphony into the world of the middle-period music:

it highlights most conspicuously the relatively widespread error that these two works are of a similar type and that Beethoven, when he wrote it, was still entirely under the influence of the Mozartian style. On the contrary, nothing is more dissimilar in form, in thought, in all respects. Mozart is likeable, gentle, gracious, spirited; he draws one to him, one likes him without dreaming of admiration; conversely, by the force and the unexpectedness of each of his movements, by the majesty of his stature, the other instils a respect which is not unmixed with terror. (attrib. Berlioz, *RGM* III/10: 6 Mar. 1836, 79)[14]

In the earlier review he implies that Beethoven's individuality is not yet fully formed; here he implies the opposite, further emphasised in the 1838 essay, where the thought of the 'parcelles d'un motif' shared between the violin sections in the Scherzo provokes comparison not with Haydn, but Weber – 'one might believe oneself witnessing the fairy games of Oberon's gracious spirits' (*RGM* V/4: 28 Jan. 1838, 34).[15] Thus in the space of four years the transition of the Second Symphony into the sound-world of the Romantic era was complete. In comparison with his remarks on the First Symphony, which he still saw as little more than an example of Mozartian *juvenilia* (despite noting the new use of wind

[11] 'déjà énormément agrandi' (*ibid.*, 134).
[12] See *RGM* VIII/12: 11 Feb. 1841, 90.
[13] 'caprices les plus piquans, les plus *imprévoyables*' (*GM* I/17: 27 Apr. 1834, 134).
[14] 'elle fait ressortir de la manière la plus évidente l'erreur assez répandue que ces deux ouvrages avaient un type commun et que Beethoven était encore tout entier, quand il l'écrivit, sous l'influence du style mozartique. Rien de plus dissemblable, au contraire, de forme, de pensées, de tout. Mozart se montre aimable, doux, gracieux, spirituel, il vous attire à lui, on l'aime sans songer à l'admirer; l'autre au contraire, par la force et l'imprévu de chacun de ses mouvements, par la majestie de sa stature, imprime un respect qui n'est pas sans mélange de terreur' (attrib. Berlioz, *RGM* III/10: 6 Mar. 1836, 79).
[15] 'on croirait assister aux jeux féeriques des gracieux esprits d'Obéron' (*RGM* V/4: 28 Jan. 1838, 34).

instruments and the timpani pedal in the slow movement), those on the
Second Symphony reveal that here he felt there was a distinct break with
tradition, greater emotional power and an exploitation of the unexpected
which demanded a new level of attention from the listener. The technique
is identical to that of Berlioz's Gluck articles: in order to gain entrance to
his personal canon, specific pieces must be susceptible of taking on a
Romantic aura; therefore, Berlioz strives to explain the meaning of
favoured works in Romantic terms. It was not until 1849, in a similar
comparison (with Haydn), that Berlioz accorded the First Symphony
truly Beethovenian status.[16]

As for the remaining two symphonies of demonstrably smaller
proportions than their respective predecessors – the Fourth and the
Eighth – Berlioz always hotly defended them against the charge of
their being Mozartian or Haydnesque. Again, he concentrated on
innovations of instrumentation and the exploitation of the unexpected,
but here we find other preoccupations which are of paramount
importance for Berlioz's Beethoven criticism as a whole: the novel use
of rhythm, metre and harmony. His attitude towards 'carrure'
immediately set him apart from the Classically minded Fétis. He
commented on the way in which Beethoven upset the symmetry of his
two opening three-bar phrases in the Allegretto scherzando of the
Eighth with half a bar's silence (during which the ear is arrested by the
change of chord in the woodwind), considering it a perfect example of
how 'the law of symmetrical phrase structure can sometimes be broken
to good effect' (*RGM* V/7: 18 Feb. 1838, 76).[17] In the Fourth
Symphony, he praised the Scherzo because of its 'duple metre phrases
forced to work within successive bars of *triple* metre' (*RGM* V/4: 28
Jan. 1838, 35),[18] and had a keen sense of the disruptive effect such
hemiolas had on the ear. His analysis of such devices was, however,
selective, and depended largely on his chosen focus for each symphony's
analysis.

Despite, or perhaps because of, Hoffmann's precedent, Berlioz did not
discuss rhythmic unities in the Fifth Symphony.[19] In this review, the
technical discussion focuses almost exclusively on Beethoven's harmonic
procedure, his use of dissonance and the harmonic ambiguity of the

---

[16] See above, pp. 86–7.

[17] 'la loi de la carrure peut être quelquefois enfreinte avec bonheur' (*RGM* V/7: 18 Feb.
1838, 76).

[18] 'phrases rythmées à deux temps, forcées d'entrer dans les combinaisons de la mesure à
trois' (*RGM* V/4: 28 Jan. 1838, 35).

[19] Hoffmann's critique of the Fifth Symphony was first published in the Leipzig *Allgemeine
musikalische Zeitung* of 4 and 11 July 1810.

transition to the finale.[20] Enmeshed with Berlioz's love of Beethoven's new use of harmony was his penchant for the 'inattendu', yet any such gestures had to be justified, both in terms of dramatic context and the logic of harmonic progression. Berlioz's need to rationalise Beethoven's harmonic innovations can be seen as part of a general justification of the composer's procedure, but also as a process by which Berlioz himself came to terms with his idol's departures from standard practice. There were, however, some harmonic acerbities in Beethoven which he could not accept: the strengthening (at bar 208) of the already dissonant chord opening the Ninth's finale was described as an 'appalling collection' of sounds (*RGM* V/9: 4 Mar. 1838, 99),[21] and he remained bemused by Beethoven's experimentation in the finale of the Eighth with the pivot note D-flat/C-sharp. He accounted for its first two appearances as the flattened submediant of F major, but subsequent appearances, leading to fragments of the theme in D-flat, C-sharp minor and finally F-sharp minor (bar 372 onwards), despite his ability to explain them theoretically, left him puzzled as to their motivation. His final comment, 'It's most odd' (*RGM* V/7: 18 Feb. 1838, 76),[22] indicates that for him the unexpected had been taken too far, and that, more importantly, the ability to justify or account for something theoretically did not automatically indicate his willingness to accept it. Yet, as Reeve points out, such criticisms do not weaken the 'admirative' style of Berlioz's criticism:

> With Fétis, the 'lapses' in Beethoven serve ultimately to prove the superiority and the perfection of Mozart. With Berlioz, these moments diminish not one iota the stature of his idol. Nor do they ever upset the admirative tone of the comments in general – which is perhaps why his criticisms go so often unnoticed. Indeed one might even maintain that the objections with Berlioz form a part of the tribute.[23]

It is in relation to the importance of theory that Berlioz's Beethoven criticism differs fundamentally from that of Fétis. For the older man, theoretical justification of innovation was of paramount importance – indeed a prerequisite for understanding – but once a problem had been solved it was almost incumbent upon him to accept its validity, though he might consider it lacking 'goût'. With Berlioz, the opposite priorities obtained: the solution of theoretical problems did not necessarily enable

---

[20] Wallace has discussed the *A travers chants* version of the 1838 review in some detail, while Reeve examines the conflicting strands of praise and censure in his remarks on harmony in relation to the other symphonies. See Wallace, *Beethoven's Critics*, 126–43, and Katherine Reeve, 'The Poetics of the Orchestra in the Writings of Hector Berlioz' (unpublished PhD dissertation, Yale University, 1978), 202ff.

[21] 'épouvantable assemblage' (*RGM* V/9: 4 Mar. 1838, 99).

[22] 'C'est fort curieux' (*RGM* V/7: 18 Feb. 1838, 76).

[23] Reeve, 'Poetics of the Orchestra', 208.

him to accept them, since the ultimate justification for an innovation was its effect and dramatic justification, not its means. Of Beethoven's use of 'musique pittoresque' in the Sixth Symphony, Berlioz said: 'To my mind, the composer's justification in such a case lies solely in the success or otherwise of his attempt' (*RGM* V/5: 4 Feb. 1838, 49).[24] Although Berlioz's pragmatic approach also meant that if an idea worked it no longer needed to have theoretical justification, the presence of such a subjective element in his criticism did not deter him from analysing difficult passages and highlighting Beethoven's ability to break compositional rules with impunity.[25] In the Seventh Symphony, it was the oscillating pedals in the first, third and fourth movements which he found particularly effective (he did not mention the extended upper pedal in the Trio). That he relished these grinding pedals and their ability to increase tension, particularly in the Seventh's finale, is apparent from his detailed descriptions of all three of them, the last and most audacious of which he admitted looked on paper like 'a fault in the clarity of the harmony' (*RGM* V/6: 11 Feb. 1838, 66).[26] Yet for him it was justified because of the force of the prevailing A major tonality, and by its admirable preparation of the coda.

In his review of the Third, Berlioz's overriding wish was to dispel the public's notion that the symphony was about military heroism. To do so, he provided an alternative (but rigid) dramatic plan – 'a hero's funeral oration' (*RGM* IV/15: 9 Apr. 1837, 122).[27] In this prototype for the Beethoven 'review-analyses' he came close to Hoffmann's technique of writing to a dramatic idea spanning the entire work. Berlioz's idea, however, had unfortunate Procrustean consequences, and such dramatisation was not a method which he used consistently again. In particular, his vision of ancient military remembrance denied the Scherzo any joyful vitality, which may explain why he did not mention the witty transformation of the triadic motif into duple metre at bar 384, even though he was acutely sensitive to such hemiolas. In 1836 he had ignored the extrovert nature of the horn writing of the Trio, finding it 'sombre and almost dreamy' (*RGM* III/17: 24 Apr. 1836, 134).[28] In 1837 he re-interpreted it

---

24 'A mon avis, la justification du compositeur n'est, en pareil cas, que dans le succès ou l'insuccès de sa tentative' (*RGM* V/5: 4 Feb. 1838, 49).
25 Reeve notes Berlioz's comments on the use of pedals in the Fifth Symphony (one of the causes of the rupture with Fétis) and also in the finale of the Eighth (bar 161 onwards), as revealing Berlioz's delight in the use of judicious chord spacing and discrete instrumentation to soften the effect of a dissonance. Reeve, 'Poetics of the Orchestra', 202–3.
26 'un défaut de clarté d'harmonie' (*RGM* V/6: 11 Feb. 1838, 66).
27 'l'oraison funèbre d'un héros' (*RGM* IV/15: 9 Apr. 1837, 122).
28 'sombre et presque rêveuse' (*RGM* III/17: 24 Apr. 1836, 134).

as 'true funeral games, constantly darkened by thoughts of mourning, games such as the warriors of the *Iliad* held around the graves of their leaders' (*RGM* IV/15: 9 Apr. 1837, 122).[29] The denial of wit's place in a work which he designated epic is surely what lies behind his refusal to accept the 'musical caprice' (*ibid.*)[30] of the 2nd horn entry just before the recapitulation of the first movement. That he could accept a similar harmonic device in the 'Pastoral' because of its whimsical dramatic justification implies that in his view the context, not the device, was at fault. Writing his 'Eroica' critique to a preconceived idea, Berlioz left himself no option but to outlaw a gesture for which his drama had no analogue; in a bizarre reversal of cause and effect, Beethoven became the victim of Berlioz's quest for dramatic realism.

In his review of the Ninth, education is Berlioz's unmistakable aim. The whole essay seeks to describe and explain the work and its motivation. The Ninth was still the least acceptable Beethoven symphony to French ears, and would not be definitively accepted in Paris for another four decades.[31] Rather than dwelling upon only the elements which interested him, Berlioz for once gave a general view of the complete work, ending with a literal translation of the 'Ode to Joy'. For him, the justification for using voices in the finale was its character as the climax of a crescendo of instrumental technique throughout the symphonies and an inner crescendo within the work itself. Given his perception (shared, for once, by Fétis) that Beethoven was unable to sustain a crescendo of excitement after the monumental transition to the Fifth's finale, Berlioz's comments on the success of the 'Ode', which he feels is largely due to the introduction of the voices, are pertinent. In terms of Berlioz's own output, particularly *Roméo et Juliette*, started in the same year as this review, they are doubly so:

Beethoven had already written eight symphonies prior to this one. In order to surpass the point he had reached with instrumental resources alone, what means remained open to him? The addition of voices to instruments. But to observe the law of crescendo and to set in relief in the work itself the power of the auxiliary force which he wanted to give to the orchestra, was it not necessary to allow the instruments to figure alone during the first part of the drama which he proposed to unfold? . . . . Given this idea, it is easy to appreciate how he was led to seek a mixed style of music which could act as a link between the two main divisions of the symphony; instrumental recitative was the bridge which he ventured to place

---

[29] 'de véritables jeux funèbres, à chaque instant assombris par des pensées de deuil, des jeux enfin comme ceux que les guerriers de l'Iliade [sic] célébraient autour des tombeaux de leurs chefs' (*RGM* IV/15: 9 Apr. 1837, 122).

[30] 'caprice musical' (*ibid.*).

[31] Discussed below, pp. 119ff.

between the choir and the orchestra, and over which the instruments passed to be joined with the voices. (*RGM* V/9: 4 Mar. 1838, 97–8)[32]

Berlioz's discussion of the first three movements uses the same approach as for the majority of the symphonies – the combination of minute technical detail with an overall interpretation – but on arrival at the finale the review's pace slows dramatically, giving a section-by-section explanation of the music's relation to the text. The description is almost devoid of technical detail, save some indications of instrumentation. Berlioz's appeal is to the emotional faculty alone, a tactic which would have led to a significantly wider dissemination and understanding of his ideas.

However, the 1838 review was not Berlioz's last word on the choral finale. Little more than a month after an essay which ostensibly represented his considered view of the work, he expressed serious misgivings about its vocal writing. The finale had been poorly received at the Conservatoire, and Berlioz attributed this in part to:

the unquestionably defective style of the vocal writing; in the resulting impossibility for singers to articulate certain notes clearly, to pronounce the words, and to give the notes the necessary full tone and volume. (*RGM* V/15: 15 Apr. 1838, 161)[33]

Nowhere else in the *Gazette* was Beethoven's competence so seriously questioned by his own supporters, although the oratorio *Christ on the Mount of Olives* generally received an adverse press because of its early composition and the decorative nature of its solo parts, which Berlioz in particular thought unworthy of their author (*RGM* VIII/29: 18 Apr.

---

[32] 'Beethoven avait écrit déjà huit symphonies avant celle-ci. Pour aller au-delà du point où il était alors parvenu à l'aide des seules ressources de l'instrumentation, quels moyens lui restaient? l'adjonction des voix aux instruments. Mais pour observer la loi du crescendo, et mettre en relief dans l'œuvre même la puissance de l'auxiliaire qu'il voulait donner à l'orchestre, n'était-il pas nécessaire de laisser encore les instruments figurer seuls sur le premier plan du tableau qu'il se proposait de dérouler? . . . . Une fois cette donnée admise, on conçoit fort bien qu'il ait été amené à chercher une musique mixte qui pût servir de liaison aux deux grandes divisions de la symphonie; le récitatif instrumental fut le pont qu'il osa jeter entre le chœur et l'orchestre, et sur lequel les instruments passèrent pour aller se joindre aux voix' (*RGM* V/9: 4 Mar. 1838, 97–8). For a discussion of the 'loi du crescendo', see Ian Kemp, '*Romeo and Juliet* and *Roméo et Juliette*', in *Berlioz Studies*, ed. Peter Bloom (Cambridge, 1992), 48–9. Fétis's comments on Beethoven's failure to sustain the 'crescendo' in the Fifth (*RGM* XIV/19: 9 May 1847, 156) may have been inspired by Berlioz. However, as early as 1822 Castil-Blaze had cited the idea of gradually increasing complexity and excitement as a desirable working principle in opera (see Gìslason, 'Castil-Blaze', 117); I have found no earlier precedent which relates to autonomous music.

[33] 'la manière incontestablement défectueuse dont les voix sont écrites; dans l'impossibilité qui en résulte pour les chanteurs d'articuler bien nettement certaines notes, de prononcer les paroles, et de donner aux sons la plénitude et la force qui leur seraient nécessaires' (*RGM* V/15: 15 Apr. 1838, 161).

1841, 226). Berlioz probably refrained from voicing the full extent of his doubts about the Ninth Symphony in his 1838 essay because the set of analyses formed a panegyric written with an eye to later publication. Individual essays are not uncritically admiring; nevertheless, to end on a note of such fundamental doubt would have resulted in an unacceptable level of anticlimax, thereby flouting his own 'loi du crescendo'.

Fétis and Blanchard

Fétis's work on Beethoven for the *Gazette* was sparse but influential, serving to undermine much of the Romantic image presented in the Schlesinger years. For twenty years, beginning with the Brandus takeover in 1846, his influence, both direct and indirect, on the journal's predominant tone, was conspicuous. In differing degrees, Blanchard and Botte followed his lead, thus helping to turn a journal which embraced modernity into one which viewed the avant-garde with (at best) ambivalence. In an essay on recent developments in symphonic composition (*RGM* XIV/19–27: 9 May – 4 Jul. 1847), Fétis countered Berlioz's arguments encouraging the Ninth's acceptance. His reasoning centred on the contamination of the autonomous movements by the choral finale's philosophical message, the failure of the cumulative process both within the work and within the finale itself, and the banality of the 'Ode to Joy' theme. In addition, he reserved particular scorn for bars 451 onwards in the finale for reasons of harmonic ineptitude and perverse modulatory practice (*RGM* XIV/23: 6 Jun. 1847, 187–8); the latter accusation also informed his opinion of the C-sharp minor quartet, alongside complaints that Beethoven flouted 'carrure' and wrote long-winded meanderings. In a detailed review of Alexandre Oulibicheff's reactionary book *Beethoven, ses critiques, ses glossateurs* (*RGM* XXIV/23–30: 7 Jun. – 26 Jul. 1857), the subject of Beethoven's deafness was again raised, and the harshness of his existence used as a weapon against his music by both the author and the reviewer.[34]

Fétis's Beethoven criticism helped delay critical acceptance of the late works. It also focused critics' minds on questions of style and periodisation. Characterising the music of each period was among Henri Blanchard's major preoccupations as a reviewer of Beethoven, forming the fundamental premise of many of his value judgements. In an extended review of the piano concertos and a selection of the instrumental sonatas, he noted that: 'What distinguishes Beethoven above all from other composers is that he appeals equally to the Romantics and

---

[34] Nevertheless, this review was the only place in the journal where Fétis was moved to defend Beethoven against a writer more conservative than himself.

the Classicists' (*RGM* XIII/31: 2 Aug. 1846, 243).[35] At this stage, Blanchard shared Fétis's scepticism about the late works; he refers here to stylistic differences between first- and second-period works (or those of the first period in which he detects elements which presage the second), carefully omitting reference to those of the third. His description of the First Piano Concerto, for instance, clearly indicates his mode of thought. The first movement is:

in the composer's Classical manner. Its melodic and harmonic outlines are clear-cut and signposted in advance by the ending of a passage with a concluding cadential trill, as in the violin concertos of Viotti. (*RGM* XIII/21: 24 May 1846, 166)[36]

By contrast, the Adagio of the Violin Sonata Op. 24 ('Spring') displays more Romantic qualities: 'a mysterious and touching melody which makes one daydream' (*RGM* XIII/31: 2 Aug. 1846, 244).[37] For Blanchard, Beethoven's music up to and including the second period showed Classical traits and the acceptable face of Romanticism; until 1852 however, his third period remained incomprehensible.

In his early reviews of the late quartets, Blanchard took his cue from Fétis, and used biographical details to prejudice readers against them. However, more important points of contact with the opinions of his older colleague concern the compositional structure of the works themselves.[38] Blanchard agreed that Beethoven's abandonment of traditional forms in the late works, which Fétis (in Cousinian vein) attributed to sheer arrogance, produced more problems than the composer could solve, resulting in diffuseness and imbalance. Reviewing an early concert of 1849 by the **Maurin**/Chevillard Quartet, he compared Op. 132 in A minor to Rousseau's *Rêveries du promeneur solitaire*: although the general rules of syntax were observed, the train of thought constantly wandered (*RGM* XVI/7: 18 Feb. 1849, 52). In the same review, he interpreted Beethoven's own questioning in the Quartet in F major Op. 135 as evidence of mental frailty. Almost paraphrasing Fétis, he noted how closely the problem was linked to formal experiment; 'traditional form, observed in his earlier works, no longer concerns him. His thought

---

[35] 'Ce qui distingue surtout Beethoven de tous les autres compositeurs, c'est qu'il plaît également aux romantiques et aux classiques' (*RGM* XIII/31: 2 Aug. 1846, 243).

[36] 'dans la manière classique de l'auteur. Les formes mélodiques et harmoniques en sont arrêtées, claires et comme prévues d'avance par la chute du trait sur la cadence finale avec trille, à la façon des concertos de violon de Viotti' (*RGM* XIII/21: 24 May 1846, 166).

[37] 'une mélodie mystérieuse et touchante qui fait rêver' (*RGM* XIII/31: 2 Aug. 1846, 244).

[38] The Parisian reception of the late Beethoven quartets has been charted by Ivan Mahaim in *Beethoven. Naissance et renaissance des derniers quatuors* (Paris, 1964). However, by selective quotation and incorrect chronology, he distorts the evidence of the press, and, in particular, falsely portrays Blanchard as consistently supercilious.

is vague; it loses its way in untrammelled developments' (*ibid.*).[39] Later that year he accused Beethoven of opening the way to the decadence of Romanticism, which rejected all traditional means of conferring order and cohesion on a work (*RGM* XVI/41: 14 Oct. 1849, 325). More unsettling still was the modulatory freedom of the late quartets, combined with the frequent delaying of cadences. Later in 1849, Blanchard observed that the first movement of Op. 130 in B-flat:

notable for its difficult, strange harmony, for the enervating delay of harmonic resolutions, for a kind of systematic hatred of concluding melodic fragments with a perfect cadence, bears witness to an exhausted imagination now devoid of lyricism, and which employed the means of method unrestrainedly and in tasteless fashion. Movements five and six, the Cavatina and the Finale, in which there still gleam a few lights of melodic inspiration, are particularly full of these indefinitely delayed cadences. (*RGM* XVI/15: 15 Apr. 1849, 116)[40]

Blanchard's reference to Beethoven's replacing inspiration with method is important as a precursor of notions of 'system' in the compositions of Schumann and Wagner, both of whom were perceived, by Fétisian critics, to have focused upon re-interpreting and developing the least promising elements of Beethoven's late manner.

Blanchard's turning point came in 1852, when he attended another Maurin/Chevillard concert, scores in hand. For the first time, it seems, he endeavoured to judge the music on the grounds of compositional technique and logicality before re-evaluating it – a rather Fétisian order of priorities which was to lead to an anti-Fétisian discovery. Blanchard's conclusions were diametrically opposed to those he had reached three years earlier. Admitting that previously he had been 'completely disoriented' (*RGM* XIX/9: 29 Feb. 1852, 67)[41] by the absence of stylistic unity compared with Beethoven's earlier, clear-cut works, he now conceded the presence of rigorous contrapuntal working, and concluded that 'the composer's powers were not failing when he wrote these works, audacious and unprecedented in the art of music' (*ibid.*, 67–8).[42] That

---

[39] 'la forme consacrée, observée dans ses précédents ouvrages[,] ne le préoccupe plus. Sa pensée est vague; elle se perd dans des développements sans mesure' (*RGM* XVI/7: 18 Feb. 1849, 52).

[40] 'remarquable par la recherche d'une harmonie étrange, par le retard fatigant des résolutions d'accord, par une sorte de haine systématique de la conclusion des parcelles de phrases de mélodie par la cadence parfaite, témoigne d'une imagination usée qui ne trouvait plus de chant, et qui employait sans mesure et sans goût les ressources de la méthode. La cinquième et sixième partie, la *cavatinna* [sic] et le *finale* dans lesquels scintillent encore plusieurs lueurs d'inspiration mélodique, abondent surtout en ces ajournements indéfinis de terminaison' (*RGM* XVI/15: 15 Apr. 1849, 116).

[41] 'tout dépaysé' (*RGM* XIX/9: 29 Feb. 1852, 67).

[42] 'l'homme n'était point déchu quand il a écrit ces œuvres audacieuses et sans précédents dans l'art musical' (*ibid.*, 67–8).

this realisation was both sudden and complete is made clear in a later review, where Blanchard looked back to its circumstances:

I admit that, accustomed to the lucid, square-cut and Classical plasticity of Haydn, Mozart and even Beethoven in his first period, this method was enough for me; but, yielding to the ever-increasing strength of the latter's genius, I listened to it anew, re-read it, and the light dawned! (*RGM* XX/3: 16 Jan. 1853, 17)[43]

From then on, Blanchard was anxious to defend Beethoven against accusations of perverse modulatory and harmonic practice, particularly (which is ironic in view of his earlier statements) in the first movement of Op. 130 in B-flat, which he now considered to contain 'heterogeneous modulations which are no less logical for that' (*RGM* XXI/6: 5 Feb. 1854, 41).[44] He also came to revel in the enharmonic audacities of the Quartet in C-sharp minor's opening fugue, particularly its stretto (*RGM* XX/3: 16 Jan. 1853, 16). Noting the formal originality of the Adagio of Op. 127 in E-flat, he discussed its 'richness of modulations, which are at once sweet, raw, unexpected, bold, yet correct and logical, and which can withstand the most exacting critical inquiry' (*RGM* XXI/13: 26 Mar. 1854, 102).[45]

After attending Maurin's rehearsals for the 1852/53 season, Blanchard inserted two preview articles for the coming series in the main body, rather than the 'Nouvelles' section, of the *Gazette*. To do so showed unprecedented enthusiasm for a chamber series, and represented a declaration of faith (*RGM* XIX/48: 28 Nov. 1852, 405; and *RGM* XX/1: 2 Jan. 1853, 4). In 1852/53 and 1854, his coverage of Maurin's work eclipsed that of any other area, centring on the freedom and variety of expression achieved by Beethoven through the innovative use of fugal and imitative techniques. Blanchard remained unsympathetic to the use of learned counterpoint for purely virtuoso ends, and placed the expression of emotion within a coherent form above all other criteria for judging a piece of music. He outlined the essential qualities of fine composition in a review of Op. 131 in C-sharp minor, a work which he now felt illustrated them perfectly; 'good compositional style resides in a profound knowledge of counterpoint and fugue, providing a bedrock for

---

[43] 'J'avoue qu'habitué à la plastique lucide, carrée et classique de Haydn, de Mozart et de Beethoven lui-même dans sa première manière, cette méthode me suffisait; mais, cédant à la force toujours ascentionnelle du génie de ce dernier, je l'entendis de nouveau, je le relus, et la lumière se fit!' (*RGM* XX/3: 16 Jan. 1853, 17).

[44] 'de modulations hétérogènes qui n'en sont pas moins logiques' (*RGM* XXI/6: 5 Feb. 1854, 41).

[45] 'richesse de modulations tout à la fois suaves et crues, inattendues, hardies, mais correctes et logiques, qui peuvent braver la critique la plus minutieuse' (*RGM* XXI/13: 26 Mar. 1854, 102).

caprice and fantasy' (*RGM* XX/3: 16 Jan. 1853, 17).[46] He detected this combination in the 'A la danza tedesca' of the Quartet in B-flat Op. 130 – a 'delicious banter' (*RGM* XXI/6: 5 Feb. 1854, 41)[47] despite its rigorously imitative style of composition. Thus Blanchard reversed his opinions whilst retaining his principles. From 1852 to 1855, Beethoven's late quartets received unprecedented coverage in the *Gazette*, sometimes reducing comment on other works played in a particular concert to a bare minimum. By October 1855, Blanchard felt he had said all he could, and the proportion of comment they received duly diminished. In 1857, he noted that the concerts had waned in popularity (*RGM* XXIV/7: 15 Feb. 1857, 49), and he, too, turned his attention to other series except when Maurin programmed an unfamiliar work. Yet by this stage he had taken his readers on a journey of discovery which both defended the quality of the late quartets and suggested avenues to their understanding. In the *Gazette*, few spans of criticism on a particular repertory take on as canonising an allure as that of Blanchard on Beethoven's late quartets. Yet Blanchard's work, like Berlioz's, was vulnerable to attack during the journal's most conservative years.

Adolphe Botte: Beethoven and New Germany

Of the *Gazette*'s other contributors writing between 1850 and 1880, only Berthold Damcke (1812–75) openly supported Blanchard's view, writing an appreciative account of Beethoven's compositional procedure in the Scherzando vivace of Op. 127 (*RGM* XIX/49: 5 Dec. 1852). With the accession of Adolphe Botte, essentially a 'dry, Classical musician', to quote Blanchard's own phrase (*RGM* XX/8: 20 Feb. 1853, 70),[48] attention focused once more on the Alard/Franchomme series or on the relatively new Armingaud/Jacquard Quartet, which specialised in the chamber music of Mendelssohn. Botte's critical stance most closely resembled that of Fétis, whom he was apt to paraphrase (though mostly without acknowledgement).[49] In comparison with both Blanchard and Bannelier, Botte was a conservative critic whose appointment during the height of the Wagner scandal led him to take refuge in the music of the

---

46 'le bon style chez un compositeur est dans la connaissance approfondie du contrepoint et de la fugue, sur laquelle peuvent s'appuyer alors le caprice et la fantaisie' (*RGM* XX/3: 16 Jan. 1853, 17).

47 'délicieux badinage' (*RGM* XXI/6: 5 Feb. 1854, 41).

48 'musicien classique sec' (*RGM* XX/8: 20 Feb. 1853, 70).

49 Fétis praised him as a 'distinguished critic' who contributed 'very fine articles' to the *Gazette* ('Critique distingué ... de fort bons articles'). Fétis, *Biographie universelle*, II, 34.

eighteenth and early nineteenth centuries. His criticism of late Beethoven stands out from that of all his colleagues in that it cannot begin to be understood independently of either its aesthetic context or Botte's own criticism of other chamber composers; it is consistently drawn against a background of anti-Wagnerian feeling catalysed by a damning article written for the journal by Fétis in 1852.[50] Botte's embarrassment at taking over reviewing the Maurin/Chevillard Quartet series from the late Blanchard is palpable; his criticism of Beethoven and Schumann verges on paranoia. In his review of the second Maurin/ Chevillard concert of 1859, which included the Quartet in F minor Op. 95 and that in A minor, Op. 132, his hostility was unconcealed and he raised the old questions of Beethoven's deafness and his wrong-headed application of philosophical ideas to music (*RGM* XXVI/5: 30 Jan. 1859, 35).

A review of a concert given by the Armingaud/Jacquard Quartet early in 1859 epitomises Botte's critical priorities. The programme included the Paris première of Schumann's Quartet in A minor Op. 41/1, the 'Kreutzer' Sonata and Haydn's Quartet in B-flat Op. 50/1.[51] Botte reserved his eulogies for the Haydn, 'whose grace, freshness, pleasant tenderness contrasted singularly with Schumann's vague unease, his feverish passion, his melodic pallor, his impotent sweep' (*RGM* XXVI/7: 13 Feb. 1859, 51).[52] However, after the Schumann, help was at hand: the 'Kreutzer' Sonata 'arrived to calm the public down again' (*ibid.*).[53] Botte's estimation of Schumann's quartet is illuminating. He complained of scholasticism combined with an overt originality which bordered on the bizarre (a term with resonances of Fétis's late-Beethoven criticism); he deemed 'monotonous' Schumann's use of similar phrases in modulating sequence, noting that, though producing constant change, such developmental technique nullified all sense of the unexpected (*ibid.*). Botte's opinion was rooted in his perception of Schumann's style as stemming from late Beethoven, as is revealed explicitly in a review of 1860 in which he compared Beethoven's earlier, expansive adagios with the modulatory perversity and frequent change of mood of Op. 130's first movement:

How we prefer their expansiveness and their natural beauty to these successions of little phrases which, if they portray disorder and fire, indicate the policy

---

[50] Fétis's Wagner criticism is analysed in Chapter 10.
[51] Identified in Fauquet, *Les Sociétés de musique de chambre*, 385.
[52] 'dont la grâce, la fraîcheur, la tendresse aimable ont singulièrement contrasté avec la vague inquiétude, la fiévreuse ardeur, la pâleur mélodique, l'élan impuissant de Schumann' (*RGM* XXVI/7: 13 Feb. 1859, 51).
[53] 'est venue rasséréner le public' (*ibid.*).

decision to effect surprise by the use of constantly uniform transitions! (*RGM* XXVII/5: 29 Jan. 1860, 35).[54]

Two ideas here are Fétisian: the notion of naturalness in relation to beauty, which is the aim of art, and the reference to the arrogance of deciding to be original. Both ideas had received new impetus in Fétis's Wagner article of 1852, though they had been central tenets of Fétis's philosophy for thirty years. At times, Botte's attitude reached a note of nostalgia as he yearned for the order and harmony of the Classical era. In so doing in a review of Mozart's Quartet in G K387, he placed the work in a realm of experience far removed, temporally, from the present:

from the opening notes of Mozart's Quartet, we find ourselves transported to one of those fortunate and fertile epochs where everything flourished, an epoch of free and still naïve expansion where genius picked simply and naturally what is best in art. (*RGM* XXVII/6: 5 Feb. 1860, 44)[55]

The sense of lost perfection was reinforced by Botte's exhorting young composers to follow an essentially Classical path. He admired Mendelssohn's music, particularly in preference to that of Schumann, and even found Schubert's expressive modulatory procedure and passionate drive too redolent of Romanticism. Moreover, the overtly demanding nature of Schubert's string writing invited the accusation that he sacrificed the expressive ideal to mere effect. In an early review, the 'Death and the Maiden' Quartet D810 was compared with an unspecified Haydn quartet in C which, despite its variation movement 'in the old style' (*RGM* XXV/50: 12 Dec. 1858, 410),[56] was enthusiastically received by the audience:

Undoubtedly the variations from Schubert's Fourth Quartet ... are effective, difficult and brilliant, and Vieuxtemps played them in masterly fashion, in the manner of a great artist; but how we prefer Haydn's! The discretion, the calm, the fresh smile of the one has been succeeded by the unease, the ardent melancholy, the rather forced joy of the other. One feels that a whole century separates them, and that unfortunately the technical progress made by instrumentalists has

---

[54] 'Combien nous préférons leur ampleur [that of the adagio movements] et leur beau naturel à ces successions de petites phrases qui, si elles peignent le désordre et la fougue, annoncent le parti pris d'étonner par des transitions toujours uniformes!' (*RGM* XXVII/ 5: 29 Jan. 1860, 35).

[55] 'on s'aperçoit, dès les premières notes du quatuor de Mozart, qu'on est transporté à l'une de ces heureuses et fertiles époques d'épanouissement, de libre et encore naïve expansion où le génie cueillait simplement et naturellement ce qu'il y a de meilleur dans un art' (*RGM* XXVII/6: 5 Feb. 1860, 44).

[56] 'à l'ancienne mode' (*RGM* XXV/50: 12 Dec. 1858, 410). The Schubert can be identified from a preview in *La France musicale* XXII/48: 28 Nov. 1858.

allowed the composer sometimes to replace the musical idea by brilliant passage-work. (*ibid.*)[57]

Whilst the vocabulary used to refer to Haydn is stereotypical, that which refers to Schubert casts him more firmly as a Romantic than was usual in the *Gazette*'s all too rare reviews of his music.[58] There is an implicit link with Botte's review of Schumann's Quartet Op. 41/1 in his reference to 'unease' in the variations, a link strengthened in his judgement of the finale, which he found 'a little too vague and uneasy, a little too tormented' (*ibid.*).[59] Botte also accused Schubert of a materialistic attitude to instrumental technique which sacrificed musical beauty to mere effect. Given his tendency to view almost everything written after Beethoven's second period as part of a general cultural decline resulting in the emotional brutalisation of performers, composers and listeners alike, it is unsurprising that Botte should exaggerate the stylistic change from Haydn to Schubert; none the less, the extent to which this is so is astounding in so young a man. He could hardly have found more reactionary Fétisian principles to emulate.

Debates about canon: *Fidelio* and the Ninth

Fidelio and the Ninth Symphony attracted particular critical attention in the *Gazette*'s later years. Conservatives among the *Gazette*'s staff suffered a humiliating defeat at the hands of a public whose enthusiasm for the Ninth reached fever pitch in the 1870s through the popularising influence of Pasdeloup and the competition between his innovative Concerts Populaires and the Conservatoire series. After Blanchard's death, the *Gazette* became distinctly more equivocal about the merits of the Ninth and the late music in general. Fétis's welcoming of Schindler's biography (*RGM* XXXII/4–8: 22 Jan. – 19 Feb. 1865) supported all the author had to say on the late quartets, and concluded that, 'the great artist's genius was burnt out before his death' (*RGM* XXXII/8: 19 Feb. 1865, 58).[60] In 1863, a review, signed

---

[57] 'Certes les variations du quatrième quatuor de Schubert ... sont d'un bel effet, difficiles et brillantes, et Vieuxtemps les a exécutées en chef d'école, en grand artiste; mais que nous leur préférons celles d'Haydn! A la discrétion, au calme, au frais sourire de l'une, a succédé l'inquiétude, l'ardente mélancolie, la joie un peu forcée de l'autre. On sent que tout un siècle les sépare, et que les progrès matériels faits par les instrumentistes ont malheureusement permis au compositeur de remplacer quelquefois l'idée par le trait à effet' (*RGM* XXV/50: 12 Dec. 1858, 410).
[58] See Chapter 6.
[59] 'un peu vague et inquiet, un peu trop tourmenté' (*ibid.*).
[60] 'le génie du grand artiste était épuisé avant sa mort' (*RGM* XXXII/8: 19 Feb. 1865, 58).

'P.S.', of Pasdeloup's performance of the Ninth, showed not only Edouard Monnais's ambivalence toward the work, but the gulf between his opinion and that of the enthusiastic public:

We, who do not yet flatter ourselves with understanding everything in a work in which there is undeniably something superhuman, made some progress listening to the interpretation which the conductor indicated to, inspired in, and demanded from his orchestra and singers. (*RGM* XXX/17: 26 Apr. 1863, 132)[61]

Monnais's use of the word 'superhuman' is evasive; in the hands of Maurice Germa, reviewing the work in 1865 under the name Maurice Cristal, it became a compliment (*RGM* XXXII/11: 12 Mar. 1865, 83). With some delight, Charles Bannelier watched the piece increase its hold on the public, expressing the hope after the Conservatoire's first 1868 performance, 'that this monumental work has finally returned to the repertoire, never again to leave it' (?Bannelier, *RGM* XXXV/5: 2 Feb. 1868, 37).[62] By 1873, he noted that at least one performance of the work each season had become obligatory 'to meet the eager demands of the listeners' (?Bannelier, *RGM* XLIII/13: 26 Mar. 1876, 101),[63] as was the case at the Concerts Populaires, where Pasdeloup 'quite rightly feels obliged, like the Conservatoire, to give a complete performance of the 'Choral' Symphony at least once each year' (?Bannelier, *RGM* XLIII/15: 9 Apr. 1876, 118).[64] Of the concert to which Pasdeloup's was a response, he exclaimed triumphantly:

Now this great work has definitively entered the current repertoire: goodwill and perseverance have prevailed over the supposed 'impossibilities' of the score, in the face of which people recoiled so easily a few years ago. (?Bannelier, *RGM* XLIII/14: 2 Apr. 1876, 109)[65]

That there had been, since 1861, a sharp improvement in the quality of the Ninth's performance is clear, especially at the Conservatoire under Ernest Deldevez, whose fastidious and exhaustive rehearsal technique

---

[61] 'Nous qui ne nous flattons pas encore de tout comprendre dans une production où il y a certainement quelque chose de surhumain, nous avons fait des progrès en écoutant l'interprétation que le chef en a dictée, inspirée, commandée à son orchestre et à ses chanteurs' (*RGM* XXX/17: 26 Apr. 1863, 132).

[62] 'que cette œuvre monumentale est revenue une bonne fois au répertoire pour ne plus le quitter' (?Bannelier, *RGM* XXXV/5: 2 Feb. 1868, 37).

[63] 'pour répondre à l'empressement des auditeurs' (?Bannelier, *RGM* XLIII/13: 26 Mar. 1876, 101).

[64] 'se croit justement obligé, comme le Conservatoire, de donner au moins une fois par an en entier la Symphonie avec chœur' (?Bannelier, *RGM* XLIII/15: 9 Apr. 1876, 118).

[65] 'Voici cette grande œuvre bien décidément entrée au répertoire courant: la bonne volonté et la persévérance ont eu raison des prétendues "impossibilités" de la partition, devant lesquelles on reculait si volontiers il y a peu d'années encore' (?Bannelier, *RGM* XLIII/14: 2 Apr. 1876, 109).

was legendary in musical circles. Performance quality seems to have been a crucial factor in securing public support; those critics, such as Botte and Monnais, who retained severe reservations about the work and who continued to discredit it in print, whether explicitly or by implication, had no effect upon the tide of contrary public opinion. The Ninth's place in the canon was assured despite them.

A major reason for critical resistance to the Ninth lay in the difficulty of its vocal parts, both solo and choral. Such criticisms, alongside more general considerations of Beethoven's skill as a vocal composer, had wider application, and were (inevitably) aired after performances of *Fidelio*, where questions of dramatic suitability were given varying emphasis depending on the critical standpoint of the reviewer in question. There is no sense of progression, however, in the *Gazette*'s reviews of *Fidelio*; an opposing pair of articles from 1845 is matched by another from 1860 and 1869 in which similar arguments are rehearsed.[66] The fracture lines are predictable: the conservatives (Héquet and Monnais) prize melodic beauty over dramatic truth and find Beethoven wanting except when he becomes Italianate; the Beethovenians (Kreutzer and **De Thémines**) make a priority of dramatic truth and are ill at ease with the accessibility of the secondary characters' music. The rôle of the orchestra provided another line of division. Kreutzer's sensitivity to the orchestra's dramatic importance was matched by both De Thémines and Héquet later. However, like Adolphe Botte, Héquet's conservatism led him to see Beethoven as the thin end of a wedge of Germanic decadence. After describing the sterility of Beethoven's invention in vocal music, Héquet made plain his opinions of modern operatic composition in Germany:

having searched extensively for a cantilena which eludes him, he is discouraged, puts the voice aside and immerses himself in the orchestra. There, he is in his element, and he constructs his fantasy. An instrumental theme is soon found; he takes it up, presents it, brings it back in twenty different guises, and subjects it to the most ingenious *imitative work* imaginable. But in the middle of these learned counterpoints the voice, encircled, strangled, is reduced merely to intoning the words. Now this is not its most appropriate rôle, nor that imposed on it by the drama. The voice is not just another instrument, it is a character, an actor. It is, above all, the voice to which the spectator listens, because the eye attracts the ear's attention, because the human spirit has its limitations, and because one

---

[66] The reviews in question are by Kreutzer (*RGM* XII/25: 22 Jun. 1845), Monnais writing as 'P.S.' – Paul Smith (*RGM* XII/26: 29 Jun. 1845), Héquet writing as Durocher (*RGM* XXVII/20: 13 May 1860) and De Thémines, under the pseudonym Elias de Rauze (*RGM* XXXVI/48: 28 Nov. 1869).

cannot give two different objects equal attention simultaneously. (*RGM* XXVII/20: 13 May 1860, 175)[67]

The presence looming in the background of this passage is undoubtedly that of Wagner, whose Parisian concerts, held early that year, were still fresh in the memory. I have illustrated how the *Gazette*'s more conservative critics, including both Botte and Fétis, saw the germ of Wagnerian modulatory and thematic processes in Beethoven's late quartets; however, Héquet's critique of *Fidelio* is the only instance of the application of such ideas to a work of the middle period.

Editing and performance practice, 1866–80

Charles Bannelier was much less hidebound than Botte, Héquet or Monnais, by his sympathy with Fétis's views on Wagner. His concert review column was more open-minded than Botte's (particularly with reference to Schumann), and Beethoven once again took centre stage in the journal's weekly criticism of concert life. In its focus on interpretation and editorial practice rather than criticism of the music itself, Bannelier's Beethoven criticism reveals the extent to which certain works were embedded in the canon; others, such as *Fidelio* and the Ninth Symphony, had still to be universally accepted. The attribution to Bannelier of unsigned articles which contain comments on interpretation (in particular, that of the music of Beethoven) is almost irrefutable, since the comments themselves reinforce ideas in three important signed articles: a review of Ernest Deldevez's *Curiosités musicales* (*RGM* XL/48: 30 Nov. 1873) and a discussion of editorial discrepancies in Beethoven's instrumental works (*RGM* XLIII/46–53: 12 Nov. – 31 Dec. 1876);[68] another Beethoven article, signed 'Ch. B.', concerns Wagner's revisions to the orchestration of the Ninth Symphony (*RGM* XLI/20–28: 17 May – 12 Jul. 1874).

Deldevez's book, born of his experience as conductor of the Conservatoire orchestra, contained the discussion of editorial anomalies and hints

---

[67] 'après avoir longtemps cherché la cantilène qui le fuit, il se rebute, laisse la voix de côté et se jette dans l'orchestre. Là il est sur son terrain, et construit sa fantaisie. Un sujet instrumental est bientôt trouvé; il s'en empare, le présente, le retourne de vingt manières différentes, et se livre au travail d'*imitations* le plus ingénieux que l'on puisse imaginer. Mais au milieu de ces savantes combinaisons, la voix, enlacée, garrotée, est réduite à psalmodier les paroles. Or, ce n'est pas là le rôle qui lui convient et que les lois du drame lui imposent. La voix n'est pas seulement un instrument, c'est un personnage, c'est un acteur. C'est elle surtout que le spectateur écoute, parce que l'œil attire l'oreille, que l'esprit humain est borné, et qu'on ne saurait donner à la fois une attention égale à deux objets différents' (*RGM* XXVII/20: 13 May 1860, 175).

[68] This article was based largely on the findings of Nottebohm, which had been published in the Leipzig *Allgemeine musikalische Zeitung* earlier in the year and thus represented the latest musicological news.

for interpretation in the orchestral music of composers from Haydn to
Beethoven, with a final chapter (to which Bannelier took exception) setting
out the case against Schumann and Wagner. As Bannelier observed, most
of the references to Beethoven had been discussed by others, but the novelty
of one comment on the Scherzo of the Fifth Symphony was striking:

> We particularly approve his [Deldevez's] comments on the manner in which the
> *poco ritardando* before the pause is played, at the beginning of this same Scherzo
> and on each return of the phrase; we have always been shocked by it. The last bar
> is dragged out so as to distort the rhythm beyond recognition. (*RGM* XL/48: 30
> Nov. 1873, 380)[69]

In later unsigned reviews, Bannelier repeatedly complained that Deldevez,
usually so careful to put his observations into practice, consistently failed
to do so here.[70] He was sceptical about the use of rubato in Beethoven's
music, and in a signed review welcomed the experimental nature of
Charles Lamoureux's interpretation of the 'Pastoral', in which he did not
make the traditional *rallentando* into each pause in the first movement,
and maintained a strict tempo in the slow movement: 'absolute metro-
nomic precision is essential in the Andante, or a magnificent poem turns
into an intolerable mess' (signed, *RGM* XXXV/7: 16 Feb. 1868, 51).[71]
However, Bannelier was far less tolerant of changes to overall tempi. His
first review of Deldevez's conducting centred on the ponderous nature of
his fast movements, a sacrifice of speed to clarity which differentiated him
from Pasdeloup (signed, *RGM* XXXIX/50: 15 Dec. 1872, 397). Though
Bannelier came to appreciate the precision of Deldevez's rehearsal and
conducting style, particularly in relation to the Ninth Symphony, he never
came to terms with his tendency to alter tempi to suit his personal taste,
prizing instead the decisions of tradition.[72]

[69] 'Nous approuvons surtout ce qu'il [Delvedez] dit de la manière dont on exécute, au
début de ce même scherzo et chaque fois que la phrase revient, le *poco ritardando* qui
précède le point d'orgue; nous en avons toujours été choqué. On traîne la dernière
mesure de façon à en rendre le rhythme absolument méconnaissable' (*RGM* XL/48: 30
Nov. 1873, 380).
[70] See, for example, *RGM* XLI/11: 15 Mar. 1874, 86.
[71] 'la plus grande précision métronomique est de rigueur dans *l'andante*, sous peine de faire
d'un magnifique poëme un gâchis insupportable' (signed, *RGM* XXXV/7: 16 Feb. 1868,
51).
[72] See especially *RGM* XLVII/4: 25 Jan. 1880, 30. Deldevez's use of slower tempi may have
restored an earlier performing tradition. Fétis complained that Habeneck took
Beethoven's symphonies and the Minuet of Mozart's Symphony in G minor K550
impossibly fast (*RGM* XXVIII/35: 1 Sep. 1861, 276). Schwarz cites the reactions of
correspondents for the *Allgemeine musikalische Zeitung* to performances of Haydn and
Mozart symphonies in Paris between 1804 and 1812. In particular, he notes that
Germans found French tempi too fast for the detailed nature of the music. Schwarz,
French Instrumental Music, 27. However, in his writings Deldevez complained of a trend
towards the slowing of tempi (Deldevez, *Mes mémoires* (Paris, 1890), 188–97), though
here he was concerned mostly with opera.

Closely connected with ideas on performance and interpretation is Bannelier's signed essay on Beethoven editions, which not only reveals many of the performance and editorial malpractices of the day, but presents a detailed and wide-ranging picture of Bannelier's critical precepts and musical opinions. Throughout, one is keenly aware of his belief in the unassailable authority of the composer's decision and of the performer's duty to render the composer's intention down to the minutest detail. Even in cases where there existed serious doubt – for example, the famous horn call at the recapitulation of the Third Symphony's first movement – Bannelier refused to condone the alteration to the second violin part recommended by both Wagner and Deldevez, even though (like them) he could find no aesthetic justification for the tonic-dominant superimposition. His reasons are revealing: since the composer both proofread the score and heard the work many times – indeed insisted to Ries on this point – his wishes, however incongruous they may seem, should be respected without question (signed, *RGM* XLIII/51: 17 Dec. 1876, 401).

The premise of respect for the composer informs Bannelier's entire article on Wagner's revisions to the orchestration of the Ninth ('Ch. B.', *RGM* XLI/20–28: 17 May – 12 Jul. 1874). The only circumstances in which Bannelier would consider changing Beethoven's text concerned the technical limitations of the instruments and players he had in mind. The rationalising of octave doublings which Beethoven had omitted because they exceeded the range available to him was the only concession Bannelier allowed ('Ch. B.', *RGM* XLI/28: 12 Jul. 1874, 219). The single Wagnerian recommendation which Bannelier accepted was by far the least significant; it concerned octave doubling in the Scherzo of the Ninth, where Wagner suggested putting the violin lines of bar 276 and the first note of bar 277 up an octave (similarly for the beginning of bar 276 in the flute) in order to preserve the original upward leap of a sixth at the height of the phrase. Bannelier justified his position by reference to Beethoven's reserve in never demanding higher than an a''' from orchestral violinists. Indicative of Bannelier's tendency to put principle above pragmatics is his argument against Wagner's rewriting of trumpet and horn parts to take advantage of the increased melodic potential of valved instruments:

The question is whether Beethoven, with valve trumpets at his disposal, would not have hesitated to use them instead of natural ones, even in these passages which are so awkwardly written, given the conspicuous difference in timbre between one instrument and the other. Wagner seems to attach no importance to this difference, any more than to the difference between the natural and the valve horn. (*ibid.*, 220)[73]

For Bannelier, the question was not that of using the upgraded version of an instrument, but of substituting a completely different tone colour as well as altering the composer's intentions. Neither, in his view, was justified.

For Botte and Fétis the acid test of a player's worth lay in the approach to the music of Haydn and Mozart; for Bannelier, not surprisingly, Beethoven's music was the touchstone. Particularly pertinent in this respect are reviews of Pierre Maurin's solo and quartet playing, which Bannelier found uneven, though shot through with genius. His recurring complaints of interpretations 'in dubious taste' (signed, *RGM* XXXIII/8: 25 Feb. 1866, 60)[74] were foreshadowed by a comment of 1854 by Fétis.[75] Bannelier provided more detailed indications of one particular fault in a review which discussed Beethoven's Quartet in E-flat Op. 127 and Mozart's Clarinet Quintet in A major K581:

We are only sorry that the four excellent players ... feel it necessary to apply the same manner of playing to Mozart's works ... Mozart's music, whose principal characteristic is the clarity and purity of its lines, is ill-suited to M. Maurin's passionate and imaginative drive; not to mention the glissandi which, in our opinion, should be banned from all music. (?Bannelier, *RGM* XLIII/13: 26 Mar. 1876, 201 [102])[76]

Fétis, commenting on the performance style of a quartet with which he was fundamentally out of sympathy, had probably been excessively harsh on Maurin over twenty years earlier. Bannelier is more trustworthy. Unlike Fétis, his criticisms are motivated not by the pitting of one quartet's repertoire against that of another, but by broader questions of interpretation. Bannelier was always wary of highly personal performances of Classical music; from his reviews of other soloists and groups,

---

[73] 'La question est de savoir si Beethoven, ayant à sa disposition la trompette à pistons, n'eût pas hésité à s'en servir au lieu de la trompette simple, même dans ces passages si gauchement écrits, vu la différence très-appréciable de timbre qui distingue ces instruments l'un de l'autre. Wagner semble n'attacher aucune importance à cette différence, non plus qu'à celle qui existe entre le cor ordinaire et le cor à pistons' ('Ch. B.', *RGM* XLI/28: 12 Jul. 1874, 220).

[74] 'd'un goût douteux' (signed, *RGM* XXXIII/8: 25 Feb. 1866, 60). See also *RGM* XLIII/3: 16 Jan. 1876, 22; *RGM* XLIV/4: 28 Jan. 1877, 30; *RGM* XLVI/6: 9 Feb. 1879, 46. The last three are unsigned.

[75] *RGM* XXI/34: 20 Aug. 1854, 270.

[76] 'Nous regrettons seulement que les quatre excellents instrumentistes ... croient devoir appliquer la même manière de jouer aux ouvrages de Mozart ... La musique de Mozart, dont le principal caractère consiste dans la clarté et la pureté des lignes, s'accommode mal des élans passionnés et fantaisistes de M. Maurin; nous ne parlons pas des glissades qui, à notre avis, devraient être bannies de toute musique' (?Bannelier, *RGM* XLIII/13: 26 Mar. 1876, 201 [102]).

notably the Müller Quartet, who made much use of rubato (signed, *RGM* XXXIII/10: 11 Mar. 1866, 74), it is clear that he sensed danger in the very idea of interpretation, especially when applied to canonic works. He thus emerges as a critic for whom the preservation of a performing tradition based as closely as possible on the composer's intentions was a primary consideration in the evaluation of contemporary performances and editions of Classical music, particularly Beethoven, but whose wish for authenticity bordered on rigidity, as though he wished that the musical canon could be frozen in time and exhibited in the manner of monuments of the static visual arts.

Questions of performance practice are the major unifying factor in reviews of virtually all Classical music in the *Gazette* after Blanchard's death. The impression given during these years is that of the consolidation of a set of precepts established in the journal in the early 1850s. Striking also during these last years is the consistency of attention devoted to Beethoven as a radical, problematic figure. Although the volume of material can be explained by his continuing popularity in concert programmes, which amply demonstrates his pre-eminence among Classical composers, it is also a measure of his capacity to arouse fierce musicological passions in a way which Haydn, for instance, could not. That there was, among the *Gazette*'s contributors, a latent, ageing rearguard ready to reverse the tenor of the journal's earlier criticism on Blanchard's death is an indication of the strength of feeling which Beethoven, in his late manner, could still inspire. The *Gazette* ended its career almost as much a Beethovenian journal as when it began, and it is fitting that one of the last articles should be a nostalgic one – a late printing of Stephen Heller's futuristic and simultaneously Schumannesque, Hoffmannesque and Berliozian skit on the rediscovery of the 'Eroica': 'Mémoire lu à l'Académie de la Nouvelle Lutèce le 13 avril 2879 par Eusebius Florestan, Secrétaire perpétuel' (*RGM* XLVI/15: 13 Apr. 1879). It immediately takes the reader back to the highly Romantic presentation of Beethoven in the *contes fantastiques* of the 1830s and 1840s which so decisively set the *Gazette* apart from its rivals. Deploying the familiar method of criticism through dialogue – Heller constructs a discussion between Napoleon and the composer over the merits and meaning of the symphony – it recaptures the highly charged emotional impact of Beethoven's music on his early French followers, and is an affectionately anachronistic effusion, bringing the *Gazette*'s Beethoven criticism full circle.

6 The Austro-German tradition III: Weber, Schubert and Mendelssohn

The music of Schubert, Weber and Mendelssohn prompted few critical battles (whether with the public or between writers of opposing persuasions) of the kinds which characterised the journal's Beethoven reception. With the exception of Botte's criticisms of Schubert, their music was perceived as neither threatening nor excessively complex (*RGM* XXV/50: 12 Dec. 1858, 410).[1] Given the *Gazette*'s natural orientation towards German music, detailed reviews of Schubert and Weber are surprisingly rare: in the former case, this largely reflects the limited Parisian familiarity with his output; the reasons for Weber's relative neglect are more difficult to define. The importance of the *Gazette*'s reviews of all three composers lies in their contribution to major debates which involved other composers, past and contemporary: the problem of a composer the perception of whose style was based on an unrepresentative selection of works; the problem of authenticity versus adaptation; the ideal nature of sacred music; and finally, the appropriate balance between technique and inspiration in composition. This chapter develops modes of reception familiar from earlier discussions, but also, particularly with regard to Mendelssohn, points to a crucial issue in both contemporary instrumental music and its criticism – the problem of dealing with Beethoven's legacy.

Weber and authenticity

For once, the finest repository of thought on one of Berlioz's idols is not Berlioz's own criticism. Given his lifelong admiration for Weber's music, weighty contributions might have been expected, but, preoccupied with Beethoven and Gluck in his Conservatoire reviews, he gives Weber scant treatment. His vocabulary, with the exception of an unsigned and stern article on one of the two symphonies in C major, which he described as 'desperately feeble' (attrib. Berlioz, *RGM* II/22: 31 May 1835, 184),[2]

---

[1] See Chapter 5.
[2] 'd'une faiblesse désespérante' (attrib. Berlioz, *RGM* II/22: 31 May 1835, 184).

none the less indicated his rapture at the novel effects Weber elicited from his orchestra. Yet the compliments addressed to Weber are illustrated in less detail than those on Beethoven or Gluck, whether on the subject of orchestration, which would seem an obvious and potentially fruitful Berliozian approach, or on the dramatic appropriateness of the operatic music. Nowhere in his reviews does Berlioz achieve or even attempt the impassioned fusion of poetic prose and technical detail which is the hallmark of his finest and most committed writing. Neither is there an independent article in the manner of his essays of 1834 on Gluck. One can only speculate as to why Berlioz neglected Weber thus; it may be because both Beethoven and Gluck, for different reasons, needed a French champion, whilst Weber was both accepted and secure. Such an interpretation would accord with Berlioz's idea of criticism as education, but hardly seems sufficient to account for such neglect, particularly given the manner in which Weber's operas were first introduced in France. By the 1830s, Castil-Blaze's adaptations of the 1820s – *Robin des bois* and *La Forêt de Senart* – were the standard source for concert excerpts from *Der Freischütz* and *Euryanthe* respectively. Such adaptations, including Castil-Blaze's *Don Giovanni* [*Don Juan*] of 1834 at the Opéra, were inimical to Berlioz's aesthetic of the artwork's integrity. Moreover, Victor Schoelcher's enraged denunciation of *Don Juan*'s inauthenticity (even though Castil-Blaze was a named editor of the journal) set a purist precedent in the journal from the outset (unsigned, *RGM* I/11–13: 16–30 Mar. 1834).[3]

Although Berlioz referred contemptuously to Castil-Blaze's versions of *Der Freischütz* and *Euryanthe*, serious attempts to shame the Société des Concerts into banishing the Castil-Blaze version of the latter's hunting chorus (whether on grounds of its aesthetic weakness or on principle) came not from him, but from Bourges and, to a lesser extent, Heller, in the 1840s. Their campaign was unsuccessful; the Société's first performance of the chorus as Weber intended it took place only in January 1879. Quite apart from the inappropriate nature of Castil-Blaze's revisions – the insertion of a new C minor section in the chorus, his changing of text, situation and overall character – for Bourges, a fundamental principle was at stake:

Whether borrowed from Weber or from another composer, whether it even has any intrinsic merit, is irrelevant. The incontestable and damnable point is that this passage does not belong to the piece as conceived by the composer. Were it a hundred times better, have we the right so to disfigure an original fragment, to

---

[3] For a discussion of this production's character and reception, see Katharine Ellis, 'Rewriting *Don Giovanni*, or "The Thieving Magpies"', *Journal of the Royal Musical Association* 119/2 (1994), 212–50.

tack on the first idea that comes to mind, to extend it, to shorten it at will, to modify an artist's thought on a capricious whim? (*RGM* XIV/16: 18 Apr. 1847, 132)[4]

By the time Léon Carvalho began his series of Weber adaptations at the Théâtre-Lyrique in 1857, Bourges was no longer writing reviews for the *Gazette*, and Gustave Héquet's *laissez-faire* attitude towards the integrity of the composer's conception did little to further Bourges's demands for the performance of Weber's operas in Paris as Weber might have recognised them: nothing short of the addition of buffo characters to *Euryanthe* (in the name of dramatic contrast) could raise his critical hackles (*RGM* XXIV/36: 6 Sep. 1857). In his 'Revue d'un demi-siècle' of 1850–1, Edouard Fétis praised Castil-Blaze, using 'traducteur' and 'arrangé' non-pejoratively, acclaiming him as an entrepreneur and cultural hero, and accusing his detractors of envy:

We must give M. Castil-Blaze his due: he always chose prudently the works on which he wished to exercise his talents as an *arranger* ... and he took marvellous advantage of the circumstances likely to aid their success. When Rossini was all the rage, he translated *Il barbiere di Sivigla* and *La gazza ladra*; at the outset of the quarrel between the Classics and the Romantics he put on *Robin des bois*, a Romantic opera if ever there was one, and which was to provoke lively debate in the artistic world ... It was a happy time for the arts when Weber's work, arranged by Castil-Blaze, had its première at the Odéon! (*RGM* XVIII/25: 22 Jun. 1851, 203)[5]

The attitudes of Fétis *fils* and Héquet, diametrically opposed to the journal's predominant standpoint in its first decade, are representative of a general shift in the journal's critical principles in the 1850s and early 1860s. The seemingly unshakeable tenets which characterised its first twelve years were progressively weakened under the Brandus brothers' direction, as a new group of critics took leading rôles in shaping its outlook. Such change is detectable in conservative attitudes towards Beethoven immediately before and after Henri Blanchard's death; on the

---

[4] 'Qu'elle soit empruntée à Weber ou à un autre compositeur, qu'elle ait même du mérite considérée en elle-même, ce n'est pas la question. Le point incontestable et condamnable, c'est que cette période n'appartient pas au morceau conçu par l'auteur. Fût-elle cent et cent fois plus belle, a-t-on le droit de défigurer ainsi un fragment original, d'y coudre le premier passage venu, de l'étendre, de le raccourcir à volonté, de modifier au gré du caprice la pensée d'un artiste?' (*RGM* XIV/16: 18 Apr. 1847, 132).

[5] 'Il faut rendre à M. Castil-Blaze cette justice qu'il a toujours choisi avec tact les ouvrages sur lesquels il voulait exercer son talent d'*arrangeur* ... et qu'il a merveilleusement tiré parti des circonstances capables d'influer sur leur succès. Lorsqu'il n'était question que de Rossini, il fit les traductions du *Barbier de Séville* et de la *Pie voleuse*; à l'origine de la querelle des classiques et des romantiques, il donna *Robin-des-Bois*, opéra romantique s'il en fut, et qui devait provoquer de vifs débats dans le monde artiste ... Heureux temps pour les arts que celui où l'œuvre de Weber, arrangé par M. Castil-Blaze[,] fit sa première apparition à l'Odéon!' (*RGM* XVIII/25: 22 Jun. 1851, 203).

problem of authentic productions of foreign operas, the purism advocated in the 1830s turned into a relativism which was reversed only with the arrival on the staff of Charles Bannelier in 1866.

It is ironic that the clearest exposition in the *Gazette* of the problems which the French created for themselves in producing Weber's stage works should have been occasioned by one of the most scrupulous (though inevitably compromised) productions: Berlioz's *Der Freischütz* of 1841. Wagner's famous essay previewed the first night and lamented the consequences, for both Berlioz and Weber, of the Académie royale's insistence upon the inclusion of recitatives and ballet (*RGM* VIII/34–5: 23–30 May 1841). In his analysis of the adaptation, which in his opinion destroyed the original balance of music and speech in the *Singspiel* and turned it into an equally unbalanced Grand opera, Wagner showed great sympathy for Weber's most prominent French supporter, and an acute awareness of the impossible situation he faced. His seriously argued essay for the *Gazette* contrasts with the Hoffmannesque and despairing mockery of its sequel, a report sent to the Dresden *Abendzeitung* of 16 and 21 June.[6] However, the main thrust of the argument is similar in both articles. In the *Gazette* article, Wagner advanced the paradox that the more expressively Berlioz set the dialogue sections, the more the drama would lose its momentum and the short musical numbers their effect. In the Dresden piece, Wagner added that Berlioz's lack of self-indulgence in this respect had courted the opposite danger too successfully: the audience had become bored. In his *Gazette* report of 13 June, Henri Blanchard had justified the effect of the new recitatives by likening Berlioz to a jeweller fashioning the perfect setting for Weber's gems (*RGM* VIII/37: 13 Jun. 1841, 302); in Wagner's view, the plainness of the new setting merely accentuated the adaptation's structural imbalance, without adding enough interest to maintain the audience's attention between numbers. Berlioz's attempt had thus failed on two counts. An equally sympathetic presentation of Berlioz's predicament was given in 1873 by Adolphe Jullien (1845–1932), who, with his customary habit of preceding important reviews with a reception history, noted with sadness the proximity of Berlioz's compromised position to that of the detested Castil-Blaze: 'And yet, here he is, putting himself in such sad company of his own free will; he has completed the masterpiece which his predecessor had arranged!' (*RGM* XL/21: 25 May 1873, 161).[7]

---

[6] See Richard Wagner, *Wagner Writes from Paris*, trans. and ed. Robert Jacobs and Geoffrey Skelton (London, 1973), 138–55.

[7] 'Et pourtant, le voilà qui, de son plein gré, se met en si triste compagnie; il complète le chef-d'œuvre que son devancier avait arrangé!' (*RGM* XL/21: 25 May 1873, 161).

Schubert

On a far smaller scale, Schubert's music was also subjected to cuts and arrangements. Early in the century, his songs were fashionable but not always treated with the critical respect the *Gazette*'s writers bestowed on established figures. In a review written in the patronising style he reserved for salon music, Blanchard sidestepped the aesthetic questions raised by the publication of three Schubert *Lieder* with 'accompagnement de violon obligé' by Alexey Lvoff (1798–1870), and was instead content with the platitude that they had 'acquired additional charm by means of the accompaniment ... with which M. Lvoff has decorated them' (*RGM* IX/ 25: 19 Jun. 1842, 251).[8] Maurice Bourges, predictably, found rather depressing the entry of Schubert's songs into the ranks of arrangers' fodder, and gave Stephen Heller a favourable review of his collection of *Quinze lieder* only on the strength of their character as transcriptions rather than arrangements (*RGM* VII/2: 5 Jan. 1840). In the hands of others, Bourges feared a wave of medleys and fantasies *à la* Henri Herz: 'For we have here the fate of all music marked with the seal of celebrity: it cannot escape this penal sanction of fashion ... And this moment of crisis has arrived for Schubert's delectable works' (*ibid.*, 18).[9]

The nature of Schubert's initial celebrity in Paris was shaped by the fact that, through the pioneering work of the tenor Adolphe Nourrit, the first genre to be introduced to Parisians was the *Lied*, which, in its lighter manifestations, could too easily be equated with the French *romance*, and treated accordingly. Reviews suggest that songs on the emotional level of 'Der Doppelgänger' or 'Der Leiermann' were rarely performed publicly; with the exception of 'Erlkönig', the songs selected were closer to the spirit of 'Das Wandern'. Whilst Bourges appreciated that there was a deep melancholy to Schubert's music, in an early biographical article, the German singing teacher and violinist Heinrich Panofka (1807–87) emphasised the composer's 'sweet warmth' (*RGM* V/41: 14 Oct. 1838, 407) and the 'beautiful dreams in ravishing songs' (*ibid.*).[10] However one-sided his understanding of the emotional range of Schubert's music, Panofka's article is unique in the *Gazette*'s history for its championing of Schubert as an innovative genius, specifically in the realm of the solo song. Panofka noted that in Germany the genre had

---

[8] 'acquis un charme de plus par l'accompagnement ... dont les a ornées M. Lvoff' (*RGM* IX/25: 19 Jun. 1842, 251).

[9] 'Car c'est là le sort de toute musique marquée du sceau de la célébrité: elle ne peut se soustraire à cette sanction pénale de la vogue ... Et ce moment de crise est arrivé pour les délicieuses conceptions de Schubert' (*RGM* VII/2: 5 Jan. 1840, 18).

[10] 'douce chaleur ... beaux rêves dans des mélodies ravissantes' (*RGM* V/41: 14 Oct. 1838, 407).

developed into something akin to a dramatic scene, but also that Schubert had added to this a new richness of harmony and 'an intimate relationship between the voice and the accompaniment' (*ibid.*).[11] In contrast to most French critics, for whom melody reigned supreme in song, his view was that such attention to the piano part added a new dimension to the interpretation of the poetry whilst avoiding the trap of turning the form into materialistic description. It thereby set a standard for future composers: '*the summary of the poetry, its character, its various sentiments, in a word, the colour of the poetic thought*, must be conveyed as much by the piano as by the voice' (*ibid.*).[12] His opinion that Schubert limited himself essentially to a single genre, apart from a few instrumental works was, of course, based on the hopelessly unrepresentative selection of Schubert's music then available in print, and had serious consequences for the reception of Schubert's output in the larger genres. The Ninth Symphony – the 'Great' C major – lay undiscovered until 1841, and throughout the *Gazette*'s lifetime the number of chamber works in circulation was pitifully small – the two piano trios, the 'Death and the Maiden' Quartet D810 (whose variations were often played separately) and the Quartet in A minor D804. The history of Schubert's discovery in France inevitably resulted in the judging of chamber and symphonic works by the yardstick of the *Lieder*.

The instrumental works which received public performance in Paris were not warmly received in the *Gazette* once the initial discovery of the 1830s had passed. Early reviews bode well for the French reception of Schubert; a review by Bélanger of the variation movement from D810, which he called 'a prayer' (*RGM* III/1: 3 Jan. 1836, 6),[13] mourned the 'immense void' occasioned by the composer's early death (*ibid.*),[14] and noted that its success was 'too flattering for us not to attempt to naturalise completely his genius in France' (*ibid.*).[15] The anonymous reviewer of the Paris première of the Piano Trio in E-flat D929 (by Franck, Alard and Chevillard in 1837) hinted at future criticisms in his comment on the unprecedented length of the finale, but otherwise found plenty to recommend:

it is with indescribable satisfaction that everyone found Schubert worthy of his reputation – that is, original and profound as in his happiest creations: in

[11] 'une liaison intime entre le chant et l'accompagnement' (*ibid.*).
[12] '*le résumé de la poésie, son caractère, ses sentiments divers, en un mot la couleur de la pensée poétique*, doit être rendu autant par l'accompagnement que par le chant' (*ibid.*).
[13] 'une prière' (*RGM* III/1: 3 Jan. 1836, 6).
[14] 'vide immense' (*ibid.*).
[15] 'trop flatteur pour qu'on ne tente pas de naturaliser tout-à-fait son génie en France' (*ibid.*). Almost nothing is known about Bélanger, except that he translated several Schubert songs.

addition, we found skilled workmanship, a closely knit style and a perfect harmony in the distribution of parts; the only reproach that we might make of the Trio is that the finale is a little long-winded. (*RGM* IV/23: 4 Jun. 1837 193)[16]

In 1858, Blanchard was considerably less generous – he preferred the essentially melodic nature of the Trio D898 in B-flat – and found that the Trio in E-flat lacked the distinguishing qualities of the *Lieder*: 'It is rather curious that the composer of so many delicious but small-scale *Lieder* which are characterised above all by moderation and concision should be a little long-winded and verbose in his instrumental music' (*RGM* XXV/ 6: 7 Feb. 1858, 44).[17] Early critics praised Schubert above all for the poetic qualities of his melodic style; his initial success in Paris as a composer of *Lieder*, added to the tendency of the French to concentrate on those songs where vocal melody, as opposed to expressive declamation, was paramount, seemed to give ample proof that lyricism in miniature was the distinguishing feature of his writing.

The earliest reports from Germany of the discovery of his symphonies and the first performance in Frankfurt of the 'Great' C major Symphony D944 in January 1841, prompted the first harsh criticism of Schubert in the *Gazette*. Since they take the form of anonymous 'Correspondance étrangère' articles it is difficult to ascertain whether they represent German or French opinion, though the third article summarises the opinions of newspapers in Hamburg (an ecstatic review) and Leipzig (negative), agreeing with the latter (*RGM* VIII/29: 18 Apr. 1841, 229–30). Not only are there complaints about the gigantic proportions of the work, but also its lack of melodic appeal: 'it contains a chaos of chords which float randomly, which deafen the ear and eventually produce chronic fatigue' (*RGM* VIII/11: 7 Feb. 1841, 85).[18] Whilst a Hamburg journal reportedly claimed that this work alone would ensure Schubert a place among the greatest German composers, the *Gazette*'s correspondent predicted its imminent demise:

We have reason to believe that these exaggerated praises will add nothing to Schubert's reputation, that the fate of his symphonies will be identical to that of

---

[16] 'c'est avec une indicible satisfaction que chacun a trouvé Schubert digne de lui-même, c'est-à-dire original et profond comme dans ses créations les plus heureuses: on a pu apprécir [sic] en outre une facture pleine de science, un style serré et une entente parfaite dans la distribution des parties; le seul reproche qu'on puisse adresser au trio, c'est un peu de longueur dans le final' (*RGM* IV/23: 4 Jun. 1837, 193). It is not known whether the French trio followed Schubert's cuts in this movement.

[17] 'Il est assez singulier que l'auteur de tant de *lieder* délicieux, mais de petite forme, qui se distinguaient surtout par la mesure, la concision, soit un peu long et verbeux dans sa musique instrumentale' (*RGM* XXV/6: 7 Feb. 1858, 44).

[18] 'il y a là un chaos d'accords qui flottent pêle-mêle, qui étourdissent et finissent par vous fatiguer cruellement' (*RGM* VIII/11: 7 Feb. 1841, 85).

those written by so many of his contemporaries, in Germany, and that in a few years they will be forgotten. (*RGM* VIII/29: 18 Apr. 1841, 229–30)[19]

The ensuing fate of the symphony in Paris tacitly confirmed this prediction: the Société des Concerts began rehearsals but abandoned any thought of performance, and the work was not presented to the Parisian public for another decade, when it was performed by François Seghers and the Société Sainte-Cécile. The author of the unsigned *Gazette* review merely continued the critical trend set ten years earlier by comparing its melodic character unfavourably with K550, the slow movement of Haydn's symphony no. 85 'La Reine' and that of Beethoven's Seventh (*RGM* XVIII/48: 30 Nov. 1851, 390). Given the importance of rhythmic drive in the work, such observations are perhaps not surprising. However, the reviewer added the incongruous charges of over-orchestration and a complexity of phrase structure which was diffuse in comparison with those models of clarity, concision and simplicity – the *Lieder*.

The only attempt at Schubert's rehabilitation as a symphonist came from **Armand Gouzien**, reviewing Pasdeloup's introduction of the 'Unfinished' D759 to a hostile audience at the Concerts Populaires in 1867 – a venture he heartily supported (*RGM* XXXIV/51: 22 Dec. 1867, 407–8). Gouzien found the work highly characteristic of the composer in its combination of sophistication, refinement and simplicity, noting its delicate and expressive use of wind instruments, and the features, particularly the use of syncopated accompaniments, which unified the two movements. Thus, Schubert's reception in nineteenth-century France was uneven: despite Adolphe Nourrit's evangelising efforts (which were confined to music of an intrinsically domestic nature), performance of Schubert's music gained neither the momentum of Beethoven's before him nor that of Wagner's after. Schubert had no champion in the realm of criticism either: no music journal of the period gave his work special attention, a factor which hindered the spread of his appeal after an auspicious, if exceptionally late, start.

Mendelssohn

By 1847, the year of his death, Mendelssohn was better established in Paris than Schubert would ever be in the period covered by this book. His piano music, regarded as good-quality salon material, was in

---

[19] 'Nous avons lieu de croire que ces éloges exagérés n'ajouteront rien à la réputation de Schubert, qu'il en sera de ses symphonies comme de celles de tant de contemporains, en Allemagne, et qu'elles seront oubliées au bout de quelques années' (*RGM* VIII/29: 18 Apr. 1841, 229–30).

circulation, the Société des Concerts's repertoire included the First and Third Symphonies and the 'Hebrides' Overture; and in chamber music circles the Octet and the Cello Sonata no. 1 in B-flat had received public performances. That the Société des Concerts, which by the late 1840s had long ceased to present its audience with challenging repertoire, embraced Mendelssohn's orchestral music (by contrast with that of Berlioz, for instance), indicates the ease of its assimilation into establishment concert life. On several occasions, Blanchard noted the links between Mendelssohn and the eighteenth century, stressing that although his style contained elements of Beethoven's first and second manner, it was essentially 'the continuation of Mozart' (*RGM* XXIII/5: 3 Feb. 1856, 35).[20] He also referred to Mendelssohn as 'Germany's contemporary Mozart' (*RGM* VIII/1: 3 Jan. 1841, 7).[21] In a review of the collection of pieces for string quartet Op. 81, he observed that the second fugue, in E-flat (Op. 81/4), was redolent of late Beethoven, but that Beethoven himself 'would not have failed to detect the good manners of *ancien-régime* nobility in Mendelssohn's muse' (*RGM* XVII/34: 25 Aug. 1850, 284).[22] The majority of the *Gazette*'s Mendelssohn reviews accepted him as Germany's most distinguished living composer, with a reputation for solid, well-crafted works. Yet, whilst his music could be accepted without difficulty, his place in the hierarchy of composers proved more difficult to define. The writings of Bourges, Fétis and Blanchard reveal uncertainty about Mendelssohn's genius, his capability for poetic expression, and the legitimacy of his major influences and their possible future application. Although his Scherzos were universally acclaimed as innovative, he was never perceived as avant-garde; indeed, among most French critics, the Romantic aspects of his compositions, particularly his tendencies toward programme music, were largely ignored in favour of more conventional stylistic traits.

Only Heller and a writer signing himself 'E.D.' detected and praised the blurred edges of Romanticism in Mendelssohn. Heller remarked that, in the A minor symphony, 'there often predominates a mysterious, indefinable rustling, which is notable in almost all his overtures, especially *Fingal's Cave*' (*RGM* XI/3: 21 Jan. 1844, 21).[23] The contributor 'E.D.', writing on the Octet in 1846, produced a uniquely Romantic critique of the first movement, using the language customarily reserved

[20] 'la continuation de Mozart' (*RGM* XXIII/5: 3 Feb. 1856, 35).

[21] 'Mozart actuel de l'Allemagne' (*RGM* VIII/1: 3 Jan. 1841, 7).

[22] 'n'aurait pas manqué de trouver une tenue de marquise de l'ancien régime à la muse de Mendelssohn' (*RGM* XVII/34: 25 Aug. 1850, 284).

[23] 'Il y règne souvent ce bruissement mystérieux, indéfinissable, qui se fait remarquer dans presque toutes ses ouvertures, surtout dans celle de *la Grotte de Fingal*' (*RGM* XI/3: 21 Jan. 1844, 21).

for the eulogising of Beethoven, and finally lapsing into the narration of a nature-inspired scenario:

the grandiose opening of this work seems like a call to mysterious revelations. Unexpected effects succeed each other rapidly. Skill alone cannot uncover the sublime; it is the divinity of the heart, inspiration, which reveals it. With this rich and powerful instrumentation, do you not suddenly believe yourself to be wandering in the depths of a virgin forest, where the spirit is filled with a religious terror[?]. And then suddenly, at the seductive aspect of a clearing which sets further into relief the majesty of what precedes and what follows, the spirit frees itself from these serious reveries. (*RGM* XIII/4: 25 Jan. 1846, 28).[24]

The author's tone and, specifically, his reference to 'religious terror' is more akin to the *Gazette*'s Beethoven criticism of the 1830s than its reception of Mendelssohn. Such views, and their manner of expression, were exceptional among Mendelssohn reviews in the *Gazette*, whose other contributors viewed him as a worthy sacred and piano music composer of limited originality and a tendency to seriousness. Hence Georges Kastner's surprise, in a review of the *Lieder ohne Worte* Op. 38, that the composer had produced a melody of 'mocking nonchalance; it took all M. Mendelssohn's talent to master thus the predominant tone of his chosen character' (*RGM* V/28: 15 Jul. 1838, 291).[25] The word 'talent' is carefully chosen: rarely, and certainly not in the obituary contributed by Bourges or in Fétis's general article of 1849, was Mendelssohn hailed as a genius. Instead, emphasis on care, conscientiousness and technical ability as his primary qualities form a unifying and, at times, pejorative, element in the reviews of many of the *Gazette*'s contributors, even those, such as Bourges, who campaigned on his behalf.

The single characteristic of Mendelssohn's style which alienated the *Gazette*'s critics was its perceived lack of spontaneity. His works approached Classical perfection, but only as the result of an excessive and detectable amount of calculation. This, for a group of critics who held that the finest music concealed by the immediacy of its expression

---

24   'le début grandiose de cet œuvre semble un appel à de mystérieuses révélations. Les effets imprévus se succèdent rapidement; l'art ne peut découvrir le sublime: c'est la divinité du cœur, c'est l'inspiration qui le révèle. A cette instrumentation large et puissante, ne vous croyez-vous pas tout d'un coup errer dans les profondeurs d'une forêt vierge, où l'esprit se pénètre d'une terreur religieuse, puis tout d'un coup il se dégage de ces rêveries sérieuses par l'aspect séduisant d'une éclaircie qui fait encore ressortir la majesté de ce qui précède et de ce qui va suivre' (*RGM* XIII/4: 25 Jan. 1846, 28). The prose style and the technique of creative criticism used in this review, coupled with a similar opinion of Mendelssohn cited in a signed review of the Piano Trio in C minor Op. 66 (*RGM* XIV/6: 7 Feb. 1847), suggest that this review may be by **J.-B. Laurens**. His signed review of Heller's *Quatre arabesques* (*RGM* XII/24: 15 Jun. 1845) contained a similar example of Schumannesque 'creative criticism', which had by then become rare in the *Gazette*.

25   'railleuse insouciance; il fallait tout le talent de M. Mendelsohn [sic] pour maîtriser ainsi la couleur prédominante du mode qu'il avait choisi' (*RGM* V/28: 15 Jul. 1838, 291).

the complexities of its workings, forever denied Mendelssohn the title of genius. Blanchard was particularly vociferous, and in a review of the Quartet in E minor Op. 44/2 referred to the first movement as 'worked-out rather than inspired', dubbing Mendelssohn 'the man with correct-ness of imagination' (*RGM* XVI/7: 18 Feb. 1849, 52).[26] Likewise, for him, the 'Italian' Symphony was 'too conscientiously harmonic, crafted too well' (*RGM* XIX/4: 25 Jan. 1852, 25).[27] His characteristic logic and clarity of phrase structure, and a perceived preoccupation with the externals of form rather than expressive content were held against him not only by Blanchard but also by Bourges. In a long obituary, Bourges blamed the strictness of Carl Zelter's teaching for producing a composer who:

often subordinates the sweep of his imagination to learned form; processes are too frequently substituted for real ideas; on several occasions, facility replaces directness and spontaneity of invention. (*RGM* XIV/48: 28 Nov. 1847, 390)[28]

Among those written by like-minded critics, one review, of 1850, stands out: Blanchard's critique of the Quartet in F minor Op. 80. Though he does not explicitly set it apart from the remainder of Mendelssohn's output by reference to its historical context (the quartet was written in the wake of the death of Mendelssohn's sister, the composer Fanny Hensel), Blanchard's language defines the work as Romantic, empha-sising its dreamy, dark and passionate elements. The work is 'coloured by that feverish animation which portrays the inner despair which every great artist carries with him, and which shortens his life, as it ruined that of Mendelssohn' (*RGM* XVII/34: 25 Aug. 1850, 284).[29]

By the middle of the century, the nature of Mendelssohn's innovation in the realm of the Scherzo was well known and appreciated. Even those who denied him originality in other areas acknowledged that, here, he had contributed something individual. In 1857, Blanchard merely mentioned that the Octet's third movement was 'deliciously graceful, mysterious and spirited' (*RGM* XXIV/5: 1 Feb. 1857, 35).[30] In 1841, basing his knowledge of Mendelssohn's style on that of the oratorio *St*

---

[26] 'plus travaillé qu'inspiré ... l'homme d'imagination correcte' (*RGM* XVI/7: 18 Feb. 1849, 52).

[27] 'trop consciusement harmonique, trop bien fait' (*RGM* XIX/4: 25 Jan. 1852, 25).

[28] 'subordonne souvent l'élan de l'imagination à la forme scientifique; le procédé se substitue trop fréquemment à la pensée réelle; l'habileté du faire remplace en plus d'une rencontre la franchise et la spontanéité de l'invention' (*RGM* XIV/48: 28 Nov. 1847, 390).

[29] 'coloré de cette animation fiévreuse qui peint le désespoir intérieur que tout grand artiste porte avec lui, et qui abrége [sic] son existence, comme elle a brisé celle de Mendelssohn' (*RGM* XVII/34: 25 Aug. 1850, 284).

[30] 'délicieux de grâce, de mystère et d'esprit' (*RGM* XXIV/5: 1 Feb. 1857, 35).

Paul, he had been surprised, and had reached conclusions similar to those of Kastner in 1838, cited above. The Scherzo:

is the most skittish, spirited banter ever heard. It would be difficult to imagine that the composer, who worked on such a large scale in *St Paul*, could chatter musically with such carefree merriment, if one did not recognise that this merriment and this charming gaiety are consistently imbued with a profound learning. (*RGM* VIII/10: 4 Feb. 1841, 75)[31]

By 1849, Blanchard had not fundamentally changed his view that Mendelssohn's Scherzo movements were the exception that proved the rule. Of the Quartet in E minor Op. 44/2 he wrote:

In the Scherzo of the quartet in question, Mendelssohn wrote like a man of genius; in the three other movements of the work, he showed himself to be a man of talent. This is the resumé of his artistic career, and the place which he has already taken in posterity. (*RGM* XVI/7: 18 Feb. 1849, 52)[32]

An overtly learned style was not valued highly outside the confines of the Conservatoire; however, it was accepted more readily in sacred music than in secular genres, provided that it did not produce an effect contrary to its text's expressive content. The notion of what constituted a suitable style for contemporary religious music exercised several critics, among whom some were prepared to accept clearly non-liturgical, dramatic compositions, whilst others campaigned, in eclectic fashion, for a rejuvenation of gothic styles; a third faction sought a return to Palestrinian purity. Bourges, an ardent campaigner for Mendelssohn's sacred music, belonged to the second category. His preview article of 1846–7 on the oratorio *St Paul* is among the *Gazette*'s most explicit documents in support of musical eclecticism (*RGM* XIII/35: 30 Aug. 1846–XIV/2: 10 Jan. 1847). Bourges praised Mendelssohn for disdaining the secular and degenerate influences of Haydn, Mozart and Beethoven, and for proving that Bach's sober reserve and Handel's simple grandeur were susceptible to nineteenth-century re-interpretation. In Fétisian vein, he stated that a performance of *St Paul* would represent one of the principal intellectual movements of the time: the search for artistic inspiration in past styles, much in the manner of German retrospective schools of painting (*RGM* XIII/35: 30 Aug. 1846, 274). Highlighting

---

[31] 'est le badinage le plus coquet, le plus spirituel qui se puisse entendre. On concevrait difficilement que le compositeur, qui a taillé dans de si larges proportions le *Paulus*, puisse bavarder musicalement avec tant de folie et de gaieté, si l'on ne reconnaissait que cette folie et cette charmante gaieté sont tout empreintes d'un profond savoir' (*RGM* VIII/10: 4 Feb. 1841, 75).

[32] 'Dans le *scherzo* du quatuor en question, Mendelssohn a procédé en homme de génie; dans les trois autres parties de cet œuvre, il s'est montré homme de talent. C'est le résumé de sa carrière artistique, et la place qu'il a déjà prise dans la postérité' (*RGM* XVI/7: 18 Feb. 1849, 52).

Mendelssohn's use of chorales, particularly the introductory prelude on 'Wachet auf', as deliberately anachronistic, he also described how the vocal writing drew closely on Bach's contrapuntal style in movements such as the crowd scene calling for Stephen's death (*RGM* XIII/36: 6 Sep. 1846, 282). Whilst Bourges made clear that *St Paul* contained weaknesses and stylistic features of which he disapproved, he viewed it not only as a success in the history of its genre, but as a success within Mendelssohn's output as he knew it. It was the ideal balance of poetry and learning, with each aiding, rather than rivalling, the other:

> To find a compromise between melodic and learned principles, to balance the demands of expression and doctrine, to succeed in clothing formal severity with poetry, to scatter a few gentle and pure reflections of primitive art, a few whiffs of the thought of past centuries, onto a conception which should be indicative of youth, even though using austere means – this was an unexpected way of rejuvenating the oratorio, of reviving the forces which had been exhausted through the gigantic strangleholds of a Bach or a Handel. (*RGM* XIII/35: 30 Aug. 1846, 274)[33]

His detailed description of each movement acts as an illustration of such critical tenets. However, Bourges forgives more here than elsewhere; less than a year after the *St Paul* article, whose overstatement is redolent of a publicity exercise, he wrote Mendelssohn's obituary. The analysis of *St Paul* praised the drawing of inspiration from the past; the obituary stated that overall, in both sacred and secular works, Mendelssohn had relied too much on the past in an attempt to avoid the banalities and clichés of modern-day compositional styles. The article claimed that the true sign of original genius in music 'consists less in creating new processes than in obtaining magnificent results from those which already exist' (*RGM* XIII/36: 6 Sep. 1846, 282);[34] the obituary withheld the title of genius from Mendelssohn for the very reason that he was essentially conservative and had founded no new compositional school. The article detected a creative equilibrium between poetry and technique; the obituary found his style, in general, too technique-oriented. That Bourges viewed *St Paul* as an exceptional work is unquestionable, but his later writings indicate an exaggerated defence. His judgement of 1847 sums up the *Gazette*'s

---

[33] 'Cimenter la paix entre le principe mélodique et le principe scientifique, contrebalancer les exigences de l'expression et de la doctrine, accommoder avec bonheur le vêtement poétique à la sévérité de la forme, semer quelques reflets doux et purs de l'art primitif, quelques émanations de la pensée des siècles écoulés sur une conception qui devait, sous des traits austères, faire preuve de jeunesse, c'était une manière inattendue de renouveler l'oratorio, de ranimer ses forces épuisées par les gigantesques étreintes d'un Bach et d'un Haendel' (*RGM* XIII/35: 30 Aug. 1846, 274).

[34] 'consiste moins à créer des procédés inconnus qu'à obtenir de magnifiques résultats de ceux qui déjà existent' (*RGM* XIII/36: 6 Sep. 1846, 282).

overall attitude: 'A man of resistance, a conservative, he perfected without inventing, sometimes modified things, but only superficially' (*RGM* XIV/48: 28 Nov. 1847, 390).[35]

As late as 1872, by which time a substantial quantity of Mendelssohn's music was firmly rooted in the repertory and had ceased to be reported in any detail, the opinion that his work lacked expressive power still prevailed. The Violin Concerto was viewed rather disparagingly as better suited to technical display than to the elevation of the soul. Reviewing **José White**'s performance of the work at the Conservatoire, Charles Bannelier explicitly compared the demands of Mendelssohn's Violin Concerto with those of Beethoven's:

This estimable artist has real qualities of style and taste; perhaps he lacks the technical accuracy and consistency of intonation which is demanded above all by a work such as this, where the effect is entirely *extrinsic*, and which demands much less feeling from the virtuoso than, for example, Beethoven's concerto. (?Bannelier, *RGM* XXXIX/19: 12 May 1872, 149)[36]

Despite Adolphe Botte's response to Schubert, quoted earlier, Schubert, Weber and Mendelssohn were never viewed as genuine Romantics. Even Blanchard, who was liable to complain of Romanticism's degeneracy at every possible opportunity, neglected to use the term in relation to any of them. Because of his operas' subject matter, Weber was perceived as the least Classical of the three, yet there is a qualitative difference between the criticism his music received and the aesthetic factioning which greeted that of Félicien David, Berlioz or the younger generation of pianists. By contrast, the tensions within Mendelssohn's reception (as opposed to his public acceptance) suggest the extent of critical unease regarding the proper direction for compositional style after Beethoven. Such unease, latent in reviews of Mendelssohn, emerges with considerable force in reviews of French responses to Beethoven's stimulus, where, in instrumental music, the extremes of Romantic programmaticism and the ossification of a Classical-inspired style drew debates about eclecticism's benefits into the open.

Such debates were, however, accompanied in the *Gazette* by less elevated concerns: despite a growing interest in non-contemporary music, publishing houses relied upon a regular succession of new, popular, titles to tempt buyers of sheet music. Most lucrative among such publications

---

[35] 'Homme de résistance, esprit conservateur, il a perfectionné, sans inventer, quelquefois modifié, mais superficiellement' (*RGM* XIV/48: 28 Nov. 1847, 390).

[36] 'Cet estimable artiste se recommande par de réelles qualités de style et de goût; il ne possède peut-être pas toute la sureté de mécanisme et d'intonation que réclame avant tout une pareille œuvre, dont l'effet est tout *en dehors*, et qui demande beaucoup moins au sentiment du virtuose que le concerto de Beethoven, par exemple' (*RGM* XXXIX/19: 12 May 1872, 149).

were self-standing piano miniatures, operatic fantasies for piano, and arrangements of new operatic favourites for various instruments. The concluding chapters of this book examine the effects of commercialism on the *Gazette*'s criticism of contemporary music, and analyse the crosscurrents between expediency and aesthetic integrity in its reception of composers as diverse as Meyerbeer and Tchaikovsky.

7   Contemporary music I: Piano music

Introduction

Although the Schlesinger/Brandus catalogue contained eighteenth- and early nineteenth-century works, the publishing house's profits derived primarily from sales of new music – in particular for the expanding markets in piano music and arrangements from popular operas. Because of their importance to the health of the business, living composers almost inevitably took their place on one of two lists: the 'sacred-cow list' or the 'son-of-a-bitch list'.[1] In the *Gazette*, the nature of many reviews (particularly in the lucrative world of opera) is explicable by reference to the commercial interests involved: Verdi, an Escudier composer, was to be denounced; Meyerbeer, a Schlesinger/Brandus composer, to be supported. Partisanship in the journal was not, however, entirely market-driven; it frequently reflected the higher artistic ideals which Schlesinger and (to a lesser exent) the Brandus brothers sought to uphold, and which they kept in uneasy equilibrium with the baser need for commercial success. Close inspection of the evidence reveals a more sophisticated structure of reception policy than Loesser implies, with some collaborators given more licence than others to express an opinion which might conflict with the publishing house's interests. Schlesinger, in particular, was adept at judging to what extent dissent among his collaborators assisted the journal's image as a forum for debate, and at what point bad publicity ceased to be beneficial. By contrast, after 1846, certain areas of reviewing were increasingly assigned exclusively to specific collaborators. Confrontation between critics was less likely when the amount of common ground for review was minimised; thus, although in 1880 the *Gazette* had nearly as disparate a collection of contributors as in 1836, the fracture lines of opinion were neither exposed nor exploited. This discussion of the journal's piano music criticism focuses upon particular episodes which illustrate the various ways in which commercially driven

---

[1] Arthur Loesser on Schlesinger's approach to contemporary music; *Men, Women and Pianos. A social history* (London, 1955), 352.

criticism was allied (with varying degrees of success) to aesthetic ideals. It examines the reception of Henri Herz, Chopin, Liszt, Thalberg, Stephen Heller and Emile Prudent in the context of the *Gazette*'s dominant modes of thought.

Henri Herz

Three major areas of criticism dominate the first years of the *Gazette*: the appreciation of Beethoven, the use of the *conte fantastique* as a vehicle for aesthetic discussion, and the war against the piano music industry. A sustained attempt was made to replace public adoration of Henri Herz's variation sets on operatic arias with the weightier music of Chopin and Heller. In this respect, the *Gazette* shared the aims of Schumann's future *Neue Zeitschrift für Musik*, which began publication in April 1834, leading the way in its deprecation of Henri Herz, Franz Hünten, Theodore Doehler and others.[2] The *Gazette*'s advertisements and small-print music reviews, however, reveal that Schlesinger did not outlaw opera-based piano music from his own catalogue. Chief among the targets for the *Gazette*'s combination of wit, hyperbole, critical parody and self-consciously literary insult was Henri [Heinrich] Herz, who was singled out from the very first issue (*GM* I/1: 5 Jan. 1834, 3–4), his reputation thereafter buffeted by a string of anonymous and derogatory articles. In opposition to *Le Pianiste*, the *Gazette*'s reviewers decried his poverty of invention and described his variation technique as the endless reformulation of a successful pattern produced by 'his variation-making machine' (*GM* I/40: 5 Oct. 1834, 321).[3] An earlier article, signed 'Le Poste', used a series of bathetic constructions to heighten the reader's sense of the absurdity of Herz's variations on the march from Auber's *Le Philtre*:

Although it contains nothing original, whether in form or content, nevertheless one finds a warm and lively energy which mitigates its equally glacial uniformity and its quite desperate poverty of invention in the three areas of melody, harmony and rhythm. (*GM* I/2: 12 Jan. 1834, 14)[4]

So extensive is the variety of conceits and so concentrated the campaign that Herz dominates the journal's piano music criticism for fully two

---

[2] Cf. Leon B. Plantinga, *Schumann as Critic* (New Haven, 1967), 21. Plantinga sees Schumann as initiating the acerbic mode of criticism lavished on minor pianist-composers; in fact, the precedent was set by the *Gazette*.
[3] 'sa machine à variations' (*GM* I/40: 5 Oct. 1834, 321).
[4] 'Quoiqu'il ne renferme rien d'original, ni dans la forme ni dans le fonds, on y découvre pourtant une énergie chaleureuse et animée, qui console un peu d'une uniformité aussi glaciale et d'une pauvreté si désespérante d'invention, sous le triple rapport de la mélodie, de l'harmonie et du rhythme' (*GM* I/2: 12 Jan. 1834, 14).

years. Such excess was entirely in Schlesinger's nature, but his reviewer rose to the challenge, confidently toying with Herz's image and even his name – his music was said to be for the fingers, not the heart (*GM* I/1: 5 Jan. 1834, 4). A parody of salon criticism mixed its genres, referring to a '*cantabile religioso* to be played on a single string' in the *Rondo militaire* on Auber's *Le Serment* (*GM* I/6: 9 Feb. 1834, 48);[5] another parody reversed salon criticism's polite superlatives: 'his concert cannot, in any way, be counted among the brilliant musical soirées of the season', and, 'The Andante, whose theme is most fortunately not developed' (*GM* I/ 13: 30 Mar. 1834, 106).[6]

In 1835, feigned disbelief that Herz's music could be worthless provided the excuse for a complete reappraisal, the climax of which was an attempt to write a creative critique *à la* Schumann of a banal piece of music. The result is gloriously meaningless. The reviewer spins words as Herz spins notes, in recurring, stereotyped, patterns:

The first reprise is sixteen bars long, and there is nothing more to say except that the final eight bars are, strictly speaking, nothing but the repeat of the first eight bars. This makes them useless at best; but what is more confusing and more detrimental to the metre is the number of bars in the second reprise, the first portion of which has eight bars whilst the second has only four. (*RGM* II/45: 8 Nov. 1835, 365)[7]

The stream of withering articles stops abruptly after a review of 27 March 1836, their consistency of tone and style suggesting the work of a single critic.[8] The evidence points mostly to François Stoepel, a founder contributor who died on 19 December 1836. The article signed 'Le Poste' is clearly Stoepel's work, since the by-line is anagrammatic. However, the other articles may be attributable on stylistic grounds. Many Herz reviews contain digressions leading back to the great German models, Beethoven, Mozart and Weber, their skill in motivic development and contrapuntal working. The review of Herz's early *Exercices et préludes* is

---

[5] '*cantabile religioso* qui doit être joué sur une seule corde' (*GM* I/6: 9 Feb. 1834, 48).

[6] 'son concert ne saurait, sous aucun rapport, être compté parmi les brillantes soirées musicales de la saison', and 'l'andante, dont fort heureusement le chant n'est pas développé' (*GM* I/13: 30 Mar. 1834, 106).

[7] 'La première reprise se compose de seize mesures, et à cela, il n'y a rien à dire, si ce n'est que les huit dernières mesures ne sont à proprement parler que la répétition des huit premières; ce qui les rend au moins inutiles; mais ce que nous trouvons de plus confus et de plus contraire au rhythme, c'est le nombre des mesures de la 2e reprise dont le premier fragment a huit mesures tandis que le second n'en a que quatre' (*RGM* II/45: 8 Nov. 1835, 365).

[8] The only tendentious article on Herz after 1836 is devoid of the facetious element which characterises the earlier tirades (unsigned, *RGM* IV/21: 21 May 1837). Its seriousness and an internal reference to the review immediately preceding it – a critique of Onslow's String Quintet no. 22 signed by Georges Kastner – suggests Kastner's authorship.

a panegyric to Beethoven and, to a lesser extent, Weber (*GM* II/6: 8 Feb. 1835); the opening article in the campaign compares Herz's accompanimental use of the orchestra with that of all three composers and finds it sadly deficient (*GM* I/1: 5 Jan. 1834, 4); the article signed 'Le Poste' shows identical characteristics, recommending that Herz abandon his fashionable career and study the works of Beethoven, Mozart and Weber.

Stoepel's signed articles give no hint that he was capable of the acidulated tone which characterises the campaign.[9] It was, of course, customary to leave potentially inflammatory articles unsigned, though such anonymity did not prevent the Herz articles provoking both a duel (between Schlesinger and Henri's brother, Jacques) and a libel case. Reviews of the 1840s are resigned and flaccid,[10] or even enthusiastic (a Fétis article on the Third Piano Concerto, *RGM* VII/12: 9 Feb. 1840). Thereafter, Herz was given easier treatment, though sometimes in a clearly stated context of 'light music' reviewing. A firm attribution for these articles is, however, complicated by Liszt, who makes passing reference to meeting with Herz in February 1837 in a letter to Marie d'Agoult: 'A rather odd incident during the evening was Herz's coming to shake my hand, saying that he had never heard me play better. Now, you know the articles I've written on Herz'.[11] The possibility thus arises that Stoepel and Liszt divided the anti-Herz campaign between them.

Chopin

While the *Gazette* spent an inordinate amount of column space in its first two years denouncing Herz in a combined show of artistic integrity and publicity-seeking, it began to set up alternative idols, to some of whom – Chopin, Heller and Alkan in particular – it remained loyal throughout its existence. Of these, the first, again provoking comparison with Schumann's *Neue Zeitschrift*, was Chopin, whose variations on 'Là ci darem la mano' Op. 2 were reviewed alongside the First Piano Concerto in a signed article by Stoepel of 21 September 1834. Stoepel's introduction can be taken as the critical premise of all the *Gazette*'s contributors:

We must place this artist among the small number of favoured geniuses who, with their goal always in sight, proceed with strength equal to their boldness,

---

[9] However, Joseph Mainzer mentions Stoepel's unfortunate tendency to alienate colleagues due to ruthless criticism of their work (*RGM* III/34: 21 Aug. 1836, 294).

[10] See Blanchard, *RGM* IX/15: 10 Apr. 1842.

[11] 'Un incident assez bizarre de la soirée, c'est Herz venant me serrer la main et me disant qu'il ne m'avait jamais entendu mieux jouer. Or, vous savez quels articles j'ai fait sur Herz'. *Correspondance de Liszt et de la Comtesse d'Agoult 1833–1840*, ed. Daniel Ollivier. 2 vols. (Paris, 1933–4), I, 181.

caring little about the doings of the attendant crowd, its desires, its needs or fashions. Let us try and follow him along his way with a critical, but friendly eye. (*GM* I/38: 21 Sep. 1834, 304)[12]

Several aspects of Chopin's image were particularly suited to Schlesinger's purpose. Firstly, he shunned the concert circuit so beloved of Liszt, Thalberg, Theodor Doehler and Friedrich Kalkbrenner, and thereby had more credibility as a serious artist whose compositions were less a vehicle for virtuosity than an artistic statement. It is, in this respect, significant that Chopin never experienced Liszt's problems in convincing Schlesinger of his worth as a composer.[13] His preference for performing to an intimate circle, and his avoidance of the large public arenas of concert life, were recommendations to a journal whose critics tended to elevate composers of piano music who had deliberately distanced themselves from the mainstream of piano virtuosi (the championing of Emile Prudent in the 1850s and 1860s was exceptional). From the first, the *Gazette*'s critics had set up a Kreislerian aristocracy of composers to whose music many would be denied spiritual access and at whose head stood the alienated Beethoven. The noble, melancholic *émigré* who disdained mass adulation was the perfect symbol for the *Gazette*'s policy for contemporary music, whatever its ostensibly educational claims. Chopin had his own public, but the *Gazette* fostered the image of social withdrawal. Secondly, Chopin was not a specialist in popular genres, particularly those based on current operatic themes, and stood apart from the commercial materialism of Herz and Henri Rosellen. He could, therefore, be championed in the journal without Schlesinger being charged with inconsistency – which could not apply to Liszt in the 1830s. Thirdly, Chopin's music was just (but only just) marketable to pianists for domestic use; Liszt's was not. Chopin reviews appear with some frequency in the 'Revue critique' column, traditionally the domain of domestic piano music. Thus, whilst he was hailed in the later 1830s as the new, regenerative force in piano composition, a puritanical instinct, intended to direct attention away from materialistic virtuosity, resulted in his being confined firmly to the salon in the pages of the *Gazette*, as though to write music that was too technically challenging was inevitably to taint the art.

Chopin's harmonic and modulatory procedure attracted most atten-

---

[12] 'Nous devons ranger cet artiste parmi le petit nombre de génies favorisés qui, le but toujours devant les yeux, marchent avec autant de force que de hardiesse, sans s'inquiéter de ce que fait la foule autour d'eux, de ce qu'elle désire, de ce qui est son besoin ou sa mode. Essayons de le suivre dans sa course d'un regard observateur, mais ami' (*GM* I/38: 21 Sep. 1834, 304).

[13] For a discussion of Liszt's relationship with Schlesinger, see Bellas, 'La Tumultueuse amitié', 7–20.

tion from the *Gazette*'s critics. The reviewer of the Mazurka in A-flat Op. 17/3 picked out the mood change effected by a sudden jump from the tonic to E major (unsigned, *GM* I/26: 29 Jun. 1834, 211); Stoepel, in his review of the First Concerto Op. 11, stressed Chopin's freedom from standard modulation patterns (*GM* I/38: 21 Sep. 1834, 305). In 1838, Blanchard attempted to characterise the localised dissonance technique of Chopin's Impromptu in A-flat Op. 29:

In the carefree progress of certain notes astonished to meet each other, and forming unprepared and unresolved dissonances, one can immediately perceive the independent spirit which presided over this pretty babbling of triplets. (*RGM* V/48: 2 Dec. 1838, 493)[14]

Blanchard's pithy description first evokes an image of Chopin's music as Brownian motion, but then immediately acknowledges the composer's control over his material. Moreover, the overall result is 'joli'. In a single sentence, Blanchard encapsulates Chopin's allure: a daring, mobile and dissonant stylistic complexity masked by large-scale accessibility. For Liszt, too, these were Chopin's strongest features. Following an aesthetic of genius which remained prevalent in France for several decades, and which condemned Mendelssohn to the ranks of the talented, Liszt stressed both Chopin's unforced originality and the hidden complexities of outwardly simple works such as the Preludes:

Admirable in their diversity, the working and skill which they contain are appreciable only on scrupulous examination. Everything seems to be a single sweep of imagination, a spontaneous inspiration. They have the liberty and greatness of manner which characterise works of genius. (*RGM* VIII/31: 2 May 1841, 246)[15]

To be credited with such ability was rare indeed in the pianistic world. However, not all of the *Gazette*'s critics were as enthusiastic as Stoepel and Liszt. The most sceptical (though not censorious) critic of Chopin and the aesthetic which he represented, was Maurice Bourges, who found a disconcerting element of detachment in the composer's veiled emotional world. A staunch supporter of Beethoven and Berlioz, Bourges disliked what he saw as the dilution of music's newly found expressive power into mere elegy and resigned melancholy. His reviews of Chopin and his followers, particularly Adolph von Henselt, are characterised by

---

[14] 'Au laissé-aller de certaines notes étonnées de se rencontrer, et qui forment des dissonances ni préparées ni résolues, on voit tout de suite l'indépendance qui a présidé à ce joli gazouillement de triolets' (*RGM* V/48: 2 Dec. 1838, 493).
[15] 'Admirables par leur diversité, le travail et le savoir qui s'y trouvent ne sont appréciables qu'à un scrupuleux examen. Tout y semble de premier jet, d'élan, de soudaine venue. Ils ont la libre et grande allure qui caractérise les œuvres du génie' (*RGM* VIII/31: 2 May 1841, 246).

weary resignation at the emotional superficiality of even the highest class of salon music. In Henselt's *Poème d'amour*, as in salon pieces of like kind, Bourges felt that profound feeling was not required,

provided that a composition has a passionate melodic drive, richness of harmony, a well-managed gradation of developments, and above all, effect, which in the end provides the victorious blow. (*RGM* VIII/54: 10 Oct. 1841, 446)[16]

In a combined review of Chopin pieces, he had difficulty pinpointing the reason for the composer's popularity, since his works 'do not take us to seventh heaven on the burning wings of enthusiasm' (*RGM* IX/16: 17 Apr. 1842, 171),[17] and stated rather patronisingly that the performance of Chopin's music demanded 'if not the soul, then at least the imagination, and simple delicacy, which is spirit's close relation' (*ibid.*).[18] Whereas Liszt praised Chopin's directness of expression, Bourges found him too mannered, particularly in his 'surprising facility for finding new forms of ornamentation' (*RGM* IX/9: 27 Feb. 1842, 82).[19] Nevertheless, he was unstinting in his praise for works such as the Third Ballade, played at Chopin's concert of 1842, which in his opinion was the composer's finest work to date (*ibid.*, 83). The importance of Bourges's response lies in his tactics and purpose. Reviewing historical styles, he judged music scrupulously by the standards of the milieu in which it was produced; here, with a different end in view, he judges by a pre-set, Beethovenian, standard wholly incompatible with the music under review. That Chopin was perceived by others to have transcended the predominant styles of his particular milieu – the salon – is irrelevant to him. Instead, Bourges attempts to direct his readers towards an altogether different aesthetic of piano music. Chopin's contemporaneity provokes him to alter fundamentally his critical rationale: criticism as appreciation becomes criticism as a statement about music's proper direction, and, as such, participates in the process of canon formation. Relativism turns to absolutism because of the prospect of influencing outcomes. Whilst Bourges's absolutism was motivated by aesthetic values, commercial gain provided the motivation for many of the *Gazette*'s prejudices.

[16] 'pourvu qu'une composition se distingue par l'allure passionnée de la mélodie, la richesse harmonique, la gradation des développements habilement ménagée, et surtout par l'effet, qui est en définitive l'argument victorieux' (*RGM* VIII/54: 10 Oct. 1841, 446).

[17] 'ne ravissent pas jusqu'au septième ciel sur les ailes brûlantes de l'enthousiasme' (*RGM* IX/16: 17 Apr. 1842, 171).

[18] 'sinon de l'âme, du moins de l'imagination, et de finesse naïve, proche parent de l'esprit' (*ibid.*).

[19] 'étonnante facilité à trouver des formes d'ornementation neuves' (*RGM* IX/9: 27 Feb. 1842, 82).

Liszt v. Fétis

There are, however, instances in the journal where aesthetic and commercial interests fuse; I shall argue later that Berlioz's reception was one such case. However, such fusion was not always born of elevated principles, as the *Gazette*'s reception of Herz illustrates; indeed, the most sophisticated example of a commercially driven aesthetic debate was an elaborately staged trick whose main events have since become legendary in Liszt reception. The most notorious episode in the history of early nineteenth-century French pianism was the Liszt/Thalberg battle of 1837. The authorship of the *Gazette* articles published in Liszt's name, and Fétis's reactionary and bitter responses, have spawned numerous studies.[20] I do not propose, therefore, to discuss the affair in detail, but to examine Schlesinger's rôle in it. Alan Walker presents the episode as a verbal duel between Marie d'Agoult/Liszt and Fétis, catalysed inadvertently by Berlioz and refereed by Schlesinger.[21] At the close of his discussion, Walker observes: 'Even the *Gazette Musicale*, normally so favourably disposed towards Liszt, produced an even-handed criticism of the "duel"' at the salons of the Princess Belgiojoso in March 1837.[22] Such even-handedness was exactly the public image Schlesinger wished to promote. Characterised by a studied impartiality, the final verdict – two victors and no vanquished – contrasts starkly with the polemics framing it (*RGM* IV/15: 9 Apr. 1837).[23] The entire discussion is itself framed by Schlesinger's footnoted comments, which are (on the surface) the epitome of editorial caution. A note to Liszt's article initiating the debate reads:

We shall insert M. Liszt's article as it stands, but with our reservations as to the discussion, where the opinion of our collaborator differs so markedly from that

---

[20] See Emile Haraszti, 'Franz Liszt – author despite himself. The history of a mystification', *Musical Quarterly* (Oct. 1947), 490–516; Serge Gut, *Franz Liszt. Les Eléments du langage musical* (Paris, 1975); Alan Walker, *Liszt: The Virtuoso Years, 1811–1847* (London, 1983), and *Liszt: The Weimar Years, 1848–1861* (London, 1989); Adrian Williams, *Portrait of Liszt by Himself and His Contemporaries* (Oxford, 1990). Letters between Liszt and Marie d'Agoult make clear that many of his signed articles were jointly written, and that they relished concealing their collaboration from friends and colleagues alike. See in particular Ollivier (ed.), *Correspondance de Liszt*, I, 188–9.

[21] Walker, *Liszt: The Virtuoso Years*, esp. 235–7.

[22] *Ibid.*, 240.

[23] Reviews on Thalberg at the Conservatoire (Joseph d'Ortigue, *RGM* IV/12: 19 Mar. 1837) and Liszt at the Opéra (Ernest Legouvé, *RGM* IV/13: 26 Mar. 1837) also form part of Schlesinger's public show of impartiality. Ernest Legouvé (1807–1903) was a poet and dramatist; he was a close friend and supporter of Berlioz.

which the *Gazette musicale* has hitherto expressed regarding M. Thalberg. (*RGM* IV/2: 8 Jan. 1837, 17)[24]

Similarly, a note to the final instalment (an open letter from Fétis to Schlesinger) indicates that the discussion is now closed. The non-negotiable nature of Schlesinger's closing gesture is intimately connected with Fétis's reproach that, in this matter, Schlesinger had been more than an impartial editor allowing freedom of critical exchange in the pages of his journal:

> More than anyone, monsieur, you know the state of play; I had written in confidence about my opinion of MM. Liszt and Thalberg: persuaded that this considered opinion might be of interest to the public, and convinced that I would express myself in a manner acceptable to the two great artists, you pressed me to write an article along those lines, and I have before me several letters in which you make insistent requests. (*RGM* IV/21: 21 May 1837, 174)[25]

Fétis felt that he had been drawn into battle, only to be left exposed. That Schlesinger had repeatedly asked for an article from Fétis cannot be verified, but the existence of Fétis's original letter is attested, albeit in slightly different terms, by Liszt himself, in a letter of 13 February 1837 to Marie d'Agoult:

> And now here comes Fétis to join the fray. Yes Fétis, the worthy professor ... is to address a letter to me in the *Gazette musicale* on the subject of my (or our) Thalberg article. Schlesinger has shown me a note which he has just received from him, in which Fétis asks if it would be convenient to insert in the *Gazette* a letter in which, he says, he will show all the respect due to an artist as great as Liszt.[26]

Liszt then states that he had authorised Schlesinger to print whatever Fétis submitted. His confidence was not misplaced. For whatever his trust in his own and Marie d'Agoult's ability to defeat Fétis, he had a staunch ally in the publisher of the *Gazette musicale*. All the evidence

---

[24] 'Nous insérons textuellement l'article de M. Liszt, en gardant toutefois nos réserves dans cette discussion où l'opinion de notre collaborateur diffère si notablement de celle que la *Gazette musicale* a émise jusqu'ici sur le compte de M. Thalberg' (*RGM* IV/2: 8 Jan. 1837, 17).

[25] 'Mieux que personne, monsieur, vous savez ce qui en est; je vous avais écrit confidentiellement mon opinion à l'égard de MM. Liszt et Thalberg: persuadé que cette opinion formulée pourrait intéresser le public, et convaincu que je m'exprimerais en termes convenables sur les deux grands artistes, vous m'avez pressé de faire un article d'après mes idées, et j'ai sous les yeux plusieurs lettres où vous me les demandiez avec instances' (*RGM* IV/21: 21 May 1837, 174).

[26] 'Et puis voilà Fétis qui va s'en mêler. Oui Fétis, le digne professeur ... doit m'adresser dans la *Gazette musicale* une lettre au sujet de mon (ou de notre) article sur Thalberg. Schlesinger m'a montré un billet qu'il venait de recevoir de lui et dans lequel il lui demande s'il conviendrait à la *Gazette* d'insérer cette lettre dans laquelle, dit-il, il saura garder toutes les convenances imposées par un aussi grand artiste que Liszt.' Ollivier (ed.), *Correspondance de Liszt*, I, 187.

points to a sequence of events in which Schlesinger, ostensibly the arbitrator, was, until Fétis threatened to reveal his machinations, working behind the scenes in support of Liszt against Thalberg and using Fétis as a pawn to inflame the controversy in print. A letter, again to Marie d'Agoult in Nohant, dated February 1837, indicates that Schlesinger was prepared to arrange a concert for Liszt at the Opéra, a fabulously prestigious venue; whatever Thalberg's chosen concert hall, it could match neither the Opéra's magnificence, nor the size and elevated status of its audience.[27] Schlesinger also took particular care to ensure the success of Liszt's chamber concerts with Alexandre Batta and Chrétien Urhan, which were reviewed enthusiastically in the *Gazette*; Liszt observed that the publisher's interest had a particular bearing on the propaganda war between himself and Thalberg:

Schlesinger is also putting himself out a little on my account; the other night he arrived at eleven o'clock to tell me that it was absolutely essential that my soirées are bursting with people, if only to put Thalberg's nose out of joint, etc., etc. I gave him a hundred tickets which he distributed (since Carnival Saturday left us little chance of a large gathering) and the hall was full and the piece on *La Juive* was showered with applause.[28]

Liszt was undoubtedly grateful for such championing from Schlesinger; moreover, his letters show the extent of his competitive spirit. Thus, the 'even-handedness' of the *Gazette*'s reviews was a fiction, and Schlesinger's footnotes to the first and last articles of the *Gazette* controversy, hypocritical. Throughout the battle, Schlesinger showed an unerring sense for publicity, exercising admirable control over his journal's public image. Far from Liszt persuading Schlesinger to print the original review,[29] the nature of the entire *Gazette* battle as an elaborate orchestration by the publisher begs the question of whether the original article might not have been written at Schlesinger's instigation. He was not above commissioning specifically tendentious articles which would, he hoped, provoke a protracted polemic. An undated letter postmarked December 1845 from Félix Danjou to Fétis relays just such a request:

Schlesinger, whom I saw yesterday, asks you most URGENTLY to send him an article for January 1st, and learning from me that I had to write to you, he asked

---

27 *Ibid.*, 190. Liszt's famous concert, however, did not take place until 19 March, a week after Thalberg's Conservatoire appearance.

28 'Schlesinger aussi se met un peu en avant pour moi; il est arrivé l'autre soir à 11 heures, pour me dire qu'il fallait absolument que mes soirées regorgent de monde, ne serait-ce que pour faire une niche à Thalberg, etc., etc. Je lui ai remis cent billets qu'il a distribués (car le samedi-gras nous laissait peu de chance de monde) et la salle a été comble et le morceau de *la Juive* couvert d'applaudissements' (*ibid.*, 183).

29 Walker, *Liszt: The Virtuoso Years*, 236.

me to ask you specifically for a series of articles entitled *The History of Music Journalism* – you have already written on this subject, but this would be in the *Gazette* and in Schlesinger's mind the initiative for a merciless war which would continue by all possible means and by all the editors AGAINST *La France musicale*.[30]

Schlesinger was thus no stranger to the business of instigating quarrels for the purposes of publicity. The Herz case displays similar qualities, and in respect of the Liszt dispute it is perhaps significant that, following the last article of the Herz campaign in March 1836, the journal had lost an important polemic element relating to one of the major issues of the day. The conclusion that the war was engineered almost completely by a publicity-seeking Schlesinger who feigned impartiality but who actively supported Liszt at the expense of both Thalberg and a supposedly revered collaborator – Fétis – is difficult to refute.

Liszt's music

However, as Jacqueline Bellas has shown, Schlesinger was less reliably supportive of Liszt than this episode might suggest.[31] Moreover, after an initial period in which D'Ortigue and Berlioz reviewed his compositions with enthusiasm, the *Gazette* showed considerable antipathy towards his music, whether for piano or orchestra, particularly once he had been linked with Wagner and the 'music of the future'. There is, however, one significant exception: Fétis's review of the *Etudes d'exécution transcendante*, celebrated for its description of Liszt as 'the most complete musician of our era' (*RGM* VIII/32: 9 May 1841, 263).[32] It is here that Fétis, with his customary smugness, attributed to the content of his own lectures on the philosophy of music (with a passing self-justification of his earlier view on Thalberg) Liszt's future importance as a composer. In his closing lecture of the 1832 series, Fétis had introduced the *ordre omnitonique*:

Liszt attended that session; he was struck by the novelty of this idea, and later it took root in his mind as an incontestable truth. So he wanted to try and apply it to piano music; and, reuniting his newly discovered modulatory formulae with modifications of Thalberg's system (which has become a necessity of the present

---

[30] 'Schlesinger que j'ai vu hier, vous prie très INSTAMMENT de lui envoyer un article pour le premier janvier et apprenant de moi que je devais vous écrire, il m'a chargé de vous demander specialement une serie d'articles intitules *Histoire du journalisme musical* – vous avez déjà traité ce sujet, mais ce serait dans la gazette et dans la pensée de Schlesinger l'initiative d'une guerre sans pitié qui se continuerait ensuite de toutes les facons et par tous les redacteurs CONTRE *la france musicale*' (BN, Dépt des manuscrits: n. a. fr. 22870/202). Original orthography.

[31] See Bellas, 'La Tumultueuse amitié'.

[32] 'le musicien le plus complet de notre époque' (*RGM* VIII/32: 9 May 1841, 263).

time), in new works, and with new effects and transcendent complexities of execution which his unbelievable facility alone could find, he formed a genre which belongs to him alone, and which resolves victoriously the question asked so often: *will Liszt become a distinguished composer?* (*ibid.*)[33]

Fétis's comment refers not to the *Etudes*, but to the then unpublished *Années de pèlerinage*, of which Liszt had given Fétis a private hearing. His reference to the 'necessity of the present time' is an allusion to Cousin's theory of transformation. Thus Fétis elected Liszt as the chosen vehicle of an epoch-making transformation in musical style. Yet his prophetic opinion had no longevity in the journal, or, indeed, in Fétis's criticism, probably because Liszt soon transcended Fétis's vision of his place in music's teleology. In particular, his development of the symphonic poem and his association with Wagner were inimical to Fétis's formalist musical aesthetics and his idealist view on the nature of genius.

In the *Gazette*'s middle years, Liszt's piano music received minimal coverage; Botte was caustic in his critique of the First Piano Concerto in E-flat (*RGM* XXVI/5: 30 Jan. 1859, 34). Bannelier's arrival as concerts reviewer in 1866 marks the final phase of Liszt's reception as a pianist-composer in the *Gazette*. Bannelier was a Hanslickian formalist, and therefore rejected the central tenets of Liszt's works from the 1840s and 1850s. Yet he was too open-minded to reject the composer out of hand. In 1879, he welcomed a project by the pianist Frédéric Lottin to present a series of recitals devoted exclusively to Liszt's music, observing that, despite Liszt's celebrity, his piano music was little known, and that, among his original compositions, some were 'intrinsically most remarkable, quite apart from their incontestable merit from the point of view of the instrument' (?Bannelier, *RGM* XLV/52: 29 Dec. 1878, 423).[34] With other works, such as the First Piano Concerto, Bannelier felt that pianism predominated excessively over musical expression.[35] On occasion, his hostility to Liszt's programmatic tendencies led him to an impasse of his own making. His review of Saint-Saëns's performance of

[33] 'Litsz [sic] assistait à cette séance; il fut frappé de la nouveauté de cette idée, et plus tard elle prit dans son esprit la consistance d'une vérité incontestable. Alors il en voulut essayer l'application à la musique de piano; et réunissant dans de nouvelles œuvres les formules neuves de modulation qu'il avait découvertes aux modifications du système de Thalberg, devenu une nécessité de l'époque actuelle, et aux effets nouveaux et combinaisons d'exécution transcendante que son habileté inouïe a pu seule trouver, il en a formé un genre qui lui appartient en propre, et qui résout victorieusement cette question si souvent posée: *Liszt sera-t-il un compositeur distingué?*' (*ibid.*). That Liszt retained immense respect for Fétis as a theorist is evident from his letters, and is discussed by Bloom. See Peter Bloom, 'François Joseph Fétis', 310ff.

[34] 'fort remarquables, intrinsèquement parlant et abstraction faite de leur mérite incontesté au point de vue de l'instrument' (?Bannelier, *RGM* XLV/52: 29 Dec. 1878, 423).

[35] *RGM* XLII/15: 11 Apr. 1875, 118; and *RGM* XLII/47: 21 Nov. 1875, 374. Both are unsigned.

the Sonata in B minor at the Salle Pleyel in April 1880 is misguided, but interestingly so. The review's preoccupations are characteristic of their author, who relates the sonata to the symphonic poem and assumes that it is programmatic. This single assumption prevents Bannelier from listening impartially, and skews his final judgement. For him, the work owes nothing to the sonata principle:

Liszt's Sonata ... is more a fantasy, a framework for a symphonic poem, than a sonata. New things require new names; why keep the classic designation for a work whose liberty of form is driven to excess? No doubt there is an underlying programme; we were not given it, but we are not too sorry, because we would probably not have appreciated to a significantly greater extent the chaotic beauties which comprise a good half of this very long musical narrative. (?Bannelier, *RGM* XLVII/17: 25 Apr. 1880, 133)[36]

Caught in his own trap of perceiving the work as a narrative continuum whose subject matter is unknown, Bannelier ceases to look for any formal logic within the musical structure, even though such coherence is exactly what he seeks. His premise that programmaticism destroys musical form blinds him to the work's very strength.

The *Gazette*'s critics never embraced Liszt's piano music because circumstances precluded it. In the 1830s, Schlesinger could not afford, aesthetically, to fête the most dazzling composer of operatic fantasies whose paler imitations his critics were at pains to denounce. If Liszt did indeed contribute to the campaign against Herz, Schlesinger would have had even more reason to avoid open support for his music. Yet at the very moment that Liszt showed himself to be a composer of intellectual weight, the Brandus takeover resulted in a Fétisian journal in which his compositions were too adventurous to be accepted. Whilst other repertoires, such as Beethoven's late music, regained their former status once Bannelier began writing regularly, the status of Liszt's programmatic (and suspected programmatic) works suffered as a result of his formalism.

Prudent and Heller

Upon the purchase of the *Gazette* by Louis Brandus, the polemical tone of its piano-music reviewing largely disappeared. In place of skirmishes involving the more colourful of Paris's virtuosi, supportive reviews of the

---

[36] 'La sonate de Liszt ... est plutôt une fantaisie, un carton de poème symphonique, qu'une sonate. Aux choses nouvelles, des noms nouveaux; pourquoi conserver l'appellation classique à une œuvre où la liberté des formes est poussée jusqu'à l'excès? Il y a, sans aucun doute, un programme sous roche; on ne nous l'a pas donné, et nous ne le regrettons pas outre mesure, car nous n'aurions probablement goûté pas beaucoup plus les beautés chaotiques qui constituent une bonne moitié de ce très long récit musical' (?Bannelier, *RGM* XLVII/17: 25 Apr. 1880, 133).

music of lesser figures, notably Stephen Heller and Emile Prudent, constituted the bulk of the *Gazette*'s piano-music coverage between 1846 and the Franco-Prussian War. Support for Prudent and Heller was expedient for the publishing house (both were Brandus composers), but also for the *Gazette*'s critics, of whom the majority were now more conservative than under Schlesinger's directorship. Both Heller and Prudent represented an acceptable compromise between virtuosity and introspection, and between accessibility and perceptible musical value; they were a *juste milieu*. Yet they both failed to live up to the destinies which their critics had marked out for them, and each, ultimately, was a disappointment to his champions.

Enthusiasm for the music and playing of Emile Prudent was not confined to the *Gazette*; he was hailed almost unanimously (and chauvinistically) in the musical press as the new head of the French virtuoso piano school. The Brandus brothers published many of his works, and it would, therefore, be surprising to find hostile reviews in the 'Revue critique' or 'Bibliographie musicale' sections of the journal. Indeed, the *Gazette* remained loyal to Prudent throughout his career, giving advance notice of his sporadic appearances in Paris, and emphasising his status as a pianist of significance. After an absence of three years from the capital, Prudent arranged a concert in February 1859 which caused Adolphe Botte to wax lyrical over a considerable development in his style. Such development seemed to:

testify to this will, this perseverance, this need for perfection with which he is endowed in the highest degree, and which prove no less the vigour of his creative faculties than his unshakeable faith in study and meditation. Emile Prudent had accustomed us to these protracted silences, to these courageous retirements, from which he always emerged greater, transformed. (*RGM* XXVI/9: 27 Feb. 1859, 65)[37]

Botte's exaggerated apologia is an exceptional case of impassioned support; elsewhere, Prudent was regarded as a fine composer writing in a style somewhere between those of Thalberg and Liszt ('B.', *RGM* XVIII/ 7: 16 Feb. 1851, 48). Never claimed as a genius (in the manner of Berlioz or Chopin), Prudent was nevertheless presented by Monnais and Botte as a master of the genre piece, a musical 'landscape painter' (*RGM* XXVI/ 12: 20 Mar. 1859, 93).[38] Yet their reviews were only superficially positive;

---

[37] 'témoigner de cette volonté, de cette persévérance, de ce besoin de perfection dont il est doué par excellence, et qui ne prouvent pas moins la vigueur de ses facultés créatrices que sa foi inébranlable dans l'étude et la méditation. Emile Prudent nous avait habitués à ces silences prolongés, à ces courageuses retraites, d'où il sortait toujours grandi, transformé' (*RGM* XXVI/9: 27 Feb. 1859, 65).

[38] 'un paysagiste' (*RGM* XXVI/12: 20 Mar. 1859, 93). Botte's phrase invites comparison with the *Gazette*'s view of Félicien David, though no such comparison was ever made in the pages of the journal.

behind the hyperbole there lay a deep-seated uncertainty about Prudent's true capacity. Botte, in the above-mentioned report on Prudent's second concert, saw promise still unfulfilled:

he has not yet spoken his last word ... he has not yet written that unique work, long-dreamed and cherished, which, in composers' lives, is the masterpiece summing up all their aspirations. (*ibid.*, 94)[39]

In the obituary notice of 7 June 1863, Edouard Monnais's evaluation of Prudent's achievements was defensive; reversing earlier reports that his style displayed a constant process of maturation, Monnais judged that Prudent had reached his zenith with the *Concerto-symphonie*, a work of his second, rather than his third, period (*RGM* XXX/23: 7 Jun. 1863, 178). Though his limitations were never identified specifically in the *Gazette*, the relative lack of weight in Prudent's compositions evidently gave cause for concern.

A similar process can be seen occurring in reviews of Stephen Heller, whose self-imposed isolation was lauded in the *Gazette* throughout its lifetime, but whose concentration on the miniature at the expense of larger forms was a persistent source of disappointment. In reviews by Bourges, Fétis, J.-B. Laurens (a close friend), Emile Mathieu de Monter, Botte and Bannelier, Heller was always a genius on the point of producing a major work, of developing to a significant extent the originality which they all detected in his compositions. An early review by Bourges of the *Six caprices sur la romance du Shérif* Op. 17, pointed to innovative details which the critic took as indicating that, in its traditional guise, the operatic fantasy, as a genre, was finally in decline.[40] In Bourges's Fétisian opinion the presence of such innovation showed 'simultaneously the public's satiety and the need for renewal, on which the artist's mind secretly works' (*RGM* VII/38: 31 May 1840, 325).[41] However, Mathieu de Monter's short biographical study of 1868 still found only the seeds of reform in Heller's style:

Heller's harmonic working shows concern and curiosity for new timbres, forms deviating from textbook formulae. His talent is a significant new starting point. (*RGM* XXXV/42: 18 Oct. 1868, 330)[42]

---

[39] 'il n'a pas encore dit son dernier mot ... il n'a pas encore écrit cet ouvrage unique, longtemps rêvé et caressé, qui, dans la vie des compositeurs, est le chef-d'œuvre résumant toutes leurs aspirations' (*ibid.*, 94).

[40] In fact, Heller continued writing operatic fantasies until 1849.

[41] 'à la fois et la satiété du public et la besoin de renouvellement qui [sic] travaille en secret la tête de l'artiste' (*RGM* VII/38: 31 May 1840, 325).

[42] 'Le travail harmonique d'Heller a le souci et la curiosité des timbres nouveaux, des formes étrangères aux formules de l'école. Son talent est un grand recommenceur' (*RGM* XXXV/42: 18 Oct. 1868, 330).

Of his supporters in the *Gazette*, Fétis was by far the most committed: Bourges at times found him too detached, thus linking him with Chopin and Henselt, and Bannelier disliked his programmatic tendencies. By contrast, Fétis set up a Trinity of French (or honorary French) pianist-composers comprising Chopin, Heller and Alkan (*RGM* XIII/24: 14 Jun. 1846, 187). He ranked Heller among the finest four piano composers of the period 1830–64, the others being Mendelssohn, Chopin and Schumann (*RGM* XXXIV/18: 5 May 1867, 144).[43] In his opinion, both Heller and Alkan were unjustly neglected, and in the pages of the journal he did much to bring them to wider attention. Yet he, too, could not conceal the fact that some of Heller's music was insipid salon material which merited the epithet he so wanted to avoid – 'light music' (*RGM* XXII/5: 4 Feb. 1855, 35).[44] Also apparent is Fetis's relief at the appearance in 1844 of the Sonata no. 2 in B minor Op. 65 as the harbinger of further, substantial pieces (*ibid.*, 37). Yet the nature of Heller's output did not change significantly, and on the publication of his Sonata no. 4 in B-flat minor Op. 143, Bannelier lamented that the work was less a sonata in the Classical sense than a loose collection of genre pieces indistinguishable from the remainder of Heller's output ('Ch. B.', *RGM* XLV/26: 30 Jun. 1878, 203). Throughout the journal's career, its critics had to content themselves with commenting on Heller's admirable disdain for public acclaim[45] and the expressive depth of his fiercely anti-virtuoso miniatures.[46]

That the *Gazette*'s critics should have been anxious for the composition of large-scale sonata-based works in an era which made the piano miniature its own is an indication of the journal's essentially Beethovenian standpoint. Even Fétis complained that Heller too often merely repeated a melody without developing it (*RGM* XIII/24: 14 Jun 1846, 188). Botte, in a review of the *Vingt-quatre nouvelles études* Op. 90, tried valiantly to bring them closer to the Germanic form by regarding them as symphonies in miniature (*RGM* XXV/47: 21 Nov. 1858, 388). The journal's critics, particularly Kastner, Kreutzer and Fétis, stated both directly and indirectly throughout its career, that piano music had fallen into a state of decadence from which any means of rescue was permitted. Hence the enthusiasm with which works such as Thalberg's Sonata in C minor Op. 56 were welcomed by both Jules Maurel (*RGM* XII/9: 2 Mar. 1845) and Henri Blanchard

---

[43] The omission here of both Thalberg and Liszt is noteworthy.

[44] 'musiquette' (XXII/5: 4 Feb. 1855, 35).

[45] E.g. Fétis, *RGM* XIV/30: 25 Jul. 1847, 244; and Botte, *RGM* XXV/47: 21 Nov. 1858, 388.

[46] Botte, *RGM* XXVII/33: 12 Aug. 1860, 283–4.

(*RGM* XIII/10: 8 Mar. 1846) in complementary reviews which, whilst emphasising different aspects of the piece, each invoked the spectre of Beethoven as a means of legitimation. Blanchard even went so far as to justify the work's lightweight finale on the grounds that short-term compromise might lead to long-term gain: 'the resurrection of the Classical sonata is something so difficult that any means are justified to restore it to public favour' (*RGM* XIII/10: 8 Mar. 1846, 78)[47]

Although some of Schumann's piano music became popular in France in the course of the century, and caused significantly fewer problems for the *Gazette*'s critics than did his chamber music or symphonies, emphasis on the sets of miniatures failed to mark him out as a regenerative influence to be followed by others.[48] In the 1870s, it was Chopin who came to be viewed as the regenerative, eclectic *juste milieu*, combining virtuosity, formal balance and depth of feeling in near-ideal proportions. Echoing the view of Ernest Legouvé, who had argued in 1838 that Chopin, rather than Liszt or Thalberg, was the finest pianist of the day,[49] Bannelier's preface to volume three of Brandus's *Répertoire de musique classique de piano* hailed him as the true source of renewal in nineteenth-century piano music:

It is to him more than to any other, more than to Thalberg, more than to Liszt himself, that the piano owes its near-arrival at its *apogee* of effect, in as much as that effect remains subordinate to the idea and does not extend beyond it. Apart from his way of making the instrument *sing*, Thalberg found only one rather mathematical combination of sonorities, an 'aural illusion' to which time has given due recognition. Liszt, an incomparably more profound artistic nature, will have left a far deeper mark; and yet he gave too much to pure virtuosity, often sacrificing the imprescriptible laws of musical thought to the desire for innovation, to the need to elevate to the heights of his marvellous powers of execution the means – too restrained for him – of Beethoven's and Weber's piano. (signed, *RGM* XLII/1: 3 Jan. 1875, 6)[50]

---

[47]   'la résurrection de la sonate classique est chose si difficile que tous les moyens sont bons pour la remettre en goût dans le public' (*RGM* XIII/10: 8 Mar. 1846, 78).

[48]   *Carnaval* quickly became a recital test-piece, but an early review by Blanchard, though respecting its originality, trivialised it as essentially educational salon music (*RGM* XII/25: 22 Jun. 1845, 205).

[49]   *RGM* V/12: 25 Mar. 1838, 135.

[50]   'C'est à lui plus qu'à tout autre, plus qu'à Thalberg, plus qu'à Liszt lui-même, que le piano doit d'être arrivé à peu près à son *summum* d'effet, en tant que l'effet demeure soumis à l'idée et ne la déborde pas. Thalberg, en dehors de sa manière de faire *chanter* l'instrument, n'a trouvé qu'une combinaison en quelque sorte mathématique de sonorités, un "trompe-l'oreille" dont le temps a fait justice. Liszt, nature artistique incomparablement supérieure, aura laissé une trace bien plus profonde; et cependant il a donné beaucoup trop à la virtuosité pure, sacrifiant souvent les droits imprescriptables de la pensée musicale au désir d'innover, au besoin d'élever jusqu'à la hauteur de sa merveilleuse puissance d'exécution les moyens trop restreints pour lui du piano de Beethoven et de Weber' (signed, *RGM* XLII/1: 3 Jan. 1875, 6). Like the Prefaces to earlier volumes, that to Volume 3 was printed in full in the *Gazette*.

By contrast, Chopin had never used virtuosity for its own sake, holding in balance the opposing forces of technical effect and musical content:

In his case, virtuosity is never isolated; however developed, however arduous, it is never repellent because one feels that it has a *raison d'être*. It summarises all one can demand of the instrument without destroying the primacy of the idea. (*ibid.*)[51]

Thus, despite the market-driven claims of the 1850s and 1860s that Heller and Prudent were on the point of creating a new and honourable school of piano composition, the *Gazette* finally returned to championing its first acknowledged genius of the piano. The aesthetic which had marked him out from Liszt in the 1830s was not that by which he was distinguished from Liszt in the 1870s, but the result was identical.

---

[51] 'La virtuosité, chez lui, n'est jamais isolée; si dévelopée, si ardue qu'elle soit, elle ne rebute pas, parce qu'on lui sent une raison d'être. Elle résume tout ce qu'on peut demander à l'instrument sans détruire la primauté de l'idée' (*ibid.*).

8 Contemporary music II: Chamber and symphonic music

In reviews of chamber and symphonic music, the *Gazette*'s policy of supporting evolution rather than revolution is even more apparent than in reviews of piano music, partly because of the greater emphasis on aesthetic, as opposed to commercial, concerns, in the reception of a repertoire which contained fewer works of crucial importance to the publishing house's fortunes. Freed from the need to present perceived weaknesses as early signs of future strength (as in their reviews of Heller and Prudent), the journal's critics could concentrate on specifically musical debates. Early championing of Berlioz did not indicate a general openness to avant-garde instrumental music; on the contrary, particularly after 1846, Berlioz was an exception to all the tenets regularly espoused by the *Gazette*'s critics. That a composer who died in 1869 and who was fundamentally opposed to the then most adventurous trends in music should be the avant-garde exception to the journal's prevailing aesthetic is significant, and represents part of a general trend towards conservatism in the Brandus *Gazette*. With the possible exception of Maurice Bourges, at no time after Berlioz's resignation as concerts reviewer did the *Gazette* employ a regular reporter with avant-garde leanings. The principal common factor among the journal's main reviewers – Monnais, Blanchard, Botte and Bannelier – is their indebtedness to Fétis, who provided a theoretical framework for judgements on the representational potential of music, harmonic, metrical and rhythmic schemes, clarity of structure, and, above all, the proper path for contemporary music. Acknowledged or not, Fétisian echoes occur with varying frequency in the work of all four critics, who with almost unflinching tenacity tried to stem the tides of Romanticism and Wagnerian influence, and to promote instead a *juste milieu* which would take the form of a re-interpretation, through autonomous music, of Beethoven. In chamber music reviews until the mid 1860s, the journal shows an unprecedentedly consistent devotion to *juste milieu* ideals, which were abundantly evident in the work of Schlesinger's house composer, Georges Onslow, from the beginning of the journal's career.

This discussion examines the problem of post-Beethovenian instrumental music, Berlioz excepted, as perceived by the *Gazette*'s critics, and analyses the effects of their eclectic and formalist modes of reception.

The *juste milieu*

There would be nothing unusual in the journal's pointing out the value of composers who followed Beethoven closely were it not that many of their works bordered on plagiarism, as Berlioz was quick to note with regard to Ferdinand Ries (*RGM* IV/13: 26 Mar. 1837, 101). Ironically, given the *Gazette*'s ostensibly Romantic aims, from as early as 1839, composers whose styles approximated to that of Ries were used as a critical shield against Romanticism, from which movement Berlioz was conveniently dissociated except in the writings of a giant such as Fétis. Until approximately 1866, the Mozartian and early Beethovenian style of chamber music and symphonies by Henri Rigel, Henri Reber, Louise Farrenc, Théodore Gouvy and Alexandre Boëly was condoned or encouraged in the journal.[1] Conservative critics did not, however, dominate completely: censorious reviews of such works were written by **Auguste Morel**, Joseph d'Ortigue and Bannelier, who cast an amused and sceptical eye over what they considered outdated, as opposed to eclectic, compositional styles. But in its middle years the *Gazette* presented its readers with a response to post-Beethovenian composition which was as alarmed as that of the traditionalist and reactionary composers whose works it discussed. Once Berlioz's voice ceased to be heard regularly in its pages, the predominant voices of both Henri Blanchard and Edouard Monnais set a new tone for the reception of Romantic instrumental music, ensuring censure for adventurous works.

Both Blanchard and Monnais believed that Romanticism was pernicious, their animosity so entrenched that on the few occasions when they referred to Romantic style as a positive characteristic, they felt the need to say so explicitly. In 1841, Blanchard defined Romanticism's faults in music; thereafter he consistently judged composers according to the degree to which their thought had been tainted:

The fatal temptations of Romanticism in music are the scorning of fugue, a pronounced antipathy towards metrical regularity, a horror of the simple, an incessant need for tortuous melody, for the use of luxuriant instrumentation, and the need to give listeners a programme which explains the composer's thought,

[1] For example: Rigel (*RM* VI/1: 3 Jan. 1839, 6–7); Reber (*RGM* VI/72: 29 Dec. 1839, 577–9; XVII/7: 17 Feb. 1850, 55; and XXVII/9: 26 Feb. 1860, 70); Farrenc (*RGM* XVII/13: 31 Mar. 1850, 109); Gouvy (*RGM* XXI/6: 5 Feb. 1854, 42) and Boëly (*RGM* XXX/15: 12 Apr. 1863, 116).

which he never formulates in a clear manner because more often than not it does not exist. (*RGM* VIII/41: 11 Jul. 1841, 337–8)[2]

Monnais's antipathy to Romanticism was even stronger. His customary position as reviewer of operatic productions, and his professional immersion in the theatrical world, may explain his incomprehension when faced with challenging instrumental music. Repeatedly, he recommended drawing back from Beethoven; in a spectacularly late expression of such conservative sentiments, he praised the Haydnesque qualities of Gounod's Second Symphony in E-flat written *c*. 1850:

Above all, we congratulate Gounod for having the good sense to compose symphonies, and for not wanting to go beyond Beethoven; for having understood that beyond him there lay an abyss, and that it was better to retreat slightly towards Haydn and Mozart, than to push onward and lose himself in outer space. (*RGM* XXIII/6: 10 Feb. 1856, 42)[3]

With the succession of Adolphe Botte to Blanchard's post in 1858, the conservative tradition continued, though Botte's fear of a Wagnerian musical future led him to concentrate on denouncing Schumann's supposed Wagnerism and positing Mendelssohn's response to Beethoven as the true way forward.

Both Monnais and Blanchard sought a *juste milieu* which would shed new light on essentially Beethovenian procedures. Such a view reinforced the journal's image as pro-Beethoven – particularly, in Blanchard's case, given that the revelation of the late quartets was still a recent experience – but it rejected outright experiment. Just as a reviewer for the *Tablettes* had warned against the emulation of Mozart in 1810, so Blanchard stated categorically that Beethoven's late quartet style should remain unique (*RGM* XX/10: 6 Mar. 1853, 82). His view linked him closely with Fétis, whose article, 'Des dernières transformations de la symphonie', viewed the dramatic symphonies of Berlioz, Douay and David as aberrations, specifically because of their descendancy from the Ninth (*RGM* XIV/19–27: 9 May – 4 Jul. 1847). The Ninth, in Fétis's view, had already taken programmaticism too far. That Blanchard's conception of renewal, echoed

---

[2] 'Les péchés mignons du romantisme en musique sont le mépris de la fugue, une antipathie bien prononcée contre le rhythme, une horreur du simple, un besoin incessant de tourmenter la mélodie, d'employer une luxueuse instrumentation, et la nécessité de donner à ses auditoires un programme explicatif de sa pensée, qu'il ne formule jamais d'une manière claire, parce que le plus souvent elle n'existe pas' (*RGM* VIII/41: 11 Jul. 1841, 337–8).

[3] 'Ce dont nous félicitons surtout Gounod, c'est d'avoir le bon esprit de faire des symphonies et de ne pas vouloir aller plus loin que Beethoven; c'est d'avoir compris qu'au delà c'était l'abîme, et que mieux valait rétrograder un peu, en se rapprochant d'Haydn et de Mozart, que marcher en avant et se perdre dans l'espace' (*RGM* XXIII/6: 10 Feb. 1856, 42).

later by Botte, was purely cosmetic, is shown in the following extract from a review of Czerny's Symphony in C minor Op. 780. Blanchard's terminology is taken from Cousin, though doubtless via Fétis:

Between this [Czerny's] imitation of fine models and the fantastic, the strange, the bizarre, which those who use them regard as the stuff of novelty, there is ... a *juste milieu*. This eclecticism comprises novelty of motif, a working-out of these motifs which is at once elegant and learned, and the use of all the fullness of modern instrumentation with which many composers are now familiar. (*RGM* XII/38: 21 Sep. 1845, 310)[4]

He detected such renewal in Mazas's Duos for two violins, highlighting the authority of 'carrure': 'this attempt at a renewal of form, which has nothing of Romantic extravagance, and in no way breaks with the regularity of either phrase structure or metre, deserves encouragement' (*RGM* V/37: 16 Sep. 1838, 374).[5] The premise of much of Blanchard's writing, as of Monnais's and Botte's, was that established forms had immutable status to which composers were required to show due respect. Those who did not, were, by definition, either arrogant, destructive iconoclasts, or incompetent dreamers. Such views conform to the Fétisian aesthetic of genius (derived from Schelling and Cousin) whereby innovation worked slowly under its own momentum through a particular composer, who might thus be termed a revolutionary *malgré lui*. In the pages of the *Gazette*, Berlioz loomed as the glaring exception to a concept which outlawed, at various stages of their careers, Schumann, Liszt, Wagner, D'Indy and Franck.

The impetus for the *Gazette*'s prevalent view of the future of instrumental music stemmed, almost inevitably, from Fétis, and was reinforced by his numerous essays, written over thirty years, on the contemporary state of composition and possible means of arresting its degeneration.[6]

---

[4] 'Entre cette manière imitative des beaux modèles et le fantasque, l'étrange, le bizarre que ceux qui les emploient prennent seuls pour de l'originalité, il existe ... un juste milieu. Cet éclecticisme consiste dans la nouveauté des motifs, le travail tout à la fois élégant et scientifique de ces motifs, et l'emploi de toutes les richesses de l'instrumentation moderne que beaucoup de compositeurs connaissent maintenant au mieux' (*RGM* XII/38: 21 Sep. 1845, 310).

[5] 'Cette tentative d'un renouvellement dans la forme, qui n'a rien de l'extravagance romantique, et qui ne brise en aucune manière ni la carrure, ni le rhythme, mérite d'être encouragée' (*RGM* V/37: 16 Sep. 1838, 374).

[6] The most important of these are: 'Dangers de la situation actuelle de la musique dramatique. Causes du mal. – Moyens de régénération' (*RGM* XII/1–13: 5 Jan. – 30 Mar. 1845); 'De la crise du goût en musique' (*RGM* XIII/1–3: 4–18 Jan. 1846); 'Des dernières transformations de la symphonie' (*RGM* XIV/19–27: 9 May – 4 Jul. 1847); 'Lettres aux compositeurs dramatiques' (*RGM* XX/47–XXI/2: 20 Nov. 1853 – 9 Jan. 1854); 'Effets des circonstances sur la situation actuelle de la musique, au point de vue de la composition. Ce qu'il faudrait faire pour améliorer cette situation' (*RGM* XXX/32–44: 9 Aug. – 1 Nov. 1863).

The excessively reverential tone of reviews of Fétis's compositions reveal much about the attitude of the *Gazette*'s contributors. Adolphe Botte's reviews are particularly interesting for their practice of judging Fétis in the language of his own antipathy to Wagner and his prescriptions for eclecticism. Each contains blatant intellectual flattery, using the poetic imagery of the 'critique admirative' style, and complimenting the composer for practising the clarity of structure he preached. Botte's review of the *Grand sextuor* is typical: 'Here ... we have main key areas: we know where we have been, where we are, and if we do not know where we are going, it is because the composer is too skilled to deny himself the charm of the unexpected' (*RGM* XXXII/1: 1 Jan. 1865, 5).[7] Botte continues by stressing Fétis's innocence with regard to a Wagnerian *bête noire*, 'these eternally *inconclusive cadences* which, always delaying what the composer seems to imply, produce, under the pretext of novelty, the monotony of surprise' (*ibid.*).[8] Botte's reference to 'l'inattendu' immediately recalls Fétis's writings on Mozart; his oxymoron – 'la monotonie de la surprise' – recalls Fétis's antipathy towards late Beethoven and Botte's own critiques of both late Beethoven and Schumann. Such reviews strengthen Fétis's image as the critical guiding light of the journal, despite his absence from Paris, and, by presenting him as a creative artist, underline his right to judge the work of others.

Virtuosity and the concerto

Larger genres offered the journal's critics the opportunity to promote their ideal of serious composition without appearing unduly conservative. Heller's description of Beethoven's Fifth Piano Concerto as a 'symphony with obbligato piano' (*RGM* XI/15: 14 Apr. 1844, 131)[9] holds the key to the *Gazette*'s concerto reviewing, which emphatically demanded that the concerto or concert piece with orchestra should be more than a loosely connected series of bravura passages, sparsely accompanied with little thought to orchestral technique. Such arguments underpinned the *Gazette*'s support for the *Concertos symphoniques* of Henri Litolff and Anton Rubinstein, and, later, Brahms's First Piano Concerto. The newer concept of the concerto can be traced to

[7] 'Ici ... il y a des tons principaux: on sait d'où l'on vient, où l'on est, et si l'on ne sait pas où l'on va, c'est que le compositeur est trop savant pour se refuser le charme de l'inattendu' (*RGM* XXXII/1: 1 Jan. 1865, 5).

[8] 'ces éternelles *cadences évitées* qui, différant toujours ce que semble promettre le compositeur, arrivent, sous prétexte de nouveauté, à la monotonie de la surprise' (*ibid.*). Botte had accused Schumann of exactly this six years earlier (*RGM* XXVI/7: 13 Feb. 1859, 51).

[9] 'symphonie avec piano obligé' (Heller, *RGM* XI/15: 14 Apr. 1844, 131).

Hoffmann's *Kreisleriana*, in which the author makes a distinction between technical piano concertos and those which are poetic and symphonic.[10] However, opportunities for the performance of symphonic concertos in Paris were limited. Traditions of programming at the Conservatoire militated against acceptance of the symphonic model, instead favouring the use of solo items as light relief from orchestral Beethoven. Often such solo items took the form of short, orchestrally accompanied, variation sets played by their composer. Despite the prominence of Beethoven's symphonies and overtures, performance of his concertos was the exception rather than the rule.[11] However, the hold of the virtuoso-composer weakened considerably during the nineteenth century; indeed, the concept of the virtuoso shifted away from that of the virtuoso-composer towards that of the virtuoso-interpreter, for whom breadth of repertoire was a defining characteristic. The sudden influx of instrumentalists playing classic works with established chamber societies in the 1850s forms part of this phenomenon.[12]

The earlier view of the virtuoso is seen in Blanchard's review of Vieuxtemps's First Concerto Op. 10, where the young violinist is set above his competitors specifically because, 'like Viotti and Kreutzer, he is a true violinist-composer' (*RGM* VIII/5: 21 Feb. 1841, 118).[13] Equally, an inability to compose well could jeopardise a performer's reputation, as in the case of Ole Bull, of whom Blanchard was scathing:

M. Ole-Bull is not yet on the same plane as Paganini. First of all, we would encourage M. Ole-Bull to take stock of this truth: that in order to be a famous violinist one must study composition seriously and be able to write extended and fine works. (*RGM* VII/13: 13 Feb. 1840, 107)[14]

In 1843, Blanchard's review of Camillo Sivori's performance of his Violin Concerto no. 2 in A major merely described the technical demands of each solo passage, a tactic he used for concertos which were essentially repetitions of the Viotti model (*RGM* X/10: 5 Mar. 1843, 82). There is no indication of censure, but Blanchard's rapturous reception of Vieuxtemps's Second Concerto as the rejuvenation of an ossifying tradition, sets his

---

[10] See E.T.A. Hoffmann, *E.T.A. Hoffmann's Musical Writings: Kreisleriana, The Poet and the Composer, Music Criticism*, trans. Martyn Clarke, ed. David Charlton (Cambridge, 1989), 101.

[11] This is what makes the young Louise Mattmann's insistence on playing Beethoven in 1844 so extraordinary (See above, Chapter 5).

[12] See Chapters 3–5.

[13] 'comme Viotti et Kreutzer, il est réellement violoniste-compositeur' (*RGM* VIII/15: 21 Feb. 1841, 118).

[14] 'M. Ole-Bull n'est pas encore sur la même ligne que Paganini. Et d'abord, nous engageons M. Ole-Bull à se pénétrer de cette vérité, que pour être un violoniste célèbre il faut travailler sérieusement la composition et savoir écrire de larges et beaux ouvrages' (*RGM* VII/13: 13 Feb. 1840, 107).

earlier reviews in perspective (*RGM* XV/32: 6 Aug. 1848, 241). In the last quarter of the century, critical priorities were reversed: in 1875, Bannelier withheld the accolade 'artist' from the cellist Joseph Servais until he had proved his merit with classic as well as virtuoso works (?Bannelier, *RGM* XLII/9: 28 Feb. 1875, 69). Three years later, when Sivori played an unspecified concert piece at Pasdeloup's Concerts Populaires, Bannelier frowned upon his compositional style, calling it an 'improbable accumulation of difficulties *à la* Paganini spicing up a formal plan *à la* Viotti' (?Bannelier, *RGM* XLV/6: 10 Feb. 1878, 45).[15] This did not, however, prevent Sivori securing one of the most enthusiastic ovations of the season.

The *Gazette*'s judgements about the value of the nineteenth-century virtuoso composer invariably focused on the tension between pure virtuosity and musical import. The ideal concept of the concerto which emerged in the *Gazette* centred not on form specifically, but on the presence of equality and dialogue between the solo instrument and the orchestra. This is apparent as early as Blanchard's review of Vieuxtemps's First Concerto, in which he complimented the composer, because: 'the orchestra plays an essential, dramatic and vivid rôle' (*RGM* VIII/15: 21 Feb. 1841, 118).[16] The same ideal was stressed in a review comparing the Seventh Concerto Op. 76 by De Bériot with Ernst's *Concerto pathétique* in F-sharp minor Op. 23, where Blanchard referred to Vieuxtemps as the most symphonic among violinist-composers (*RGM* XVIII/31: 3 Aug. 1851, 253–4). However, in 1862, Botte observed that Vieuxtemps's procedure, as shown in a concerto in A minor (probably Op. 37, the 'Grétry'), was insufficiently developmental, and that it gave showmanship unacceptable priority over musical content (*RGM* XXIX/49: 7 Dec. 1862, 394). His conclusion may have been informed by new movements in the pianistic world, where Anton Rubinstein's concertos and works bearing the new genre label of 'concerto symphonique' were interpreted by the *Gazette*'s critics as indicating a move towards the fusion of virtuosity with large-scale symphonic thought and strong emotional content. It is no coincidence that Henri Litolff's reappearance in Paris (after an absence of over a decade) was greeted enthusiastically with cries of Beethovenian ardour. Monnais, reviewing his *Concerto symphonique* no. 4 Op. 102 declared that in it 'the composer had absorbed the virtuoso, although the latter had gained, rather than lost, in power' (*RGM* XXV/8: 21 Feb. 1858, 59).[17] Monnais's move away

---

[15] 'invraisemblable accumulation de difficultés à la Paganini accidentant un canevas à la Viotti' (?Bannelier, *RGM* XLV/6: 10 Feb. 1878, 45).

[16] 'l'orchestre joue un rôle essentiel, dramatique, coloré' (*RGM* VIII/15: 21 Feb. 1841, 118).

[17] 'le compositeur avait absorbé le virtuose, quoique ce dernier eût plutôt gagné que perdu en puissance' (*RGM* XXV/8: 21 Feb. 1858, 59).

from lauding virtuosity for its own sake is important; moreover, he agreed with an earlier article by Berthold Damcke (*RGM* XXV/6: 7 Feb. 1858) that Litolff's developmental procedure stemmed squarely from middle-period Beethoven. No greater recommendation could have been desired.

Schumann and Brahms

In the 1870s, Bannelier's unsigned reviews of Schumann's Cello Concerto (given its Paris première by **Henri Poëncet**) and Brahms's First Piano Concerto (premièred by Wilhelmine Szarvády) drew the balance of the *Gazette*'s criticism still further towards the orchestra and towards a brand of artistic élitism akin to that of its early years. Bannelier praised Poëncet's humility for playing a work which is 'too symphonic and lacking in brilliance for most performers to lay claim to it' (?Bannelier, *RGM* XXXVII/16: 17 Apr. 1870, 124–5).[18] Three reviews of the Brahms concentrate on the work's symphonic, Beethovenian nature, the ungrateful difficulty of its solo part (requiring the self-effacement of the virtuoso), and its unpopularity with audiences. The first article calls the work 'almost a symphony with solo piano' and finds the outer movements inspired by Beethoven, the central Adagio (which Bannelier calls the Andante) inspired by Mozart (?Bannelier, *RGM* XLIII/15: 9 Apr. 1876, 118);[19] the second concentrates on the soloist's rôle:

In no way does this greater fusion within the whole result in a weakening of the soloist's rôle; on the contrary, if this rôle loses something in the way of brilliance, it is much more difficult to play well, and of a more elevated musical interest than the technical feats which are the essence of the non-symphonic concerto. (?Bannelier, *RGM* XLIII/20: 14 May 1876, 158)[20]

After Szarvády's first performance of the work at the Châtelet concert series, Bannelier claimed: 'artists will always take an interest in this concerto; the ordinary public ... does not seem disposed to adopt it' (?Bannelier, *RGM* XLVI/44: 2 Nov. 1879, 359).[21] Regarding both Brahms and Schumann, Bannelier was echoing Maurice Bourges's ideas

[18] 'trop symphonique et trop peu brillante pour que la généralité des exécutants y jette son dévolu' (?Bannelier, *RGM* XXXVII/16: 17 Apr. 1870, 124–5).

[19] 'presque une symphonie avec piano principal' (?Bannelier, *RGM* XLIII/15: 9 Apr. 1876, 118).

[20] 'Il ne résulte en aucune façon, de cette fusion plus grande dans l'ensemble un amoindrissement du rôle de l'exécutant; au contraire, ce rôle, s'il perd quelque chose du côté de l'éclat, est beaucoup plus difficile à bien tenir et d'un plus haut intérêt musical que dans les hauts faits de mécanisme qui sont l'essence du concerto non symphonique' (?Bannelier, *RGM* XLIII/20: 14 May 1876, 158).

[21] 'Les artistes s'intéresseront toujours à ce concerto; le public ordinaire ... ne paraît pas disposé à l'adopter' (?Bannelier, *RGM* XLVI/44: 2 Nov. 1879, 359).

on Beethoven's concertos, articulated as early as 1848. Bourges had noted that the non-soloistic nature of Beethoven's Fourth Piano Concerto made particular demands on the pianist:

In general, this concerto is not the most favourable to the virtuoso's personal success. Passages brusquely cut off, sudden interruptions by the orchestra often turn public attention away from the pianist, and somehow deny him applause to the benefit of the ensemble. Only a true artist can accept such unpropitious circumstances without being disadvantaged. (*RGM* XV/6: 6 Feb. 1848, 42)[22]

Schumann's music came to prominence in Paris only after his death. Both Adolphe Botte and Edouard Monnais viewed him as a Wagnerite (an opinion Bannelier was later at pains to dispel) and thus a prime representative both of musical decadence in Germany and of arrogant, self-styled genius. Fauquet, citing the example of Scudo, explains the case against Wagner and Schumann as resting on two objections: their perceived obscurity of style and their lack of melodic gift.[23] The problem is more complex: the *Gazette*'s critics had a significantly longer list of grievances against Schumann, but applied them only to orchestral and chamber music, leaving the piano works and songs as models of concision, clarity and effortless inspiration against which to pitch the later works. For these, Botte and Monnais showed little mercy until forced into submission by public opinion. The ability to compose with effortless inspiration, closely related to the ability to conceal art, was yet another influential ideal of genius to which Fétis's followers subscribed, and by whose standards composers as disparate as Schumann and D'Indy suffered. Firstly, Schumann was charged with an incapacity for such spontaneity, and a propensity for excessively academic writing which was not altogether successful. Botte berated the Piano Quintet's finale:

where a constant preoccupation with technique, where the prolixity of imitation, where the fugal style, treated with some hesitation, betrays a pen unaccustomed to the elegance and skilled part-writing of counterpoint. (*RGM* XXIX/12: 23 Mar. 1862, 96)[24]

Similarly, in 1865 Monnais found the overture to *Genoveva* 'poor and wretched; one can feel the labour in it, the will, but not inspiration and

---

22 'En général, ce concerto n'est pas le plus favorable au succès personnel du virtuose. Les périodes brusquement tranchées, les interruptions subites de l'orchestre détournent souvent du pianiste l'attention publique et lui valent en quelque sorte l'applaudissement au profit de l'ensemble. Il n'y a qu'un véritable artiste qui puisse accepter sans désavantage ces chances peu propices' (*RGM* XV/6: 6 Feb. 1848, 42).

23 See Fauquet, *Les Sociétés de musique de chambre*, 164.

24 'où une constante préoccupation de science, où la prolixité des imitations, où le style fugué, manié avec une certaine hésitation, trahit une plume peu accoutumée aux élégances et aux savantes combinaisons du contre-point' (*RGM* XXIX/12: 23 Mar. 1862, 96).

genius' (*RGM* XXXII/46: 12 Nov. 1865, 370);[25] he commented similarly after the Paris première of the 'Rhenish' Symphony in 1857 (*RGM* XXIV/4: 25 Jan. 1857, 26). The contrast with Botte's opinion of two unspecified *Lieder*, sung at the same concert as the performance of the Piano Quintet cited above, is stark. Here, 'the melody ... is distinguished, expressive and dreamy; its accompaniment is truly exquisite' (*RGM* XXIX/12: 23 Mar. 1862, 96).[26] Two weeks later, after Clara Schumann's second Paris concert, Botte set up a similar comparison between one of the violin sonatas (he does not indicate which) and *Carnaval* (*RGM* XXIX/14: 6 Apr. 1862, 116). The fracture lines of Schumann's acceptance among conservatives thus run parallel to those of Schubert: the miniaturist is elevated at the expense of the large-scale composer. Both Monnais and Botte also detected links between Schumann and Beethoven: Schumann's late works were frequently discredited as the products of an unhealthy genius who had produced much of note in earlier life (Blanchard, *RGM* XXIII/2: 13 Jan. 1856, 11); Monnais's obituary of 1856 portrayed him as a misguided dreamer attempting, in madness, to push music farther than its nature could permit (*RGM* XXIII/39: 28 Sep. 1856, 313–14).

Signs of a rehabilitation of Schumann's posthumous reputation in the journal appear only in 1865, after the Paris première of the Piano Concerto played by Saint-Saëns. Maurice Germa (writing as Cristal) accused Parisians of listening to it with prejudiced ears, and, in his assessment of the work, emphasised positive aspects whilst avoiding an uncritically admiring stance:

> The musical idea is presented with clarity, its development is attractive, the main theme's return is always prepared with originality, and if the general character is too agitated and disjointed, one cannot justifiably accuse it of monotony or timidity. (*RGM* XXXII/5: 29 Jan. 1865, 35)[27]

Whilst Bannelier, in a report of Alfred Jaëll's performance of the work the following year, found the structure of the piece too repetitious – two fast movements each with a slower introduction (?Bannelier, *RGM* XXXIII/15: 15 Apr. 1866, 118) – by 1877 it had achieved classic status in the repertoire alongside the Piano Quintet: 'With a hallowed work such as that, there is nothing more to be said' (?Bannelier, *RGM* XLIV/4: 28

25 'pauvre et triste, on y sent le travail, la volonté, mais non l'inspiration et le génie' (*RGM* XXXII/46: 12 Nov. 1865, 370).

26 'La mélodie ... est distinguée, expressive et rêveuse; l'accompagnement en est réellement exquis' (*RGM* XXIX/12: 23 Mar. 1862, 96).

27 'L'idée musicale est exposée avec clarté, les développements en sont attrayants, le retour de l'idée principale est toujours originalement préparé, et si l'allure générale a trop d'agitation et de soubresauts, on ne peut moins l'accuser ni de monotonie ni de timidité' (*RGM* XXXII/5: 29 Jan. 1865, 35).

Jan. 1877, 30).[28] Bannelier's late concert reviews consistently overturned the judgements of Botte and Monnais in the 1850s and 1860s regarding the chamber and the orchestral works, also defending the Third and Fourth Symphonies on their introduction to the public. After a stormy reception of the latter, Bannelier criticised a portion of the audience at Pasdeloup's Concerts Populaires, who:

on principle, evidently, believed themselves duty bound to shout disapproval last Sunday after the first movement of Schumann's Symphony in D minor. Such people always equate Schumann with Wagner, and their musical education seems far from complete. (signed, *RGM* XL/43: 26 Oct. 1873, 341)[29]

His wish that Schumann be given a fair hearing meant that conductors who made compromises in the name of promoting his works also risked attack. When Colonne programmed the 'Rhenish' without its finale, Bannelier complained of 'mutilation' and infidelity to the composer's intention:

The majority of Schumann's works are characterised by a cohesion, a unity of thought which means that they cannot be dismembered. Perhaps this unity is often overworked and too strictly imposed; none the less it is one of the principal features of the master's work. (?Bannelier, *RGM* XLII/9: 28 Feb. 1875, 69)[30]

Adolphe Jullien was similarly appalled at Pasdeloup's cuts in his supposedly complete performance of *Faust* in 1880 (*RGM* XLVII/10: 7 Mar. 1880, 74). Whilst Bannelier's reviews of Schumann's work reveal fairness of judgement, he was not committed to the composer in the manner of Jullien, instead detaching himself slightly from the music. It is, therefore, ironic that the composer whose ideals were so closely united with those of the *Gazette* in its years of Romanticism, and who, on the basis of the review of piano music signed by Liszt in 1837 seemed set for stardom in the journal (*RGM* IV/46: 12 Nov. 1837), should have been so tardily accepted.

In 1874, Adolphe Jullien introduced the *Gazette*'s readers to a composer whom he presented as Schumann's successor: Johannes Brahms. His music review of the cantata *Rinaldo* stressed Brahms's

[28] 'D'une œuvre consacrée comme celle-là, il n'y a plus rien à dire' (?Bannelier, *RGM* XLIV/4: 28 Jan. 1877, 30).
[29] 'qui a cru devoir, dimanche dernier, par principe évidemment, *chuter* après le premier morceau de la symphonie en *ré mineur* de Schumann. Ceux-là en sont toujours à l'assimilation Schumann–Wagner, et leur éducation musicale ne paraît pas près d'être terminée' (signed, *RGM* XL/43: 26 Oct. 1873, 341).
[30] 'La plupart des œuvres de Schumann se font remarquer par une cohésion, une unité de pensée qui fait qu'on ne peut les démembrer. Cette unité est souvent trop cherchée peut-être et trop voulue; elle n'en est pas moins un des principaux caractères de l'œuvre du maître' (?Bannelier, *RGM* XLII/9: 28 Feb. 1875, 69).

originality and his proven success in every major genre except opera (*RGM* XLI/52: 27 Dec. 1874). However, as Bannelier's reviews of the First Piano Concerto suggest, public acceptance of Brahms was not immediate. In 1875, the Serenade in D Op. 11 was coldly received, and Bannelier made a distinction between the quality of Brahms's orchestral and chamber works:

On the strength of what we know of him in France, Brahms does not seem to merit ranking among the masters of the orchestra; he is far superior in the realm of chamber music. The Serenade received a rather cool reception. (?Bannelier, *RGM* XLII/3: 17 Jan. 1875, 22)[31]

Bannelier was supportive of Brahms's music, though he detected rather too much asceticism in it.[32] Despite his evident respect for Hanslick, his reviews neither showed overt partisanship nor located Brahms's music within the rivalries which divided musical Vienna; indeed, on the level of musical style, he never even made an explicit distinction between Brahms's autonomous music on the one hand, and the programmaticism of the New Germans on the other. In April 1880, he welcomed a concert devoted entirely to Brahms's chamber music and songs organised by the pianist Mme Français at the Salle Pleyel, and dubbed it 'a real act of artistic courage' (?Bannelier, *RGM* XLVII/15: 11 Apr. 1880, 118).[33] The concert included the Violin Sonata and Piano Quartet in A major, two songs and the Piano Sonata Op. 2 in F-sharp minor, of whose merits Bannelier was unconvinced, since he found its developmental sections too laboured. His reaction is unsurprising given the Lisztian character of the work, and his positive response to the enterprise contrasts sharply with his reception of Félix Lottin's Liszt series of the previous year.

Bannelier's final appreciation of Brahms's music brought his style close to a *juste milieu* ideal to which Bannelier himself did not subscribe:

Brahms's Second Symphony, with which M. Pasdeloup opened the sixth Concert Populaire, remains the very considerable work of a man of talent who handles the Classical form admirably and is even able to extend and modernise it; however, just as at its first performance, it left the impression of being no more than a pleasant and deeply felt work. Superior in small pieces, in chamber music,

---

[31] 'Brahms ne semble pas, au moins d'après ce qu'on connaît de lui en France, devoir prendre rang parmi les maîtres d'orchestre; il est de beaucoup supérieur dans la musique de chambre. La Sérénade n'a reçu qu'un accueil assez froid (?Bannelier, *RGM* XLII/3: 17 Jan. 1875, 22).

[32] Cf. an unsigned review of the Piano Quartet in A major Op. 26 which he was pleased to find lacked any hint of 'sécheresse' (?Bannelier, *RGM* XLIV/8: 25 Feb. 1877, 62).

[33] 'un véritable acte de courage artistique' (?Bannelier, *RGM* XLVII/15: 11 Apr. 1880, 118). Nothing is known about Mme Français.

Brahms seems entirely lacking in the gift of symphonic composition. (?Bannelier, *RGM* XLVII/48: 28 Nov. 1880, 383)[34]

Bannelier's reception of Brahms invites comparison with that of Botte and Monnais writing on Schubert and Schumann: he sees Brahms as a master of the smaller forms and disparages his ability in larger genres, whilst emphasising his formal traditionalism and, by implication, his Beethovenian ancestry. In reviews of the First Piano Concerto, the link with Beethoven is made explicit (?Bannelier, *RGM* XLIII/15 and 20: 9 Apr. and 14 May 1876). Bannelier never used the term *juste milieu*, which was thoroughly outdated by the time he began his critical career; nevertheless, his vision of contemporary music was entirely compatible with the concept as used by Blanchard in the 1840s. Seen in the context of the journal's intellectual history, Bannelier's comments on Brahms's handling of form represent the continuation of a long-established wish for instrumental music to develop from middle-period Beethoven but to remain within recognisable formal bounds. Yet Bannelier is uncertain about Brahms's merit for reasons identical to those of Bourges and Fétis regarding Mendelssohn in the 1840s: he senses talent where he would like to find genius. With hindsight, it is difficult not to see in Mendelssohn and Brahms the most sophisticated expression of the *juste milieu* for which the *Gazette*'s Fétisian critics had longed. Yet neither composer was accepted and applauded unreservedly because they were perceived as lacking precisely the element of audacity which the *juste milieu* explicitly rejected. Ultimately, the post-Beethovenian *juste milieu* was an elusive ideal.

The problem of programme music

As much on aesthetic as on stylistic grounds, programme music divided the *Gazette*'s critics. The brief flowering in France of the Dramatic or Ode Symphony in the hands of Emile Douay, Félicien David and Louis Lacombe, received a mixed reception ranging from delight (at the appearance of a long-awaited complement to Berlioz), to the condemnation of all programme music. Fétis contributed the most decisive condemnation in the final instalment of his 'Dernières transformations de la symphonie' (*RGM* XIV/19–27: 9 May – 4 Jul. 1847). He wrote of

---

[34] 'La symphonie en *ré* de Brahms, que M. Pasdeloup a fait entendre au début du sixième concert populaire, reste le travail fort remarquable d'un homme de talent qui manie admirablement la forme classique et sait même lui donner de l'extension et la moderniser; mais, pas plus qu'à la première audition, elle n'a laissé [que] l'impression d'une œuvre géniale et profondément sentie. Brahms, supérieur dans les petites pièces, dans la musique de chambre, ne semble décidément point doué pour la symphonie' (?Bannelier, *RGM* XLVII/48: 28 Nov. 1880, 383).

Berlioz as composing dramatic music for orchestra under the misnomers of symphonies and overtures; the use of such designations for anything but an 'orchestral sonata' was anathema to him (*RGM* XIV/27: 4 Jul. 1847, 218).[35] Moreover, he suggested that programmatic composers chose their genre as a retreat from the greater demands of both dramatic and autonomous music. The descriptive composer, an avid lover of effects, lacked the sustained inspiration demanded by drama, and therefore preferred to restrict himself to 'a succession of musical tableaux whose duration is limited only by the composer's imagination' (*ibid.*, 218–19).[36] Such formalism was advanced with equal aesthetic conviction by Charles Bannelier in the 1860s and 1870s. However, the undeniable success of Félicien David's *Le Désert* in 1844 showed the Berliozian side of the journal's criticism.

Bourges, welcoming *Le Désert* after its première, recalls Schumann's famous 'Hats off, gentlemen, a genius!' to herald Chopin's Op. 2:

Make way, gentlemen, make way I say! Open ranks; move aside. Make way again, give me some room! For here's the news: Unto us is born a great composer, a man of singular power, extraordinary temper, one of those very rare talents who without warning holds an entire hall spellbound, who imperiously shakes it to its roots, who masters it, who wrenches cries of enthusiasm from it and secures an astonishing degree of popularity in under two hours. (*RGM* XI/50: 15 Dec. 1844, 413)[37]

Bourges was wary of claiming that David had eclipsed all who preceded him, since to adopt such a stance would be to betray Berlioz.[38] Nevertheless, he hoped that David's success indicated a bright future for French instrumental music, and there are no signs of aesthetic displeasure at the composer's use of descriptive techniques. Whilst not sharing Bourges's enthusiasm for David, Blanchard wrote an encouraging review of Lacombe's *Manfred*, though he sidestepped the main aesthetic issue by concentrating on the work's delicate (and thus acceptable) Romanticism (*RGM* XIV/13: 28 Mar. 1847, 102–3). By contrast, Gustave Héquet's reviews of David's *Christophe Colomb* ('G. H.', *RGM* XIV/11: 14 Mar.

---

[35] 'sonate d'orchestre' (*RGM* XIV/27: 4 Jul. 1847, 218).

[36] 'une suite de tableaux musicaux, dont la durée n'est limitée que par la fantaisie du compositeur' (*ibid.*, 218–19).

[37] 'Place, messieurs, place, vous dis-je! Ouvrez vos rangs; écartez-vous. Place, encore une fois, et place large et belle! car voici: Un grand compositeur nous est né, un homme d'une singulière puissance, d'une trempe extraordinaire, un de ces talents si rares, qui fascinent tout d'un coup une salle entière, qui la secouent impérieusement, qui la maîtrisent, qui lui arrachent des cris d'enthousiasme et conquièrent en moins de deux heures une étonnante popularité' (*RGM* XI/50: 15 Dec. 1844, 413).

[38] The most prominent periodical making exaggerated claims for David was his publisher's house journal, *La France musicale*. See in particular 'Un Nouveau Génie' (*FM* VII/50: 15 Dec. 1844, 362).

1847) and Douay's *Jeanne* and *La Chasse royale* ('G. H.', *RGM* XIV/15: 11 Apr. 1847) were scathing about the notion of descriptive music. With his customary lack of sophistication, Héquet reduced the concept to absurdity:

Nowadays we have musicians who paint, musicians who narrate, musicians who preach, and we should not be surprised to learn that a musician of the centre-left is at this very moment preparing a symphony on the incompatability of state-paid posts and standing for parliament. (*RGM* XIV/15: 11 Apr. 1847, 121)[39]

As far as the *Gazette*'s critics were concerned, David never equalled *Le Désert*, merely recomposing it in pale imitations such as the disastrous *Moïse au Sinaï* (the review of *RGM* XIII/13: 29 Mar. 1846 is diplomatically signed '***') and the more fortunate *Christophe Colomb*. In the later decades of the century the journal noted the success of further performances but made no attempt to rehabilitate David in the regular repertory, and often referred to the limitations of his talent, a trend set by Edouard Monnais in a review of the oratorio *L'Eden* in 1848: 'This is the second time he has made the mistake of choosing a theme far too robust for the nature of his talent' ('R.', *RGM* XV/35: 27 Aug. 1848, 265).[40] Berlioz, in one of his last articles, found the use of block-chord harmony and the overt simplicity too populist (he did not mention Saint-Simonian music-making) (*RGM* XVI/5: 4 Feb. 1849, 36). By contrast, Blanchard saw this style of word-setting as Handelian – 'in a placid and backward-looking Handelian style' (*RGM* XVI/7: 18 Feb. 1849, 53).[41] In 1855, Blanchard made it clear that David's heyday was over, describing *Christophe Colomb* as merely 'estimable', its composer 'worthy ... conscientious and often inspired (*RGM* XXII/39: 30 Sep. 1855, 299).[42] This performance at the Conservatoire was poorly attended; thereafter, only *Le Désert* showed signs of lasting popularity.

However, the problem of programmatic music arose with greatest vehemence over the Lisztian symphonic poem and the considerable French response to it at the hands of Saint-Saëns, Massenet and D'Indy. In the *Gazette*, the critic most concerned with the symphonic poem's development was Bannelier, for whom its wider context posed a critical dilemma. Bannelier excitedly observed the emergence of a new branch of

---

[39] 'Nous avons aujourd'hui des musiciens qui peignent, des musiciens qui racontent, des musiciens qui prêchent, et nous ne serions pas étonnés d'apprendre qu'un musicien centre gauche prépare en ce moment même une symphonie sur l'incompatibilité des fonctions salariées et de la députation' ('G.H.', *RGM* XIV/15: 11 Apr. 1847, 121).

[40] 'Voici la seconde fois qu'il se trompe en choisissant un thème beaucoup trop fort pour la nature de son talent' ('R.', *RGM* XV/35: 27 Aug. 1848, 265). The first occasion was *Moïse*.

[41] 'en style placide et rétrospectif à la Hændel' (*RGM* XVI/7: 18 Feb. 1849, 53).

[42] 'estimable ... consciencieux et souvent inspiré' (*RGM* XXII/39: 30 Sep. 1855, 299).

French music – the flowering of a long-awaited indigenous school of instrumental composition of which the French could be proud, beginning in the early 1860s and gaining momentum with the foundation of the Société Nationale de Musique in 1871. Yet, as a formalist, he remained opposed to many of its defining characteristics. Bannelier translated Hanslick's *Vom Musikalisch-Schönen* for the *Gazette* ('Ch. B.', *RGM* XLIV/10–28: 11 Mar. – 15 Jul. 1877); moreover, he showed a Fétisian antipathy to materialism in music, believing that attempts at graphic representation deprived music of its essential appeal to the emotions and the imagination.

That the unsigned concert reviews column from 1867 onwards is the work of Charles Bannelier has been argued earlier; evidence within the coverage of new music, particularly that of programme music, further supports this attribution. Bannelier's war against music's conceptualisation was unremitting, and a small number of critical devices appeared regularly. Although few of his signed articles contained subject matter that might reveal an antipathy towards programme music, those that did so advanced arguments wholly consistent with those of unsigned articles. In a music review of Heller's five piano pieces Op. 140 – the *Voyage autour de ma chambre* – Bannelier observed:

Music has no such need of precision: how many works, whose authors believed they had to specify their meaning with care, would benefit from being heard without any particular preoccupation, the soul open to any impression! ('Ch. B.', *RGM* XLIV/10: 11 Mar. 1877, 75)[43]

For Bannelier, instrumental music stood or fell purely on its musical merits; the suitability of that music to its programme was irrelevant when he came to judge a particular piece. His policy with Saint-Saëns's *Le Rouet d'Omphale*, a work whose popularity he could not deny, was invariably to separate its worthlessness as description from its purely musical logic, which he found praiseworthy:

we have already and frequently said, if this piece contains the skill of a master in the art of writing, we do not admit the genre, and so long as we see him producing works such as the *Rouet d'Omphale* and *Phaëton*, we shall repeat that M. Saint-Saëns is on the wrong road. (?Bannelier, *RGM* XLI/10: 8 Mar. 1874, 78)[44]

---

[43] 'La musique n'a pas tant besoin de préciser: combien d'œuvres, dont leurs auteurs ont cru devoir spécifier avec soin la signification, gagneraient à être entendues sans préoccupation aucune, l'âme ouverte à toutes les impressions!' ('Ch. B.', *RGM* XLIV/10: 11 Mar. 1877, 75).

[44] 'nous l'avons déjà dit souvent, s'il y a dans ce morceau le faire d'un maître en l'art d'écrire, nous n'admettons point le genre, et nous répéterons que M. Saint-Saëns fait fausse route, tant que nous lui verrons produire des œuvres comme *le Rouet d'Omphale* et *Phaëton*' (?Bannelier, *RGM* XLI/10: 8 Mar. 1874, 78).

The following year, Bannelier had not changed his opinion:

In terms of absolute music, it is a very charming piece. What a pity that the composer gave it a title which relates to a descriptive programme – unfortunately in the materialistic sense of the word – and that he wished to translate the untranslatable! (?Bannelier, *RGM* XLII/52: 26 Dec. 1875, 415)[45]

And a year later:

The materialistically descriptive leanings of this piece, which we have already lamented, do not prevent us from recognising that it is constructed with the hand of a master and is pretty in effect. (?Bannelier, *RGM* XLIII/10: 5 Mar. 1876, 76)[46]

Bannelier's practice thus consistently upheld the theory that whilst formal coherence and purely musical quality could partially redeem a programmatic piece, looseness of form could not be justified in terms of the programme. A piece which sacrificed form to content was beyond hope. That he felt that the latter was the most likely outcome in any programmatic work is demonstrated in an unsigned review of Saint-Saëns's pioneering concert of Liszt's tone poems and the 'Dante' Symphony in March 1878. Bannelier presented Liszt as forging a new genre which completely rejected Classical and even Romantic ideals, and whose main fault was: 'the indeterminate poetic element which, in this kind of composition, replaces more specific beauties (formal unity, developmental interest) which are essential in a classic work' (?Bannelier, *RGM* XLV/12: 24 Mar. 1878, 94).[47] Bannelier's tendency to suspect the presence of a programme when a work made no formal sense to him followed from his intellectual separation of form and content. The practice itself was Berliozian in nature, though re-interpreted and systematised. Berlioz, too, thought that a programmatic piece should be able to stand alone as autonomous music – his defence of the 'Pastoral' in 1838 comes to mind: 'And by God! if you do not like this programme, if it goes against the grain, irritates you, get rid of it and listen to the symphony as you would listen to autonomous music' (*RGM* V/5: 4 Feb. 1838, 49).[48] Yet

[45] 'Absolument parlant, c'est un bien charmant morceau. Quel dommage que le compositeur y ait attaché un titre qui appelle un programme déscriptif, – malheureusement dans le sens matériel du mot, – et qu'il ait voulu traduire l'intraduisible!' (?Bannelier, *RGM* XLII/52: 26 Dec. 1875, 415).

[46] 'Les tendances matériellement déscriptives de ce morceau, que nous avons déjà regrettées, ne nous empêchent pas de reconnaître qu'il est construit de main de maître et d'un joli effet' (?Bannelier, *RGM* XLIII/10: 5 Mar. 1876, 76).

[47] 'l'élément poétique indéterminé qui, dans ce genre de composition, remplace les beautés d'ordre plus précis (l'unité du plan, l'intérêt du développement) essentielles dans l'œuvre classique' (?Bannelier, *RGM* XLV/12: 24 Mar. 1878, 94).

[48] 'Eh! pour dieu, si ce programme vous déplait, vous contrarie, vous irrite, jettez-le, et écoutez la symphonie comme une musique sans objet déterminé' (*RGM* V/5: 4 Feb. 1838, 49).

Berlioz would never have used the argument to denounce a programmatic work in the manner of Bannelier, because he acknowledged the influence of the programme on the work's shape. Bannelier wilfully separated content and form. Having stripped the work of its programme, he proceeded to judge it as autonomous music; his review of *Danse macabre* gave a detailed description of the piece, only once relating its mood changes to a possible signification intended by the composer (?Bannelier, *RGM* XLII/5: 31 Jan. 1875, 37).

With the music of Vincent d'Indy, Bannelier used other arguments whose truculence may indicate his sense of a lost cause. The view which emerges from his reviews of *La Forêt enchantée* and the Schiller trilogy of symphonic poems – *Piccolomini, La Mort de Wallenstein* and *Le Camp de Wallenstein* – is that the 'bastard genre' of the programme symphony is too lowly for 'a first rate musician' (?Bannelier, *RGM* XLV/19: 12 May 1878, 149).[49] Flattery is used in an attempt to set a talented composer back on the right path – opera. Bannelier thus shows his conviction that the conceptualisation of orchestral music inevitably takes it close to the dramatic, rather than heightening the expression of the symphonic. In 1880 this conviction is expressed even more strongly:

The fact is that the symphonic poem serves only as a kind of distraction for certain composers, prevented by a thousand obstacles from 'hitting the stage'; however, the orchestra will only ever be an unfaithful or limited interpreter of their dramatic aspirations. They should face up to this and take their stand. (?Bannelier, *RGM* XLVII/12: 21 Mar. 1880, 93)[50]

In comparison, the enthusiasm with which Bannelier had welcomed the 'liberty of imagination' of D'Indy's Piano Quartet the previous month is significant (?Bannelier, *RGM* XLVII/6: 8 Feb. 1880, 46).[51]

Running parallel with his reception of the New French School was Bannelier's response to new composition in Russia. In the last three years of the *Gazette*, three writers contributed major articles on Russian music: Camille Benoît reviewed Tchaikovsky's early works up to Op. 30 (*RGM* XLIV/24–5: 17–24 Jun. 1877), César Cui contributed a highly tendentious and partisan history of music in Russia (*RGM* XLV/19–XLVII/40: 12 May 1878 – 3 Oct. 1880), and Bannelier reviewed the Paris premières

---

[49] 'genre bâtard ... un musicien de premier ordre' (?Bannelier, *RGM* XLV/19: 12 May 1878, 149).

[50] 'Le poème symphonique, il est vrai, ne sert que quelque sorte que de dérivatif à certains compositeurs, empêchés par mille obstacles de 'faire du théâtre'; l'orchestre ne sera cependant jamais qu'un infidèle ou insuffisant interprète de leurs aspirations dramatiques, il faut bien qu'ils se le disent et qu'ils en prennent leur parti' (?Bannelier, *RGM* XLVII/12: 21 Mar. 1880, 93).

[51] 'liberté de fantaisie' (?Bannelier, *RGM* XLVII/6: 8 Feb. 1880, 46). The work was not definitively completed until 1888.

of works by (in particular) Tchaikovsky and Rimsky-Korsakov. Cui's article was commissioned – presumably by Bannelier, who was by then the chief editor of the journal – but his attacks on the more Westernised of Russia's composers were such that when he openly refused to discuss a large proportion of Rubinstein's output on the grounds that it was not truly 'Russian', Bannelier was moved to add an editorial footnote dissociating the journal's editors from his views (?Bannelier, *RGM* XLVII/35: 29 Aug. 1880, 273). As a postscript to the article, Bannelier provided an appreciation of Cui's own compositions (signed, *RGM* XLVII/40: 3 Oct. 1880, 314–16). Bannelier's reviews of Rimsky-Korsakov and Tchaikovsky share the hallmarks of his Saint-Saëns criticism. Referring to *Sadko*, which was played at the third of the Russian concerts at the 1878 Exposition universelle, he effected the same separation between its quality as autonomous music and the misguidedness of its programmatically inclined composer:

Apart from its flaw of asking of music what it cannot [give] – the translation of the action of an entire Russian popular legend – this work is not only thought out and composed in masterly fashion, but also imbued with all the poetry of the North. (?Bannelier, *RGM* XLV/49: 29 Sep. 1878, 314)[52]

Reviewing Tchaikovsky's fantasy overture *Romeo and Juliet* and the symphonic fantasia *Francesca da Rimini,* Bannelier's approach was to emphasise their stylistic proximity to the New German School: *Romeo and Juliet* lacked clarity, but showed Tchaikovsky's strength as an orchestrator (*RGM* XLIII/51: 17 Dec. 1876, 406); the first section of *Francesca da Rimini* was totally descriptive 'in the material sense of the word', and reminiscent of Liszt ('C.B.', *RGM* XLV/45: 10 Nov. 1878, 363).[53] Bannelier recognised Tchaikovsky's ability in *Francesca* and *Romeo* to write music which emphasised the purely emotional, but saw such music spoiled by its programmatic context.

Of the Tchaikovsky overtures played in Paris at this time, only his symphonic fantasia *The Tempest* was published by Brandus. Two reviews – one of the score, the other of a performance – illustrate both a cleavage among the *Gazette*'s writers, and the (limited) extent to which Bannelier's criticism was susceptible to compromise in the interests of the publishing house. In the same year that he had complained of *Sadko*'s programmaticism and *Francesca*'s materialism (thus allying himself with the indifferent public response), Bannelier predicted a Berliozian future of

---

[52] 'Cette œuvre, à part le tort qu'elle a de demander à la musique, qui n'en peut mais [sic], la traduction du programme tout entier d'une légende populaire russe, est non-seulement tracée et exécutée de main de maître, mais encore imprégnée de toute la poésie du Nord' (?Bannelier, *RGM* XLV/39: 29 Sep. 1878, 314).

[53] 'dans le sens matériel du mot' ('C.B.', *RGM* XLV/45: 10 Nov. 1878, 363).

late recognition for *The Tempest*, giving it a carefully worded welcome. He found it 'rich in new and bold ideas', and continued: 'We know little "programme music" which has such power of inspiration and which is orchestrated with such intuition for effects' (?Bannelier, *RGM* XLV/38: 22 Sep. 1878, 305).[54] By contrast, Camille Benoît's music review of the piano duet version indicated that he had no qualms about the work's programmatic nature. Benoît was staunchly supportive of the New German School, and attended the first Bayreuth festival.[55] Revelling in *The Tempest*'s expressive programmaticism, he produced a piece of criticism in the narrative, Romantic tradition. At the beginning of the work:

The sea swells, majestic, calm; above the persistent rhythm of the basses is placed a melody for the horns; it dominates the murmur of divided violins, as if the mysterious and grave voice of the waters hovered above the obedient waves: from far off come muffled cries in reply. (*RGM* XLIV/24: 17 Jun. 1877, 189)[56]

The contrast here between the views of Bannelier and Benoît is minimised by the factor of commercial interest. At their extreme, their respective aesthetic positions on programme music were wholly incompatible, as were those of Bannelier and a former contributor – the Wagnerian and champion of the Lisztian symphonic poem, Armand Gouzien. Yet with Benoît, potential conflict within the journal was averted through a fleeting and market-driven *rapprochement* between a supporter of formalism and a supporter of the New German School, to which Tchaikovsky was perceived by supporters of both sides to be allied.

Non-programmatic music of the New French School

It is unsurprising that Bannelier should locate the regeneration of post-war French instrumental music in chamber works and non-programmatic orchestral pieces. More generally, the need for specifically French innovation had been felt as early as 1844: it is implicit both in the generally exaggerated reaction to David's *Le Désert*, which seemed to combine novelty with the accessibility which Berlioz haughtily disdained, and in Bourges's depressed statement of July 1846, soon after the failure of David's *Moïse*, that only dramatic music had potential for innovation:

---

[54] 'riche d'idées, d'effets neufs et hardis. Nous ne connaissons pas beaucoup de "musique à programme" ayant cette puissance de souffle et orchestrée avec cette intuition des effets' (?Bannelier, *RGM* XLV/38: 22 Sep. 1878, 305).

[55] See Albert Lavignac, *Le Voyage artistique à Bayreuth*. 1897, 5th edn (Paris, 1903), 549.

[56] 'La mer se soulève majestueuse, calme; sur le rhythme persistant des basses se pose le chant des cors; il domine le murmure des violons divisés, comme si la voix mystérieuse et grave de l'esprit des eaux planait au-dessus des vagues obéissantes: de lointains [sic], de sourds appels lui répondent' (*RGM* XLIV/24: 17 Jun. 1877, 189).

'since concert music, with all-too-rare exceptions, is producing nothing but pitiable trivialities' (*RGM* XIII/30: 26 Jul. 1846, 236).[57] However, after the Franco-Prussian War, Emile Mathieu de Monter glimpsed signs of change and looked forward to a new symphonic school.

> Must we then despair and mourn over the final invasions of the buffo genre, when we see public opinion moving gradually towards pure music (which lives only by and for itself, creating magic illusions with no outside help) and tasting the purest intellectual joys in these serene regions? The great charm of the Symphony, and its irresistible influence, is to leave ample room for individual interpretation and to make the listener believe for a moment that he thinks and sings, when he only listens. (*RGM* XXXIX/1: 7 Jan. 1872, 3)[58]

Two years later, Bannelier made a similar point, but was able to speak with more confidence of 'an artistic future which would have seemed an impossible dream a few years ago' (signed, *RGM* XLI/1: 4 Jan. 1874, 1).[59]

The roots of this change lie with Franck and Saint-Saëns. Their music, sometimes berated on account of overt Romanticism, was eventually welcomed. Saint-Saëns was the more prominent, partly because of his career as a concert pianist. However, he was always viewed as an uneven composer, whereas once Franck had established a reputation based around a few works, he maintained it. During Botte's years as reviewer, Saint-Saëns lost the ground he had gained with Blanchard, for whom he was one of the few composers of whom the word 'Romantic' could be used in a non-pejorative sense. Botte accused him of Schumannesque writing: cadential retardations, the abuse of dissonance and a lack of emotion, beauty and limpidity (*RGM* XXVII/16: 15 Apr. 1860, 142). Only in Bannelier's reviews did he regain some recognition; the Piano Quintet Op. 14 of 1855, the very work so harshly treated by Botte, was adjudged 'altogether magnificent, especially in its fugal finale' (signed, *RGM* XXXIII/17: 29 Apr. 1866, 130).[60] Bannelier reserved his highest praise for the Piano Quartet in B-flat Op. 41, in which all the qualities he

---

57 'puisque celle de concert, à de trop rares exceptions près, ne vit que de pitoyables trivialités' (*RGM* XIII/30: 26 Jul. 1846, 236).
58 'Faut-il donc se désespérer et broyer du noir, devant les derniers envahissements du genre bouffe, lorsqu'on voit le sentiment public se porter peu à peu vers la musique pure, qui ne vit que d'elle et pour elle, en créant de magiques illusions, sans aucun concours étranger, et goûter en ces régions sereines les plus pures jouissances intellectuelles? Le grand charme de la Symphonie et son influence irrésistible est de laisser une large place à l'interprétation individuelle et de faire croire un moment qu'il pense et qu'il chante à celui qui ne fait qu'écouter' (*RGM* XXXIX/1: 7 Jan. 1872, 3).
59 'un avenir artistique qui nous eût paru, il y a quelques années, une chimère irréalisable' (signed, *RGM* XLI/1: 4 Jan. 1874, 1).
60 'magnifique dans toutes ses parties et surtout dans son finale fugué' (signed, *RGM* XXXIII/17: 29 Apr. 1866, 130).

demanded of a fine chamber work were united: 'this quartet of elevated conception, fine ideas, the greatest skill in development, originality of form and strength of colour' (?Bannelier XLII/11: 14 Mar. 1875, 85).[61] By contrast, he found Saint-Saëns's concertos and solo works uneven, and objected to the mixing of styles in the Fourth Piano Concerto in C minor Op. 44, which was both formally weak and stylistically wilful; 'it is an orchestral fantasy with solo piano rather than a concerto; it even contains purely symphonic music' (?Bannelier, *RGM* XLII/45: 7 Nov. 1875, 358).[62]

During the 1870s the music of Lalo, De Castillon and Massenet gained significant popularity, with Fauré emerging as a significant figure at the end of the decade. Of these, Bannelier viewed De Castillon as a supremely talented débutant, Massenet as a populist composer of orchestral suites, and Lalo as a maturing, serious, artist. The intense passion of Lalo's Cello Sonata in A minor and the exploratory nature of its expressive writing for both cello and piano appealed to him ('C.B.', *RGM* XL/14: 6 Apr. 1873, 108), whilst in 1878 he noted that its 'irreproachable structure enabled the composer's thought to be followed with ease through developments which were at times very complex' (?Bannelier, *RGM* XLV/8: 24 Feb. 1878, 62).[63] Bannelier invariably noted the logicality of Lalo's structural thinking, which he regarded as clarified Schumann;[64] the Violin Concerto Op. 20, *Symphonie espagnole* Op. 21 and Cello Concerto all received his sanction. Of Fauré he was more censorious, partly because of a lack of dynamism in Fauré's style, which he found painfully apparent in fast, traditionally weighty, movements. However, a review in 1878 of the Violin Sonata in A major Op. 13 praised the 'subtle and penetrating fragrance' of its inner movements (?Bannelier, *RGM* XLV/27: 7 Jul. 1878, 214),[65] and he was similarly supportive of the inner movements of the First Piano Quartet Op. 15 (?Bannelier, *RGM* XLVII/21: 23 May 1880, 165). Timidity was a characteristic to which Bannelier could not warm, and he accused Fauré of it in the first movements of both the Piano Quartet and the Violin Concerto Op. 14 (which remained unfinished):

[61] 'ce quatuor d'une conception élevée, d'idées heureuses, d'une extrême habileté dans le développement, avec une originalité de forme et une puissance de couleur' (?Bannelier, *RGM* XLII/11: 14 Mar. 1875, 85).

[62] 'c'est une fantaisie pour orchestre et piano principal bien plus qu'un concerto; on y trouve même le style de la symphonie pure' (?Bannelier, *RGM* XLII/45: 7 Nov. 1875, 358).

[63] 'structure irréprochable permet de suivre sans fatigue la pensée de l'auteur à tracer des développements parfois très-complexes' (?Bannelier, *RGM* XLV/8: 24 Feb. 1878, 62).

[64] See ?Bannelier, *RGM* XLIV/50: 16 Dec. 1877, 398.

[65] 'subtil et pénétrant parfum' (?Bannelier, *RGM* XLV/27: 7 Jul. 1878, 214).

The second movement is as rich in invention, as full of charm and even passion as the first is dull, monotonous and lacking in effect. If the proposed finale is worthy of the slow movement, we advise M. Fauré to rewrite the opening Allegro from scratch. (?Bannelier, *RGM* XLVII/16: 18 Apr. 1880, 125)[66]

Of particular interest here is Bannelier's tacit expectation of a Germanic interpretation of formal balance in the outer movements of a sonata structure. The characteristic *demi-teinte* of Fauré, shared by Chausson, and a major stylistic feature of French music at the turn of the century, was not viewed as a welcome innovation of national style, but an inability to conform to a Germanic standard whose right to supremacy Bannelier seems not to have questioned.

The clearest evidence for regeneration in French instrumental music appeared during the showcase year – 1878 – when concerts of French chamber and orchestral music were arranged as part of the Exposition universelle. The juxtaposition of old and new produced stark contrasts, and set the achievement of the New French School in perspective. Bannelier's column 'Nouvelles musicales de l'exposition', referred explicitly to works of the post-Beethovenian *juste milieu* as historical phenomena. The revered Georges Onslow's Twelfth Quintet, programmed in the opening chamber concert, was the first to be re-evaluated as an historical artefact: 'intrinsically, it is a work of real value, especially if one thinks back to the time when it first appeared' (?Bannelier, *RGM* XLV/23: 9 Jun. 1878, 181).[67] Similarly, Léon Kreutzer's Quartet in D minor, taking inspiration from Beethoven and Boccherini by turns, was 'in places a little backward in style' (?Bannelier, *RGM* XLV/33: 18 Aug. 1878, 260).[68] Bannelier disparaged Reber's Symphony in D minor of 1858; 'without being truly symphonic, [it] could be played as a pretty intermezzo' (?Bannelier, *RGM* XLV/28: 14 Jul. 1878, 221),[69] whilst his scorn for Gouvy and David was unreserved:

M. Gouvy's muse, by turns sentimental or warlike, recalls the semi-Romanticism of the first quarter of the century, which had its day and breathed out its novel fragrance, stale now and for evermore ... Félicien David's 'character-piece quintets' are infantile and interminable; these kinds of miniature landscapes, a

[66] 'Autant le premier est terne, monotone, sans effet, autant le second est riche d'invention, plein de charme et même de passion. Si le finale futur est digne du mouvement lent, nous conseillerons à M. Fauré de refaire en entier le premier allegro' (?Bannelier, *RGM* XLVII/16: 18 Apr. 1880, 125).

[67] 'intrinsèquement, c'est une œuvre de réelle valeur, surtout si on se reporte à la période musicale où elle a paru' (?Bannelier, *RGM* XLV/23: 9 Jun. 1878, 181).

[68] 'un peu rétrograde par le style dans certaines parties' (?Bannelier, *RGM* XLV/33: 18 Aug. 1878, 260).

[69] 'sans être tout à fait symphonique, [elle] pourrait être donné comme un joli intermezzo' (?Bannelier, *RGM* XLV/28: 14 Jul. 1878, 221).

dubious innovation, call neither for great melodic invention, nor for powers of ensemble writing. (*ibid.*, 222)[70]

Criticism of contemporary instrumental and orchestral music in the *Gazette* was relatively untainted by commercial considerations. Much of the discussion, whether of performances or published music, centred on aesthetic issues relating to form and content, revealing the extent to which Fétis's theories pervaded later thought on a wide range of composers. With opera, the financial stakes for any publishing house were considerably higher, and their use of journals to advertise their latest works injected much opera criticism with a sense of polemic sharper even than that found in reviews of piano music. Opera criticism is, in aesthetic terms, the most compromised and inglorious of the discipline's arenas in the nineteenth century.

---

[70] 'la muse de M. Gouvy, tour à tour sentimentale ou guerrière, nous rappelle souvent le demi-romantisme contemporain du premier quart de ce siècle, qui eut son heure de vogue et exhala son parfum de nouveauté, éventé maintenant et pour toujours ... Les *quintettes de genre*, de Félicien David, sont enfantins et interminables; ces sortes de paysages-miniatures, innovation très-contestable, ne demandent ni grande invention mélodique, ni grande force de conception d'ensemble' (*ibid.*, 222).

9   Contemporary music III: Opera

Together with piano music, the sale of vocal scores, separate numbers, and arrangements of popular arias from current operas provided the major source of income for music publishers in nineteenth-century Paris. For any publishing house with its own journal, the criticism of such works was inextricably tied to the business's financial needs. The adulation of house composers and the denigration of those of rival firms became a priority. Despite initial claims to provide its readers with unbiased criticism, the *Gazette* was no exception to this phenomenon; contributors whose opinion ran counter to the party line were forced into ambiguity and evasion in order to avoid a censorious editorial footnote. Among the Schlesinger/Brandus composers, Meyerbeer and Halévy were by far the most revered; their antithesis from the Escudier camp was Verdi, against whom the Brandus brothers waged a critical war which made them worthy successors to the fearless Schlesinger, until critical opinion from within and public acceptance from without forced them to modify the journal's position. This chapter focuses primarily on composers – among them Meyerbeer, Halévy, Verdi, Offenbach and Lecocq – whose receptions best illuminate the problem of critical integrity compromised by commercial interest and rivalry.

Meyerbeer

The most lucrative house composer for Schlesinger and the Brandus brothers was Meyerbeer. Although the *Gazette*'s reviews never degenerated into unsubstantiated eulogy, it is nevertheless clear that he could do no wrong; both Schlesinger and Brandus exploited every opportunity to promote his works, whether large- or small-scale. Yet their task was difficult: although the grand operas remained in the repertory alongside *L'Etoile du Nord* and *Le Pardon de Ploërmel*, Meyerbeer's production rate was slow, and his demands on the various directors of the Opéra were such that a work could take several years to reach the stage. Thus, Schlesinger and later directors of the journal had to fill in the sizeable gaps between new operas with inflated critiques of small pieces, and milk operatic premières to the last drop. The receptions of *Le Prophète* in 1849 and *L'Africaine* in 1865 are cases in point, with preview information to arouse audience curiosity, and numerous follow-up articles and reviews from abroad to prevent interest decreasing in works whose novelty value had diminished.

There are, however, cracks in the journal's support. These are at their most apparent in the early, Romantic years of the journal, during which *Les Huguenots* received its première and became the height of operatic fashion. *Les Huguenots* was, in the most obvious sense, an eclectic opera. Meyerbeer's use of the chorale 'Ein feste Burg' at strategic points constituted more than an exercise in local colour; in particular, the overture, a set of variations on the chorale melody, was a neo-Baroque work. Schlesinger's ideal reviewer would have been Fétis, who had been welcomed officially to the editorial team in January 1836, just two months before the première; however, it was Berlioz, as the journal's most prominent and established reviewer, who wrote articles on *Les Huguenots* (*RGM* III/6: 7 Feb. 1836 and *RGM* III/10–12: 6–20 Mar. 1836). Berlioz was diplomatically evasive in his review for the *Gazette*. His defence of the beginning of Act II, quoted earlier, reads as a sleight of hand;[1] other comments are couched more clearly in Berlioz's 'evasive' manner, not least his remark that the libretto is 'so richly decorated by the musician' (*RGM* III/10: 6 Mar. 1836, 74).[2] Much of the review is lukewarm, conforming to Kerry Murphy's category of 'secondary praise'.[3] Later to become its most famous scene (with the Act IV love duet), the only section of the opera to inspire him to something approaching his poetic 'style admiratif' was the Act IV chorus 'Dieu le veut, Dieu l'ordonne', known as the 'Bénédiction des poignards'. Whilst Berlioz found other scenes, such as the superimposition of three choruses in Act III, praiseworthy, his language was more restrained. Moreover, the article's second and third instalments repeat much of the material of the first, and contain extensive comments on Meyerbeer's instrumentational originality, possibly as a ploy to avoid discussing the music itself.[4] Of

---

[1] See above, p. 29.

[2] 'si richement brodé par le musicien' (*RGM* III/10: 6 Mar. 1836, 74). On the implications of 'broder', see Kerry Murphy, *Hector Berlioz*, 97. Murphy categorises Berlioz's critical language on pp. 152–6.

[3] Murphy, *Hector Berlioz*, 155. Murphy analyses reviews of *Les Huguenots* on pp. 118–33.

[4] Berlioz was genuinely admiring of Meyerbeer's sensitivity to orchestral colour, and included several examples from the operas in his *Grand traité d'instrumentation* of 1843. His first article on Meyerbeer for the *Gazette* was on instrumentation in *Robert-le-diable* (*GM* II/28: 12 Jul. 1835).

Act II and parts of Act V Berlioz is openly censorious. It is significant that the preamble of the three-instalment article is its most rhetorically enthusiastic part, portraying Meyerbeer as a Romantic figure, misunderstood but defiant, and happy for posterity to judge in his favour if the audiences of the present are insufficiently educated to do so.[5] Although the review undoubtedly contains tensions, Berlioz manages to remain consistent with the *Gazette*'s general stance towards Meyerbeer – staunch support in the interests of the publishing house's financial security. He wrote no more Meyerbeer reviews for the *Gazette* (although he reviewed *Le Prophète* for the *Journal des débats*); later grand operas were reviewed in detail by Fétis and Georges Kastner (*Le Prophète*) or Edouard Monnais and Maurice Bourges (*L'Africaine*), all of whom found it easier to be unequivocal in their support.

Particularly anxious to show his allegiance, Fétis was a strong ally to Louis Brandus's cause. An episode of 1847, parts of which remain a mystery, illustrates both Fétis's willingness to have criticisms of Meyerbeer tempered editorially, and Meyerbeer's concern over his image in the *Gazette*. On 18 August, Fétis wrote to Brandus regarding an article which he had just written for the *Gazette*:

Please cast an eye over the paragraph which relates to Meyerbeer: it could be that you have information which conflicts with my ideas, and that these latter are contrary to your interests; in this case, arrange the paragraph as you would wish, so long as I am not made to contradict myself within the article.[6]

Fétis's article undoubtedly contained material which criticised Meyerbeer. On 24 August, Meyerbeer wrote from Franzensbad to his Paris confidant, Louis Gouin:

I am surprised to find the *Revue musicale*, which wants to publish my new works, accepting diatribes against me such as that of Fétis, which you mention in your letter. If the article is indeed as you indicate, Brandus's employee's cutting of

---

[5] Though there may be a sting in the tail, since Berlioz's final comment on Meyerbeer's belief in himself is ambiguous: 'Experience has proved to what extent he was right' ('L'expérience a prouvé jusqu'à quel point il avait raison') (*RGM* III/10: 6 Mar. 1836, 73).

[6] 'Veuillez jetter un coup d'œil sur le paragraphe relatif à Meyerbeer: il se pourrait que vous eussiez des données qui seraient en opposition avec mes idées, et que celles-ci fussent contraires à vos intérêts; dans ce cas, faites arranger le paragraphe comme vous l'entendrez, pourvu qu'on ne me mette pas en contradiction avec moi-même dans le sens de l'article.' Letter of 18 August 1847 from Fétis to Louis Brandus, quoted in Daniel Fryklund, *Contribution à la connaissance de la correspondence de Fétis* (Stockholm, 1930), 7.

eight lines is not enough. He should have stripped out EVERYTHING in there which worked against me. Kindly send me the article when it is printed.[7]

The ensuing sequence of events is not known; however, the *Gazette* contains no article which obviously relates to the above letters, and it is highly likely that Fétis withdrew the piece. Meyerbeer's letter illustrates his close supervision (by proxy) of his reception in the *Gazette* – even before it reached the journal's pages – and suggests that he wielded considerable influence over the journal's criticism; moreover, Fétis's willingness to allow his prose to be altered in accordance with Brandus's (or Meyerbeer's) requirements, provides striking evidence of the extent to which he and Brandus co-operated.

Yet Fétis's championing of Meyerbeer brought its own problems. His review of *Le Prophète* in 1849, accompanied by a lavish number of music examples, constituted a thinly veiled advertisement for the work (*RGM* XVI/16–22: 22 Apr. – 3 Jun. 1849). Yet, despite Fétis's praise for Meyerbeer's reminiscence technique, sense of drama, unerring knack for local colour, wisdom in making Scribe's libretto more musical, and skill in instrumentation, as an exercise in publicity the review is marred by the sheer force of Fétis's personality – in particular, his tone of self-congratulatory vindication as Meyerbeer's first champion in Paris (*RGM* XVI/18: 6 May 1849, 138). Moreover, towards the end of the final instalment, Fétis characteristically refers to his own work as the spark for Meyerbeer's innovation:

In my course of 1832 on the philosophy of music, I said that future transforma-tions of the art lie in the exploration of the immense domain of rhythm, of which we hardly know the first thing: Meyerbeer seems to share my opinion. (*RGM* XVI/22: 3 Jun. 1849, 169)[8]

Far more effective as publicity, and more detailed concerning the dramatic character of the music, was Georges Kastner's analysis of *Le Prophète*'s full score (*RGM* XVII/5–15: 3 Feb. – 14 Apr. 1850). Here, Kastner appears to have suspended his customary reserve (most of his

---

[7] 'Je m'étonne que la revue musicale qui veut éditer mes nouvelles Ouvrages accueille des diatribes contre moi comme celle de Fétis dont Vous me faites mention dans votre lettre. Si l'article est fort comme Vous me le dites, il ne suffit pas que l'associé de Brandus en ait coupé 8 lignes. Il en aurait du élaguer TOUT ce qu'il y était là dedans contre moi. Ayez la bonté de m'envoyer cet article quand il sera imprimé.' Quoted in Heinz and Gudrun Becker, *Giacomo Meyerbeer: Briefwechsel und Tagebücher*, 4 vols. (Berlin, 1960–), IV, 298. The employee to whom Meyerbeer refers is Deschamps d'Hanneucourt, then the *Gazette*'s director.

[8] 'Dans le cours de philosophie de la musique que j'ai fait en 1832, j'ai dit que les transformations de l'art se trouveront dans le rhythme et dans l'exploration de son immense domaine, dont les abords seulement sont connus: Meyerbeer semble partager mon opinion' (*RGM* XVI/22: 3 Jun. 1849, 169).

articles are rather dry music reviews) in a critique which combined detailed analysis with poetic enthusiasm. Two passages are outstanding: his description of a dominant pedal as a symbol of the crowd's increasing discontent in Act I (no. 3), and that of the frustrated D major cadence which accompanies Jean de Leyde's tactical disowning of his mother in Act IV (Finale, section B). In the former, with its initial 'drawing in' of the reader and its fusion of analysis and metaphor, Kastner's style and technique could almost be mistaken for Berlioz:

Listen to these panting notes, this G, this A [A-flat], repeated in lugubrious and monotonous fashion above the ardent and lively semiquaver idea in the cellos, violas and bassoons (p.39). Could it not be said that they sound the toxin of revolt in [the people's] souls? Gradually increasing in volume as the orchestra comes to life, the first of these notes finally establishes its sovereignty within the harmonic totality (p.41). There, it occupies every position: it is at the bottom, in the middle, at the top. Held by the horns in C, the ophicleide, the flute and piccolo; sounded by the timpani and the trumpets, restated, in tremolo, by the violas and the first violins, it has the formidable aspect of a dominant pedal multiplied four, five, six times over five octaves. The G, this terrible G, is the pivot around which popular anger revolves. It is the great voice of the storm which dominates every other voice. (*RGM* XVII/7: 17 Feb. 1850, 54)[9]

The strength of Kastner's description for Brandus's purposes is that it does not preach through hackneyed superlatives; rather, the critic's enthusiasm and admiration for the composer are embedded in its very syntax. In addition to focusing on specifically dramatic moments of the score, Kastner broached more general questions concerning Meyerbeer's style and practice; in particular, he discussed Meyerbeer's facility in historical pastiche – a subject which reappeared in Maurice Bourges's analysis of *L'Africaine* in 1865.

Kastner was a 'theorist-critic'. Bourges, by contrast, was an 'historian-critic', and his historical interest was the major driving force of his analysis of the score of *L'Africaine*, which argued that Meyerbeer's achievement lay in his ability to use a wide variety of styles to dramatic

---

[9] 'Entendez ces notes haletantes, ce *sol*, ce *la*, répétées d'une façon lugubre et monotone sur le dessin ardent et mouvementé en doubles croches des violoncelles, des altos et des bassons (p.39.)[.] Ne dirait-on pas qu'elles sonnent dans les âmes le tocsin de la révolte? Augmentant peu à peu d'intensité à mesure que l'orchestre s'anime, la première de ces notes finit par s'établir en souveraine dans l'ensemble harmonique (p.41). Là elle occupe toutes les positions: elle est au grave, au médium, à l'aigu. Tenue par les cors en *ut*, l'ophicléide, la grande et la petite flûte; donnée par les timbales et les trompettes, repercutée en *tremolo* par les altos et les premiers violons, elle offre l'aspect formidable d'une pédale de dominante quadruplée, quintuplée, sextuplée dans l'étendue de cinq octaves. Le *sol*, ce terrible *sol* est le pivot sur lequel tourne la rage populaire. C'est la grande voix de l'ouragan qui domine toutes les autres voix' (*RGM* XVII/7; 17 Feb. 1850, 54).

ends (*RGM* XXXII/21–5: 21 May – 18 Jun. 1865).[10] Through comparisons of specific parts of the opera with the style and general character of Rameau's *Castor et Pollux* and *Zoroastre*, Gluck's *Armide*, Mozart's *La clemenza di Tito*, and a reference to *basso continuo*, the portrayal of 'Meyerbeer the eclectic' was given new impetus. Consistent with this portrayal, Bourges outlined aspects of Meyerbeer's work which, though rooted in tradition, extended the boundaries of the art. One such was his experimentation with different phrase lengths, through which Bourges saw him as achieving greater fidelity of expression (*RGM* XXXII/22: 28 May 1865, 171); another was his experimentation with superimposed rhythms. Bourges saw the roots of Meyerbeer's practice in Beethoven. Of the duet for Sélika and Inès in Act V, he noted that its skill lay in:

the essentially symphonic ability to combine several very disparate rhythms, and to make them work together in such a way that not one of them causes confusion, and that each contributes to the homogeneity of the whole without losing its characteristic individuality. (*RGM* XXXII/25: 18 Jun. 1865, 198)[11]

That this is overstating the case only increases the importance of Bourges's statement as a means of justifying Meyerbeer's procedure. Similarly, Bourges staunchly defended his unusual use of harmony (or the lack of it). Just as Kastner had, on dramatic grounds, argued in favour of the parallel fifths of the anabaptists' plotting in Act II of *Le Prophète* (*RGM* XVII/9: 3 Mar. 1850, 70), so Bourges picked out the 'invocation' music of Act IV and the bare unison opening of Act V for special praise. Marie Escudier isolated exactly the same passages in his review of the public dress rehearsal (*FM* XXIX/18: 30 Apr. 1865, 133). His agenda, however, was different. Bourges was anxious to link Meyerbeer's music to historical traditions whilst at the same time lauding its originality; Escudier noted that the roots of several passages lay in Meyerbeer's earlier works, thereby casting doubt on his level of invention. The 'invocation' recalled the 'Bénédiction des poignards' in Act IV of *Les Huguenots*; the cabaletta (Escudier's term) of Nelusco's aria in Act II (no. 5b) replicated 'certain phrases from *Robert* in a rather slavish manner' (*ibid.*);[12] the introduction to Act III was too reminiscent of a passage from *Le Prophète* (*FM* XXIX/19: 7 May 1865, 142). At the end of his review of the première, Escudier wrote an appreciation of

---

10 Bourges mentions having seen sketches, and gives a broad idea of the main dates of the work's composition (*RGM* XXXII/25: 18 Jun. 1865, 197). At no point does he mention Fétis's involvement in completing the opera.

11 'la faculté, essentiellement symphonique, de combiner et de faire marcher simultanément plusieurs rhythmes très-divers, de telle sorte que pas un n'amène de confusion, et que chacun concourt à l'homogénéité de l'ensemble sans perdre son individualité caractéristique' (*ibid.*, 198).

12 'un peu trop servilement certaines phrases de *Robert*' (*FM* XXIX/18: 30 Apr. 1865, 133).

Meyerbeer's contribution to opera which was, in its even-handedness of praise and criticism, markedly cooler than that of Bourges (*ibid.*, 143). Berlioz's review of *Les Huguenots* excepted, to read reviews of Meyerbeer's operas in the *Gazette* is to encounter a solid mass of support. In particular, Bourges's review of *L'Africaine*, which contains not one hint of adverse criticism, is a testimony to the talents of the publishing house's most lucrative and popular composer.

Halévy

The irony of the *Gazette*'s position on opera (shared by Schlesinger and the Brandus brothers) was that the lucrative elements of stylistic elevation, popularity and productivity were indeed present among their house composers, but not consistently in combination. Had Halévy's productivity been allied to Meyerbeer's box office stardom, the publishing house's finances would have been significantly healthier. Halévy's swiftness of composition meant that the business regularly had a major new opera whose attendant publications would tempt the public, but his unevenness meant that he and the publishing house were open to attack: it left to the *Gazette*'s critics the job of shoring up his reputation after each 'succès d'estime'. Whilst house critics fought to promote Halévy as the head of a new French school of operatic composition based on the principle of eclecticism, his detractors accused him of inherently unmelodious, overly learned, writing, and indecent compositional haste. That the *Gazette*'s critics were aware of these problems is clear from their reviews, some of which are too defensive for genuine apologias.

In a six-instalment article on *Charles VI* (*RGM* IX/15–29: 9 Apr. – 16 Jul. 1843) which ostensibly hailed Halévy as the leading light of French opera, Henri Blanchard came perilously close to conceding defeat on every adverse criticism commonly aimed at the composer. He began by assessing Halévy's significance as a composer of opera:

A man found himself in a position whereby, filled with the good and sane doctrines of Cherubini and Méhul, avoiding the well-worn tracks of composers who concentrate on writing to please M. Musard ... equally, avoiding the metaphysical ramblings of contemporary music, which, strictly speaking, is not music, a man found himself in this position, and this man was M. Halévy, who through instinct and skill, founded musical eclecticism. (*RGM* IX/15: 9 Apr. 1843, 124)[13]

[13] 'Un homme s'est trouvé dans cet état de choses qui, nourri des bonnes et saines doctrines de Cherubini et de Méhul, évitant les sentiers battus des compositeurs qui se préoccupent, en écrivant, de plaire à M. Musard ... évitant également les divagations métaphysiques de la musique actuelle, qui, à proprement parler, n'est pas de la musique, un homme s'est trouvé, et cet homme c'est M. Halévy, qui a fait instinctivement et scientifiquement de l'éclectisme musical' (*RGM* IX/15: 9 Apr. 1843, 124).

Blanchard's following comments have much in common with those of Castil-Blaze and Escudier (*La France musicale*) and Emile Dardonville (*Le Monde musical*). He feels obliged to defend Halévy against the charge, levelled by Dardonville,[14] of writing too quickly and forcing his talent immediately after *La Reine de Chypre* (first performed in December 1841). Castil-Blaze had made a similar point after the première of *La Reine*:

> M. Halévy is in too much of a hurry, and in the whole world at the moment, there is only one man who can hurry and who can be hurried with impunity. With due respect to painters and poets, among all artists only Rossini has real genius; only genius can work fast and well. (*FM* IV/52: 26 Dec. 1841, 468)[15]

Such a reference to Rossini was guaranteed to enrage Schlesinger. Similarly, both Castil-Blaze and Dardonville had noted an absence of melodic flow in Halévy's compositions; Castil-Blaze remarked sardonically that *La Reine* was 'homeopathic music, a tiny fraction of melody poured into an ocean of chords, albeit well-chosen chords' (*ibid.*).[16] In a review of *Lazzarone*, Dardonville equalled his cutting tone; 'New, gracious and original melodies were conspicuous by their absence in M. Halévy's new score' (*MM* V/14: 3 Apr. 1844, 54).[17] Blanchard, in response to what was a traditional criticism of Halévy's style, tried but failed utterly to prove the composer's melodic pre-eminence; 'his works abound in melody, and we can prove it in *Charles VI*, in which each act has two or three which are direct and at the same time full of distinction' (*RGM* X/20: 14 May 1843, 164).[18] Allied to the view of Halévy's melodic style as unnatural was the problem of the orchestra's melodic and motivic importance. Here, Blanchard was ambivalent. He noted the rich orchestral palette in *Charles VI*, and called orchestral melody a higher form of melody, particularly when it took the form of a recurring theme having dramatic importance of its own; but in the first instalment he cited Grétry's complaint that Mozart put the statue in the orchestra and the pedestal on stage (*RGM* X/15: 9 Apr. 1843, 124), which inevitably coloured the supportive tone of the third instalment. Halévy's complexity of musical thought, later dismissed by Escudier as 'a muddle of

---

14 *MM* IV/12: 23 Mar. 1843, 42. Nothing is known about Emile Dardonville.
15 'M. Halévy se presse trop, et dans le monde entier en ce moment, il n'y a qu'un homme qui puisse se presser et que l'on puisse impunément presser. Dans tout le peuple artiste, n'en déplaise aux peintres, aux poètes, Rossini seul a du génie; le génie seul peut aller vite et faire bien' (*FM* IV/52: 26 Dec. 1841, 468).
16 'la musique homœopathique, un dix-millionième de mélodie versé dans un océan d'accords, bien ajustés, d'ailleurs' (*ibid.*).
17 'Les mélodies neuves, gracieuses et originales, ont brillé par leur absence dans la nouvelle partition de M. Halévy' (*MM* V/14: 3 Apr. 1844, 54).
18 'le chant abonde en ses ouvrages, et nous pourrions en donner la preuve dans *Charles VI*, dont chaque acte en renferme deux ou trois pleins de franchise en même temps que de distinction' (*RGM* X/20: 14 May 1843, 164).

combinations' (*FM* IX/6: 8 Feb. 1846, 42) was not convincingly defended either.[19] Of the entr'acte to Act IV of *Charles VI*, Blanchard remarked upon its 'richly complex thought, sometimes laboured, a little tortuous' (*RGM* X/26: 25 Jun. 1843, 215–16).[20]

Between the spectacular success of *La Juive* and *Les Mousquetaires de la reine*, Halévy's operas, particularly his opéras-comiques, were not widely acclaimed. Yet they were each treated in the *Gazette* as signs of a new, potentially influential, development in the composer's style. Comparisons with the *Gazette*'s reception of Heller and Prudent are difficult to resist. Such tactics are present in Blanchard's reviews of *Les Treize* and *Le Shérif* in 1839;[21] they reappear, reinforced by the confidence of vindication, in Fétis's retrospective essay following the success of *Les Mousquetaires* in 1846. Fétis viewed *L'Eclair* and *La Reine de Chypre* as innovative, and portrayed Halévy as experimenting with enharmonic practices and techniques of instrumentation which he refined to their utmost in *Les Mousquetaires*:

It is, somehow, the eclectic work in which the feelings which had directed the artist in previous phases of his career have come together within certain limits; it is the product of taste and experience, the manifestation of talent in its maturity. (*RGM* XIII/38: 20 Sep. 1846, 297)[22]

Yet even here, Fétis, who ought to be writing a glowing review on the publication of the full score of the work, cannot allow Halévy the title of genius. Moreover, towards the end of the article, which is judgemental where a 'style admiratif' would have been more appropriate, he finds that the vocal phrases of Roland's aria in Act II 'seem to lack naturalness and nobility' (*ibid.*, 298),[23] and complains that the score lacks stylistic unity, veering between over-sophistication and banality:

particularly in final cadences, in a complexity of phrase which falls slightly into affectation and is far from natural, due to fear of vulgarity; finally, in a certain excess of fast tempi, which is clearly done in the publisher's interests. (*ibid.*, 299)[24]

---

[19] 'combinaisons embrouillées' (*FM* IX/6: 8 Feb. 1846, 42). Escudier was referring back to *La Reine de Chypre* and *Charles VI* in a review of *Les Mousquetaires de la reine*.

[20] 'pensée richement complexe, et quelquefois recherchée, un peu tourmentée' (*RGM* X/26: 25 Jun. 1843, 215–16).

[21] *Les Treize*: *RM* VI/16: 18 Apr. 1839; *Le Shérif*: *RGM* VI/45–8: 5–22 Sep. 1839.

[22] 'C'est en quelque sorte l'œuvre d'éclectisme où viennent se coordonner dans de certaines limites les sentiments qui avaient dirigé l'artiste dans les phases précédentes de sa carrière; c'est le produit du goût et de l'expérience, la manifestation du talent dans sa maturité' (*RGM* XIII/38: 20 Sep. 1846, 297).

[23] 'semblent manquer de naturel et de noblesse' (*ibid.*, 298).

[24] 'particulièrement dans les cadences finales, dans une recherche de phrases qui tombe un peu dans l'afféterie et s'éloigne du naturel, par crainte de la vulgarité; enfin dans un certain excès de mouvements animés, qui est évidemment la part faite aux intérêts de l'éditeur' (*ibid.*, 299).

Such ambivalence seeping into ostensibly adulatory reviews throws Wagner's supportive article on *La Reine de Chypre* into sharp relief (*RGM* IX/9–18: 27 Feb. – 1 May 1842). The *Gazette* article was not the first Wagner had written on *La Reine*: an article had already appeared in the Dresden *Abendzeitung* of 26 and 29 January 1842. Comparison of the two reveals widely differing priorities, and an unmistakable element of tactical flattery in the *Gazette* review, which would have served Schlesinger's ends well, though only indirectly. It is far more adulatory than the Dresden review, which concentrates on the libretto and deals with the music almost as an afterthought.[25] The *Gazette* review inverts this relationship, spending little time on the libretto (which had already been discussed by Blanchard in *RGM* VIII/65: 26 Dec. 1841), and giving a glowing account of Halévy's place in French music, followed by discussion of the most noteworthy parts of the score – in particular the gondoliers' scene at the beginning of Act II. Wagner's argument, that the regeneration of German and Italian opera is dependent upon emulation of the French model as shown in *La Reine*, and his citing of Donizetti's finest (and French) opera, *La Favorite*, as the prime example of this tendency,[26] can be read as a suggestion that the Opéra management might have given him the chance to reveal his own debt to French operatic tradition. In this fully signed article he even naturalises himself as a Frenchman, referring to the Opéra as 'our great lyric stage' (*RGM* IX/9: 27 Feb. 1842, 76),[27] and expresses the wish that French opera houses 'will some day be open to true talents; and that then all those who have at heart the interests of great and true music drama will take Halévy as their model' (*RGM* IX/11: 13 Mar. 1842, 102).[28] In an uncommon fit of modesty, when describing the current state of operatic composition in Germany he neglects to mention any of his own works, focusing instead on Mendelssohn's weak dramatic talent. In an attempt to inflate French national pride, German operatic composition is portrayed as being at a desperately low ebb, with no hope of regeneration from within. Wagner's interpretation thus conflicts with his ideas on operatic composition as presented two years earlier in the Hoffmannesque story 'Une visite à Beethoven' (*RGM* VII/65–9: 19 Nov. – 3 Dec. 1840), where he used Beethoven as a mouthpiece for his own radicalism:

---

[25] The Dresden review is translated in Wagner, *Wagner Writes from Paris*, 163–77.

[26] This opinion of Donizetti's *La Favorite* changed later: in *Mein Leben* he described it as 'a flat and basically un-French pot-boiler'. Wagner, *My Life*, trans. Andrew Gray, ed. Mary Whittall (Cambridge, 1983), 197.

[27] 'notre grande scène lyrique' (*RGM* IX/9: 27 Feb. 1842, 76).

[28] 's'ouvriront quelque jour aux vrais talents; et qu'alors tous ceux qui ont à cœur les intérêts du grand et véritable drame musical, prennent Halévy pour modèle' (*RGM* IX/ 11: 13 Mar. 1842, 102).

If I were to write a score on the basis of my own instincts, nobody would want to hear it, because I wouldn't include ariettas or duets, or any of the traditional baggage which people use nowadays to put together an opera. (*RGM* VII/69: 3 Dec. 1840, 584)[29]

Wagner's comments of 1842 on the state of opera in Germany were published just three weeks before he and Minna left Paris – hence the gap between instalments two and three (13 March and 24 April). One wonders whether Wagner was still hoping for an offer from the Opéra's director, Léon Pillet, despite the humiliation of having sold his scenario for *Le Vaisseau fantôme* to him in 1841 (after which the commission was given to Dietsch), or whether reproach is implied. Whatever the intention, Wagner's main motivation for praising Halévy in such hyperbolic terms was not necessarily to please Schlesinger or to write his sincere opinion of Halévy, but to further his own ends. It is ironic that his review should be the most consistently laudatory that the *Gazette* ever published on Halévy's music.

Verdi

La France musicale spent the first half of the 1840s attacking Halévy, granting him a positive review only after the success of *Les Mousquetaires de la reine*. The *Gazette* retaliated regarding Verdi, whose reception in the *Gazette* up to 1854 caused considerable embarrassment to those writing later, since the success of *Il trovatore* was such that it could not be ignored, even by a journal with generally anti-Italian leanings.[30] The *Gazette*'s hostility was motivated purely by commercial rivalry. Reviews antedating the Ricordi/Escudier deal of May 1845, which gave the Escudier brothers sole French rights to Verdi's scores, contrast sharply with those written shortly afterwards. An early, unsigned, article picks Verdi out from his Italian contemporaries as, potentially, a worthy, and above all, dramatic, successor to Donizetti. The author is not uncritical of Verdi's *Nabucodonosor*, but detects ability and originality:

Verdi steers clear of the usual route; it is not with bravura arias, but with ensembles and choruses that he seeks his effects . . .

Nabucodonosor is written in a noble and imposing style; choruses form its essential part, and the composer develops a great power of expression in them;

---

[29] 'Si j'écrivais une partition conformément à mes propres instincts, personne ne voudrait l'entendre, car je n'y mettrais ni ariettes ni duos, ni rien de tout ce bagage convenu qui sert aujourd'hui à fabriquer un opéra' (*RGM* VII/69: 3 Dec. 1840, 584).

[30] Donizetti was the exception to Schlesinger's anti-Italian policy in publishing opera. In October 1850, Louis Brandus added a significant number of works by Rossini, Bellini and Donizetti to his stock through a merger with Troupenas, thereby weakening the publishing house's Germanic bias.

but the solo numbers do not maintain the same high level; drama takes precedence over song, and one searches the score in vain for pieces with seductive and facile melodies, which capture public attention immediately and stay in the memory easily. The young composer has proved that he has a fertile imagination, refined taste combined with serious study and a perfect knowledge of the resources of his art. (*RGM* X/24: 11 Jun. 1843, 203)[31]

The closing comments of the above quotation are of prime importance, since it was on grounds of bad taste and supposed incompetence that Verdi was attacked later, not least by Fétis in his essay 'De la crise du goût en musique' (*RGM* XIII/1–3: 4–18 Jan. 1846). However, the first attack came from Edouard Monnais (writing as 'R.') in a review of the same opera, known from 1844 as *Nabucco*. He instantly alighted on the Escudiers and their 'Verdistes':

And none the less a new sect, comprising half a dozen fanatics, tried to establish itself, on the pretext that a new god had just appeared! In this regard we shall mention that there is a most spirited journal ... (*RGM* XII/44: 2 Nov. 1845, 357)[32]

The journal in question was, of course, *La France musicale*, whose article, signed 'Escudier', gave a better idea of audience reaction to the work (Monnais neglected to mention two encores), and praised the clarity, elegance and originality of the score, particularly its orchestration and Verdi's ability to balance voices against the orchestra (*FM* VIII/42: 19 Oct. 1845, 329–30). [Léon] Escudier's tone was triumphant. By contrast, Monnais complained of 'noise, lots of noise, nothing but noise' (*RGM* XII/44: 2 Nov. 1845, 358),[33] and claimed that Verdi over-wrote for the brass section. He disparaged even those numbers which were an unqualified success, dismissed Act IV as 'completely and utterly worthless' (*ibid.*, 359),[34] and predicted only brief fame for a composer with a chronically weak melodic style.

In order to strengthen the case against Verdi, Brandus used the weight

---

[31] 'Verdi s'écarte de la route ordinaire; ce n'est point par des airs de bravoure, mais par les morceaux d'ensemble et par les chœurs qu'il cherche à produire de l'effet ...
Nabuccodonosor [sic] est une œuvre d'un style noble et imposant; les chœurs en forment la partie essentielle, et l'auteur y développe une grande puissance d'expression; mais les solos ne se soutiennent pas à la même hauteur; le drame l'emporte sur le chant, et on cherche en vain dans la partition les morceaux à mélodies séduisantes et faciles, qui captivent tout d'abord l'attention du public et se retrouvent aisément dans la mémoire. Le jeune compositeur a fait preuve d'une imagination féconde, d'un goût très fin, auxquelles qualités se joignent des études sérieuses et une connaissance parfaite des ressources de son art' (*RGM* X/24: 11 Jun. 1843, 203).

[32] 'Et pourtant une secte nouvelle, composée d'une demi-douzaine de fanatiques, a essayé de se montrer, sous prétexte qu'un nouveau dieu venait d'apparaître! A ce propos nous dirons qu'il existe un très spirituel journal' (*RGM* XII/44: 2 Nov. 1845, 357).

[33] 'du bruit, beaucoup de bruit, toujours du bruit' (*ibid.*, 358).

[34] 'd'une complète et incontestable nullité' (*ibid.*, 359).

of Fétis's opinion and that of the Florentine critic Alessandro Gagliardi, a staunch follower of Donizetti and an upholder of the pure Italian tradition. Gagliardi's first article served Brandus's purposes perfectly, since it combined Verdi's denunciation with enough criticism of the French tradition (by implication, the eclectic style) to give readers the illusion of impartiality. The following passage from an essay on music in Rome elicited an editorial footnote reminding the reader of the author's inevitable national prejudice:

his [Verdi's] point of departure is not his own country; one might say that above all he has modelled himself on the new French school in which there is a little of everything, except naturalness, spontaneity, bountiful inspiration, in a word, except genius, unless it is Rossini who wields the pen. (*RGM* XIII/21: 24 May 1846, 164)[35]

In this article and his review of *Macbeth*'s Florentine première (*RGM* XIV/13: 28 Mar. 1847) – the only hostile review of the opera to appear in the French press[36] – Gagliardi complained of vulgarity, poverty of musical content and over-use of the brass, which had drowned out the vocal lines. In the 1846 article, Verdi's use of unison choruses, soon to become a hobbyhorse in the *Gazette*, was also condemned as regressive. Such tirades continued unabated, despite the embarrassment of writing a dismissive review after *Jérusalem*'s success at the Opéra (*RGM* XIV/48: 28 Nov. 1847). However, there were signs that the *Gazette*'s unity of opinion was about to crack: the unsigned author remarked that one of his 'excellent colleagues' had attempted to persuade him to change his mind (*ibid.*, 385).[37]

Fétis's profoundly reactionary attitude in an article of 1850 (*RGM* XVII/37–39: 15–29 Sep. 1850) has been discussed by Massino Mila.[38] The only aspects new to the *Gazette*'s established policy are his references to the artistic and political climate of which Verdi is a product, and which, in Fétis's opinion, have alone precipitated his success. In 1846, his tone was one of disappointment that a potentially fine musician should find his talent being compromised:

Had he lived in another time, Verdi might well have yielded to his own feeling, and, developing the principal quality which he received from nature, he would

---

[35] 'son point de départ n'est pas dans son pays; on dirait qu'il s'est surtout formé à cette nouvelle école française où il entre un peu de tout, sauf le naturel, la spontanéité, la fréquence de l'inspiration, en un mot sauf le génie, à moins pourtant que ce ne soit Rossini qui tienne la plume' (*RGM* XIII/21: 24 May 1846, 164).

[36] See David Rosen and Andrew Porter (eds.), *Verdi's Macbeth. A Sourcebook* (Cambridge, 1984), 376–9 and 60 n. 3.

[37] 'excellents confrères' (*RGM* XIV/48: 28 Nov. 1847, 385).

[38] Massino Mila, 'Fétis e Verdi, ovvero gli infortuni della critica', *Atti del IIIo congresso internazionale di studi Verdiani, Milano, Piccola Scala, 1972* (Parma, 1974), 12–17.

have turned it into the distinctive characteristic of his talent. (*RGM* XIII/1: 4 Jan. 1846, 4)[39]

In 1846, Fétis viewed Verdi as still capable of redeeming himself; he need only 'descend into himself and listen only to his own inspiration' (*ibid.*),[40] thus divorcing himself from a pernicious environment. By 1850, Fétis's opinion had hardened, his tone considerably more trenchant. After relating Verdi's initial success to his society's need for a musical symbol of twenty-five years of revolutionary violence, he stated that the composer's music was now changing to reflect less bellicose sentiments, particularly in *Luisa Miller* (*RGM* XVII/37: 15 Sep. 1850, 310). However, Verdi now appeared unequal to the task, showing signs of the 'painful labour' (*RGM* XVII/39: 29 Sep. 1850, 322)[41] which distinguished his lowly talent from the genius of Bellini, Rossini, Donizetti and even Mercadante. Fétis denigrated his limited repertoire of rhythmic accompanimental figures, adding the now predictable complaints of too many unison choruses and banal brass writing.

The height of the *Gazette*'s opposition occurred when Louis Brandus paraphrased a negative report on *Rigoletto* from *The Times*, including the statement: 'This opera has precious little chance of staying in the repertoire' (*RGM* XX/21: 22 May 1853, 191),[42] to which the Escudiers took exception. Brandus's response was an impassioned defence of his staff – Monnais in particular – and included the delightfully misguided statement that '*Rigoletto* is dead, dead for good!!!' (*RGM* XX/23: 5 Jun. 1853, 101 [201]).[43] The most important aspect of Brandus's article, however, was its direct and indirect references to the work of Maurice Bourges.

Of the *Gazette*'s regular critics of the 1840s and 1850s, Bourges was the most independent. His review of *I due Foscari* (*RGM* XIII/51: 20 Dec. 1846), whilst reporting the failure of an uneven work, mentioned three numbers which were 'really noteworthy and sincerely applauded' (*ibid.*, 403),[44] and questioned the wisdom of the Italiens' administration in staging one of Verdi's weakest scores. Despite the weight of Fétis's judgement two years earlier, Bourges's review of *Luisa Miller* campaigned for Verdi's reappraisal, given the 'transformation in the

[39] 'Venu dans un autre temps, Verdi se serait vraisemblablement abandonné à son sentiment propre, et développant la qualité principale qu'il a reçue de la nature, il en aurait fait le caractère distinctif de son talent' (*RGM* XIII/1: 4 Jan. 1846, 4).

[40] 'descendre en soi-même et de n'écouter que ses inspirations' (*ibid.*).

[41] 'pénible travail' (*RGM* XVII/39: 29 Sep. 1850, 322).

[42] 'cet opéra n'a guères chance de se maintenir au répertoire' (*RGM* XX/21: 22 May 1853, 191).

[43] '*Rigoletto* est mort, mort à tout jamais!!!' (*RGM* XX/23: 5 Jun. 1853, 101 [201]).

[44] 'réellement remarquables et sincèrement applaudis' (*RGM* XIII/51: 20 Dec. 1846, 403).

maestro's style' which the opera was claimed to represent (*RGM* XIX/50: 12 Dec. 1852, 460).[45] By his own admission, the review was 'much more *pro* than *con*' (*ibid.*, 461).[46] The review of *Luisa Miller* is not Bourges's best work – the short, clipped, style in this and the *Foscari* review contrasts sharply with his customarily expansive prose; he appears deliberately to couch his views in understated language. However, he is detailed concerning the opera's musical and musico-dramatic quality, and finds much to praise. Needless to say, this was not the kind of review Louis Brandus required, and although he printed it without an admonitory footnote, his riposte to Escudier referred to it as over-indulgent towards Verdi:

Yes, I repent and accuse myself of having been untruthful, moreover quite recently, regarding *Luisa Miller*, performed at two Paris opera houses, and having allowed my subscribers to believe that this double fiasco of such a vaunted work was almost a success! (*RGM* XX/23: 5 Jun. 1853, 102 [202])[47]

It may, therefore, be that the contributor who had tried to change the mind of the unsigned reviewer of *Jérusalem* in 1847 was Maurice Bourges.

After the Paris première of *Il trovatore*, Edouard Monnais wrote a review of appeasement: 'This is the moment to prove to Verdi that we are not biased against him and that we do not oppose him as a matter of policy' (*RGM* XXI/53: 31 Dec. 1854, 421).[48] He maintained the consistency of the journal's critical attitude by emphasising that Verdi was merely the finest living composer in a country whose current compositional standards were low, and that he was inferior to his predecessors. Nevertheless, Monnais acknowledged signs of increased sophistication in *Il trovatore*. His 'Revue de l'année 1854' (*RGM* XXII/ 1: 7 Jan. 1855) showed even more generosity, saying that it had 'brilliantly marked the theatre's second season' (*ibid.*, 2)[49] and that it would have a secure future in the repertoire. Although subsequent reviews of *Les Vêpres siciliennes*[50] and *Un ballo in maschera*[51] were to indicate that Verdi's style required further refinement, Monnais was genuinely enthusiastic concerning both *La traviata* (XXIII/50: 14 Dec.

---

[45] 'transformation de la manière du maestro' (*RGM* XIX/50: 12 Dec. 1852, 460).
[46] 'bien plutôt favorable que contraire' (*ibid.*, 461).
[47] 'Oui, je me repens et m'accuse d'avoir manqué à la vérité, tout récemment encore, à l'occasion de cette *Luisa Miller*, jouée sur deux théâtres de Paris, et d'avoir laissé croire à mes abonnés que ce double fiasco d'une œuvre tant vantée était presque un succès!' (*RGM* XX/23: 5 Jun. 1853, 102 [202]).
[48] 'Voici le moment de prouver à Verdi que nous n'avons pas contre lui de parti pris et que nous lui faisons pas d'opposition systématique' (*RGM* XXI/53: 31 Dec. 1854, 421).
[49] 'brillamment marqué la seconde saison du théâtre' (*RGM* XXII/1: 7 Jan. 1855, 2).
[50] Bourges, *RGM* XXII/24: 17 Jun. 1855.
[51] Monnais, *RGM* XXVIII/3: 20 Jan. 1861.

1856, 398) and, in a complete reversal of Brandus's opinion of 1853, *Rigoletto*. Here, he alighted on the famous Act III quartet which, 'comprising two duets which interlace without becoming entangled, is undoubtedly one of the most beautiful things the art of music has produced' (*RGM* XXIV/4: 25 Jan. 1857, 26).[52] He did not, however, retract any of the *Gazette*'s earlier judgements, since he still viewed everything antedating *Luisa Miller* (1849) as obscure *juvenilia*.[53] By 1867, Verdi's position was unassailable; reviewing *Don Carlos*, Monnais wrote, 'as for the music, Verdi's name alone suffices to recommend it' (*RGM* XXXIV/11: 17 Mar. 1867, 83).[54]

After Monnais's death the following year, opera reviewing passed to a new generation of contributors who had not been involved in the Verdian squabbles of 1846 or 1853. Supportive of his work, they simultaneously continued the *Gazette*'s tradition of retrospective disparagement. Monnais's reviews of the 1860s set a precedent by which only Verdi's latest operas secured approval. In a reversal of the *Gazette*'s attitude to house composers, in whom transitional stylistic features were welcomed as evidence of potential, Verdi's increasing sophistication was used as an excuse to dismiss his earlier efforts, thereby undermining his status. From 1869, the works of the early 1850s were consistently disparaged by the standards of his most recent output. H. Lavoix *fils*, reviewing *Un ballo in maschera*, complained of the formlessness of earlier works: 'All its numbers are written with a skill, a regard for form, the absence of which, unfortunately, one regrets too often in *Rigoletto* and above all in *Il trovatore*' (*RGM* XXXVI/47: 21 Nov. 1869, 377).[55] In 1874, Adolphe Jullien claimed that Verdi's decisive change of style had occurred between 1861 and 1866 (*La forza del destino* and *Don Carlos*), when the composer ceased to be stubbornly isolationist and began to take account of stylistic currents in the rest of Europe, notably those represented by Meyerbeer, Berlioz and Wagner (*RGM* XLI/11: 15 Mar. 1874, 81). Two years later, **Paul Bernard** remarked of *La forza del destino* that: ' We shall find only the old Verdi, the Verdi of *Il trovatore*, less felicitous, less inspired' (*RGM* XLIII/45: 5 Nov. 1876, 354).[56]

---

[52] 'composé de deux duos qui s'entrelacent sans se confondre, est, sans aucun doute, une des plus belles choses que l'art musical ait enfantées' (*RGM* XXIV/4: 25 Jan. 1857, 26).

[53] See Monnais on *I lombardi* (*RGM* XXX/3: 18 Jan. 1863, 17) and *Ernani* (*RGM* XXX/51: 20 Dec. 1863, 403).

[54] 'quant à la musique, le nom de Verdi suffit à la recommander' (*RGM* XXXIV/11: 17 Mar. 1867, 83).

[55] 'Tous les morceaux y sont conduits avec une habileté, un souci de la forme, dont on regrette malheureusement trop souvent l'absence dans *Rigoletto* et surtout dans *le Trouvère*' (*RGM* XXXVI/47: 21 Nov. 1869, 377).

[56] 'Nous ne trouverons que le Verdi des anciens jours, le Verdi du *Trovatore*, moins heureux, moins inspiré' (*RGM* XLIII/45: 5 Nov. 1876, 354).

Bernard was not, however, in agreement with Jullien; a few months earlier he had pushed the starting point for Verdi's maturity further still – to 1870–1 – designating *Aida* the curtain-raiser to the composer's second period (*RGM* XLIII/18: 30 Apr. 1876, 137). That Verdi's style developed enormously throughout his career is irrefutable; nevertheless the *Gazette*'s systematic consigning of progressively later works to the oblivion of a first period ensured that in each review his achievement was tainted with the memory of past banalities.

Late nineteenth-century French composers

Part of the reason behind Verdi's sudden success in France may lie in the perceived demise of indigenous opera in the latter half of the century. After Meyerbeer's death in 1864, the *Gazette*'s critics saw French opera as in crisis, despite the continuing steady work of Ambroise Thomas. In his annual review of musical life in 1866, Edouard Monnais suggested that increased interest in early music might be a prime contributory factor. He referred, specifically, to the three productions of *Don Giovanni* which had dominated the year's operatic fare:

The taste for music has not ceased to make itself felt with ever-increasing force; but it must be remarked that, without meaning to attack anyone, the more general taste turns towards early masterpieces, the fewer new works appear. Is this progress or weakness? Celebrated composers write less than ever before, and our newcomers have difficulty making themselves known. Could it be that due to admiring the beautiful, to admiring the classic, we shall have brought ourselves to the point where we no longer dare do anything new? (*RGM* XXXIV/1: 6 Jan. 1867, 1)[57]

As far as the *Gazette*'s critics were concerned, David and Gounod could not begin to approach the full-blooded drama of Verdi's and Meyerbeer's scores. Gounod was adversely received by critics as divergent in their general outlook as Bourges, Héquet, Monnais, Jullien, Bernard and Bannelier. Many criticisms reveal more about their writers than about Gounod himself: it is unsurprising to find Monnais hinting at Wagnerisms in *La Reine de Saba* (Paul Smith, *RGM* XXIX/9: 2 Mar. 1862, 70), and expressing relief at their relative scarcity in *Mireille* (Paul Smith, *RGM* XXXI/13: 27 Mar. 1864, 100) – Monnais shared Botte's

---

[57] 'Le goût de la musique n'a pas cessé de s'y manifester avec une force toujours croissante; mais, il faut bien le remarquer, sans en faire un grief contre qui que ce soit, plus le goût général se tourne vers les anciens chefs-d'œuvre, moins il s'en produit de nouveaux. Est-ce un progrès ou une défaillance? Les compositeurs renommés composent moins que jamais, et les nouveaux venus ne se montrent qu'à peine. Est-ce qu'à force d'admirer le beau, d'adorer le classique, nous nous serions formés à tel point que nous n'oserions plus rien faire du neuf?' (*RGM* XXXIV/1: 6 Jan. 1867, 1).

paranoia concerning the New German School and its influence.[58] Reviewing *Sapho*, Gounod's first opera, in 1851, Bourges saw promise; in Berliozian style, he found mitigating circumstances in the libretto for the work's dramatic weakness. Nevertheless, he complained about the opera's monotonous, formless arioso, and its often inappropriately retrospective style (*RGM* XVII/16: 20 Apr. 1851). Three years later, only the orchestral introduction to *La Nonne sanglante* roused Bourges to poetic prose, though in it he detected shades of Meyerbeer's *Le Prophète* (*RGM* XXI/44: 29 Oct. 1854, 350); other parts he adjudged either too derivative (he judged the transfiguration scene of Act II a flagrant reminiscence of the sunrise in David's *Le Désert*) or laboured (the page's *couplets*, also in Act II). In the eyes of the *Gazette*'s critics, Gounod's promise remained largely unfulfilled. His most favourable reception in the *Gazette* came from Gustave Héquet (writing as Durocher) after the première of *Faust* at the Théâtre-Lyrique in 1859. Héquet found the work uneven, the first two acts generally inferior to Acts III, IV and V. His detailed comments on individual numbers continued a trend (set by Bourges) which was to be a common thread of reviews of his work: reference to his penchant for evoking past styles, from Lully to Sacchini. Bourges had found *Sapho* over-endowed with such references; for Héquet, who was infinitely more conservative as a critic, Gounod's ability to write 'period' music drew praise. He judged the chorus of old men in Act II to be:

one of the most noteworthy numbers in the entire work. There is nothing more original, better turned, more spirited or finer than this little old-time melody, of which Grétry would have been proud. (*RGM* XXVI/13: 27 Mar. 1859, 102)[59]

By the 1870s, reviews by Bannelier and Jullien were harsh; Bernard, another conservative, was more constructive, but represented the minority view. Though the Brandus brothers never published a Gounod opera (Choudens was Gounod's principal publisher), there is no evidence that the *Gazette*'s response to his music was part of a campaign *à la* Verdi. All the journal's critics acknowledged the general phenomenon of

[58] Christian Goubault notes that the reception of Gounod's music was conditioned by the ascendancy first of Italian, then German, opera, in the second half of the century: he was perceived as too German during a vogue for Italian opera and too Italian when Wagnerism was at its height. See Christian Goubault, *La Critique musicale dans la presse française de 1870 à 1914* (Geneva, 1984), 334. However, Monnais excepted, there are few indications of Gounod's being perceived as too Germanic in the *Gazette* in the 1850s and 1860s; criticism centred on aspects other than national trends in composition.

[59] 'un des morceaux les plus remarquables de l'ouvrage. Rien de plus original, rien de mieux tourné, rien de plus spirituel et de plus fin que cette petite mélodie vieillotte que Grétry eût été fier d'avoir trouvée' (*RGM* XXVI/13: 27 Mar. 1859, 102). Héquet was similarly supportive of the Lullian flavour of *Le Médecin malgré lui* (*RGM* XXV/3: 17 Jan. 1858, 18).

Gounod's talent, particularly in his opulent use of the orchestra, but were in varying degrees disconcerted by his unevenness, and a chameleon-like diversity of style which was increasingly perceived as derivative. Writing on the ruinous production of *Jeanne d'Arc* at Offenbach's Théâtre de la Gaîté in 1873, Jullien detected a change of style in Gounod's work – away from the boldness of Schumann and Berlioz (with backward glances at Handel and Bach) and towards a studied simplicity: 'Now he affects an extreme simplicity, and to the extent that he throws off his richness of instrumental apparel he leaves the workings bare. He was too richly ornamented before; now he is too banal and empty' (*RGM* XL/46: 16 Nov. 1873, 363).[60] Added to this was the charge of a lack of originality. Bannelier was no more generous reviewing *Polyeucte* in 1878, complaining of indiscreet orchestration and the 'slight musical worth' of parts of the work (*RGM* XLV/41: 13 Oct. 1878, 326).[61] Only Bernard, in a review of a revival of *Philémon et Baucis* in 1876, attempted to redress the balance, by presenting Gounod as a modernist whose works were only beginning to be understood properly and who had, in the past, 'borne the flag of regeneration' (*RGM* XLIII/21: 21 Mar. 1876, 161).[62]

In the 1870s, the rise to prominence of Saint-Saëns, Joncières and Reyer was treated with interest by Jullien and Bannelier, but was eclipsed in 1875 by the appearance at the Opéra-Comique of *Carmen*, and the posthumous standing of its composer. Paul Bernard gave the première a mixed reception (*RGM* XLII/10: 7 Mar. 1875), hailing Bizet as a new French model, since he 'showed himself truly worthy of the task which was given him' (*ibid.*, 73), but complaining that the choruses were 'tortured and ambitious' (*ibid.*, 74).[63] However, in true French style Bizet's stock rose sharply on his death, and in an unsigned obituary he was described as first-rate, both as an opera composer and symphonist (?Bannelier, *RGM* XLII/23: 6 Jun. 1875, 183). This view was reinforced the following year, when, in a review of Ernest Guiraud's *Piccolino* at the Opéra-Comique, Bernard lamented the sorry state of French operatic composition in the wake of its leader-elect's death:

If ... we consider who might outlive Meyerbeer, Rossini, Hérold, Halévy, Auber, we are forced to agree that at present we seem to have impotence and stagnation,

[60] 'Il affecte maintenant une simplicité extrême, et à mesure qu'il rejette sa riche parure instrumentale il met à nu le procédé. Il faisait trop précieux autrefois, il fait trop banal et trop vide aujourd'hui' (*RGM* XL/46: 16 Nov. 1873, 363).
[61] 'bien mince valeur musicale' (*RGM* XLV/41: 13 Oct. 1878, 326).
[62] 'arborer le drapeau d'une rénovation' (*RGM* XLIII/21: 21 Mar. 1876, 161).
[63] 's'est véritablement montré à la hauteur de la tâche qui lui était confiée' (*RGM* XLII/10: 7 Mar. 1875, 73), 'tourmentés et ambitieux' (*ibid.*, 74).

that the art of musical drama seems to have entered an era of paralysis. (*RGM* XLIII/16: 16 Apr. 1876, 121)[64]

Carmen alone had given French opera a new and dignified direction; but Verdi, that 'musical genius ... who ... remains powerfully creative and none the less retains the ability to interest and move the masses' remained pre-eminent (Bernard, *RGM* XLVIII/18: 30 Apr. 1876, 137).[65] *Le Wagnérisme* had not yet arrived.

Offenbach and Lecocq

The sense of operatic impoverishment in the 1860s, intensified after Bizet's death in 1875, was heightened still more by the activities and influence of Jacques Offenbach. From presenting tiny semi-staged interludes in public recitals at the Salle Herz, the former cellist built what in the operetta year of 1868 seemed an unassailable empire: he had created, and remained the ultimate exponent of, a new genre. His ostensible intention, as claimed in the introduction to his competition for a one-act operetta, was to re-create the true spirit of opéra-comique (*RGM* XXIII/29: 20 Jul. 1856). In the *Gazette*, Offenbach's venture was heartily encouraged by the critics who were customarily responsible for the reviewing of light opera, particularly **Edouard Déaddé** (pseudonym D.-A.-D. Saint-Yves), Gustave Héquet (pseudonym Léon Durocher) and **Emile Abraham** (pseudonym Adrien Laroque). By contrast, critics who supported more serious forms disparaged the genre and looked forward to its demise. In his review of the year 1868, Emile Mathieu de Monter noted the pernicious effect of operetta's success on public taste:

'Give me your play', say the young composers to the vaudeville hacks, 'and I will tack on a few arias.' The result is a score. Operetta is triumphant. Everything sings, sounds and resounds. From austere and pure art, we have arrived at an elegant promiscuity. (*RGM* XXXVI/1: 3 Jan. 1869, 1)[66]

However, in the 1850s the novelty of Offenbach's conception elicited nothing but enthusiasm from the *Gazette*'s critics, provided that a work's

---

[64] 'Si ... on cherche qui pourra survivre aux Meyerbeer, aux Rossini, aux Hérold, aux Halévy, aux Auber, on en arrive à être forcé de convenir qu'en ce moment, il semble y avoir impuissance et stagnation, que l'art dramatique musical paraît entrer dans une ère de marasme' (*RGM* XLIII/16: 16 Apr. 1876, 121).

[65] 'génie musical ... qui ... reste puissamment créateur et conserve quand même le don d'intéresser et de remuer les masses' (Bernard on *Aida*, *RGM* XLVIII/18: 30 Apr. 1876, 137).

[66] ' "Donnez-moi votre pièce, disent les jeunes compositeurs aux vaudevillistes, j'y coudrai quelques airs." Le résultat, c'est une partition. L'opérette est victorieuse. Tout chante, sonne et resonne. De l'art austère et pur, nous en sommes venus à une élégante promiscuité' (*RGM* XXXVI/1: 3 Jan. 1869, 1).

subject matter did not descend too far towards the farcical or the *risqué*, a feature of Hervé's and Delibes's productions which invariably met with censure.[67] From the first, Offenbach's ability to parody a wide variety of styles was commented upon by Monnais and Héquet, who particularly admired the wit of this practice, but never interpreted it as a satirical commentary on the state of French operatic composition. Whilst the strictures under which Offenbach was allowed to set up his theatre offered little room for grandiose writing, early reviews linked his work with a wish to return to the old, pure, opéra-comique style: 'More than anyone, Offenbach has the knack for this vital and light genre of our old opéra-comique, which he has decided to restore to us' wrote Déaddé of *Le 66!* ('D.', *RGM* XXIII/31: 3 Aug. 1856, 247).[68] The more substantial of Offenbach's works were published by Brandus: Gemmy made particular efforts to promote *La Périchole* in 1868, printing a separate article on the music by one of his more established critics, Paul Bernard (*RGM* XXXV/52: 27 Dec. 1868). The only critic who disagreed radically with the view that operetta should aspire to the condition of opéra-comique was Déaddé's successor, Emile Abraham, who, in a review of Jules Duprato's *La Tour du Chien-Vert*, complained that the music 'is not an operetta, but a failed opéra-comique' (*RGM* XXXVIII/49: 31 Dec. 1871, 376).[69]

The Brandus house's most prominent operetta composer in the 1870s was Charles Lecocq, who was unfailingly promoted as the genre's saviour. Offenbach, his fortune lost, had sailed to America. Lecocq's works were reviewed with a fervour redolent of Halévy's reception in the 1840s – even, in the case of *Kosiki*, using the popular press's traditional ploy of printing extracts from favourable reviews in other papers (*RGM* XLIII/44: 29 Oct. 1876). The very rarity of these outbursts of publicity, with their full-page advertisements for arrangements of the work in question, places in perspective the reviews of H. Lavoix *fils*, who with increasing determination hailed Lecocq as a reformer:

Never has M. Ch. Lecocq given the public a work more carefully structured, more felicitous in melody, than *La Marjolaine*. Operetta's buffoonery has given way to a refined, delicate musical style which is agreeable both to the public and

[67] Hervé's real name was Florimond Ronger.
[68] 'Offenbach a, plus que personne, l'instinct de ce genre vif et léger de notre ancien opéra comique qu'il a pris à tâche de nous rendre' ('D.', *RGM* XXIII/31: 3 Aug. 1856, 247). The attribution of articles signed 'D.' to Edouard Déaddé rests on the disappearance both of this initial and his signed column (D.-A.-D. Saint-Yves), customarily entitled 'Revue des théâtres', almost simultaneously in 1870, coupled with an obituary notice at the resumption of publication in 1871 (*RGM* XXXVIII/36: 1 Oct. 1871, 272), after which Emile Abraham (Adrien Laroque) takes over the reviewing for his operetta column.
[69] 'n'est pas un opéra-bouffe, mais un opéra-comique manqué' (*RGM* XXXVIII/49: 31 Dec. 1871, 376).

to musicians. This little muse of opera buffa, svelte and clear, laughing with silvery directness but without crudity, boldly continues its way towards opéra-comique, and it is M. Lecocq who leads her by the hand. (*RGM* XLIV/6: 11 Feb. 1877, 43)[70]

Yet it was clear that the golden years of French operetta had long since disappeared, and that genre did not contain the seeds of renewal in French opera. In 1880, writing Offenbach's obituary, a critic signed 'B.' refused to judge his merit definitively. Only time, he felt, could make, 'a correct distinction between what should be definitively forbidden on the grounds of good taste and a healthy aesthetic, and what should be retained as truly, wisely and finely artistic' (?Bannelier, *RGM* XLVII/41: 10 Oct. 1880, 325).[71] Whilst he suspected the presence of more in the latter category than was currently acknowledged, he gave no indication that Offenbach's promised regeneration had occurred.

Criticism of contemporary French and Italian opera showed the *Gazette* at its most partial; the publishing house's financial dependence upon opera-related publications caused aesthetic ideals to be sacrificed to commercial exigencies. At times, the journal's opera criticism closely resembled both pure advertisement and *parti pris* denigration; as Michael Corleone might have said of the *Gazette*'s attempts to destroy Verdi, 'it's not personal ... it's strictly business'. Such impersonality detracted from the quality of the *Gazette*'s criticism (*qua* criticism) because it restricted the field of vision and encouraged the perception of polar categories. For different reasons respectively, the *Gazette*'s criticism of the New German School and Berlioz transcended such market-driven practices, bringing the aesthetics of the canon to the fore once again. The next two chapters discuss their reception in a journal which increasingly yielded to Fétisian conservatism.

---

[70] 'Jamais M. Ch. Lecocq n'a donné au public une œuvre plus soignée de forme, plus heureuse de mélodie que *la Marjolaine*. La bouffonnerie de l'opérette a fait place à une musique fine, délicate, qui plaît à la fois et au public et aux musiciens. Elle continue hardiment sa route vers l'opéra comique, cette petite muse de l'opéra bouffe, à l'allure svelte et dégagée, au rire franc et argentin sans grossièreté, et c'est M. Lecocq qui la conduit par la main' (*RGM* XLIV/6: 11 Feb. 1877, 43).

[71] 'un juste départ entre ce qu'il convient de proscrire sans retour, au nom du bon goût et de la saine esthétique, et ce qu'il y a lieu de retenir comme vraiment, sagement et finement artistique' (?Bannelier, *RGM* XLVII/41: 10 Oct. 1880, 325).

10 Contemporary music IV: The music of the future

In 1852, Fétis wrote what turned out to be his most influential article for the *Gazette*. Entitled 'Richard Wagner – sa vie, son système de rénovation de l'opéra, ses oeuvres comme poète et comme musicien, son parti en Allemagne, appréciation de la valeur de ses idées' (*RGM* XIX/ 23–32: 6 Jun. – 8 Aug. 1852), it set the tone of the journal's subsequent criticism not only of Wagner but of Liszt and, for a period, Schumann.[1] Georges Servières attacked Fétis for so poisoning the composer's reputation in France:

This study is extremely important, firstly as an exposition, but particularly due to its influence on later judgements made in the press and by artists. Although he did not invent the legend of the *music of the future*, in this series of articles (which Baudelaire called an *indigestible and abominable pamphlet*), Fétis put about all the ideas on Wagner which were most likely to frighten off those who admired Auber and Halévy. With great skill, he highlighted those elements of the composer's style which are furthest removed from the formal conventions of French opera, and through perfidious quotations ... succeeded in arousing routine's innate distrust of innovative theories.[2]

Fétis's essay attacked Wagner using criteria familiar from his earlier criticism: that self-styled genius was mere arrogance, and self-styled reformism misguided; that programme music was a wrong path, since it weakened the autonomy of the art and increased its tendency to materialism; that 'carrure' was a natural law, and clearly delineated

---

[1] Adolphe Botte's criticism of Schumann's chamber music and Charles Bannelier's of Liszt's piano music and the symphonic poem, are informed by the content of Fétis's articles.

[2] 'Cette étude présente une extrême importance, d'abord comme développement, mais surtout en raison de l'influence qu'elle a exercée sur les jugements ultérieurs de la presse et des artistes. Bien que n'ayant pas inventé la légende de la *musique de l'avenir*, Fétis, dans cette série d'articles que Baudelaire traite *d'indigeste et abominable pamphlet*, a répandu sur le compte de Wagner toutes les idées les plus propres à effaroucher les admirateurs d'Auber et Halévy. Avec une grande habileté, il mit en relief ce qui, dans les tendances du compositeur, s'éloigne le plus de la forme conventionnelle de l'opéra français et, par des citations perfides ... sut éveiller les défiances innées de la routine à l'égard des théories novatrices'. Georges Servières, *Richard Wagner jugé en France* (Paris, 1887), 25–6.

melody essential to music's comprehensibility; that an aesthetic of beauty – the ideal – should always prevail over an aesthetic of realism and dramatic truth; that, in opera, music should always be superior to poetry; finally, that the use of a compositional system was a sign of weakness, indicating a lack of genius, imagination and spontaneity of expression. For much of the essay, Fétis engaged minimally with the music itself, reviewing instead the aesthetic of which he claimed it was the product. In the final instalment, which observed Berlioz's 'loi du crescendo', he made the wild gesture of dubbing Wagner a Comtian positivist:

Like him, such philosophers suppress genius and substitute the action of the will; like him, they reject the ideal; finally, like him they want to restrict sensitivity's emotions and imagination's fantasies in favour of clarity of ideas. (*RGM* XIX/32: 8 Aug. 1852, 259)[3]

Fétis's attack on Comtian positivism, its atheism, and its negation of the continuing value of historical traditions, is the product of extreme circumstances. Despite the attractions of both an evolutionary theory which could find parallels in the development of Western harmony and tonality, and a methodological rigour which could only enhance the status of musicology, Fétis did not underestimate the materialism and anti-historicism inherent in Comte's system. For Fétis, Wagner's conception of opera amounted to vandalism against tradition and a threat to the hard-won status of autonomous music at the top of the Romantic artistic hierarchy: his emphasis on truth reduced music to the status and limited goals of language (*RGM* XIX/30: 25 Jul. 1852, 243). In a series of 'Lettres aux compositeurs dramatiques' (*RGM* XX/47–XXI/2: 20 Nov. 1853 – 9 Jan. 1854), Fétis provided several attacks which complemented and clarified those of his 1852 Wagner essay. In the second letter, he argued that dramatic music's purpose should be the ideal, and posited the industrial, commercial, systemic (and therefore materialist) music of Wagner as its antithesis (*RGM* XX/50: 11 Dec. 1853, 427–8); he also contrasted the emotional qualities of great music with Wagner's purely sensationalist concerns (*ibid.*, 427). Later, in a passage remarkable for its proximity to the famous denunciation of Berlioz's impotent revolutionary strivings in the *Revue musicale* of 15 December 1832, he reinforced the anti-Comtian message of 1852. Apart from those who compose for the soul and those who compose to give pleasure, he detected a third category:

---

[3] 'Comme lui, ces philosophes suppriment le génie et lui substituent l'action de la force vitale; comme lui, ils repoussent l'idéal; comme lui, enfin, ils veulent limiter les émotions de la sensibilité et les fantaisies de l'imagination au profit de la clarté des idées' (*RGM* XIX/32: 8 Aug. 1852, 259).

There is another class of artists who, wishing to give the art a direction which is not its own, and who, lacking the genius necessary for the realisation (at least in part) of the revolution which they they have in mind to bring about, detach themselves from the very art of whose transformation they dreamed. Such men are persuaded that a system is a creation, and that one makes music from calculated propositions. They see doing something different from what was done before as inspiration, and they seem to give determination a value equal to that of ideas in the attainment of their goal. (*ibid.*, 429)[4]

Wagner was the most advanced of this group, and in Fétis's opinion his goal – the *Gesamtkunstwerk* – was itself misguided: a monstrous and artificial whole in which every constituent element was weakened (*ibid.*). In the third letter, Fétis reintroduced ideas of truth versus beauty to the debates concerning Romanticism. Ostensibly, his subject was that of form in dramatic music, but Wagner's formlessness, and its antecedents, were uppermost in Fétis's mind:

This system has not arisen now for the first time; it is the inseparable acolyte of what is known as Romanticism, a word which, in certain minds, signifies scorn for all rules and all experience, the negation of the beautiful as a category, the adoration of the true or of what is taken for it, and the cult of the ugly, inasmuch as it is present in the true. (*RGM* XX/52: 25 Dec. 1853, 444)[5]

In the *Gazette*'s pages, the mildly pejorative word 'procédé' was used to describe the approach of talented composers such as Mendelssohn; the word 'système', infinitely more damning – particularly when used as proof of adherence to the theory of materialism – was used consistently in relation to Wagner. Further, influential, elements of Fétis's essays of 1852–4 were his personalisation of academic dispute and his equation of the man with the music. Unlike Cousin, who taught that great men's personal lives should not be scrutinised, since they invariably appeared vulgar and contemptible in comparison with their public deeds, Fétis, when it suited him, demanded equal integrity in life and art.[6] Whilst Wagner, in his direct and indirect attacks on the French, did nothing to endear himself personally to the nation, the close links which were

---

[4] 'Il est une autre classe d'artistes qui, voulant donner à l'art une direction qui n'est pas la sienne, et qui, n'ayant pas le génie nécessaire pour la réalisation, au moins en partie, de la révolution qu'ils ont le dessein d'accomplir, se placent en dehors de ce même art dont ils ont rêvé la transformation. Ces hommes se sont persuadé qu'un système est une création, et qu'on fait de la musique de propos délibéré. Faire autre chose que ce qu'on a fait avant eux leur paraît une inspiration, et la volonté leur semble avoir la même valeur que les idées pour atteindre leur but' (*RGM* XX/50: 11 Dec. 1853, 429).

[5] 'Ce système, ce n'est pas d'aujourd'hui qu'il se produit pour la première fois; il est inséparable acolyte de ce qu'on appelle le romantisme, mot qui, pour certains esprits, signifie le mépris de toutes règles et de toute expérience, la negation du beau comme type, l'adoration du vrai ou de ce qu'on prend pour lui, et le culte du laid, en tant qu'il est dans le vrai' (*RGM* XX/52: 25 Dec. 1853, 444).

[6] See Cousin, *Cours de philosophie*, Leçon X, 24–6.

perceived between biography and musical evaluation served only to heighten antagonism towards him, particularly after *Eine Kapitulation* of 1870.

Wagner's treatment in the decade prior to Fétis's attack could hardly provide a sharper contrast, with foreign reports stressing the success and popularity of his scores in German cities. It is not, of course, inconceivable that some of the early, enthusiastic reviews were submitted by Wagner himself, since he would still have been in contact with Schlesinger after his departure from Paris in 1842. Reports from Dresden in 1843 are markedly more laudatory than those from elsewhere. There are signs of self-advertisement in reviews of *Der fliegende Holländer*: 'This is the second work from the pen of this young musician-poet, whose genius was revealed with so much brilliance in the opera *Rienzi*' (*RGM* X/3: 15 Jan. 1843, 26).[7] A second report stressed that the work had been a success, despite its challenging novelty (*RGM* X/9: 26 Feb. 1843, 73), and noted that Wagner was a deserving and popular choice as the new conductor at Dresden; a third reported a royal compliment paid to Wagner on the occasion of the Dresden festival (*RGM* X/30: 23 Jul. 1843, 261). A similar procedure occurs regarding early performances of *Tannhäuser* in 1845, where each report closes by drawing attention to Wagner's popularity.

Such notices, all confined to the 'Nouvelles' section of the journal, continued until 1850, when the journal carried an extract from Gérard de Nerval's essay on the Weimar performances of *Lohengrin* (*RGM* XVII/38: 22 Sep. 1850, 316–17), which ended with the suggestion that it was not Wagner's most successful work. In two reviews, the first following the performance of the overture *Christophe Colomb* at a concert organised by the *Gazette* (*RGM* VIII/11: 7 Feb. 1841, 80–1), the second in 1850 after the Société Sainte-Cécile's performance of the *Tannhäuser* overture, Henri Blanchard voiced misgivings about the direction Wagner's music had taken. His description of *Tannhäuser* as 'Romantic in the strongest sense of the word' (*RGM* XVII/48: 1 Dec. 1850, 398),[8] was a warning in itself. Nevertheless, Blanchard's argument was expressed in impersonal terms; he saw *Tannhäuser* as another manifestation of a movement of which he disapproved on principle. Eight years later, his response to the same overture was characterised by hostility and sarcasm. Blanchard found the work banal and lacking in melody. He added: 'The public listened to this strange work in a religious silence; they even applauded, which is most

---

[7] 'C'est la deuxième pièce sortie de la plume de ce jeune musicien-poète, dont le génie s'est révélé tout récemment avec tant d'éclat, dans l'opéra de *Rienzi*' (*RGM* X/3: 15 Jan. 1843, 26).

[8] 'romantique dans toute la force de cette expression' (*RGM* XVII/48: 1 Dec. 1850, 398).

gracious of them' (*RGM* XXV/6: 7 Feb. 1858, 44).[9] The use of religious imagery is significant. The journal's critics customarily used such allusions in their writings on Beethoven and, later, on Berlioz, viewing them as priests of their school of composition; by contrast, Wagner's self-deification was unacceptable, and his followers were sarcastically dubbed 'M. R. Wagner's sect' in a report from the *Gazette*'s Munich correspondent on rehearsals for the première of *Tristan* (*RGM* XXXII/23: 4 Jun. 1865, 186).[10] Much of the difference between Blanchard's two reviews can be explained by reference to Fétis's articles, whose publication instantly transformed the criticism of Wagner's music into a series of personal attacks and sarcastic insults. The extent of Fétis's power can be gauged by the credo which Edouard Monnais included in a review of Wagner's first Paris concert of 1860. After posing questions concerning Wagner's theory and practice, the nature of his melodic style and the ultimate value of his work, Monnais (writing as 'Smith') continued:

We do not need to concern ourselves with it: all these things have been related, explained, discussed with such authority of knowledge and reasoning by our illustrious collaborator, M. Fétis, that our task is more than fulfilled in advance. Who else but he could add anything to the fine and profound study which he published in this very journal? Therein lies our profession of faith; therein are our doctrines, and we know no others. (*RGM* XXVII/5: 29 Jan. 1860, 33)[11]

The concept of art transforming itself through genius rather than genius setting out to transform art was one of the most influential of Fétis's arguments against Wagner and his circle, partly because it fitted with the *Gazette*'s by then general maxim of evolution, without revolution, in music. After the second performance of *Tannhäuser* in 1861, Monnais judged that Wagner's failure was thoroughly deserved and equally predictable:

We had no doubts as to the outcome which awaited his foolhardy enterprise here. One does not with impunity try to change everything which exists, in the theatre and elsewhere, to replace it with vague conceptions which rest only upon abstract reasoning. The art of music needs no reshaping. (*RGM* XXVIII/12: 24 Mar. 1861, 89)[12]

[9] 'Le public a écouté dans un silence religieux cette œuvre étrange; il a même applaudi, ce qui est très-poli de sa part' (*RGM* XXV/6: 7 Feb. 1858, 44).

[10] 'la secte de M. R. Wagner' (*RGM* XXXII/23: 4 Jun. 1865, 186).

[11] 'Nous n'avons pas à nous en occuper: toutes ces choses ont été racontées, exposées, discutées avec une telle autorité de science et de raison par notre illustre collaborateur, M. Fétis, que notre tâche est plus que remplie d'avance. Quel autre que lui pourrait ajouter quelque chose aux belles et profondes études qu'il a publiées dans ce journal même? Là est notre profession de foi; là sont nos doctrines, et nous ne saurions en avoir d'autres' (*RGM* XXVII/5: 29 Jan. 1860, 33).

[12] 'Nous ne doutions pas du résultat qui attendait chez nous sa téméraire entreprise. On n'essaye pas impunément de changer tout ce qui existe, au théâtre ou ailleurs, pour y substituer de vagues conceptions qui ne reposent que sur des raisonnements abstraits. L'art musical n'est plus à refaire' (*RGM* XXVIII/12: 24 Mar. 1861, 89).

Fétis's son Edouard expressed similar opinions in his article 'Du nouveau en musique' (*RGM* XXXV/4: 26 Jan. 1868), and hinted prophetically at the danger of a chasm appearing between the composer and the public: 'if we must have novelty in music, we must not have too much of it; we must not reach the point of worrying music lovers in the perception of certain sensations which please them' (*ibid.*, 26).[13] Towards the close of the article, he outlined the difficulty of following the harmonic, melodic and metrical procedure of a composer who set out specifically to trick the ear; he accused Wagner of egotism, self-conscious novelty, and an obscurantist style which had much in common with German philosophy. Fétis *fils* used the fact that music is a temporal art to demonstrate the inadmissible nature of intellectually complex works:

One can study the pages of a book at leisure; one can reflect for hours or whole days on the allegorical significance of a picture; but music does not stop to let one penetrate the mystery of its workings; one must take it in, understand it as it goes by. If it is not intelligible, if the idea does not distinguish itself from among the surrounding sonorities, it is merely noise. (*ibid.*, 27)[14]

Edouard Fétis's standpoint, of course, represents a rejection – indeed an inversion – of one of the *Gazette*'s longest-established tenets: the policy of encouraging the public to come to terms with difficult works by making the effort to hear them a number of times with an open mind. It implies that the journal's conception of genius as superior to the majority of humanity has been abandoned, and outlaws its identification with the socially alienated artist writing for posterity, a major feature of the *Gazette*'s Beethoven criticism. Moreover, it denies criticism itself any capacity to bring the public and the avant-garde closer together, and thus argues its own uselessness. Few of the *Gazette*'s reviews presented their readers with such nihilism.

In the late 1860s, Charles Bannelier's attitude to Wagner was one of restrained hostility. He could not condone the composer's personal behaviour, but campaigned in the *Gazette* for an end to the rioting which became a common feature of Pasdeloup's Concerts Populaires whenever a piece by Wagner was programmed, arguing that the qualities of the man and the musician should be kept apart.[15] There may be vestiges here

---

[13] 's'il faut du nouveau en musique, il n'en faut pas trop; il n'en faut pas au point de troubler les amateurs dans la perception de certaines sensations qui leur plaisent' (*RGM* XXXV/4: 26 Jan. 1868, 26).

[14] 'On peut étudier à loisir les pages d'un livre; on peut réfléchir des heures et des jours entiers sur le sens allégorique d'une composition picturale; mais la musique ne s'arrête pas pour laisser pénétrer le mystère de ses combinaisons; il faut la saisir, la comprendre au passage. Si elle n'est point intelligible, si l'idée ne se dégage pas de l'ensemble des sonorités, elle n'est qu'un bruit' (*ibid.*, 27).

[15] See 'Ch. B.', *RGM* XLIII/45: 5 Nov. 1876, 357; and ?Bannelier, *RGM* XLVI/20: 18 May 1879, 157–8.

of the idea, present in Cousin and reinforced in the *Gazette*'s *contes* (in particular Balzac's 'Gambara' of 1837), that genius could be excused from the necessity of living up to accepted moral codes, though Bannelier never wrote anything explicitly to this effect. His response to Wagner, particularly the later works, is interesting for its increasing openness. His review of *Rienzi*'s première at the Théâtre-Lyrique in 1869 was conciliatory, though this could be due solely to the opera's relatively conventional style (signed, *RGM* XXXVI/15: 11 Apr. 1869). Similarly, his acceptance of *Die Meistersinger*, whose première he attended in Munich, may have been helped by the misapprehension that the work's composition antedated that of *Lohengrin*: Bannelier picked out the most traditional passages for praise (signed, *RGM* XXXV/26–7: 28 Jun. – 5 Jul. 1868). Bannelier was less severe on Wagner than Georges Servières would have us believe:[16] he praised Pasdeloup's perseverance in continuing a Wagnerian crusade in the teeth of fearsome opposition from the audience, and often, such as in a report on Siegfried's 'Funeral March', questioned not the quality of the music but the advisability of taking it out of its dramatic context ('Ch. B.', *RGM* XLIII/45: 5 Nov. 1876, 357–8). Far from suggesting hostility, such comments beg comparison with those of Berlioz on the fate of Gluck extracts at the Société des Concerts. The articles of 1879 and 1880 suggest that Bannelier is drawn to Wagner more than he would care to admit; the prelude to *Tristan* 'shows, undoubtedly, the hand of a master' (?Banne-lier, *RGM* XLVI/15: 13 Apr. 1879, 118),[17] although (in an echo of Fétis and Botte) Bannelier cannot accept its uniformity of modulatory procedure. He criticises *Siegfried Idyll*, programmed by Colonne, as monotonous for similar reasons (?Bannelier, *RGM* XLVII/47: 21 Nov. 1880, 374). Yet a final review of *Die Walküre*'s closing scene praises its expressive power, even when taken out of its dramatic context:

Here, passion speaks a language of extreme intensity … invoking the aid of harmony whose audacity borders on strangeness, a powerful orchestration which is at times almost violent. Alongside impenetrable enigmas, it cannot be denied that here we have some very beautiful passages: the orchestral peroration is one such, and in its sweet and penetrating charm [it] contrasts with the remainder. (?Bannelier, *RGM* XLVII/52: 26 Dec. 1880, 414)[18]

[16] See Servières, *Richard Wagner*, (Paris, 1887), 133, 145.
[17] 'porte, sans aucun doute, la griffe d'un maître' (?Bannelier, *RGM* XLVI/15: 13 Apr. 1879, 118).
[18] 'La passion y parle un langage d'une intensité extrême … en appelant à son aide une harmonie hardie jusqu'à l'étrangeté, une instrumentation puissante parfois jusqu'à la violence. A côté de véritables énigmes, il y a là de fortes belles pages, on ne saurait le nier: le morceau d'orchestre de la péroraison en est une, et fait contraste avec le reste par son charme doux et pénétrant' (?Bannelier, *RGM* XLVII/52: 26 Dec. 1880, 414).

Two reviews stand out from a general background of polemic and unease in the journal: an uncharacteristically positive report on *Tannhäuser* in Frankfurt from Gustave Héquet (Durocher, *RGM* XXIV/40: 4 Oct. 1857, 323–4) and a review of the *Ring* (*RGM* XLIII/36–7: 3–10 Sep. 1876) signed 'N...'.[19] Héquet's article, which is not entirely laudatory, begins with positive comments and moves towards censure. However, unlike Monnais and Fétis, Héquet does not proceed from a viewpoint of unassailable French superiority, and he takes seriously the positive response of the Frankfurt audience.[20] Still further removed from the *Gazette*'s usual response to Wagner's late music is the *Ring* review, which lifts the journal's reviewing towards genuine enthusiasm. A studiously objective preview article states that a detailed series of reviews will be provided by 'Un correspondant spécial' (?Bannelier, *RGM* XLIII/33: 13 Aug. 1876, 260). The first of these reviews deals mostly with the general reception of the four works (unsigned, *RGM* XLIII/35: 27 Aug. 1876, 278); the second, in two instalments signed 'N...', talks of the 'real poetry' of the prelude to *Das Rheingold* (*RGM* XLIII/36: 3 Sep. 1876, 285),[21] the 'great expressive and descriptive intensity' of the close of *Die Walküre* (*RGM* XLIII/37: 10 Sep. 1876, 292),[22] and the exquisite, Mendelssohnian delicacy of the forest murmurs and the woodbird scene in *Siegfried* (*ibid.*); moreover, the critic refers to Act III of *Götterdämmerung* as 'one of the finest things written for the lyric stage' (*ibid.*, 293),[23] concluding that, despite his tendency to musical verbosity, 'In many respects Wagner the musician is a man of genius' (*ibid.*, 294).[24]

As described here, the review may seem severely out of step with the tenor of the journal's Wagner criticism, even that of Bannelier; however, when discussing Wagner's compositional procedure, the reviewer is ambivalent in ways which coincide precisely with Bannelier's views. A formalist, Bannelier was highly sceptical of programme music's merits; 'N...' expresses a similar sentiment regarding the depiction of Nibelheim:

[19]   The author's identity is unknown.
[20]   Quoting the critic Adolphe Giacomelli, Servières states that Héquet was one of the two leaders of the cabal which tried to bring the Paris performance down in 1861 (the other, as attested by Baudelaire, was the *Revue des deux mondes*'s reactionary critic, Paul Scudo). See Servières, *Richard Wagner*, 83. Such an interpretation implies that Héquet's view hardened considerably between 1857 and 1861; it is unfortunate that there are no articles in the *Gazette* which might explain why.
[21]   'véritable poésie' (*RGM* XLIII/36: 3 Sep. 1876, 285).
[22]   'grande intensité expressive et descriptive' (*RGM* XLIII/37: 10 Sep. 1876, 292).
[23]   'une des plus belles choses écrites pour la scène lyrique' (*ibid.*, 293).
[24]   'Wagner musicien est, par bien des côtés, un homme de génie' (*ibid.*, 294).

antipathetic to this generalised use of musical imitation, I shall make my reservations here once and for all; given which, I willingly admit that, of its type, the piece in question is perfectly successful. (*RGM* XLIII/36: 3 Sep. 1876, 285)[25]

In his account of *Das Rheingold*, the *Ring* reviewer gives a brief explanation of Wagner's thematic technique. However, he sees the function of the *Leitmotiv* as either a 'visiting card' or a reminiscence motif referring to specific events; there is no hint of a psychological interpretation of the technique. His interpretation leads to the complaint that certain orchestral passages, such as Siegfried's 'Rhine Journey' and the 'Funeral March', and the main vocal narratives of *Götterdämmerung*, are nothing more than mosaics, although Wagner's skill in their arrangement is never doubted. After Siegfried and Brünnhilde's farewell, which the critic praises highly, 'the main motives heard so far throughout the cycle are brought back, most ingeniously moreover, in one of those goulashes of which Wagner is so fond' (*RGM* XLIII/37: 10 Sep. 1876, 293).[26] Siegfried's conversation with the Rhinemaidens 'provides another pretext for the reunion of all the motives heard earlier at each point in the hero's life' (*ibid.*).[27] Bannelier may have taken his cue from the opinion of the Bayreuth correspondent: in a review of Siegfried's 'Funeral March' at the Concerts Populaires, he wrote: 'It is a mosaic constructed, and very well constructed, from motives already heard, particularly in *Siegfried*' ('Ch. B.', *RGM* XLIII/45: 5 Nov. 1876, 358).[28]

The nature of the *Gazette*'s Wagner criticism in 1880 might suggest that, had it continued publication, it might have been transformed (along the lines of *Le Ménestrel*) into a journal supportive of Wagner's work. Yet the evidence militates against such a view, setting Bannelier's criticism in perspective. In its final decade, the *Gazette* had three committed supporters of the New Germany on its staff: Camille Benoît (1877–80), Adolphe Jullien (1870/71–80) and Ernest Reyer (1868–80). Yet none wrote a signed article on Wagner's music, and, on the basis of the 1876 review of the *Ring* in Bayreuth as the zenith of the journal's enthusiasm (excepting the likely self-promotion of 1843–5), none wrote

---

[25] 'réfractaire à cet emploi généralisé de l'imitation par les sons, je fais ici mes réserves une fois pour toutes; moyennant quoi, je reconnais volontiers que le morceau en question est parfaitement réussi en son genre' (*RGM* XLIII/36: 3 Sep. 1876, 285).

[26] 'les principaux motifs entendus jusqu'ici dans toute la tétralogie sont rappelés, fort ingénieusement du reste, dans une de ces *ollas-podridas* comme Wagner les aime' (*RGM* XLIII/37: 10 Sep. 1876, 293).

[27] 'sert de nouveau prétexte à la réunion de tous les motifs entendus précédemment, à chaque période de la vie du héros' (*ibid.*).

[28] 'C'est une mosaïque faite, et fort bien faite, avec des motifs déjà entendus, particulièrement dans *Siegfried*' ('Ch. B.', *RGM* XLIII/45: 5 Nov. 1876, 358). There is no evidence to suggest that 'N...' is Bannelier, whose only known attendance at Bayreuth was at the festival of 1886. See Albert Lavignac, *Le Voyage artistique*, 552.

unsigned articles either, despite Camille Benoît's presence at the 1876 festival. Moreover, from 1865 to 1869, Armand Gouzien contributed to the journal, but wrote neither on Wagner nor on the composer who was, in the 1870s, to become his idol – Liszt.[29] The probability that these four authors were, at the very least, not encouraged to write articles on Wagner for the *Gazette*, is high.

The impression is strengthened in examining the gulf between the *Gazette*'s criticism of the New Germans and the work of the same critics when they wrote for other publications. Armand Gouzien's Bayreuth reviews provide an example of his evangelistic approach;[30] so, too, does his welcoming of the Lisztian symphonic poem in 1879, at a time when Bannelier continued to argue fiercely against the genre's validity. The *Journal de musique* viewed the symphonic poem as a new genre allowing the nineteenth century to break free from the symphony and overture. An unsigned article entitled 'Liszt and Saint-Saëns', which is undoubtedly by Gouzien himself, claimed that Beethoven and Berlioz had only developed the symphony; by contrast, Liszt had surpassed it:

This brilliant and fertile creation will be his greatest claim to fame in posterity, and when time has worn away the bright trace of the greatest pianist that ever was, inscribed on his golden book will be the name of the emancipator of instrumental music. (?Gouzien, *JM* IV/181: 15 Nov. 1879, 2)[31]

Gouzien then outlined the genre's formal principles, noting the combination of unity and variety afforded by the use of sections in different tempi bound together by the transformation of themes (*ibid.*).

Yet in the 1870s, Wagnerism could not be completely contained, even though it escaped only indirectly onto the *Gazette*'s pages. The journal's most strongly Wagnerian article is Adolphe Jullien's review of a revival of Reyer's opéra-comique *La Statue* in a revised form (*RGM* XLV/17: 28 Apr. 1878). Jullien attempts to find *La Statue* a place in both the

[29] Armand Gouzien published a set of articles in the *Journal de musique*, of which he was chief editor (*JM* I/12–13: 19–26 Aug. 1876). Reyer never attended Bayreuth; Jullien was not present at the first festival (see Servières, *Richard Wagner*, 190). Benoît attended in both 1876 and 1882. See Lavignac, *Le Voyage artistique*, 549–50. However, the *Gazette* articles seem too formalist to be Benoît's.

[30] Though, paradoxically, they end on a note of depressed confusion at *Götterdämmerung*'s complexity.

[31] 'Cette création brillante et féconde sera dans la postérité son plus beau titre de gloire, et quand le temps aura effacé la trace lumineuse du plus grand pianiste qui fut jamais, il inscrira sur son livre d'or le nom de l'émancipateur de la musique instrumentale' (?Gouzien, *JM* IV/181: 15 Nov. 1879, 2). An extraordinarily uneven periodical, the *Journal de musique* provided its readers with coffee-table journalism on every subject except that of the New German School, which prompted long and intellectually complex articles signed by Gouzien. On this subject, the style and aesthetically supportive content of Gouzien's unsigned articles makes them indistinguishable from those which are signed.

modernist and the traditionalist camps: he legitimises it in the eyes of the traditionalists by stressing its descendancy from the great tradition of Grétry; at the same time he highlights the challenging (i.e. Wagnerian) nature of its style for the audience of the opéra-comique. Jullien is careful not to mention Wagner by name until the middle of the article, referring only to the characteristic procedures of Reyer's writing, 'the extreme purity of vocal melody divested of any parasitic ornament, roulade or cadential pause' (ibid., 129).[32] Yet he cannot resist an evangelistic outburst on the proper direction for opera, which can be located in:

the very structure of his work, this continuity of the musical texture, tightened even more by new recitatives in such a way that one cannot tell where a recitative finishes or where an aria begins, this excellent arrangement, which responds so well to the ideal of lyric drama. (ibid.)[33]

This is the only such defence of the Wagnerian ideal of unending melody in the entire Gazette; its critics were otherwise unanimous in condemning the absence of clarity in a formal procedure which, as they saw it, had no obvious lines of demarcation, whether in opera or instrumental music.

As in other journals, Wagner's detractors in the Gazette saw his influence as almost omnipresent; a composer often stood or fell on his perceived acceptance or rejection of Wagnerian doctrine. Adolphe Botte's Schumann criticism of the 1850s and 1860s illustrates the extent of such responses, which (understandably) gathered momentum after the Franco-Prussian War. Determined to keep the genre innocent of Wagnerian elements, Paul Bernard, in his opéra-comique reviews of 1872, showed the level of obsession reached by the journal's more conservative critics. He detected Wagnerian influence even in Emile Paladilhe's Le Passant:

Unfortunately, almost all our young musicians covet a kiss from modern Germany's muse, and in my view this muse seems too little the daughter of Apollo and too much the offspring of M. Wagner and others. The result is what I shall call the school of musical labyrinths. (RGM XXXIX/17: 28 Apr. 1872, 130)[34]

Unreservedly supportive reviews of Aimé (Louis) Maillart and Massenet, written later the same year, were conditioned by the same consideration

---

[32] 'le caractère si pur de la mélodie vocale expurgée de tout ornement parasite, roulade ou point d'orgue' (RGM XLV/17: 28 Apr. 1878, 129).

[33] 'le plan même de son œuvre, cette continuité de la trame musicale, encore resserrée par des récits nouveaux, de telle façon qu'on ne sache ni où le récit finit, ni où l'air commence, cette disposition excellente, et qui répond si bien à l'idéal parfait du drame lyrique' (ibid.).

[34] 'Malheureusement, presque tous nos jeunes musiciens ambitionnent le baiser de la muse germanique moderne, et cette muse-là me semble bien peu fille d'Apollon et beaucoup trop parente de MM. Wagner et consorts. Il en résulte ce que j'appellerai l'école du labyrinthe musical' (RGM XXXIX/17: 28 Apr. 1872, 130).

in inverse: that both works appeared free of such pernicious elements.[35] There are other instances of the practice: Adolphe Botte's articles on Fétis, Berthold Damcke's defence of Henri Litolff (*RGM* XXV/6: 7 Feb. 1858, 45–6), Bannelier's review of Massenet's overture *Phèdre* (?Bannelier, *RGM* XLI/9: 1 Mar. 1874, 69), and the discussions from 1876 of the Wagnerism or otherwise of *Aida* (Bernard, *RGM* XLIII/18: 30 Apr. 1876, 138; Ch. Bannelier, *RGM* XLVII/13: 28 Mar. 1880).[36] Of those composers who were actively associated with the 'music of the future', Liszt received the harshest criticism in the *Gazette*, particularly with reference to the symphonic poems. Saint-Saëns, a follower of the school in the larger genres, was also subjected to censure. In 1877, an unsigned report of *Samson et Dalila*'s success in Weimar praised Saint-Saëns for utilising Wagnerian techniques in a non-plagiaristic manner; an editorial introduction emphasised that the *Gazette* reserved judgement on the issue because of: 'the critic's standpoint. In such cases, one cannot be too circumspect' (?Bannelier, *RGM* XLIV/49: 9 Dec. 1877, 387).[37] Two years later, on the performance of an aria from *Etienne Marcel*, Bannelier was equally ambivalent:

It has a gentle and poetic melancholy; but its unclear form, in comparison with our dramatic customs, the predominance, almost throughout the piece, of what might be called threnody, disorient the listener a little. (?Bannelier, *RGM* XLVI/ 8: 23 Feb. 1879, 61)[38]

Such opinions are hardly supportive; nevertheless they contrast sharply with the stern advice given to Saint-Saëns in 1870 on his Piano Concerto no. 3 in E-flat Op. 29, where, the finale excepted, Bannelier saw nothing but 'a regrettable aberration; it is comparable to everything incoherent and tormented in Liszt's late manner. There is nothing to gain in this path, along which the finest masters lose their originality' (?Bannelier, *RGM* XXXVII/13: 27 Mar. 1870, 100).[39]

Wagner's profile in the journal describes a concave arc which reaches its lowest point in the 1850s and recovers partially over the next thirty years. Though he contributed briefly to the journal in the 1840s, he never

[35] Maillart: *RGM* XXXIX/26: 30 Jun. 1872; Massenet: *RGM* XXXIX/48 [49]: 8 Dec. 1872.

[36] See also Servières, *Richard Wagner*, 176 ff.

[37] 'le point de vue critique auquel il [the critic] s'est placé. En pareille matière, on ne saurait être trop circonspect' (?Bannelier, *RGM* XLIV/49: 9 Dec. 1877, 387). The report was reprinted from *L'Indépendance belge*.

[38] 'Il est d'une mélancolie douce et poétique; mais sa forme peu arrêtée, eu égard aux habitudes de notre théâtre, la prédominance, dans presque tout le morceau, de ce qu'on est convenu d'appeler mélopée, déroutent un peu l'auditeur' (?Bannelier, *RGM* XLVI/8: 23 Feb. 1879, 61).

[39] 'une regrettable aberration; c'est á comparer á tout ce que la dernière manière de Liszt a d'incohérent et de tourmenté. Il n'y a rien á gagner dans cette voie, et les meilleures natures y perdent leur originalité' (?Bannelier, *RGM* XXXVII/13: 27 Mar. 1870, 100).

gained a following among its staff, and the strength of Fétisian influence in the 1850s was such that he and his followers were, thereafter, always viewed warily. By contrast, Berlioz had significant influence on the journal's opinions from the outset, and was associated from the beginning with a journal whose tenets were, in part, fundamentally opposed to those of his fiercest critic on the *Revue musicale*. Moreover, Schlesinger and the Brandus brothers published his works.[40] Among the contemporary composers reviewed in the *Gazette*, Berlioz's reception is the most complex, drawing together the strands of aesthetic and personal allegiance, Fétisian influence, commercial interest, and the relation between critics and performers in securing acceptance for a member of the avant-garde.

[40] During Schlesinger's absences from Paris in the late 1830s, Berlioz became acting director of the journal. Several letters in the period August 1836–October 1837 attest to this. See Hector Berlioz, *Correspondance générale*, ed. Pierre Citron, 5 vols. (Paris, 1972–), II, nos. 476, 493, 498, 508 and 511.

11   Contemporary music V: Berlioz

Writing in 1893, Adolphe Jullien described an article by Fétis in the *Revue musicale* of 15 December 1832:

This study thus contains, conveniently grouped, all the arguments (among which some are pretty specious) which could be presented to the public to discredit the author of the *Fantastique*; in taking them up and sharpening them, the master's enemies managed to forge well-tempered arms which they could make use of for thirty, forty, fifty years without their becoming blunt. It is they who harassed Berlioz, who crippled him with stinging wounds; it was Fétis who armed them.[1]

The symmetrical relationship of this opinion to that of Servières on Wagner is apparent. However, Berlioz's fate in the *Gazette* could hardly have differed more; explaining the unparalleled complexity of his reception produces a micro-history of the entire journal. The reception of Berlioz in the *Gazette* is exceptional. As a contributor (and as director during Schlesinger's absence), in the 1830s he had enormous power over the *Gazette*'s message; despite the fact that he did not publish exclusively with Schlesinger, as a composer he could, in the years up to 1846, depend upon constructive reviews from colleagues of whom many were personal friends. Alongside Beethoven, he was, from the outset, presented as the *Gazette*'s finest composer – the embodiment of the genius as presented in Schlesinger's *contes*. Alone among avant-garde Romantics, he survived a Fétisian shift in the journal's critical

---

[1] 'Cette étude renferme ainsi, très adroitement groupés, tous les arguments, dont quelques-uns assez spécieux, qu'on pouvait présenter au public pour discréditer l'auteur de la *Fantastique*; en les reprenant, en les aiguisant, les ennemis du maître arrivèrent à se forger des armes bien trempées et dont ils purent faire usage pendant trente, quarante, cinquante ans, sans les émousser. Ce sont eux qui ont harcelé Berlioz, qui l'ont criblé de blessures cuisantes; c'est Fétis qui les avait armés.' Adolphe Jullien, *Musique, mélanges d'histoire et de critique musicale et dramatique*, 2nd edn (Paris, [1900], 218–19). The article in question was a review of the *Symphonie fantastique* and the *Retour à la vie*, written in response to Berlioz's public humiliation of Fétis for 'correcting' the text of Beethoven's symphonies (*RM* VIe année, no. 46: 15 Dec. 1832, 365–7). See Bloom, 'Berlioz and the Critic', 240–65.

aesthetic which outlawed Schumann, Liszt and Wagner; in 1880, he was still the *Gazette*'s most celebrated nineteenth-century composer.

Berlioz's reception represents one of the few areas of criticism where Fétis's influence was countered effectively. By November 1835, when the *Gazette* took over Fétis's *Revue*, the journal's Berliozian character, together with its welcoming of Romanticism, was well established. Moreover, Berlioz's prominence among the staff stifled any discontent which might have arisen among Schlesinger's contributors. By the Brandus takeover of 1846 and, more importantly, Fétis's attack of 1852 on Wagner, the supportive tone of Berlioz criticism had too much momentum to be modified – still less, reversed. The extent of Berlioz's in-house support inevitably drew accusations of partiality and 'coterie';[2] that such charges were largely unjustified was one of the journal's greatest strengths. The *Gazette* rarely published uncritical eulogies of Berlioz's works in the manner of *La France musicale*'s reception of Félicien David; rather, the journal's critics appear, corporately or not, to have believed that a composer of Berlioz's calibre should be criticised at the highest level. However, critics unsympathetic to Berlioz's cause rarely reviewed either his concerts or the monumental series of performances of his major works staged by Colonne and (with less evangelism) Pasdeloup in the 1870s. There were few occasions when Monnais had a chance to express his ambivalence or Fétis his hostility. Blanchard, too, generally avoided reviewing Berlioz; in 1851, Léon Kreutzer reported on a concert by Berlioz's Grande Société Philharmonique, whilst Blanchard reviewed all the week's remaining concerts (*RGM* XVIII/14: 6 Apr. 1851). With the exception of opinions on Berlioz's degeneracy written by Fétis in the context of other subjects,[3] Berlioz's critics consistently took his status as a genius as their fundamental premise, and made strenuous attempts to educate their readers to accept him as such.

However, such support did not prevent the publication of reviews, by Heller and Kreutzer in particular, which questioned the composer's practice. The strength of the *Gazette*'s approach to Berlioz lay in its inverse partisanship, whereby the strongest criticisms of his music came from those who were known to be wedded to his cause. The ploy has a calculated honesty combined with the advantage of preventing rare passages of eulogy, such as Bottée de Toulmon's famous account of the Requiem (*RGM* IV/50: 10 Dec. 1837), from appearing too cloying. The *Gazette* gave Berlioz more concentrated

---

[2] *FM* II/1: 3 Jan. 1839, 1. The charge of 'coterie' is not levelled directly either at the *Gazette* or at Berlioz; however, the *Gazette* is the only plausible candidate.

[3] See in particular his 'Dernières transformations de la symphonie' (*RGM* XIV/19–27: 9 May – 4 Jul. 1847), discussed in Chapter 8.

exposure than any other composer, including Beethoven. Although its coverage of Berlioz's output was uneven, no other composer's works were analysed at such length by so many different contributors, both as a result of their being performed, or (more importantly) in independent articles written for general interest. Emphasis on certain works sets in perspective the scant attention given to others. Some of those neglected were downplayed for diplomatic reasons: the failure of *Benvenuto Cellini* was given minimal coverage in 1838, and the work never recovered much stature in the journal. Other omissions were more closely linked with aesthetic issues: there was, in the journal's forty-seven-year history, no significant independent article on the *Fantastique* or on *Lélio*; other major works, including *Les Troyens*, *Béatrice et Bénédict*, and *Les Nuits d'été*, each received a single, lengthy article. By contrast, *Roméo*, the Requiem and *La Damnation* received extensive coverage, since they were the works which the journal's critics acknowledged as those on which Berlioz's reputation should rest, and for which they attempted to ensure posterity. Criticism's educational rôle was of paramount importance: until a work had been understood and accepted by the public, the *Gazette*'s critics felt it their duty to continue explaining the nature of its qualities. The public's sustained antipathy to Berlioz's output meant that expository and evaluative criticism of selected works persisted until well after Colonne and Pasdeloup had begun to turn the tide of public opinion in the 1870s.

The *Gazette*'s early reviews are unashamedly Romantic in tone. Berlioz embodied the ideal of the fusion of the arts: equally adept at writing words and notes, he was presented both as a poet and a painter in sound. The trend is exemplified by an unsigned article of December 1834, probably written by François Stoepel.[4] The critic outlined three methods of composition: the purely musical, the imitative and the poetic. Dismissing autonomous music as one-dimensional,[5] and the imitative as primarily an historical phenomenon, he gave the palm to the poetic, in which he saw the mundane compositional decisions of autonomous music enriched and ennobled by an overarching poetic idea:

> where the musician develops a broad aesthetic theme, penetrates all its most diverse facets to reveal in his harmony the feelings which inspired his imagination, in such a way as to arouse in us the same feelings, to elevate us with him to the lofty plane of his ideas, to let us rise, like him, to the fullness of excitement, to let us suffer his own pain, finally to let us groan like him in all the agonies of despair.

---

[4] For a defence of this attribution, see Appendix 5.

[5] Despite his laudatory reviews of Onslow's chamber music, discussed in Chapter 2.

This is precisely what characterises Berlioz's manner. This composer is a poet above all. (?Stoepel, *GM* I/52: 28 Dec. 1834, 425)[6]

In 1834, an unsigned reviewer of Berlioz's second concert compared his instrumentation to the subtle treatment of colour and light by a fine painter (*GM* I/49: 7 Dec. 1834, 395);[7] in the eyes of Heller, writing on the *Fantastique*, fusion of the arts was Berlioz's main achievement: 'with artists such as Berlioz, poetry, music and painting exist simultaneously' (*RGM* V/48: 2 Dec. 1838, 492).[8] As late as 1854, Maurice Bourges suggested that the most appropriate preparation for listening to *L'Enfance du Christ* was to take:

a special stroll round the Louvre ... the sight of most of these expressive paintings, particularly the earliest and the most naïve, would be an excellent preparation for listening better to the new score and feeling it more keenly. (*RGM* XXI/51: 17 Dec. 1854, 406)[9]

The *Gazette*'s articles of the 1830s presented Berlioz through the positive means of highlighting his strengths; later articles showed more defensiveness and, implicitly or explicitly, attempted to counter Fétisian arguments. Berlioz's situation was the inverse analogue of Wagner's: careful selection (or perhaps unopposed self-selection) of critics reviewing Berlioz's music, and diplomatic silence over unsuccessful premières, indicated the journal's partisanship. Those critics who came most under the Fétisian spell were all but silent on the subject of his music. Ironically, they comprised the journal's mainstay reviewers, their contributions spanning its entire life: Blanchard, Monnais, and, to a certain extent, Bannelier. However, their opinions can be deduced from their comments on other Romantic or modernist composers. Blanchard's definition of Romanticism in 1841, for instance, constituted a list of Berlioz's

---

6 'où le musicien s'échauffe sur une grande idée esthétique, s'en pénètre sous toutes ses faces les plus diverses, pour nous révéler ensuite par ses accords les sentimens qui ont enflammé son imagination, de manière à éveiller en nous les mêmes sentimens, à nous élever avec lui jusqu'à la hauteur de ses idées, à nous faire monter comme lui jusqu'au comble de l'enthousiasme, à nous faire souffrir de sa propre douleur, de manière enfin à ce que nous gémissions comme lui dans toutes les angoisses du désespoir. C'est là précisément ce qui caractérise la manière de Berlioz. Ce compositeur est poète avant tout' (?Stoepel, *GM* I/52: 28 Dec. 1834, 425).

7 The reappearance of comments on the contrast between Berlioz's wild, energetic music and his ability to write passages of exquisite serenity again suggests the authorship of Stoepel. See below, p. 226.

8 'chez des artistes comme Berlioz il y a tout à la fois de la poésie, de la musique et de la peinture' (*RGM* V/48: 2 Dec. 1838, 492).

9 'une promenade spéciale au musée du Louvre', where 'la vue de la plupart de ces peintures expressives, surtout des plus anciennes et des plus naïves, serait une excellente préparation pour mieux écouter et sentir la partition nouvelle' (*RGM* XXI/51: 17 Dec. 1854, 406).

perceived sins (*RGM* VIII/41: 11 Jul. 1841, 337–8).[10] As part of his definition, he presented all the major charges against which Berlioz was to be defended in the *Gazette*: the implicit charge of formlessness in Romantic music, the perceived need for 'carrure', the question of noisy orchestration (related to Fétis's complaints about music's increasing materialism) and the problem of programme music.

The following year, Maurice Bourges attempted to expose the over-reaction of such comments. Blanchard had reviewed Berlioz's first concert of 1842, referring to *Harold*'s 'vague meditations' (*RGM* IX/6: 6 Feb. 1842, 53),[11] citing other critics' negative opinions of the *Rêverie et caprice*, and displaying his own ambivalence by describing Berlioz as:

the eccentric, exceptional musician, whom some proclaim the Shakespeare of modern art, whilst others say he is only the Scarron; Berlioz who, according to one person, sumptuously displays the rich, vibrant, warm and luxuriant tones of Rubens on his musical palette, or who, according to another, is nothing but a grotesque Callot. (*ibid.*, 53–4)[12]

In a review of the composer's second concert, Bourges poured scorn upon those critics (including, by implication, Blanchard) who claimed to find the simplest of his works incomprehensible. The *Rêverie et caprice* was one such piece: 'Frankly, you would have to be prejudiced beyond belief to call a simple romance divided into two couplets, each containing two tempi (an Adagio in $\frac{6}{8}$ and an Allegro vivace in $\frac{3}{8}$) *unprecedented, incomprehensible*' (*RGM* IX/8: 20 Feb. 1842, 68).[13] A month later, he continued the battle in an article on Berlioz and form (*RGM* IX/13: 27 Mar. 1842). His weapon was dry, bar-by-bar descriptive analysis which, partly because of its Fétisian associations, was rarely used in the *Gazette*. Bourges's aim was to expose doubters through the use of their own means. He discussed the 'Scène aux champs' and the *Marche funèbre*, detailing their formal outlines, their key schemes, thematic ideas and overall unity. His examples were carefully chosen to dispel the idea that a

[10] See Chapter 8, pp. 161–2.

[11] 'vagues méditations' (*RGM* IX/6: 6 Feb. 1842, 53).

[12] 'Berlioz, le musicien excentrique, exceptionnel, que quelques uns proclament le Shakspeare de l'art moderne, pendant que d'autres disent qu'il n'en est que le Scarron; Berlioz qui, suivant celui-ci, étale fastueusement sur sa palette musicale les tons riches, animés, chauds et luxuriants de Rubens, ou qui, selon celui-là, n'est qu'un grotesque Callot' (*ibid.*, 53–4). Paul Scarron (1610–60), French picaresque novelist; Jacques Callot (1592–1635), French artist, famous for etchings. Given E. T. A. Hoffmann's enthusiasm for the Romantic fantasy of Callot's etchings (they form the subject of prefatory material to *Kreisleriana*), and Berlioz's respect for Hoffmann, Blanchard's comparison is not wholly successful.

[13] 'Franchement il faut être prévenu outre mesure pour traiter d'*inouïe*, d'*incompréhensible*, une simple romance divisée en deux couplets, dont chacun renferme deux mouvements, l'un adagio à $\frac{6}{8}$, l'autre allegro vivace à $\frac{3}{8}$' (*RGM* IX/8: 20 Feb. 1842, 68).

descriptive movement must necessarily lack formal cohesion, and to stress the traditional elements of the *Marche*'s form. Bourges repeated the 'descriptive analysis' technique in a review of the première of *Le Carnaval romain* (*RGM* XI/6: 11 Feb. 1844).

The overture, in A major, is divided into three sections. The first, a very fast Allegro in $\frac{6}{8}$, briefly states the energetic theme which later plays such a significant rôle. The second is an Andante in C major in $\frac{3}{4}$. We noticed with admiration the skilful variations in the presentation of a delicious melody taken from the vocal trio of *Benvenuto Cellini*. Stated first by the cor anglais with a pizzicato offbeat accompaniment, then repeated in E major by the violas underneath a counter-melody in the first flute and clarinet, this noble theme reappears in canon at the octave to surprisingly rich effect. The group of bassoons, cellos and violas, which state it together, is imitated at a beat's distance by the violins, the flutes and the oboes together. The expansive and full wind writing, which floats in varied patterns under this majestic theme, acquires a more piquant interest by the unusual rhythm and the carnival-like sonority of two *tambours de basque*, cymbals, timpani and triangle. The third section, Allegro vivace in $\frac{6}{8}$, begins muted with a phrase which is delicate, light, murmuring and mysteriously frisky in character. This section of the overture, written with such skilful use of wind instruments, contrasts well with the explosion of the *fortissimo*, which bursts out in E major. There is nothing warmer, more vigorous, more intoxicated than the second, delirious, wanton theme. There is nothing more amazing or more skilled than the way he treats it. The electric shock given by this outstanding idea, grows in intensity after the development, where the two motifs of the Allegro are heard again and again, combined, contrasted with a hundred beauties of detail which cannot be included in such a brief analysis. (*RGM* XI/16: 11 Feb. 1844, 43–44)[14]

[14] 'Trois mouvements successifs divisent l'ouverture écrite en *la* majeur. Le premier, *allegro* très vif à six-huit, fait pressentir brièvement la mélodie fougueuse qui joue plus loin un si grand rôle. Le second est un *andante* à trois temps en *ut* majeur. On y a remarqué avec admiration les dispositions habilement variées dans lesquelles M. Berlioz présente un chant délicieux extrait du trio vocal de *Benvenuto Cellini*. Récitée d'abord par le cor anglais avec un accompagnement à contre-temps du quatuor *pizzicato*, puis reproduite en *mi* majeur par les altos sous un contre-sujet de première flûte et de première clarinette, cette noble mélodie reparaît traitée en canon à l'octave avec une richesse d'effet surprenante. Le groupe de bassons, des violoncelles et des altos, qui la disent ensemble, est imité à un temps de distance par les violons, les flûtes et les hautbois réunis. L'harmonie large et pleine, qui flotte en dessins variés sous ce chant majestueux, acquiert un intérêt plus piquant par le rhythme singulier et la sonorité toute carnavalesque de deux tambours de basque, des cymbales, des tymbales [sic] et du triangle. Le troisième mouvement, *allegro vivace* à six-huit, débute avec sourdines par une phrase fine, légère, chuchotante, et d'une couleur mystérieusement folâtre. Cette partie de l'ouverture, écrite avec un ménagement très adroit des effets d'instruments à vent, est heureusement opposé à l'explosion du *fortissimo*, qui éclate en *mi* majeur. Rien de plus chaud, de plus vigoureux, de plus ivre que ce second thème délirant, échevelé. Rien de plus éblouissant et aussi de plus habile que l'art avec lequel l'auteur l'a traité. La secousse électrique imprimée par cette pensée étourdissante redouble d'intensité après le développement intermédiaire, où les deux motifs de l'allegro passent et repassent, mélangés, contrastés avec cent beautés de détail qui échappent à une analyse rapide' (*RGM* XI/16: 11 Feb. 1844, 43–44).

Bourges begins in a neutral, descriptive vein redolent of Fétis. In his assessment of the first two sections, he emphasises elements of structure, of melodic repetition (which Berlioz's music was deemed to lack) and counterpoint. However, when he reaches the Allegro vivace, the speed and character of his prose is transformed into a 'critique admirative' in the tradition of Berlioz himself – a compliment which would have been lost on none of the *Gazette*'s readers, nor on the composer. The move from technical description to a poetic fusion of analysis, evaluation and interpretation is undoubtedly calculated, but this does not detract from its effect, which is to draw the reader into the excitement of the music as if against his or her better judgement. As Bourges states earlier in the review, the public will eventually judge the piece on its emotional, not its formal, merits; his prose invites exactly this response. There could have been no better antidote to the carping of anti-Berliozian critics.

In 1852, twenty years after hinting that a theory analogous to that of the four stages of harmony could be formulated for rhythm and metre, Fétis wrote 'Du développement futur de la musique dans le domaine du rhythme' (*RGM* XIX/35–52: 29 Aug. – 26 Dec. 1852), in which he outlined a series of innovations in rhythm and metre (including the use of irregular metres) which would enrich future composition. During publication of this series, Léon Kreutzer contributed an analysis of Berlioz's Requiem (*RGM* XIX/43–7: 24 Oct. – 21 Nov. 1852) in which he directly attacked the musicologist's pretensions as a prophet of musical style. Throughout his analysis, Kreutzer returned to the subject of Berlioz's innovative practice. Referring to the rhythmic originality of the *Kyrie* he claimed: 'In the realm of rhythm, Berlioz is an innovator; and with reference to this branch of the art, inspiration had long dictated to him what theory now teaches' (*RGM* XIX/44: 31 Oct. 1852, 370).[15] Despite such irritated outbursts, even Kreutzer found the influence of Fétis inescapable. An examination of the extent of his influence on the *Gazette*'s critiques of Berlioz shows an interesting combination of hostility and tacit agreement among the journal's Berliozian contributors, Kreutzer included. Fétis supported the notion that true genius composed spontaneously. He was, in consequence, suspicious of revisions or works which seemed to betray a difficult gestation; his only exception to the rule appears to have been Meyerbeer. The aesthetic of spontaneity which prevailed among the *Gazette*'s critics occasionally worked against Berlioz, as with those parts of *La Damnation* which were revised from the *Huit scènes de Faust*. Kreutzer marshalled this very argument to express

---

[15] 'Dans le domaine du rhythme Berlioz est un novateur; et à propos de cette branche de l'art, l'inspiration depuis longtemps lui avait dicté ce qu'enseigne aujourd'hui la théorie' (*RGM* XIX/44: 31 Oct. 1852, 370).

his disapproval of the 'Easter Hymn', stating in words which Fétis himself could have used: 'To conceive, execute, and all this in an almost immediate thought process, such is the ideal goal to which an artist in full possession of creative genius, of creative strength, can aspire' (*RGM* XXII/4: 28 Jan. 1855, 27).[16] He also felt that the thematic developments of the ball scene in *Roméo et Juliette*, 'seem to indicate painful labour' (*RGM* XV/11: 12 Mar. 1848, 81).[17] By contrast, the celebrated duet between Ursula and Hero at the close of Act I of *Béatrice et Bénédict* was described by a reviewer signing himself 'Z.', as 'one of those things which are found, not sought' (*RGM* XXIX/33: 17 Aug. 1862, 269).[18] Even as late as 1873, Bannelier criticised the 'Marche au supplice' because it 'has no directness and feels too laboured' (?Bannelier, *RGM* XL/45: 9 Nov. 1873, 358).[19]

The charge of materialism, like that of formlessness, was one on which the *Gazette*'s critics deliberately focused. Berlioz's programmaticism, his gift for dramatic realism and his love of extremes (of tessitura and volume) all rendered the subject inescapable. His penchant for large orchestras featuring massed brass left him open to ridicule and caricature on the ground that he materialised music by sheer force of sound, brutalising the senses and using effect to conceal poverty of invention. The *Gazette*'s critics never denied his passion for the grand gesture;[20] however, they contrasted it with his supreme delicacy in handling small forces. Once more the trend was set by Stoepel, in a signed review of the *Neuf mélodies irlandaises* which noted of No. 5, 'La belle voyageuse', that Berlioz had two complementary sides to his nature. After emphasising the raw energy of his genius, Stoepel observed: 'when a genius of such temper once tackles this sphere [the graceful style], he appears to abandon himself to it with a magic spell, and everything he produces then breathes the divine delight of pure joy, of delicious ecstasy' (*GM* I/21: 25 May 1834, 170).[21] The 'Mab' scherzetto, the *Roméo et Juliette* Scherzo and the sylphs' scene in Part II of *La Damnation* never failed to provoke enthusiasm, whilst critics in general hailed *L'Enfance du Christ*

---

[16] 'Concevoir, exécuter, et cela par un acte presque immédiat de la pensée, tel est le but idéal que peut se proposer un artiste en pleine possession du génie qui crée, de la force qui réalise' (*RGM* XXII/4: 28 Jan. 1855, 27).

[17] 'semblent dénoter un travail pénible' (*RGM* XV/11: 12 Mar. 1848, 81).

[18] 'une de ces choses trouvées et non cherchées' (*RGM* XXIX/33: 17 Aug. 1862, 269).

[19] 'n'a pas l'allure franche et sent trop le travail' (?Bannelier, *RGM* XL/45: 9 Nov. 1873, 358).

[20] See Bourges on the *Te Deum* (*RGM* XXII/18: 6 May 1855, 138).

[21] 'quand un génie d'une telle trempe aborde une fois cette sphère [le genre gracieux], il paraît s'y abandonner avec un charme magique, et tout ce qu'il produit alors respire la divine jouissance d'une joie pure, d'une extase délicieuse' (*GM* I/21: 25 May 1834, 170).

as the beginning of a second period in Berlioz's style, on account of its tenderness and delicacy. Critics such as Fétis, who complained of the increasing 'bruit' of modern orchestration, were thus answered.

More vexed was the issue of music's representational potential. The most complex elements in Berlioz's reception in the *Gazette* concern the proper place and limits of programme music. The extreme nature of Stoepel's concept of poetic music (quoted earlier) was not shared by all the *Gazette*'s critics, some of whom stated or implied that they would like to see an abstract symphony from Berlioz's pen.[22] However, instrumental music's ability to convey ideas, and Berlioz's supremacy in this area, were never doubted. In his open letter to Schumann after the première of *Roméo et Juliette*, Stephen Heller defended the composer's descriptive style, stating that: 'To my mind, Berlioz demands no more effects of music than it can provide' (*RGM* VI/69: 19 Dec. 1839, 546).[23] He had already declared his allegiance the previous year in an article on the *Symphonie fantastique*, in which he described his conversion to the programmatic procedures at work therein, claiming that Berlioz's sureness of expression was such that the music alone drew him involuntarily to images consistent with the content of the programme (*RGM* V/48: 2 Dec. 1838, 492).

Yet there were times when the worst pejorative term for descriptive music – materialism – was used with reference to Berlioz. Only Heller could justify what critics perceived as the sacrifice of form to content and emotion to truth in the tomb scene of *Roméo et Juliette*. **Charles Merruau** felt that it contained, 'the defects of Berlioz's first style' (*RGM* VI/63: 28 Nov. 1839, 499),[24] by which he probably meant the *Symphonie fantastique*, a work which was never enthusiastically acclaimed in the *Gazette*, and which in its later years was treated patronisingly as among Berlioz's *juvenilia*. In 1848, Kreutzer complained that the tomb scene represented programme music's worst excesses, saying that it exceeded the power of music and did nothing to further Berlioz's cause: 'this is materialising the art, and gives M. Berlioz's critics reason to ask how he might express the colour of his trees' (*RGM* XV/11: 12 Mar. 1848, 82).[25] Kreutzer recommended that it be cut.

[22] See, for example, Merruau, *RGM* VI/63: 28 Nov. 1839, 499; and Kreutzer, *RGM* XV/11: 12 Mar. 1848, 82.

[23] 'Berlioz, à mon sens, ne demande nullement à la musique plus d'effets qu'elle n'en peut fournir' (*RGM* VI/69: 19 Dec. 1839, 546). Heller's open letter is translated almost in full in Julian Rushton, *Berlioz:* Roméo et Juliette (Cambridge, 1994), 60–9.

[24] 'les défauts de la première manière de Berlioz' (*RGM* VI/63: 28 Nov. 1839, 499).

[25] 'voilà qui est matérialiser l'art, et qui peut donner raison aux critiques demandant comment M. Berlioz exprimerait la couleur de ses arbres' (*RGM* XV/11: 12 Mar. 1848, 82).

Jullien, writing in 1875, agreed, although he dared not recommend the work's mutilation:

Berlioz *materialised* the entire scene; he even wanted to paint somewhere Romeo's successive gulps and the first attacks of the poison; but the staging or the gestures which he imagined and which he described by turns with a rapid violin or cello figure, by a sigh on the clarinet or a timpani roll, are a closed book for the listener. This piece lies entirely outside the confines of the symphony. (*RGM* XLII/49: 5 Dec. 1875, 389)[26]

The exception to such critical opinion was Heller, in his open letter to Schumann (*RGM* VI/69–70: 19–22 Dec. 1839) in which he freely admitted that Berlioz had written theatrical orchestral music – 'you could imagine yourself at the rehearsal of the most dramatic of operas, played by the orchestra and during which the stage remained empty' (*RGM* VI/70: 22 Dec. 1839, 561).[27] Heller noted that this was 'at once a reproach and a compliment' (*ibid.*),[28] since, although the music alone could not convey detail, it contained the essence of tragedy. He drew out the thematic associations within the tomb scene, referring to the return of the love theme as a major unifying factor; lastly, he stated that the power and expressive force of the music compensated for the absence of a much-needed explanatory text.

Heller's view of Berlioz's programmatic procedures was not, however, universally accepted. In an uneasy introduction to a detailed essay on *La Damnation de Faust* (*RGM* XXI/49–XXII/13: 3 Dec. 1854 – 1 Apr. 1855), Léon Kreutzer attempted to bring *La Damnation, Roméo et Juliette* and the *Symphonie fantastique* into the realm of autonomous music, arguing that their distance from theatre music was proof of their status as pure, uncompromised musical expression. In the course of his discussion, Kreutzer made a point which Berlioz's opponents systematically ignored, and which would have been clarified by a cursory reading of the composer's essay 'De l'imitation musicale', which had appeared in the *Gazette* in 1837 (*RGM* IV/1–2: 1–8 Jan.). Kreutzer argued that descriptive music could take various forms, ranging from the concretely imitative to the poetically suggestive, and that Berlioz's idea of using music to create an image analogous to that of a stimulus from

---

[26] 'Berlioz a *matérialisé* toute la scène; il a même voulu peindre quelque part les gorgées successives bues par Roméo et les premières atteintes du poison; mais les jeux de scène ou les gestes qu'il se représentait et qu'il décrivait un à un par tel trait rapide de violons ou de violoncelles, par un soupir de clarinette ou un roulement de timbale, sont lettre close pour l'auditeur. Ce morceau sort absolument du cadre de la symphonie' (*RGM* XLII/49: 5 Dec. 1875, 389).

[27] 'l'on pourrait se croire à la répétition d'un opéra des plus dramatiques exécutée par l'orchestre et durant laquelle la scène resterait vide' (*RGM* VI/70: 22 Dec. 1839, 561).

[28] 'un reproche et un éloge tout à la fois' (*ibid.*).

another art did not cause his purely musical inspiration to be compromised to the extent that his detractors liked to claim. The absence of theatrical trappings, the fundamentally emotional, rather than sensual or material, nature of his descriptive manner, left him almost free from constraint:

once this is accepted (this slight hindrance, if you like, to the liberty of thought), the composer is absolutely free in his ideas, his forms, his developments; he need make no concessions to anyone. (*RGM* XXII/2: 14 Jan. 1855, 10)[29]

However, Kreutzer's unease lies only just under the surface. In 1848, he had appealed to Berlioz for an abstract symphony that would silence his detractors once and for all – 'a symphony, as he alone can make them, but in which there would be no element of drama' (*RGM* XV/11: 12 Mar. 1848, 82);[30] the argument Kreutzer presented in 1855 smacks of an aesthetic *volte-face* occasioned by the realisation that no such work would be forthcoming. Formalist arguments aside, part of Kreutzer's dilemma stems from the historical legacy of Hoffmann, and the claim that pure instrumental music was superior to that defiled by texts. Such thinking, though in conflict with ideals of the fusion of the arts, was inextricably linked with the Beethovenian tenor of the journal's early criticism. As France's greatest symphonist and Beethoven's perceived successor, it was natural that Berlioz should be judged by an aesthetic of autonomous music. In his last significant article on Berlioz for the *Gazette*, Kreutzer's intention in 1855 was to alter the aesthetic to suit the composer, in order that Berlioz's reputation might be saved from the stigma of materialism.

The idea of Berlioz as a composer who could express more with notes alone than with words was a Hoffmannesque and, until the 1870s, consistently held opinion in the *Gazette*, coming to grief only when faced with the overt narrative in the tomb scene of *Roméo et Juliette*. This concept, together with Berlioz's own stated reasons for the purely instrumental slow movement in *Roméo*, informs Georges Kastner's

[29] 'une fois cette donnée (cette légère entrave à la liberté de la pensée, si l'on veut) acceptée, le compositeur reste absolument libre de son idée, de ses formes, de ses développements; il n'a aucune concession à faire à qui que ce soit' (*RGM* XXII/2: 14 Jan. 1855, 10). In 1980 Jacques Barzun drew the opposite conclusion with essentially the same intention of weakening the perception of Berlioz's output as unusually programmatic. He argued that the extent of external influences on 'absolute' music makes futile the traditional view of absolute and programme music in opposition to each other. All music is therefore programmatic. (See 'The Meaning of Meaning in Music: Berlioz Once More', *Musical Quarterly* LXVI/1 (Jan. 1980), 1–20.) However, these are not Kreutzer's aesthetic premises; nor does he have the benefit of knowing that Berlioz's posterity is assured.

[30] 'une symphonie, comme seul il sait les faire, mais dont le drame sera absent' (*RGM* XV/11: 12 Mar. 1848, 82).

comparison of the love scenes here and in *La Damnation de Faust*: 'In the "balcony scene", Romeo and Juliet are, by their very absence, far more present than Faust and Marguerite in the scene from *Faust*' (*RGM* XXII/ 6: 11 Feb. 1855, 43).[31] Such paradoxes fuelled the irony that the journal's critics viewed Berlioz's operas as driven by their music and his symphonies as driven by their drama. The journal's most extended study of Berlioz, a 32–instalment assessment of his life and works by Emile Mathieu de Monter (*RGM* XXXVI/24–XXXVII/27: 13 Jun. 1869 – 3 Jul. 1870), made this very point concerning *Les Troyens*:

> The calculated slowness of progressions whose goal cannot be glimpsed, sometimes leads *The Trojans* to the plains of monotony. This score, too much that of a symphonist to be well written for the voices, is more interesting to read than to listen to; above all, more interesting to hear in concert excerpts than in its complete form on stage. (*RGM* XXXVII/4: 23 Jan. 1870, 26)[32]

A criticism more inimical to Berlioz's operatic aesthetic could hardly have been devised by his worst enemies. Adolphe Jullien, one of the *Gazette*'s most ardent supporters of Berlioz, but also one of his most exacting critics, complained of the supremacy of music over drama in *La Prise de Troie*, particularly the extended and largely static octet following the news of Laocoön's death (*RGM* XLVI/50: 14 Dec. 1879, 405). Jullien was not alone in viewing Berlioz, ultimately, as France's greatest symphonist; even in those works which contained substantial vocal parts, the extent to which critics focused their attention on the orchestra is striking. Heller noted of the finale to *Roméo et Juliette* that, despite its operatic style, Berlioz allowed music to take precedence over drama (*RGM* VI/70: 22 Dec. 1839, 561).

The prevailing view of Berlioz as a symphonist rather than as a composer of opera had a decisive effect on the manner of his reception. Precisely because he did not have a reputation as an operatic composer, the Branduses and Schlesinger knew that Berlioz would not make their fortune; in the journal, the hyperbole of opera advertising – lavished on Meyerbeer, Halévy and Lecocq – was redundant. Instead, the *Gazette*'s critics concentrated on educating a future public. Berlioz's weakness as a source of commercial gain is put in focus by the journal's response to his death. He died at the moment when the Brandus house was revelling in

---

[31] 'Dans la Scène au balcon, Roméo et Juliette, par leur absence même, sont bien plus présents que Faust et Marguerite dans la scène de *Faust*' (*RGM* XXII/6: 11 Feb. 1855, 43).

[32] 'La lenteur calculée de progressions dont on n'entrevoit pas le but final égare parfois *les Troyens* dans les steppes de la monotonie. Cette partition, trop d'un symphoniste pour être bien traitée sous le rapport vocal, est plus curieuse à lire qu'à entendre; surtout plus intéressante à entendre en fragments au concert, que dans sa totalité à la scène' (*RGM* XXXVII/4: 23 Jan. 1870, 26).

the success of a new acquisition – Rossini's *Petite messe solennelle*. Although news of Berlioz's death made the front page, it was swamped, in column space and adulatory language, by eulogistic reports, many gathered from other papers, of Rossini's work. In contrast with the journal's emotional response to the deaths of Rossini and Meyerbeer, Berlioz's obituary by Mathieu de Monter was sombre and understated, though his massive 32-instalment tribute was still to come. Nevertheless, even in death Berlioz was overcome by the pressures of a hostile market.

The irony of Berlioz's death being upstaged by Rossini's church music would not have been lost on Berlioz's supporters in the *Gazette*, among whom there were several apologists for the Requiem as sign of the revitalisation of monumental sacred music in France. Part of such revitalisation took the form of a stylistic eclecticism which several critics detected in Berlioz's work. Though the term 'eclecticism' was not used in reviews of Berlioz's sacred music, his use of ancient styles for dramatic effect caused comment. Maurice Bourges's review of *L'Enfance* (the same as that in which he recommended that prospective listeners view the old masters at the Louvre) is characterised by its comparisons of various parts of the work with composers from Palestrina to Handel and Le Sueur:

What is immediately striking is the archaic character which predominates from start to finish; the systematic search for sixteenth- and seventeenth-century forms of the art, such as the relatively strict imitation, the fugal style, the suspensions, the harmonic progressions far removed from modern tonality. (*RGM* XXI/51: 17 Dec. 1854, 406)[33]

Secular works also possessed eclectic qualities. From the 1870s, rarely did a performance of *La Damnation* pass without a reference to the archaic simplicity of the 'Chanson du Roi de Thulé'. In 1872, Jullien admired its 'archaic forms' (*RGM* XXXIX/10: 10 Mar. 1872, 75);[34] later he referred to its gothic simplicity (*RGM* XLIV/8: 25 Feb. 1877, 60). Such comments drew attention away from Berlioz the Romantic and presented him almost as a neo-Classicist. It was Jullien who, in 1879, portrayed Berlioz as returning to the Classicism of two of his first idols – Gluck and Spontini – in a review of *La Prise de Troie* which presented his career as the absorption of the arch-Romantic into the Classicist, beginning with *L'Enfance* and continuing with the Gluckian regularity of

---

[33] 'Ce qui frappe tout d'abord, c'est le caractère d'archaïsme qui y règne d'un bout à l'autre; c'est la recherche systématique des formes de l'art au XVIe et XVIIe siècles, telles que les imitations plus ou moins serrées, le style fugué, les suspensions, les successions harmoniques peu sympathiques à la tonalité moderne' (*RGM* XXI/51: 17 Dec. 1854, 406).

[34] 'formes archaïques' (*RGM* XXXIX/10: 10 Mar. 1872, 75).

parts of *Béatrice et Bénédict*; Jullien, however, saw Berlioz's Classicism at its zenith in *Les Troyens*:

Late in life, Berlioz ... had a fine attack of Classicism, and it is here that we can see how the stormy lessons with his master Le Sueur had a real influence on this undisciplined pupil. Of the four composers whom Berlioz adored as sovereign gods of music, and whom he made his absolute models, two inspired him most at the beginning of his career: Beethoven and Weber, and two at the end: Gluck and Spontini. (*RGM* XLVI/50: 14 Dec. 1879, 404–5)[35]

The final phase of the *Gazette*'s Berlioz criticism coincides with that period of growing confidence when critical enthusiasm was bolstered by visible progress in the concert arena – the 1870s. When Berlioz wrote to his sister Adèle of his audacity in treating *Roméo et Juliette* as an opera and presenting three closely spaced performances in 1839, he must have been aware of how necessary a measure it was to give a work of such novelty the benefit of repeated hearings.[36] Despite the occasional performance of extracts of his works in Paris up to his death, Berlioz's reputation had floundered partly because he had no opera in the standard repertory. That the momentum necessary for a work to enter the repertory had not been achieved accounts for the numerous substantial essays the *Gazette* printed on the same work. The need for repeat performances carried over into criticism: at the end of his essay on the Requiem, Léon Kreutzer wrote: 'Nobody will blame me for these long expositions on a work which is already old' (*RGM* XIX/47: 21 Nov. 1852, 397).[37] Though old, the work was relatively unfamiliar to the journal's readers.

The real reason behind the acceptance of Berlioz in France lies with the director of the Concerts du Châtelet, Edouard Colonne. He programmed weekly performances of the large-scale orchestral and choral works from 1875 and, by giving *La Damnation* eleven hearings between February 1877 and January 1878, performed what Bannelier, referring to Colonne's intention to perform all the major works, uncut, in the 1877/78 season, termed a 'work of reparation in which the public gives him the greatest encouragement' (?Bannelier, *RGM* XLIV/44: 4 Nov. 1877, 350).[38] Whilst Pasdeloup's attention was split between

---

[35] 'Berlioz, sur le tard de sa vie ... fut pris d'un bel accès de classicisme, et c'est alors qu'on put voir combien les leçons à bâtons rompus de son maître Lesueur avaient eu d'influence réelle sur cet élève indiscipliné. Des quatre compositeurs que Berlioz adorait comme les dieux souverains de la musique et dont il avait fait ses modèles absolus, deux l'inspirèrent de préférence au début de sa carrière: Beethoven et Weber, et deux à la fin: Gluck et Spontini' (*RGM* XLVI/50: 14 Dec. 1879, 404–5).

[36] Berlioz, *Correspondance générale*, II, no. 697.

[37] 'On ne me blâmera pas de ces longs développements donnés à une œuvre déjà ancienne' (*RGM* XIX/47: 21 Nov. 1852, 397).

[38] 'œuvre de réparation à laquelle le public l'encourage de son mieux' (?Bannelier, *RGM* XLIV/44: 4 Nov. 1877, 350).

championing Berlioz and Wagner, and the Conservatoire put on expurgated versions which would not frighten its 'timid public' (signed, *RGM* XLII/50: 12 Dec. 1875, 398),[39] Colonne concentrated on French music (and specifically Berlioz) almost to the extent of forming a cult for the appreciation of his music. In the *Gazette*, Adolphe Jullien was the obvious candidate as reviewer both of these concerts and those of the Concerts Populaires, which often ran performances in tandem with the Concerts du Châtelet. Though Bannelier prepared a piano duet version of the *Fantastique* and clearly respected Berlioz's work, he wrote the briefest of comments on his music in the journal, and never reviewed the evangelising concerts of Pasdeloup and Colonne. Jullien, however, commanded a significant amount of column space on a regular basis.

Of all the composers reviewed in the *Gazette*, Berlioz was the most problematic. An avowed reformer, he was welcomed during the Schlesinger years but, as the hold of Fétisian ideas strengthened in the late 1840s and 1850s, had increasingly to be defended against the tide of adverse criticism. By the 1870s, when his reputation was at last becoming secure, aesthetic goals had shifted and he was accepted in part as a composer with inherently Classical leanings. The idea of programme music was applauded, but selectively; early Romantic works such as the *Fantastique*, *Lélio* and *Harold* were quietly forgotten, and works intended for the canon – *Roméo*, *La Damnation*, *L'Enfance* and the Requiem – over-exposed. The Classicism of *Les Troyens* excepted, the operas were never given wholehearted support. The *Gazette* portrayed Berlioz more in its own image than in a manner he would have accepted as reflecting his own priorities.

By 1880 the *Gazette* revealed a serious imbalance in its coverage of and opinions on contemporary music. On the one hand, Berlioz's immense popularity was reflected in Jullien's criticism, which often highlighted the dramatic and descriptive in his style and made few negative value-judgements on the validity of programme music. Simultaneously, Saint-Saëns and D'Indy were criticised for following programmatic procedures which were seen to have come from Liszt, and which were never related in the journal to the tradition of Berlioz's works of the 1830s and 1840s. Following the Franco-Prussian War, the Germanic and French strands in symphonic music were kept out of conflict purely by the designation of different reviewers for each, much as Gemmy and Louis Brandus's need to publicise the operettas of Offenbach and Lecocq was maintained in

---

[39] 'public timoré' (signed, *RGM* XLII/50: 12 Dec. 1875, 398).

peaceful co-existence with the disgust of De Monter and Bannelier at the genre's degeneracy and its dubious implications for public taste. The sense of debate, so much a part of the early *Gazette*, had disappeared. Although there was no less a sense of critical conflict among collaborators in the years up to 1880 than when the journal first appeared, the existence of such conflict was tacitly denied by what appears to have been an editorial policy of non-aggression, in which the reviewing of most composers showed only one side of a debate. Such a policy represented a complete reversal of Schlesinger's tactic, which was to encourage discussion, even if it threatened to develop beyond the confines of a critical dispute, as in 1837. The most extreme manifestation of a non-aggression policy in the 1860s and 1870s was the presence of four silent sympathisers of New German composition on the staff of a journal which remained officially antipathetic to the 'music of the future'. Although tensions between commercial interest and critical integrity showed through, particularly in the journal's operatic criticism, and an element of hypocrisy is evident in its advertising of operatic arrangements for piano by composers only marginally superior to Henri Herz, the *Gazette* managed, by detailed reviewing, to justify its opinions in a way which other journals with less musically educated readerships (and reviewers) could not. In Berlioz's case, the demands of public education, the need for criticism to do justice to an acknowledged genius and, ironically, Berlioz's own operatic failures, enabled the *Gazette*'s criticism to transcend the demands of commercialism. The very stringency of the reviews of Jullien, Heller and Kreutzer proved their commitment to Berlioz's cause.

Conclusion

For works which the public can hear every day at the theatre, in the concert hall, in the salon, works where its tastes, its instincts, are flattered, often to the detriment of the true and the beautiful, the critic is only a clerk; he has no mission other than to gather together the support and report opinion; to change it, to modify it, even, would be an impossible task. For works which belong more truly to the realm of art, the critic's mission becomes nobler and more serious. He questions the thought of the composer, penetrates it, unveils it; he is the connecting link which joins the composer to the public; it is up to him not to let his attention wander onto a thousand details which he will pick up later, but to concentrate on the true beauties. (*RGM* XIX/43: 24 Oct. 1852, 357)[1]

So wrote Léon Kreutzer of the demands Berlioz's music made upon critics and criticism. He thus stressed the element of mission in his rôle as a critic, and his function as a vehicle through whose work the public might understand, appreciate and, finally, judge, works which were initially beyond its comprehension. The *Gazette*'s strength as an educative force lay in the ability and willingness of its critics to accept their rôle as defined by Kreutzer; some of its most compelling episodes resulted from the abandonment, often for commercial reasons, of the same principles.

In his obituary notice for the *Gazette*, Léon Escudier paid tribute to its directors for their continuity of purpose during the half-century of its life (*L'Art musical* XX/1: 6 Jan. 1881, 7). Although to imply an unbroken tradition was excessively reverential, several major questions, with their attendant conflicts, preoccupied the journal's critics throughout its

---

[1] 'Pour les œuvres que le public a l'occasion d'entendre tous les jours au théâtre, au concert, au salon, œuvres où ses goûts, ses instincts sont flattés, au détriment souvent du vrai et du beau, le critique n'est qu'un greffier; il n'a d'autre mission que de recueillir les suffrages et de constater l'opinion; la changer, la modifier, même, serait une tâche impossible. Pour les œuvres qui appartiennent plus réellement au domaine de l'art, la mission du critique devient plus sérieuse et plus noble, [sic] il interroge la pensée du compositeur, la pénètre, la dévoile; il est le trait d'union qui joint le compositeur au public; c'est à lui de ne pas laisser l'attention s'éparpiller sur mille détails qu'elle embrassera plus tard, mais de la concentrer sur les véritables beautés' (*RGM* XIX/43: 24 Oct. 1852, 357).

career. The concept of criticism as an educative discipline remained constant from the journal's Beethoven criticism in the 1830s to that of Berlioz in the 1870s. Increasingly, the educative ideal became tied to that of the formation of a musical canon whose aesthetic quality had been tested by critics and was deemed irreproachable. Arguments over contemporary music, when not sullied by purely commercial interests, thus centred not only around a composer's present status, but on the question of probable posthumous worth. The most revealing of the *Gazette*'s discussions are those in which the aesthetic tenets of composition are questioned: its reception of late Beethoven, Wagner and programmatic music are cases in point. The *Gazette*'s enthusiasm for early music is also linked with the growth of the canon, though here the question is complicated by the increasing autonomy of musicology, which gradually ceased to view performance as, necessarily, the natural or even the desired consequence of its investigations. In musicology, the educative spirit was paramount, but the discipline's self-justifying nature did little to promote music composed before 1600 as more than a curiosity. Even Fétis, renowned for his love of Renaissance music, fostered such a view by consigning to the Dark Ages of his *ordre unitonique* all music which antedated the use of the dominant seventh, adjudging it harmonically incomplete. The influence of Fétis's theories, alongside a shortage of available scores, ensured that, even by 1880, no Renaissance work had achieved the public acclaim which welcomed the oratorios of Handel and the *St Matthew Passion* to Paris in the 1870s. Indeed, any attempt to repeat Lamoureux's experiment using earlier music was explicitly discouraged by the *Gazette*'s historians as necessarily doomed to failure. Sacred music of the Renaissance escaped such disparagement only when maintained within its traditional liturgical context, thus reinforcing the essential nature of the canon as a secular phenomenon.

Early acceptance of the notion of a musical canon focused on music dating from around 1780 onwards. Although earlier music was a familiar component of sacred repertoires, it had to be re-evaluated in the concert hall in order to become part of the canon. That judgement was suspended when sacred works were performed in a sacred context is indicated by the critics themselves. In 1878, Adolphe Jullien highlighted the irony of public acceptance of Berlioz's Requiem as compared with its immediate rejection of other, secular, works. Despite relatively few performances, the Requiem had eked its way into the repertoire because it had been presented in religious and ceremonial contexts in which the immediate voicing of public opinion was forbidden:

Doubtless it is due to the enforced silence of the audience that the Requiem succeeded in being performed several times in Paris ... without the public seeming to become annoyed, while *La Damnation de Faust*, a much more diverse, vital creation, more theatrical and consequently closer to general taste, had been judged and condemned without possibility of appeal after two performances. (*RGM* XLV/12: 24 Mar. 1878, 89)[2]

Such re-evaluation was brought about by performers, critics and the public. With early music, a spirit of revival permeated both the performance and criticism of works which had fallen into disuse. Until a work had been assimilated, the need for re-examination and re-evaluation brought about a blurring of the distinctions between music criticism and musicology. Though none of the journal's critics used the term 'canon', 'classique' was used in the 1830s to refer to Haydn and Mozart, and later, to Beethoven. By 1870, the perceived goal of art music – acceptance into the 'répertoire' as a prelude to becoming part of the canon – indicated a clear sense of a hierarchy of works. The existence of such a hierarchy was appreciated by the 1860s. Gustave Héquet was ambivalent about the stagnant nature of the Société des Concerts's programming policy; whilst admitting that its concerts lacked variety, he none the less feared that the standard repertoire was under threat from diversification (*RGM* XXX/8: 22 Feb. 1863, 60). His fear of musical stagnation was mingled with relief that a newly established repertoire was protected from the consequences of an enforced return to an aesthetic of disposable music – the very aesthetic against which early nineteenth-century critics had fought successfully.

Whilst opera and domestic piano music were always potentially ephemeral genres, chamber and concert music expanded to accommodate the retention of the old alongside the addition of the new. Despite its inevitable coverage of operatic premières, throughout its career the heart of the *Gazette*'s criticism lay in its reviews of concert life. The scale of its coverage of chamber and orchestral concerts was unsurpassed, revealing its nearly unwavering commitment to an aesthetic of intemporal beauty. Its essential character as a Beethovenian journal remained constant, despite the presence of critics such as Monnais and Botte, for whom Beethoven was a dangerous influence. For forty-seven years, Beethoven was the touchstone of its criticism. By contrast, the place of Haydn and Mozart was progressively coloured by historicist considerations. Yet Beethoven's consistently high profile in the *Gazette*

---

[2] 'C'est, sans doute, en raison du silence forcé de l'auditoire que le *Requiem* a pu être exécuté plusieurs fois à Paris ... sans que le public ait paru s'en fâcher, tandis que *la Damnation de Faust*, cette création beaucoup plus variée, plus vivante, plus théâtrale enfin et par conséquent plus dans le goût général, avait été jugée et condamnée sans appel possible en deux auditions' (*RGM* XLV/12: 24 Mar. 1878, 89).

inevitably helped alter the journal's critical position as the years progressed. Starting out as a Romantic, modernist publication committed to the finest music produced by Germany, it ended its career rejecting all that 'la nouvelle Allemagne' represented, and took the opportunity of its most distinguished house composer's death to offer him as an alternative idol: Berlioz became a Beethovenian who had rejected the excesses of Romanticism for a purer, more Classical mode of expression.

Central to the shift from German Romanticism to French Classicism was the influence of Fétis, though he would not have accepted the choice of Berlioz as the journal's flagbearer. His view of genius as a non-egotistical vessel represented a rejection of the ideas illustrated in the journal's first decade, where Romantic ideas of the status of the artist were combined uneasily with the utopian view of music's elevated place in society. Elitist and individualist ideas of the genius writing for posterity gave way to a Fétisian model influenced by Cousin's philosophies and outdated utopian ideals of music as balanced, clear, and accessible, its creators serving their audience. During the journal's most conservative years – 1858–65 – the impact of these ideas jeopardised even Beethoven's reputation. The equation of Romanticism with the uglier sides of realism and materialism led to its denigration in the work of Monnais and Blanchard, who used the term to indicate a comprehensive rejection of proper musical values. New compositional systems, whether in the guise of programmaticism or new approaches to thematic and modulatory procedure, were seen as inimical to true inspiration and as a cover for poverty of musical thought. Such opinions were increasingly echoed in the journal once Schlesinger had sold it to Louis Brandus in 1846. In differing degrees, Blanchard, Botte, Bourges, Héquet, Monnais, and Bannelier – the journal's main concert reviewers in the Brandus years – were Fétisian critics. To Fétis's Cousinian notion of eclecticism as the use of older styles to rejuvenate contemporary music (an early theory of neo-Classicism), Blanchard, Botte and Monnais added the narrower concept of a desired *juste milieu* in instrumental music – a style based on the re-interpretation of middle-period Beethoven. The emergence of this view in the 1840s helps to articulate the fundamental change in the journal's character from modernism to conservatism. Just as Fétis believed in the need for change without a denial of Classical stylistic values, so the *Gazette*'s espousal of its own brand of eclecticism allied it to evolution rather than revolution. Monnais, the most reactionary of the journal's critics (in that he was equally suspicious of contemporary and early music as legitimate constituents of the canon), even suggested that stasis was to be preferred:

In the progress of art, as in that of society, there are three tendencies which manifest themselves continually and reciprocally, although seeming to contradict one another. One person wants always to forge ahead; another always to turn back; the third asks only to stay put. It is clear that only with the last would the world and art remain stationary, but also that with the other two they would inevitably break down. (*RGM* XXI/33: 13 Aug. 1854, 265)[3]

The journal's focus on the Viennese classics as music's rightful core repertory came to prejudice it against the Romanticism it had originally supported. Fétis's influential formalist theories, which threatened to undermine the strong position Berlioz enjoyed throughout the career of the journal, recommended that the extra-musical tendencies of Romanticism be regarded as an aberration necessarily destructive to formal purity. Hence the difficulty Bannelier experienced in dealing with Liszt's later works and the efflorescence of his innovations in the French symphonic poem, and his insistence on judging programmatic works by the formal standards of autonomous music. By laying emphasis on Beethoven's middle-period works as the seed of future music, and accepting the late works only as inimitable, the *Gazette*'s post-1846 critics, Bannelier and Jullien excepted, also rejected the orchestral output of Schumann, particularly once his name had been linked with that of Wagner. Such antipathy to modern German music, combined with a perceived absence of innovation in French music up to around 1870, explains the journal's critical conservatism in its reviewing of new instrumental music between Blanchard's death in 1858 and Bannelier's arrival in 1866, during which time the opinions of Monnais, Botte and Héquet held sway.

The *Gazette*'s lack of critical spark in its middle years was exacerbated by the then limited resources of music criticism. French critics never aspired to German models of analysis, being content with an informative combination of description and interpretation which made little use of technical language except in the hands of Berlioz or a theorist such as Georges Kastner. The equation of analysis with destructive dissection was common in the 1830s, and remained so almost until the end of the century in France. In the late 1840s, Conservatoire concert reviews ceased in the *Gazette*, primarily because the public needed no further introduction to works it already knew, and because critics had nothing to add to previous discussions. A critical stalemate was broken by the entry

---

[3] 'Dans la marche de l'art, comme dans celle de la société, il y a trois tendances qui se manifestent sans cesse et se servent réciproquement, tout en ayant l'air de se contrarier. Celui-ci veut toujours s'élancer en avant; celui-là toujours retourner en arrière; le troisième ne demande qu'à rester en place. Il est clair qu'avec le dernier seulement le monde et l'art demeureraient stationnaires, mais aussi qu'avec les deux autres ils se briseraient infailliblement' (*RGM* XXI/33: 13 Aug. 1854, 265).

of virtuosi as interpreters of canonic works, and by their increasing emphasis on rejuvenating the classics by means of expressive devices. The rejection of established performing traditions in favour of personal interpretation opened the way for new critical responses which effected a separation between musicology and music criticism as practised today; attention turned from the value of the music itself (which was no longer open to question) to its manner of performance. Journals which concentrated on contemporary music tended to give interpretation less attention, since it was tangential to the business of artistic evaluation and demanded more technical detail than was traditional in commentaries on (particularly) operatic stars. Such concert criticism is inseparable from the concept of canon. From the 1850s, the criticism of interpretation became a feature of the *Gazette*'s concert reviews of Classical and early music. Its use can be taken as evidence of the assimilation by the public of a particular work or genre, and of the status, as perceived by the critic, of the work in question. Here again, emphasis was placed on the maintenance of tradition, where possible, though that which can be viewed as conservatism on the part of Botte and Bannelier was also related to the concept, instilled in the journal's criticism from the days of Berlioz, of the importance of preserving the integrity of the composer's intention. Modernisation by interpretation was irrelevant to those who believed that a work's beauty was permanent, immutable, or rooted in its own time; their voices rose in protest at the disrespect shown by acclaimed virtuosi to the artwork's status. Whilst the work of Héquet and even Fétis provide glaring exceptions to the journal's upholding of these tenets, the majority view prevailed, not only in reviews of performances, but also in reviews of new editions and theoretical articles.

Chamber and symphonic music had limited commercial value for a nineteenth-century French publisher; by contrast, piano music, operatic vocal scores and arrangements were infinitely more lucrative. It is in the criticism of contemporary music in these genres that the main inconsistencies of the *Gazette*'s critical approach appear. The journal's attack on Herz in 1834–6 must be weighed against its support for other salon composers, including Emile Prudent; the complaints of Bannelier and De Monter on operetta's degeneracy are aesthetically incompatible with the publishing house's full-page advertisements for the works of Lecocq and Offenbach; the campaign against Verdi was essentially an attempt to hamper a rival publisher's success, and general disapproval of the secularisation of sacred music was compromised by the journal's hyperbolic welcoming of Rossini's (and Gemmy Brandus's) *Petite messe solennelle*. Such conflicts of artistic and commercial interest are to be expected in a journal part of whose function is to advertise house products. Yet in some cases excessive praise backfires, reinforcing the view of the journal's opponents. Attempts to establish Halévy as France's premier opera composer in the 1840s failed because the *Gazette*'s critics tacitly confirmed the accusations of his detractors. Similarly doomed was the setting up of Heller and Prudent as geniuses on a Beethovenian scale, despite the absence of major works in their output. Whilst other journals succeeded in brazen praise of their house composers, particularly the Escudiers with Verdi and David, the greater critical conscience of most of the *Gazette*'s writers allowed doubts to creep into otherwise eulogistic language, or vice versa. Only rarely were they chastised in print. Yet editorial control was carefully managed, both before and after 1846. The moulding of the work of numerous contributors of differing critical quality and persuasion into a journal which had clear ideals without being narrowly partisan was achieved with greatest success by Schlesinger, whose galaxy of Romantic contributors edged Fétis out of the limelight. The theoretical perspective set up through the early *contes fantastiques*, which posited an aristocracy of artist-critics from which professional theorists and hacks were excluded, kept his influence at bay. Fétis appears to have enjoyed a warmer relationship with the Brandus brothers than with Schlesinger: it was from 1846 that his ideas began to have appreciable influence on the aesthetic premises which informed critiques of new music. The concept of the *juste milieu*, present from the outset in the *Gazette*'s support for its house composers Onslow and Meyerbeer, became a talisman with which to ward off the evil spirit of Romanticism.

The strongest unifying element of the *Gazette*'s critical history is the Belgian musicologist, whose connection with the journal, at first antagonistic, and always physically separated, was intellectually inescapable even after his death. The journal, which in 1834 professed to be the antithesis of the stately *Revue musicale*, ceased publication in 1880 showing more of its predecessor's characteristics than Schlesinger would have wished, criticising contemporary music according to Fétisian principles and, from the 1860s, devoting an increasing amount of column space to scholarly historical articles. Whilst the *Gazette*'s stance on Berlioz was too well established to be overturned, Fétis's essay of 1852 on Wagner marks a turning point in its history – the first rejection of a modernist – and a paradigm for the tone of its future criticism. It is ironic, yet fitting, that in this respect the *Gazette* should have preserved so precisely the Fétisian dichotomy between modernistic theory and conservative practice: the Wagnerian prophecies of Balzac's *Gambara* and Wagner's own *Beethoven*, so enthusiastically welcomed in 1837 and 1840 respectively, were rejected upon their realisation. The superficial unity of intent represented by the journal's lifelong support for Beethoven and Berlioz only accentuates the change in their perception as Classical rather than Romantic. For the *Gazette*, the price of upholding a musical canon by the invocation of Fétisian ideals was the sacrifice of its modernist identity.

Appendix 1: Principal contributors to the *Gazette*

This appendix lists all named editors and the most prominent of those who contributed occasionally. Many articles in the *Gazette* were initialled, but the identity of some of these authors is unknown. Moreover, foreign correspondents did not usually sign their work. The most likely foreign correspondents among the contributors listed below are Davison (London), Gruneisen (London), Rellstab (Berlin) and Wartel (Vienna), but their precise years of activity for the journal are impossible to establish. Thus, a blank against a particular name means only that no definitively attributable article has been found for that year. Moreover, the fact of being listed on the editorial board is no guarantee that a particular writer was attached to the journal: Schlesinger in particular retained 'star' names on the masthead long after they ceased to have any connection with the *Gazette*. For the years 1850 and 1852, no writer is recorded as being an official editor because no annual or masthead listing is given. Germanic names and initials have been preserved in the Frenchified forms in which they originally appeared. Contributions are listed under the author's byline; thus, for instance, contributions signed by Edouard Monnais and Paul Smith, Arthur Pougin and Maurice Gray, or Gustave Héquet and Léon Durocher, are listed separately, to show in which years a particular writer used particular names.

Key: 0 Listed editor, no known contributions;   # Editor and known contributor;   = Known contributor.

Notes to Appendix 1 may be found on pp. 253–4.

	1834	'35	'36	'37	'38	'39¹	'40	'41	'42	'43	'44	'45	'46	'47	'48	'49	'50	'51	'52	'53	'54	'55	'56	'57	'58
Adam, Adolphe	#	#	0	0	#	#	#	0	0	0	0	0	0	0	0	0	0	0	=	0	0	#	#	#	#
Anders, G. E.	#	#	0	0	#	#	#	0	0	0	0	0	0	0	0	0	0	0	=	0	0	#	#		
Auger, Hippolyte																							#		
Balzac, Honoré de			#	0																					
Bannelier, Charles																								#	#
Beaulieu																								#	#
Beauquier, Charles																									#
Bénédict, G.					=		0	0	0	0	#	0	0	0	0		0			0	#	#	#	0	#
Bénédit, G.²				=	=		0	0	0	0							=	0							
Benoist, François		#	#	0	0	0	0	0	0	0	#	0	0	0	0										
Benoît, Camille	#	#	#	#	#	#	#	#	#	#	#	#	#	#	#	#	#	#	#	#	#	#	#	#	#
Berlioz, Hector			#	0	#	#	#	#	#	#	#	#	#	#	#		0			0					
Bernard, Paul												#													
Berton, H.-M.	#	#	0	#	0	0	0	0	0	0	0	0													
Bertrand, Edouard			#	#	#	#	#	#	#	#	#	#	#	#	#	#	#	#	=	#	#	#	#	#	#
Blanchard, Henri							=																		
Blaze de Bury, Henri																									#
Botte, Adolphe				=																					
Bottée de Toulmon, Auguste		#		#																					
Bourgault-Ducoudray, L.-A.					#	#	#	#	#	#	#	#	#	#	#	#	=	#	#	#	=	#	0	#	#
Bourges, Maurice					#	#	0	0	#	#	#	#	#	#	#	#	=	#	#	#	=	#	#	#	#
Bousquet, Georges	#	#	#	0	0	0	0														0				
Castil-Blaze	#	#	#	#	#	#	#													#					
Champfleury, Jules (pseud.)					#	0												#							
Chasles, Philarète																							#		
Chavée, Honoré																									
Chouquet, Gustave																									
Comettant, Oscar																		=							
Cristal, Maurice³																		#							
Cui, César																									

Name	1834	'35	'36	'37	'38	'39	'40	'41	'42	'43	'44	'45	'46	'47	'48	'49	'50	'51	'52	'53	'54	'55	'56	'57	'58
Damcke, Berthold																		#	=	#	#	#	#	0	#
Danjou, Félix		#	#	#	#	#	0	#	#	#	#	#	0	#	#	0									
David, Ernest																					0	0			
Davison, J. W.													0												
Desarbres, Nérée																		#		0	0				
Deschamps, Ernest													0	0	0	0									
Desprez, Adrien							#																		
Diaz[4]		=	=																						
Duesberg, Joseph		#	#	#	0	#	0	#	0	0	0	0	0	0	0	0	0	0		0	#	0	#	#	#
Dumas, Alexandre			#	#		#																			
Durand, Auguste																							#	#	#
Durocher, Léon[5]																							#		#
Durutte, Camille		#	#	#	#	#		0	#	#	#	#	#							#	#	#			#
Elwart, Antoine		#	#	#	#	#	0	#	0	#	#	#	#	0	0	0	=	#			0	0			#
Fétis, Edouard		#	#	#	#	#	#	#	#	#	#	#	#	#	0	=	=	#	=	#	0	#	0	0	#
Fétis, F.-J.	#	#	#	#	#	#	#	#	#	#	#	#	#	#	#	#	#	#	=	#	#	#	#	#	#
Filloneau, Ernest																									
Fouque, Octave																						#			
Gathy, Auguste									=																
Gollmick, Karl																									
Gouzien, Armand																									
Gray, Maurice[6]																									
Gruneisen, Charles																				#					
Guémer, A.	#																								
Guéroult, Adolphe				#	#	#	#[7]	#																	
Guichard											#	0												#	
Guillou, Joseph	#	0	#		#	#	=	#	0	0	0					=				#	#	0			
Halévy, Fromental		=	=	=																					
Heine, Henri	0	#	#	#	#	#	#	#	0	#	#	#	0	0	0	0	0	0		#	#	0			
Heller, Stephen		#	#																						

	1834	'35	'36	'37	'38	'39	'40	'41	'42	'43	'44	'45	'46	'47	'48	'49	'50	'51	'52	'53	'54	'55	'56	'57	'58
Héquet, Gustave														0	0	0		#	=	#	#	#	#	0	0
Hess, Charles-Léon																									
D'Indy, Vincent																	0								
Janin, Jules	#	#	#	#	#	0	#	#	#	#	#	#	#	#	#	#									
Jullien, Adolphe																				#	#	#	#	#	#
Kastner, Georges			=	#	#	#	#	#	#	#	#	#	#	#	#	#		#	0	#	#	0	#	#	
Kreutzer, Léon										#	0	=	0	0				=	=	#					
Lacome, Paul																									#
Lafage, J. Adrien de		=	#	#	#		0	#	0	#	0	0	0	#	#	#		#	=	#	#	#	#		
Lamazou, (L'Abbé)																					#	#			
Laroque, Adrien[8]																									
Latapie													#												
Laurens, J.-B.					=							=		#	0										
Lauzières, Achille de[9]																#									
Lavoix fils, Henri																									
Lecomte, J.-L.-M.					=		#	#	0			0	0	#	0										
Legouvé, Ernest					=	=																			
Lenz, W. de																									
Lepic, Germanus (pseud.)		#	#	#	0				=	=			=			0									
Le Sueur, J.-F.	0	0	0	=																					
Liszt, Franz	0	#	#	#	#	#	#	#	#	#	0	0	#	0	0										
Madelaine, Stéphen de la (pseud.)	#	#	#	#	#																				
Mainzer, Joseph		#	#										#	#											
Martin d'Angers, Julien									0	0		#	#	#											
Marx, A. B.	#	0	0	0	0	0	0	0	0	0	0	0	0	0	0	0									
Massougnes, Georges de																									
Mathieu de Monter, Emile																							#	#	
Maurel, Jules								#	#	0							0	0	0				#		
Meifred, Joseph																		#							
Méreaux, Amédée					=												=		0		0				

Name	1834	'35	'36	'37	'38	'39	'40	'41	'42	'43	'44	'45	'46	'47	'48	'49	'50	'51	'52	'53	'54	'55	'56	'57	'58
Merruau, Charles		#	0	0																		0	0	0	0
Méry, Joseph				#		=															=				
Monnais, Edouard	#	#	#	#	#		0	0	0	0	0	0	0	0	0	0					=				0
Morel, Auguste			#	#	=	#	0	0										#		0	0	0	0	0	0
Moskowa, Prince de la[10]																	=				0				
Nerval, Gérard de								#																	
Neukomm, Edmond																									
D'Ortigue, Joseph		#	#	#	#	0	0	0	0					=	#	0		#		0	0	#		#	0
Panofka, Henri		0	#	#	#	#	0	0						=	0	#						0	0	0	0
Parmentier, Théodore																									
Pontécoulant, Adolphe, Comte de					=															#	#	0[11]	#	0	0
Pougin, Arthur																									
Prévost, Hippolyte					#	#	0																		
Radau, R.																									
Rauze, Elias de[12]				#	0		0	0	0	0	0	0	0	0	0	0	=	#	=	#	#	#	#	0	=
Rellstab, Ludwig							#																		
Reyer, Ernest																									
Richard, Paulin[13]	#	0	0	#	0																				
Roger, Louis																									
Ruelle, Ch.-Em.																									
Saint-Etienne, Sylvain													0				0		#						
Saint-Félix, Jules de[14]		0		=													=	#					#		
Saint-Hugué, Edme de								0																	
Saint-Yves, D.-A.-D.[15]			#	0	0	0	0	0	0	0	0	0	0	0	0	0						#	#	#	#
Sand, George			#	#					#																
Sauvage, Thomas					0						0	0	0	0	0	0									
Schlesinger, Maurice[16]											0	0	0	0	0	0									
Schumann, Robert											0	0	0												
Schwab, F. M. L.					0						0	0	0	0	0	0									
Séligmann, Paul																		=				#	#	#	=

	1834	'35	'36	'37	'38	'39	'40	'41	'42	'43	'44	'45	'46	'47	'48	'49	'50	'51	'52	'53	'54	'55	'56	'57	'58
Seyfried, J.-G.	#	0	0	0	0	0	0																		
Smith, Paul[17]							#	#	#	#	#	#	#	#	#	=	=	#	=	#	#	#	#	#	#
Spazier, O.																									
Specht, A.	#	#					#	#	#	#	#	0	0	0	0	0									
Stoepel, François					#																				
Strunz, Jacques																									
Thurner, A.																									
Viardot, Louis																						#	#		
Villemot							#	#	#													#	#		
Wagner, Richard																									
Wartel, Thérèse[18]																	=				=	=			=
Weber, Johannes																									
Wekerlin, J.-B.																									

	1859	'60	'61	'62	'63	'64	'65	'66	'67	'68	'69	'70/'71	'72	'73	'74	'75	'76	'77	'78	'79	'80
Adam, Adolphe	#																				
Anders, G. E.		0																			
Auger, Hippolyte																					
Balzac, Honoré de																					
Bannelier, Charles								#	#	#	#	#	#	#	#	#	#	#	#	#	#
Beaulieu					=	=															
Beauquier, Charles	#	0	0	0	0	0	0	0	0	0	0	0	0	0	0	0	0	0	0	0	0
Bénédict, G.	0	0	0	0	0	0	0	0	#	0	0	0									
Bénédit, G.											0	0									
Benoist, François																					
Benoît, Camille																	#	#		#	#
Berlioz, Hector	#		#	#	0	0	#	#	0	#	#	#	#								
Bernard, Paul								0	#	#	#	#	#	#	#	#	#	#	#	#	
Berton, H.-M.	#																				
Bertrand, Edouard		0	0	0	0	0	0	0	0												
Blanchard, Henri							0	0	0												
Blaze de Bury, Henri									0												
Botte, Adolphe	#		#	#	#	#	#	#	0												
Bottée de Toulmon, Auguste	#																				
Bourgault-Ducoudray, L.-A.	#	0	#	0	0		#	#	#	#	#	#	0	0	0	0	0	#	#	#	0
Bourges, Maurice													0	0	0	0	0	0	0		
Bousquet, Georges																					
Castil-Blaze																					
Champfleury, Jules (pseud.)																					
Chasles, Philarète																					
Chavée, Honoré																					
Chouquet, Gustave				#	#	#	#	#	0	0	0		0	0	#	0	0	0	0	0	#
Comettant, Oscar				0	0	0	0	0	#	#	0		0	0	0	0	0	0	0	0	0
Cristal, Maurice															=						
Cui, César																		=	=	=	=

Name	1859	'60	'61	'62	'63	'64	'65	'66	'67	'68	'69	'70/'71	'72	'73	'74	'75	'76	'77	'78	'79	'80
Damcke, Berthold	#	0	0	0	0	0	0								#	#	=	0	0	0	0
Danjou, Félix					=																
David, Ernest											#	#	#	#	#	#	0	0	0	0	0
Davison, J. W.										#	0										
Desarbres, Nérée																					
Deschamps, Ernest					#	0															
Desprez, Adrien											#	#	#	#	0						
Diaz																					
Duesberg, Joseph	#	#	#	#	#																
Dumas, Alexandre						#	#	#													
Durand, Auguste	#	#	#	#	#	#	#														
Durocher, Léon	#	#	#	#	#	#	#	#													
Durutte, Camille	#	#	#	#	#	#	#	#	#	#	#	#	#	#	#	#	=				
Elwart, Antoine	#	0				#	#	#	#	#	#	#	0	0	0	0	0	0	0	0	0
Fétis, Edouard									#	#	0	0	0	0	(=)[19]	0	0	0	0	0	0
Fétis, F.-J.	#	#		=					#	#	#	#	#	#	#	#	0	0			
Filloneau, Ernest				=										=	#	#	#	0	0	#	#
Fouque, Octave																					
Gathy, Auguste		=																			
Gollmick, Karl																					
Gouzien, Armand								#	#	=	0	0									
Gray, Maurice									#	=	0										
Gruneisen, Charles										=											
Guémer, A.																					
Guéroult, Adolphe																					
Guichard																					
Guillou, Joseph																					
Halévy, Fromental																					
Heine, Henri						=															
Heller, Stephen								#	#	0	0		0	0	0	0	0	0	0	#[20]	0

	1859	'60	'61	'62	'63	'64	'65	'66	'67	'68	'69	'70/'71	'72	'73	'74	'75	'76	'77	'78	'79	'80
Héquet, Gustave	0	#	0	0	0	#	#														
Hess, Charles-Léon													0								
D'Indy, Vincent																				=	
Janin, Jules												#									
Jullien, Adolphe	#	#										#	#	#	#	#	#	#	#	#	#
Kastner, Georges			#	0	0	0	0	#	0												
Kreutzer, Léon			=	#	0	0		0	0					0							
Lacome, Paul			#	0																	=
Lafage, J. Adrien de	#	#																			
Lamazou, (L'Abbé)																					
Laroque, Adrien																#	#	#	#	#	#
Latapie																					
Laurens, J.-B.																					
Lauzières, Achille de										0	0										
Lavoix fils, Henri											#	#	#	#	#	#	#	#	#		
Lecomte, J.-L.-M.																					
Legouvé, Ernest																					
Lenz, W. de											0	0	0	0	0	0	0	0			
Lepic, Germanus (pseud.)																					
Le Sueur, J.-F.																					
Liszt, Franz																					
Madelaine, Stéphen de la (pseud.)																					
Mainzer, Joseph																					
Martin d'Angers, Julien																					
Marx, A. B.																					
Massougnes, Georges de																					
Mathieu de Monter, Emile		#	#	#	#	#	0	#			#	#	#	#	#	#	#	#	#		
Maurel, Jules																		#	#	0	0
Meifred, Joseph																					
Méreaux, Amédée		=																			

	1859	’60	’61	’62	’63	’64	’65	’66	’67	’68	’69	’70/’71	’72	’73	’74	’75	’76	’77	’78	’79	’80
Merruau, Charles		0	0	0																	
Méry, Joseph																					
Monnais, Edouard					#	0	0	0	0	0											
Morel, Auguste																					
Moskowa, Prince de la																					
Nerval, Gérard de																					
Neukomm, Edmond									#			#	#	#	#	#	0	0	0	0	
D'Ortigue, Joseph		=[21]							0		0										
Panofka, Henri																					
Parmentier, Théodore	0	#		0	0	0	0	0	0												
Pontécoulant, Adolphe, Comte de			=															=			
Pougin, Arthur			#	#	#	#	0	#	#	#	#	#									
Prévost, Hippolyte																					
Radau, R.																#	#			0	0
Rauze, Elias de											#		#								
Rellstab, Ludwig											#										
Reyer, Ernest									#		0	0	0	0	0	0	#	#	0	0	0
Richard, Paulin						=															
Roger, Louis																					
Ruelle, Ch.-Em.											#	#		#	#	#	#	#	#	#	0
Saint-Etienne, Sylvain																					
Saint-Félix, Jules de																					
Saint-Hugué, Edme de																					
Saint-Yves, D.-A.-D.	#		#	#	#	#	#	#	#	#	#	#									
Sand, George																					
Sauvage, Thomas								#	#	#	#	#	0	#	#	0					
Schlesinger, Maurice																					
Schumann, Robert							=	=													
Schwab, F. M. L.	#	0	0																		
Séligmann, Paul																					

	1859	'60	'61	'62	'63	'64	'65	'66	'67	'68	'69	'70/'71	'72	'73	'74	'75	'76	'77	'78	'79	'80
Seyfried, J.-G.																					
Smith, Paul		#	#	#	#	#	#	#	#												
Spazier, O.																					
Specht, A.																					
Stoepel, François																					
Strunz, Jacques																					
Thurner, A.									=		#	#		0							
Viardot, Louis											#	#									
Villemot																					
Wagner, Richard																					
Wartel, Thérèse	#	0																			
Weber, Johannes																=	=	=		#	#
Wekerlin, J.-B.																				#	#

1 This column combines contributors to the *Revue musicale* and the *Revue et Gazette musicale*.
2 Bénédict and Bénédit are probably both Pierre-Gustave Bénédit.
3 Pseudonym for Maurice Germa.
4 Pseudonym for Henri Blanchard.
5 Pseudonym for Gustave Héquet.
6 Pseudonym for Arthur Pougin.
7 Named as 'Ad. Geroux,' but almost certainly Adolphe Guéroult.
8 Pseudonym for Emile Abraham.
9 Pseudonym for Mark de Thémines.
10 Joseph-Napoléon Ney, Prince de la Moskowa (1803–57).
11 Parmentier is unlikely to have contributed unsigned articles; he was fighting in the Crimea from May to December (*RGM* XXII/19: 13 May 1855, 150; and *RGM* XXII/51: 23 Dec. 1855, 403).
12 Pseudonym for Mark de Thémines.
13 Signed 'P. R.'.
14 Full name: Jules de Saint-Félix d'Amoureux.
15 Pseudonym for Edouard Déaddé. From 1856, Déaddé also signed articles 'D.'.
16 Schlesinger was intimately involved in all aspects of the journal's production, but his name appeared on the lists of editors only from 1845. After

his sale of the business to Louis Brandus in 1846, Schlesinger's name appeared in the years indicated. Contributions attributable to the Brandus brothers are exceptionally rare.

17 Pseudonym for Edouard Monnais.
18 According to Antoine Elwart, Thérèse Wartel sent occasional contributions from Vienna for several years up to around 1860. See Elwart, *Histoire de la Société des concerts du Conservatoire impérial de musique, avec dessins, musique, plans, portraits, notices biographiques, etc.* (Paris, 1860), 222.
19 Articles published posthumously in 1874.
20 Older works reprinted.
21 One article, signed 'Jules d'Ortigue'.

Appendix 2: Personalia

ABRAHAM, ÉMILE (1833–1907)

Playwright, theatre administrator and theatre critic. His last known play dates from 1881. Editor of *L'Entr'acte* and contributor to the *Petit journal*. Wrote for the *Gazette* under the pseudonym Adrien Laroque.

BANNELIER, CHARLES (1840–99)

Trained as a scientist, then switched to music. Studied composition at the Paris Conservatoire. Prepared piano duet version of the *Symphonie fantastique*. A Hanslickian – he translated *Vom Musikalisch-Schönen* into French and serialised it in the *Gazette* in 1877. His movements after 1880 are not known.

BATTA, ALEXANDRE (1816–1902)

Dutch cellist and composer. Studied in Brussels. As a performer, specialist in the piano trio repertoire. Regular partners included: Liszt and Urhan; his brother Laurent and the violinist Seghers; Vieuxtemps and Rosa Escudier-Kastner (the Société des Trios Anciens et Modernes, 1865–8). Awarded the Légion d'honneur in 1875.

BERNARD, PAUL (1827–79)

Composer of piano music, songs and operas. Studied at the Paris Conservatoire from 1843. Piano pupil of Gambaro and Thalberg; harmony and composition pupil of Elwart, later Halévy. Also contributed to *Le Ménestrel*.

BOTTE, ADOLPHE (1823–93→)

Composer of piano music and songs, critic. Studied at the Paris Conservatoire from 1837, where he was a piano pupil of Zimmermann and also studied counterpoint and fugue. Moved to Rouen in 1842, where he began activities as a critic, returning to Paris in 1854. Also wrote for the *Messager des théâtres* as A. de Pavilly.

BOURGES, (JEAN-)MAURICE (1812–81)

Composer, writer, critic. Trained in literature at Bordeaux; later studied composition with Auguste Barbereau. His most successful opera, *Sultana*, was produced at the Opéra-Comique in 1846. One of the *Gazette*'s finest historian-critics, with a reviewing style probably modelled on that of Berlioz.

CHAULIEU (MARTIN, CHARLES, *DIT*) (1788–1849)

Composer and piano teacher. Trained with Louis Adam and Catel at the Conservatoire, winning first prizes in harmony and piano in 1805 and 1806. Thereafter concentrated on composition and teaching. Moved to London *c*. 1840, and died there.

COCATRIX (*c*. 1770–?)

Amateur musician who arrived in Paris from La Rochelle in 1797, staying until the end of 1804. Worked in the Bureau de la Marine before setting up the *Correspondance des amateurs musiciens* with a retailer, Armand Seguin.

DAVID, ERNEST (1824–86)

Failing health from around 1870 forced him to abandon a career in business and to work from home. His book *La Musique chez les juifs* (1873) gained him recognition. Biographical articles, especially of old Italian masters, were his principal contribution to the *Gazette*.

DÉADDÉ, ÉDOUARD (1810–70)

Playwright, novelist, theatre director. He wrote most of his work in collaboration, often with his brother. Over a hundred stage works exist.

DELACOUR, VINCENT-CONRAD-FÉLIX (J. DELACOUR): (1808–40)

French harpist and composer. Pupil of Fétis in counterpoint and fugue at the Conservatoire, but left for Italy in 1827 before completing his studies. After an appointment as harpist in Berlin, returned to Paris to study composition with Berton from 1833, winning second prize in the Prix de Rome of 1835.

DELOFFRE, (LOUIS-MICHEL-)ADOLPHE (1817–76)

French violinist and theatre conductor. Studied violin with Bellon, Lafont and Baillot. Conductor at the Théâtre-Lyrique from 1852; at the Opéra-Comique from 1868 until his death.

DELSARTE, FRANÇOIS (1811–71)

Singer specialising in early music, particularly Gluck. A pupil at Alexandre Choron's Institution royale de musique classique et religieuse. Organiser of important concert series featuring the music of Lully, Rameau and Gluck.

FANART, LOUIS (1807–83)

Trained as an organist in Reims; subsequently studied at the Paris Conservatoire. Returned to Reims in 1830, set up a Société Philharmonique there in 1833 and founded the Reims Conservatoire in 1844, directing it until 1852. Published works included an organ treatise and a collection of easy liturgical music for choir.

GEOFFROY, JULIEN-LOUIS (1743–1814)

Writer and theatre critic. Professor of Rhetoric at the Collège Mazarin from 1779. A Royalist – contributed to L'Année littéraire, later retitled L'Ami du Roi. On the arrest in 1792 of Royou, a central figure on the journal's staff, Geoffroy fled Paris, teaching in an outlying district. Returned to Paris in 1800, set up L'Année littéraire again, and took up his post at the Débats.

GERMA, MAURICE (1827–87)

Historian-critic. Wrote widely under the pseudonym Maurice Cristal. After two years of Law study in Toulouse, moved to Paris. Published a series of stories and poems: La Légende d'amour (Paris, 1854). An unsuccessful composer. Once established in Paris, he researched into literature of music. Approached the writing of music history through the concept of national schools.

GOUZIEN, ARMAND (1839–92)

Singer, composer, critic and civil servant. Contributed to a wide variety of general and specialist journals. Founded the Revue des lettres et des arts (1867–8) with Villiers de L'Isle-Adam. Edited the Journal de musique (1876–82). Inspector of Fine Arts from 1881, then Commissioner for National Theatres.

HÉQUET, GUSTAVE (1803–65)

Writer, critic, composer. First career in Law. Largely self-taught, he began composing in the 1830s. His dramatic scena Le Roi Lear was performed by the Société des Concerts in 1844, but his first major stage work did not appear until 1856. Music critic of Le National 1841–51; closely associated with Troupenas's La Mélodie 1842–3. Also wrote for La France musicale and Le Ménestrel. His pseudonym for the Gazette was Léon Durocher.

KALKBRENNER, CHRISTIAN (1755–1806)

Composer and writer on music. After a career in Germany, became choirmaster at the Paris Opéra in 1798 and remained in Paris until his death. Compositions include an opera, symphonies, a piano concerto and piano sonatas. Father of the pianist Friedrich Kalkbrenner (1785–1849).

LAINEZ, ÉTIENNE (1753–1822)

Principal tenor at the Opéra for thirty years from 1783. Taught lyric declamation at the Paris Conservatoire from 1816.

LAURENS, J.-B. (1801–90)

Artist, amateur musician and composer, antiquarian and writer. Secretary of the Faculty of Medicine at Montpellier. Enthusiastic connoisseur of early music (from early Baroque onwards). Close friend and confidant of Stephen Heller; supporter of Mendelssohn.

LAVOIX, H. FILS (1846–97)

Librarian, writer. His most successful work, the *Histoire de l'instrumentation depuis 1500 à nos jours* (1878), won the Concours Bordin awarded by the Académie des beaux-arts. Contributed to *Le Monde artiste, Le Moniteur universel* and *La Chronique musicale*. His last known work, *L'Histoire de la musique*, appeared in 1885. Several articles for the *Gazette* were also published independently.

LEBOUC, CHARLES-JOSEPH (1822–93)

Cellist and composer. Trained in cello and composition at the Paris Conservatoire; played in the Société des Concerts orchestra and the Paris Opéra orchestra. With the singer Paulin, founded the Soirées de Musique Classique in 1855 and ran them singlehandedly from 1857.

MASSART, (LOUISE-)AGLAÉ (NÉE MASSON) (1827–87)

Pianist and teacher. Trained at the Paris Conservatoire. A renowned interpreter of Beethoven; also premièred Léon Kreutzer's Piano Concerto in 1861. Married to the Belgian violinist Lambert Massart (1811–92); their household became a popular meeting-place for musicians. Both taught at the Paris Conservatoire; Aglaé took Louise Farrenc's post on the latter's retirement in 1872.

MATHIEU DE MONTER, ÉMILE (1835–81)

Studied medicine and music at Strasbourg. Contributed to *L'Europe artiste, Le Messager des théâtres, L'Orchestre, L'Orphéon* and London's *The Musical World*.

Specialised in reviews of choral and sacred music; his views on the proper nature of sacred music matched those of Berlioz. His interest in sacred music is reflected in his major work, *Louis Lambillotte et ses frères* (Paris, 1871).

MATTMANN, LOUISE (1826–61)

Pianist. A child prodigy 'discovered' by the Duchesse d'Orléans in 1837 and taught by Friedrich Kalkbrenner. Like Aglaé Massart (q.v.), renowned for her playing of Beethoven. Played Mozart and Beethoven concertos with the Société des Concerts orchestra, but concentrated mainly on chamber work, especially with Armingaud, Maurin and Lebouc (q.v.). Died in poverty.

MAURIN, JEAN-PIERRE (1822–94)

Violinist. Studied at the Paris Conservatoire with Baillot (he was one of his last pupils) and Habeneck. Founded the Société des Derniers Quatuors de Beethoven (the Maurin/Chevillard Quartet) in 1852.

MERRUAU, CHARLES (1807–82)

After a university career teaching rhetoric, history and humanities, became chief editor of *Le Temps*, then *Le Constitutionnel*, under the directorship of Louis Véron. Cousin invited him to become Secretary-General of Public Instruction in 1840. From 1850, Secretary-General of the Prefecture of the Seine. Received the Légion d'honneur in 1854.

MONNAIS, EDOUARD (1798–1868)

Degree in Law. Collaborated on theatrical works in Paris from 1826. Deputy Director of the Paris Opéra from 1839; Commissioner for National Theatres and the Conservatoire from 1840. Wrote for the *Gazette* from 1835 to his death, mostly under the pseudonym Paul Smith or the initals 'P. S.' and 'R.'. Slavish follower of Fétis regarding music after Mozart; antipathetic to early music.

MOREL, AUGUSTE-FRANÇOIS (1809–81)

Composer and critic. Worked in Paris from 1836 to 1860 and then became Director of the Marseilles Conservatoire (his home town). Supporter and friend of Berlioz.

POËNCET, HENRI (c.1844–73)

Principal cellist (solo) at the Concerts Populaires, and member of the Lamoureux Quartet from 1867–8. Taught at the Dijon Conservatoire for around four years before his death.

POISOT, CHARLES-ÉMILE (1822–1902)

Composer, historian. Learned piano in Dijon with a pupil of Liszt. Arrived in Paris in 1834; ten years later entered the Conservatoire as Halévy's student. His compositions include romances, short operas, salon music for piano and a piano trio dedicated to Onslow. Returned to Dijon in 1852 and devoted more time to teaching and writing.

STOEPEL, FRANÇOIS (1794–1836)

Prussian piano/music theory teacher. Held a series of posts in Germany (some of them created for or by him) before settling in Paris. Some small-scale and didactic compositions. A founder contributor to the *Gazette*, sometimes using the pseudonym Le Poste. Wrote many of the journal's key early articles, establishing its critical allegiances.

SZARVÁDY, WILHELMINE (NÉE CLAUSS) (1834–1907)

Pianist, born and trained in Prague. Moved to Paris in 1852. Toured Europe as a soloist, later settled in Paris. Champion of Schumann's music. Widely admired for breadth of repertoire (Scarlatti–Brahms) and respect for composer's intentions.

TARDIEU DE MALLEVILLE, CHARLOTTE (NÉE D'ARPENTIGNY MALLEVILLE) (1830–90)

Pianist and composer. Pupil of Amédée Méreaux, from whom she may have derived her abiding interest in early music (she rarely played music by living composers). Most renowned as a Mozartian and as a resident or guest pianist for Paris chamber societies. Regularly organised four chamber concerts per year in the salles Sax, Pleyel or Erard from 1849 to 1869.

THÉMINES, MARK DE (1818–94)

Son of the renowned General Pons de Lauzières-Thémines. Spent thirty years as a journalist in Paris, working for *La Patrie*. Signed political articles 'De Lauzières' and musical ones 'De Thémines'. A specialist in translating opera libretti from French into Italian and vice versa.

URHAN, CHRÉTIEN (1790–1845)

Violinist and viola player. A member of the Baillot Quartet, and rose to solo violinist in the Opéra orchestra. He was the first viola soloist in *Harold in Italy* in 1834. Primarily known as a chamber player.

WHITE, JOSÉ (LOS DOLORES, SILVESTRE DE, *DIT*) (1836–1918)

Cuban violinist and composer. A pupil of Delphin Alard at the Paris Conservatoire. Active as a chamber musician in Paris; it is not known when he left. Worked in the imperial court of Brazil until 1889, when he returned to Paris.

Appendix 3: *Contes, nouvelles*, dialogues and other short literature in Schlesinger's *Gazette musicale*, 1834–46[1]

1834

Jules Janin, 'Le Dîner de Beethoven' – *conte fantastique* (I/1–2: 5–12 Jan.).

F. Halévy, 'Ali-Baba, et Sainte Cécile' (I/3:19 Jan.).

*C. M. de Weber, 'Songe de Charles-Marie de Weber, par lui-même' (I/4: 26 Jan.).

Jules Janin, 'Hoffman' [sic] – *conte fantastique* (I/13–14: 30 Mar. – 6 Apr.).

Hector Berlioz, 'Le Suicide par enthousiasme' – *nouvelle* (I/29–32: 20 Jul. – 10 Aug.).

Jules Janin, 'L'Homme vert' – *conte fantastique* (I/50: 14 Dec.).

*Unsigned, 'Haendel' – *conte* (I/52: 28 Dec.). Translation from *Neue Zeitschrift für Musik*.

1835

Jules Janin, 'Le Concert dans la maison' – *conte fantastique* (II/1: 4 Jan.).

Joseph Méry, 'La Fontaine d'Ivoire' (II/4: 25 Jan.).

Jules de Saint-Félix, 'Le Meilleur de mes amis' – *histoire musicale* (II/5: 1 Feb.).

Unsigned, 'Le Concert de Hummel. Extrait du journal d'un voyageur' (II/6: 8 Feb.). Translated by Dumont.

Joseph Méry, '*La Norma* au Carlo Felice' (II/8: 22 Feb.).

Frédéric Mab (pseud.) 'Les Cygnes chantent en mourant' (II/10–14: 8 Mar. – 5 Apr.).

Alexandre Dumas, 'La Juive' (II/17–18: 26 Apr. – 3 May).

Adolphe Adam, 'La Répétition générale d'*Iphigénie en Tauride*' (II/21: 24 May).

Stéphen de la Madelaine (pseud.), 'L'Auteur de *Charmante Gabrielle*' (II/44: 1 Nov.).

'Comment l'opéra fut introduit en France' (II/47: 22 Nov.).

Adolphe Adam, 'Un Début en province' (II/52: 27 Dec.).

1836

*E.T.A. Hoffmann, 'Lettre du chat Murr (E.T.A. Hoffmann) au rédacteur de la *Gazette musicale de Berlin*' (III/1: 3 Jan.).

*C.M. de Weber, 'La Loche' – *conte fantastique* (III/5–6: 31 Jan. – 7 Feb.).

---

[1] Short, anecdotal/biographical narratives, of which Edouard Monnais provided several in the 1840s, are not included in this list, though literary open letters are. Asterisked titles are known not to have been commissioned specifically for the journal.

Samuel Bach (pseud. for Théophile de Ferrière), 'Le Vieux râcleur' (III/7: 14 Feb.).

Samuel Bach, 'Divagations musicales de Samuel Bach. Brand-Sachs' (III/17–18: 24 Apr. – 1 May).

Jules Janin, 'Gabrielli' [sic] (III/20–24: 15 May – 12 Jun.).

Jules Janin, 'Stradella, ou le poète et le musicien' (III/28: 10 Jul.).

Stéphen de la Madelaine, 'Corelli' – *nouvelle* (III/46: 13 Nov.).

Jules Janin, 'Gaffarelli' [sic] (III/50: 41 [11] Dec.).

Stéphen de la Madelaine, 'La Vieillesse de Guillaume Dufay' (III/52: 25 Dec.).

1837

George Sand, 'Le Contrabandier' – *histoire lyrique* (IV/1: 1 Jan.).

Stéphen de la Madelaine, 'Francesca' – *nouvelle* (IV/5: 28 Jan.).

'Les Psaumes de Josquin' – *nouvelle* (IV/14–16: 1–16 Apr.).

'La Jeunesse de Bassini' (IV/19–22: 7–28 May).

Honoré de Balzac, 'Gambara' – *étude philosophique* (IV/30–34: 23 Jul. – 20 Aug.).

Antoine Elwart, 'Faute d'un piano! Chronique musicale de l'Hôtel Bazancourt' (IV/35: 27 Aug.).

Margeanville, 'Il ne faut pas jouer avec le feu' (IV/36–8: 3–17 Sep.).

Hector Berlioz ,'Le Premier opéra – *nouvelle* (IV/40–1: 1–8 Oct.).

Alexandre Dumas, 'Histoire d'un ténor' (IV/43–49: 22 Oct. – 3 Dec.).

Jules David, 'Le Musicien du régiment' (IV/51–2: 17–24 Dec.).

1838

*Henri Heine, 'Lettres confidentielles' (extracts) (V/3–5: 21 Jan. – 4 Feb.).

Franz Liszt [with Marie d'Agoult], 'Lettres d'un bachélier ès-musique' (V/6–35: 11 Feb. – 2 Sep.).

Henri Panofka, 'Sonate en *la* mineur de Beethoven. Extrait du journal d'un artiste' (V/23: 10 Jun.).

Stéphen de la Madelaine, 'Le Maître de chapelle de François Ier. Chronique du XVe siècle' (V/24–5: 17–24 Jun.).

Félicien Mallefille, 'Les Exilés. – Un Chemin' (V/36: 9 Sep.).

1839

All entries published in the *RGM*, not the *RM*.

Franz Liszt [with Marie d'Agoult], 'Lettres d'un bachélier ès-musique' (VI/2–15: 13 Jan. – 14 Apr.).

*Felice Romani, 'Ode à Paganini' (VI/47: 15 Sep.). Translated by Hector Berlioz.

*E. T. A. Hoffmann, 'Le Poëte et le compositeur' (VI/58–9: 10–14 Nov.).

1840

Richard Wagner, 'Une visite à Beethoven' (VII/65–9: 19 Nov. – 3 Dec.).

1841

Richard Wagner, 'Un musicien étranger à Paris' (VIII/9–12: 31 Jan. – 11 Feb.).
Henri Blanchard, 'Chieng et Sering, ou les nouveaux Siamois' (VIII/17: 28 Feb.).
Paul Smith (pseud. for Edouard Monnais), 'De Paris à Rome et de Rome à Paris (VIII/26: 1 Apr.).
Paul Smith, 'Un aveugle' (VIII/23: 21 Mar.).
Werner (pseud. for Richard Wagner), 'Caprices esthétiques. Extraits du journal d'un musicien défunt. Le musicien et la publicité' (VIII/26: 1 Apr.).
*Ludwig Tieck, 'Un mélomane' (extract) (VIII/32: 9 May).
Henri Blanchard, 'La valse, ou les deux prisonniers' (VIII/44: 1 Aug.).
Paul Smith, 'Galerie ancienne et moderne' (VIII/46–55: 15 Aug. – 17 Oct.).
Paul Smith, 'Un Requiem' (VIII/56: 24 Oct.).
Richard Wagner, 'Une soirée heureuse. Fantaisie sur la musique pittoresque' (VIII/56–8: 24 Oct. – 7 Nov.).
A. Specht, 'Mœurs musicales. Le Mari de la cantatrice' (VIII/59: 14 Nov.).
Paul Smith, 'Un nom d'artiste' (VIII/64: 19 Dec.).

1842

Paul Smith, 'Esquisses de la vie d'artiste' (IX/14–48: 3 Apr. – 29 Nov.).
Jules Lecomte, 'Le Joueur de viole, et le pigéon de la place Saint-Marc, histoire vénitienne' (IX/24–32: 12 Jun. – 7 Aug.).
Henri Blanchard, 'Ludwig, ou l'élève de Weber' (IX/49–50: 4–11 Dec.).

1843

Henri Blanchard, 'Un songe d'un nuit d'hiver' (X/1: 1 Jan.).
George Sand, 'Carl' (X/1–3: 1–15 Jan.). Music by F. Halévy.
Paul Smith, 'Petits mystères d'une soirée musicale' (X/7–11: 12 Feb. – 12 Mar.).
Edouard Fétis, 'Un Cabinet de curiosités musicales' (X/13–14: 26 Mar. – 2 Apr.).
Paul Smith, 'Le Luthier et l'artiste' (X/22–5: 28 May – 18 Jun.).
Maurice Bourges, 'Une Mélodie' (X/29–30: 16–23 Jul.).
Edouard Fétis, 'La Querelle de la basse viole, du violon et du violoncelle' (X/45: 5 Nov.).
Hector Berlioz, 'Idylle' (X/49: 3 Dec.).
Paul Smith, 'Le Docteur Matanasius' (X/50–51: 10–17 Dec.).

1844

Henri Blanchard, 'L'Actrice et l'étudiant' (XI/2–8: 14 Jan. – 25 Feb.).
Hector Berlioz, 'Euphonia, ou la ville musicale' (XI/7–30: 14 Jan. – 28 Jul.).
Maurice Bourges, 'Une Occasion (XI/15–16: 14–21 Apr.).
Paul Smith, 'Portefeuille de deux cantatrices' (XI/40–XII/20: 6 Oct. 1844 – 18 May 1845).

1845

Paul Smith, 'Portefeuille de deux cantatrices' (cont'd from 1844).
Maurice Bourges, 'Souvenirs d'un octogénaire' (XII/25–41: 22 Jun. – 12 Oct.).
Unsigned, 'Une Soirée à plaisir' (XII/38: 21 Sep.).
Paul Smith, 'Les Elèves de Baron de Bage [Bagge]' (XII/48: 30 Nov.).

1846

Paul Smith, 'Vouloir et Pouvoir' (XIII/1: 4 Jan.).

Appendix 4: Publishing history of the *Gazette*

PUBLICATION

5 Jan. 1834 – 28 Aug 1870, 1 Oct. 1871 – 31 Dec. 1880 (*GM* 5 Jan. 1834 – 25 Oct. 1835; *RGM* 1 Nov. 1835 – 31 Dec. 1880).

PERIODICITY

Weekly (twice weekly 3 Jan. 1839 – 11 Apr 1841). After an irregular experiment with twice-weekly publication at the end of 1838, from 3 January to 27 June 1839 there was a regular midweek issue entitled the *Revue musicale*, with separate subscription arrangements and numbering but many shared contributors; the weekend issue continued as the *Revue et Gazette musicale* and was not available for subscription independently of the *Revue*. Schlesinger let it be known that Fétis was editorially responsible for the *Revue*, though this has proved impossible to substantiate.[1] After 27 June 1839 the midweek edition continued under the title *Revue et Gazette musicale*.

PROPRIETORS (direction of the publishing house)

Maurice Schlesinger: Jan. 1834 – Jan. 1846
Louis Brandus: 18 Jan. 1846 – May 1852
Louis and Gemmy Brandus: Jun. 1852 – Aug. 1854
Gemmy Brandus and Sélim Dufour: Aug. 1854 – Jul. 1872
Gemmy Brandus: Jul. 1872 – Feb. 1873
Louis Brandus: ?Feb. 1873 – Dec. 1880

DIRECTORS (by issue)

Maurice Schlesinger: 5 Jan. 1834 – 29 Dec. 1839 (also director of *Revue musicale* 3 Jan. – 27 Jun. 1839)
A. Specht: 2 Jan. – 27 Dec. 1840
Maurice Schlesinger: 3 Jan. 1841 – 11 Jan. 1846
Pierre-Charles-Ernest Deschamps d'Hanneucourt: 18 Jan. 1846 – 17 Apr. 1853[2]

---

[1] Schlesinger's tactics are indicated in a letter of 23 February 1839 from the Escudier brothers to Fétis, in which they attempted (unsuccessfully) to persuade him to defect to *La France musicale* (BN), Dépt des manuscrits: Papiers Fétis, n. a. fr. 22871/45).

[2] He used two versions of his name: D. d'Hanneucourt (1846–8) and Ernest Deschamps (1849–53). He was the son of the solicitor Pierre-Jean Deschamps.

Lazare (Louis) Brandus: 24 Apr. – 25 Dec. 1853[3]
Louis Dubreuilh: 1 Jan. 1854 – 28 Dec. 1856[4]
Sélim (Samuel) Dufour – 4 Jan. 1857 – 21 Jul. 1872[5]
Gemmy Brandus: 28 Jul. 1872 – 9 Feb. 1873[6]
Louis Brandus: 16 Feb. 1873 – 31 Dec. 1880[7]

ADMINISTRATOR

Edouard Philippe – 1 Oct. 1871 – 31 Oct. 1880

CHIEF EDITOR

Exact dates unknown. 1841–6 Schlesinger signed himself director and editor in chief; from 7 November 1880 Charles Bannelier was named as chief editor, though he had acted in this capacity for several years.[8] *Le Ménestrel* indicates that Fétis (Edouard?) and Edouard Monnais also acted as chief editors (*Le Ménestrel* XLVII/6: 2 Jan. 1881, 44).

SUBSCRIPTION OFFICE

1834–48: 97 rue Richelieu (in 1839 the *Revue musicale* office was at 10 bd des Italiens)
1849 – Jun. 1851: 87 (renumbered from 97) rue Richelieu
Jun. 1851 – Dec. 1880: 1 bd des Italiens[9]

SUBSCRIPTION RATES

A variety of subscription modes operated. The annual subscription rates for Paris were:

1834–44: 30F[10]
1845–7: 24F
1848–80: 24F

Rates for the provinces and abroad fluctuated more frequently.

3   Brandus stated his intention to take control of the paper on 21 April 1853 (AN: F[18] 413/51). For an explanation of the legal procedure by which directors of journals were registered, see 'Press regulations', below.
4   Dubreuilh stated his intention to take control of the journal on 30 December 1853 (AN: F[18] 413/53).
5   Dufour, who died on 25 July 1872, was a partner in the publishing house from August 1854, having already been closely involved with the Russian side of the business for two years.
6   A letter from the Préfecture de Police to the Ministre de l'Intérieur dated 14 August 1872 states that Brandus's notification of a change of director was submitted on 1 August (AN: F[18] 413/54).
7   Louis Brandus's notification of directorsip was not submitted until 26 June 1873 (AN paris: F[18] 413/56).
8   See *Dictionnaire de biographie française* (Paris, 1933–), 76.
9   From August 1851, the main publishing-house address was 103 rue Richelieu.
10 Subscription for the *Revue musicale* only – 20F.

FOREIGN OUTLETS

A foreign subscription office is first mentioned in 1837 (Leipzig), though subscription rates included foreign tariffs from 1834. No details of foreign outlets until 1848, which named offices in London (2), St Petersburg, New York, Lisbon, Madrid, Rome, Amsterdam, Berlin, Stockholm and Vienna. In 1853 Geneva and Brussels were added; from 1855 all specific references to foreign outlets disappeared.

PRINT RUNS AND SUBSCRIPTION RATES

Sketchy information on print runs is available, most of it contained in government documents of the Administration de l'Enregistrement et des Domaines, whose estimates were based on the quantity of paper submitted for stamp duty by each journal each month. The archival sources relevant to the *Gazette* are AN: BB[17] A 99/14, BB[17] A 103/4, BB[17] A 118/1 and BB[17] A 145/1.[11] Comparative figures for the most prestigious music journals, calculated from documents in BB[17], are available for 1836–8, 1840–1 and 1845–6 (see Table 1). The figures should be treated as rough estimates.

Table 1

	1836	1837	1838	1840	1841	1845	1846
France musicale	–	–	632	690	905	2142	1642
Gazette musicale	600	413	456	773	687[12]	798	792
Ménestrel	608	623	503	555	433	802	449

(Sources: AN: BB[17] A 99/14, BB[7] A 103/4, BB[17] A 118/1 and BB[17] A 145/1.)

On 3 January 1834 the printer Lachevardière stated his intention to print 2,000 copies of the *Gazette* in the first instance (AN: F[18] 89 B).

Figures from the Administration des Postes give a more accurate indication of numbers of subscribers in the provinces in isolated months of 1840–1 and 1846–7 (see Tables 2 and 3)

Table 2

	Nov. 1840	Dec. 1840	Nov. 1841	Dec. 1841
France musicale	309	332	843	933
Gazette musicale	359	348	345	264
Ménestrel	285	391	269	264

(Sources: AN: BB[17] A 115/11 (1840) and BB[17] A 118/2 (1841).)

[11] The figures have been analysed, though with some misinterpretations, by H. Robert Cohen, 'The 19th-Century French Press and the Music Historian: archival sources and bibliographical resources', *Nineteenth-Century Music* VII/2 (Fall 1983), 136–42, and (as part of a more general study) in Pierre Albert, Gilles Feyel and François Picard, *Documents sur l'histoire de la presse nationale aux XIXe et XXe siècles* (Paris, 1977).

[12] Due to variation in the *Gazette's* periodicity in 1841, this figure is particularly problematic.

Table 3

	Nov. 1846	Dec. 1846	Jan. 1847	Feb. 1847	Jul. 1847	Aug. 1847
France musicale	1365	1362	1312	1283	1054	1054
Gazette musicale	455	421	404	395	388	382
Ménestrel	338	351	369	330	330	329

(Source: AN: BB[17] A 148/1.)

ACCOUNTS

The only known accounts which are publicly available concern 1852–3 and 1854–7, and are conserved at the Centre des archives contemporaines, Fontainebleau: Dossiers Dufour: MC XXIII, D.C. 173 and MC XLII, D.C. 21. Shareholders' reports prepared by Sélim Dufour and Gemmy Brandus consistently stress the utility of maintaining publication of the *Gazette*, even though it frequently ran at a loss (the only known exception was 1852/53, when the *Gazette* made modest profits of 1014.65F (MC XXIII D.C. 173).[13]

PRESS REGULATIONS

Throughout its publication, the *Gazette* was subject to scrutiny under the provisions of press laws of varying degrees of restriction. In practice, the non-political nature of most music journals meant that they were rarely viewed as threatening to any government in power during the period 1800–80; their owners could state their intention to publish a journal which was 'non-politique' and thus be exempted from the high 'cautionnements' demanded of daily newspapers and political periodicals. By the terms of the law of 18 July 1828 any political journal which appeared more than twice per week was subject to a 'cautionnement of 6,000 francs; the figure was reduced proportionately for journals which appeared less frequently. By the law of 17 February 1852 the highest 'cautionnement' (for Paris and Ile de France papers appearing four times or more per week) was 50,000 francs.

Major press laws of the period specified the procedures for registering a journal prior to publication. The 'droit d'impression' application submitted to the Préfecture de Police (and then passed to the Ministre de l'Intérieur) required the supplicant to give the full title and subtitle of the journal, its periodicity, the names of its proprietor and printer, and to submit two specimen copies. Detailed records of these applications are held at the Archives nationales, Paris (F[18]). From 1828 to the 1860s this procedure appears to have been a formality; later, particularly after the Franco-Prussian War, each prospective proprietor (or new

---

[13] For an analysis of these documents and their significance, see Anik Devriès, 'La maison Brandus. Heurs et malheurs d'un commerce d'éditions musicales au XIXe siècle', *Revue de musicologie* LXX/1 (1984), 51–82. Devriès's analysis of the contents of MC XXIII D.C. 173 (pp. 57–8) is, however, flawed, since it presents quotations from a single shareholders' prospectus (probably dating from the end of 1854) as though from several similar documents dating from different years.

proprietor of an established journal) was vetted, though no application among those consulted in F^{18} was refused outright.

Documents relating to the *Gazette* (F^{18} 413/44–57) include 'droit d'impression' applications from 1841 to 1873 and letters discussing the fines incurred by Schlesinger for defaulting on the stamp duty payable on each copy of the journal (F^{18} 413/45–9). The original application of 1834 is not present; presumably Schlesinger's application of 1841 was necessary because he had taken back the directorship from Specht. Assuming sole directorship of the *Gazette* in 1872 after Sélim Dufour's death, Gemmy Brandus, a Prussian (though naturalised French), applied to continue publishing the journal (F^{18} 413/54); an amusingly inaccurate report, which stated that the publishing house had been founded in 1827 by F.-J. Fétis, was duly provided by the Ministre de l'Intérieur (F^{18} 413/55). The report on Louis the following year gave more detail on his political views – in particular, that he had, during the Franco-Prussian War, dismissed an employee whom he believed to be a Prussian sympathiser (F^{18} 413/57).

Appendix 5: Pseudonyms and attributions

Pseudonym or initial	Name
Maurice Cristal	Maurice Germa
Diaz	Henri Blanchard
Léon Durocher	Gustave Héquet
Maurice Gray	Arthur Pougin
J.J.J.	Henri Blanchard
Adrien Laroque	Emile Abraham
Achille de Lauzières	Mark de Thémines
Stéphen de la Madelaine	Etienne-Jean-Baptiste-Nicolas Madelaine
P.P. (in *TP*)	Pierre Porro
P.R.	Paulin Richard
Le Poste	François Stoepel
R.	Edouard Monnais
Elias de Rauze	Mark de Thémines
D.A.D. Saint-Yves	Edouard Déaddé
Paul Smith	Edouard Monnais

ATTRIBUTION OF ANONYMOUS ARTICLES

Unsigned articles in nineteenth-century journals are an occupational hazard for scholars, and their attribution on stylistic grounds alone will always be tendentious. In order not to disrupt the flow of the main text, the nature of the evidence surrounding two attributions is set out below.

CHARLES BANNELIER

The unity of style and attitude towards a wide variety of musical issues in the unsigned concert reviews column from 1867 onwards, compared with the opinions and interests shown in signed articles by Charles Bannelier, points almost beyond doubt to his authorship. Until 1867 the concert reviews column was generally signed or initialled and placed in the main body of the text; from January 1867 it was printed in smaller type under a heading such as 'Concerts de la semaine', or subsumed under the 'Nouvelles' section of the journal unless an event, such as the opening performance of a major concert series, was deemed particularly important. Such exceptional reviews were almost invariably initialled or signed – many of them by Bannelier (the initials 'C.B.' and 'Ch. B.' still hold for Bannelier even after the Franco-Prussian War, when Charles Beauquier joined the editorial staff, and despite the advent of Camille Benoît in 1877). A comparison of these signed reviews, along with other articles in the main body of the journal, provides a substantial corpus of internal evidence which points to Bannelier's sole authorship of the 'Nouvelles' column from 1867 to 1880. In his signed articles, certain preoccupations appear repeatedly: sensitivity to performance style and a tendency to pick out a single detail of a piece, much in the manner of Berlioz, but almost always connected with interpretation; the necessity for historical validation of a point of stylistic principle in performance; the importance of strict editorial procedure; an enthusiasm for Baroque music, particularly Bach; a mistrust of Wagner but a clear and emphatic separation of his ideals from those of Schumann; reverence for Beethoven, including the late works; support for new French instrumental music combined with ambivalence towards the Lisztian symphonic poem and programmatic music in general; finally, the first use in the *Gazette* of consistently specific designations of works where there could be some doubt, even in the cluttered context of programme listings. In any week's reviews from 1867 onwards, the majority of these preoccupations can be found.

Reviews in the 'Nouvelles' column were generally of two kinds: brief, journalistic reports, or reviews which discussed the music in detail. Bannelier could not have attended the whole of every concert which received attention (of which some clashed); it is probable that those concerts which received fuller notices were those he attended, and that he relied on reporters for information on other events. Nevertheless, the consistency of authorial tone in both reviews and reports suggests that the entire column passed through one person's hands. In the absence of irrefutable documentary evidence for Bannelier's authorship of these reviews, I have maintained a distinction between signed and unsigned articles throughout this study.

FRANÇOIS STOEPEL

The attribution of the article 'Troisième concert de M. Berlioz' (*GM* I/52: 28 Dec. 1834, 324–6) rests mainly on the recurrence here of an identical explanation of the process of composition to that in Stoepel's signed article on Onslow (*GM* I/ 19: 11 May 1834). The Onslow article distinguishes between the composition of absolute music and that of dramatic orchestral music, citing Beethoven, Weber and Berlioz as composers of the second category but warning against the equation of this with puerile, imitative music. The tactics in both articles are identical:

Composers of the first category set to work with this thought: 'I wish to write a string quartet ... Usually a quartet begins with an Allegro: I might also write a short introduction. But no! Let the Allegro start straight away with energy and freshness! (*GM* I/19: 11 May 1834, 151)[1]

---

[1] 'Les compositeurs qui se trouvent dans le premier cas se mettent au travail avec cette pensée: '*Je veux écrire un quatuor pour des instrumens à cordes* ... *C'est ordinairement par un* allegro *que commence tout quatuor: je pourrai bien faire aussi une courte introduction. Mais non, que l'*allegro *prenne tout de suite son essor avec énergie et fraîcheur!*' (*GM* I/19: 11 May 1834, 151).

This compares with:

In compositions of pure music, the composer limits himself to saying: I am going to write a symphony which begins with a brilliant allegro; after that there will be a gracious adagio, then a scherzo in the modern style, and to finish, a finale alla polacca. (unsigned, *GM* I/52: 28 Dec. 1834, 425)[2]

Although the Berlioz review is signed 'P.R.', a note to the index for 1834 indicates that the initials for Paulin Richard were appended in error.

---

[2] 'Dans les compositions purement musicales, le compositeur se borne à se dire: Je vais faire une symphonie qui commencera par un allégro [sic] brillant; viendra ensuite un adagio gracioso, puis un scherzo comme on fait aujourd'hui et pour terminer, un finale alla polacca' (unsigned, *GM* I/52: 28 Dec. 1834, 425).

Bibliography

ARCHIVAL AND MANUSCRIPT SOURCES

ARCHIVES NATIONALES, PARIS (C.A.R.A.N.)

F^{18} 89 (B), F^{18} 316–423. Imprimerie, librairie, presse, censure.
BB^{17} A 86, BB^{17} A 90, BB^{17} A 92, BB^{17} A 99–100, BB^{17} A 103–4, BB^{17} A 109, BB^{17} A 115, BB^{17} A 118, BB^{17} A 145, BB^{17} A 148. Ministère de la Justice. Cabinet particulier du ministre (1815–48).
BB^{18} 1396 Ministère de la Justice. Correspondance générale de la Division criminelle.

CENTRE DES ARCHIVES CONTEMPORAINES, FONTAINEBLEAU

MC XXIII, D.C. 173 Dossier Dufour; MC XLII, D.C. 21 Dossier Dufour.

BIBLIOTHÈQUE NATIONALE, PARIS

Département de musique: Lettres autographes.
Département des manuscrits: n. a. fr. 22870–1 (Papiers Fétis).

NINETEENTH-CENTURY NEWSPAPERS AND JOURNALS

L'Abeille musicale
L'Art musical
La Correspondance des amateurs musiciens
La Décade philosophique
La France musicale
Journal de musique (1770–77)
Journal de musique (1876–82)
Journal des débats (Journal de l'Empire)
Le Ménestrel
Le Monde musical
Les Quatre saisons du Parnasse
Revue de Paris
Revue musicale
(Revue et) Gazette musicale de Paris

Sentiment d'un harmonophile
Les Tablettes de Polymnie

SECONDARY SOURCES

Aitken, Shelagh: 'Music and the Popular Press: Music criticism in Paris during the First Empire' (unpublished PhD dissertation, Northwestern University, 1987).

Albert, Pierre; Feyel, Gilles; Picard, François: *Documents sur l'histoire de la presse nationale aux XIXe et XXe siècles* (Paris, 1977).

Allen, James Smith: *Popular French Romanticism. Authors, Readers and Books in the 19th Century* (New York, 1981).

Allen, Warren D.: *Philosophies of Music History* (1939). 2nd edn (New York, 1962).

Arlin, Mary I.: 'Fétis' Contribution to Practical and Historical Music Theory', *Revue belge de musicologie* XXVI–XXVII (1972–3), 106–15.

Bailbé, Joseph Marc: *Le Roman et la musique en France sous la monarchie de juillet* (Paris, 1969).

Balzac, Honoré de: *Le Chef d'œuvre inconnu, Gambara, Massimilla Doni*, ed. Marc Eigeldinger and Max Milner (Paris, 1981).

Barricelli, Jean-Pierre: 'Autour de Gambara I: Balzac et Meyerbeer', *Année balzacienne* (1967), 157–63.

Barzun, Jacques: *Berlioz and the Romantic Century*. 2 vols. (London, 1951).

'The Meaning of Meaning in Music: Berlioz Once More', *Musical Quarterly* LXVI/1 (Jan. 1980), 1–20.

Beardsley, Monroe C.: *Aesthetics from Classical Greece to the Present. A Short History* (Alabama, 1966).

Becker, Heinz and Gudrun: *Giacomo Meyerbeer: Briefwechsel und Tagebücher*. 4 vols. (Berlin, 1960–).

Giacomo Meyerbeer. A Life in Letters, trans. Mark Violette (Bromley, 1989).

Becq, Annie: *Genèse de l'esthétique moderne: de la raison classique à l'imagination créatrice, 1680 à 1814*. 2 vols. (Pisa, 1984).

Bellas, Jacqueline: 'La Tumultueuse amitié de Franz Liszt et de Maurice Schlesinger', *Littératures* XII (Nov. 1965), Annales publiés trimestriellement par la Faculté des lettres et des sciences humaines de Toulouse. Nouvelle série, t. I, fasc. III, 7–20.

Berlioz, Hector: *Grand traité d'instrumentation et d'orchestration modernes* (Paris, 1843).

Voyage musical en Allemagne et en Italie (Paris, 1844).

Les Soirées de l'orchestre (Paris, 1852).

Les Grotesques de la musique (Paris, 1859).

A travers chants (Paris, 1862).

Correspondance générale, ed. Pierre Citron. 5 vols. (Paris, 1972–).

The Art of Music and Other Essays (A travers chants), trans. and ed. Elizabeth Csicsery-Rónay (Bloomington and Indianapolis, 1994).

Bernard, Elisabeth: 'Jules Pasdeloup et les concerts populaires', *Revue de musicologie* LVII (1971), 150–78.

Bloom, Peter: 'François-Joseph Fétis and the *Revue musicale* (1827–1835)' (unpublished PhD dissertation, University of Pennsylvania, 1972).

'Critical reaction to Beethoven in France: F. J. Fétis', *Revue belge de musicologie* XXVI–XXVII (1972–3), 67–83.

'Friends and Admirers: Meyerbeer and Fétis', *Revue belge de musicologie*, XXXII–XXXIII (1978–9), 174–87.

'Berlioz and the Critic: La Damnation de Fétis', *Studies in Musicology in Honor of Otto E. Albrecht*, ed. J. W. Hill (Kassel etc., 1980), 240–65.

'The Public for Orchestral Music in the Nineteenth Century', *The Orchestra: Origins and Transformations*, ed. J. Peyser (New York, 1986), 251–81.

'A Review of Fétis's *Revue musicale*', *Music in Paris in the Eighteen-Thirties*, ed. Bloom (Stuyvesant, 1987).

(ed.): *Berlioz Studies* (Cambridge, 1992).

Boime, Albert: *Thomas Couture and the Eclectic Vision* (New Haven and London, 1980).

Bonnaure, Jacques: 'Monsieur Scribe ou le romantisme du juste milieu', *L'Avant scène: opéra* 100 (Jul. 1987), 88–93.

Bouverot, Danielle: 'L'"expression" en peinture et en musique (1830–1850)', *Romantisme* no. 71 (1991), 69–84.

Boyd, Malcolm (ed.): *Music and the French Revolution* (Cambridge, 1992).

Boyé: *L'Expression musicale mise au rang des chimères* (Paris and Amsterdam, 1779).

Brody, Elaine: *Paris. The Musical Kaleidoscope, 1870–1925* (London, 1987).

Brzoska, Matthias: '"Mahomet" et "Robert-le-Diable": l'esthétique musicale dans "Gambara"', *Année balzacienne* (1983), 51–78.

Bujić, Bojan (ed.): *Music in European Thought 1851–1912* (Cambridge, 1988).

Burnham, Scott: 'Criticism, Faith and the *Idee*: A. B. Marx's Early Reception of Beethoven', *Nineteenth-Century Music* XIII/3 (Spring 1990), 183–92.

Cabanis, A.: *La Presse sous le Consulat et l'Empire (1799–1814)* (Paris, 1975).

Cannone, Belinda: *Philosophies de la musique (1752–1789)* (Paris, 1990).

La Réception des opéras de Mozart dans la presse parisienne (1793–1829) (Paris, 1991).

Carlez, Jules: *Framery. Littérateur-Musicien (1745–1810)* (Caen, 1893).

Castex, P.-G.: *Le Conte fantastique en France de Nodier à Maupassant* (Paris, 1951).

Chabanon, Michel Paul Gui de: *De la musique considérée en elle-même et dans ses rapports avec la parole, les langues, la poésie et le théâtre* (Paris, 1785).

Champfleury, Jules: *Grandes figures d'hier et d'aujourd'hui* (Paris, 1861).

'Richard Wagner and After the Battle', trans. Palomba Paves-Yashinsky, *Nineteenth-Century Music* XIII/1 (Summer 1989), 18–27.

Charlton, D. G.: *Positivist Thought in France during the Second Empire, 1852–1870* (Oxford, 1959).

(ed.): *France: A Companion to French studies* (London, 1972).

(ed.): *The French Romantics* (Cambridge, 1984).

Charlton, David: *Grétry and the Growth of Opéra-Comique* (Cambridge, 1986).

'Cherubini: A Critical Anthology, 1788–1801', *Research Chronicle*, 26 (1993), 95–127.

Citron, Pierre: 'Autour de Gambara II. "Gambara", Struntz et Beethoven', *Année balzacienne* (1967), 165–70.

Claudon, F.: 'Balzac et Beethoven', *Année balzacienne* (1971), 101–7.

Cohen, H. Robert: 'Berlioz on the Opéra (1829–1849): A study in Music Criticism' (unpublished PhD dissertation, New York University, 1973). Summarised as: 'H. Berlioz critique musical. Ses écrits sur l'Opéra de Paris, de 1829 à 1849', *Revue de musicologie* (1977), 17–34.

'The 19th-Century French Press and the Music Historian: Archival Sources and Bibliographical Resources', *Nineteenth-Century Music* VII/2 (Fall 1983), 136–42.

Comte, Auguste: *Cours de philosophie positive.* 6 vols. (Paris, 1830–42).

Cooper, Jeffrey: *The Rise of Instrumental Music and Concert Series in Paris, 1828–71* (Ann Arbor, 1983).

Coudroy, Marie-Hélène: *La Critique parisienne des 'grands opéras' de Meyerbeer. Robert le Diable – Les Huguenots – Le Prophète – L'Africaine* (Saarbrücken, 1988).

Cousin, Victor: *Fragmens philosophiques* (Paris, 1826).

Cours de philosophie. Introduction à la philosophie (Paris, 1828)

Cours de l'histoire de la philosophie. Cours de 1829. Histoire de la philosophie du XVIIIᵉ siècle. 2 vols. (Paris, 1829).

Cours de l'histoire de la philosophie moderne. Nouvelle édition, revue et corrigée. 5 vols. (Paris, 1846).

Du vrai, du beau et du bien (Paris, 1853)

Cowart, Georgia (ed.): *French Musical Thought 1600–1800* (Ann Arbor, 1989).

Cramer, Ch. Fr.: *Anecdotes sur Mozart. Traduites de l'allemand* (Paris, 1801).

Crosten, William L.: *French Grand Opera. An Art and a Business* (New York, 1948).

Curtiss, Mina: 'Fromental Halévy', *Musical Quarterly* XXXIX (1953), 196–214.

Dahlhaus, Carl: *Realism in Nineteenth-Century Music*, trans. Mary Whittall (Cambridge, 1985).

The Idea of Absolute Music, trans. Roger Lustig (London, 1989).

Dandelot, Arthur: *La Société des concerts du Conservatoire* (Paris, 1898).

Deldevez, E.-M.-E.: *Curiosités musicales. Notes, analyses. Interpretation de certaines particuliarités contenues dans les œuvres des grands maîtres* (Paris, 1873).

La Société des concerts 1860 à 1885 (Conservatoire National de Musique) (Paris, 1887).

Mes mémoires (Paris, 1890).

Desgranges, Ch.-M.: *Le Romantisme et la critique. La Presse littéraire sous la Restauration, 1815–1830.* 2nd edn (Paris, 1907).

Devriès, Anik: 'Un éditeur de musique "à la tête ardente". Maurice Schlesinger', *Fontes Artis Musicae* 27/3–4 (Jul. – Dec. 1980), 125–36.

'La maison Brandus. Heurs et malheurs d'un commerce d'éditions musicales au XIXe siècle', *Revue de musicologie* LXX/1 (1984), 51–82.

Devriès, Anik; Lesure, François: *Dictionnaire des éditeurs de musique français.* 2 vols. (Geneva, 1979–88).

Diaz, José-Luis: 'L'*Artiste* romantique en perspective', *Romantisme* no. 54 (1986), 5–23.

Dictionnaire de biographie française (Paris, 1933–).

Didier, Béatrice: 'Hector Berlioz et l'art de la nouvelle', *Romantisme* no. 12 (1976), 19–26.

Eckart-Bäcker, Ursula: *Frankreichs Musik zwischen Romantik und Moderne. Die Zeit im Spiegel der Kritik* (Regensburg, 1965).

Edwards, Paul (ed.): *The Encyclopedia of Philosophy* (New York and London, 1967).

Ellis, Katharine: 'Rewriting *Don Giovanni*, or "The Thieving Magpies"', *Journal of the Royal Musical Association* 119/2 (1994), 212–50.

Elwart, Antoine: *Histoire de la Société des concerts du Conservatoire impérial de musique, avec dessins, musique, plans, portraits, notices biographiques, etc.* (Paris, 1860).

Histoire des concerts populaires de musique classique. 2nd edn (Paris, 1864).

Fauquet, Joël-Marie: *Les Sociétés de musique de chambre à Paris de la restauration à 1870* (Paris, 1986).

'Berlioz's version of Gluck's *Orphée*', *Berlioz Studies*, ed. Peter Bloom (Cambridge, 1992), 198–253.

Fellinger, Imogen: 'Periodicals', *New Grove Dictionary of Music and Musicians* XIV (London, 1980), 4407–535.

Fétis, François-Joseph: *La Musique mise à la portée de tout le monde* (1830). 3rd edn (Paris, 1847).

Biographie universelle des musiciens et bibliographie générale de la musique. 2nd edn. (Paris, 1860–5), Supplément et complément, ed. Arthur Pougin. 2 vols. (Paris, 1878–80).

Fétis, François-Joseph; Moscheles, Ignaz: *Méthode des méthodes de piano* (Paris, [1840]).

Fizaine, J.-C.: 'Génie et folie dans *Louis Lambert, Gambara* et *Massimilla Doni*', *Revue des sciences humaines* XLIV/3 (1979), 61–75.

Flaubert, Gustave: *L'Education sentimentale*, ed. Peter Wetherill (Paris, 1984).

Friedland, Bea: *Louise Farrenc (1804–1875) composer, performer, scholar* (Ann Arbor, 1980).

Fryklund, Daniel: *Contribution à la connaissance de la correspondance de Fétis* (Stockholm, 1930).

Fubini, Enrico: *The History of Musical Aesthetics*, trans. Michael Hatwell (London, 1991).

Fulcher, Jane: 'Musical Aesthetics and Social Philosophy in France 1848–1870' (PhD dissertation, Columbia University, 1976).

'Le Socialisme utopique et la critique musicale en France sous le second Empire', *Revue internationale de musique française* V/14 (Jun. 1984), 63–8.

The Nation's Image: French Grand Opera as Politics and Politicized Art (Cambridge, 1987).

Gail, Jean-François: Réflexions sur le goût musical en France (Paris, 1832).

Garceau, Hélène: 'Notes sur la presse musicale religieuse en France de 1827 à 1861', *Periodica Musica* (Spring 1984), 6–13.

Gasperini, A. de: *La Nouvelle Allemagne musicale: Richard Wagner* (Paris, 1865).

Gíslason, Donald G.: 'Castil-Blaze, *De l'opéra en France* and the Feuilletons of the *Journal des Débats* (1820–1832)', (unpublished PhD dissertation, University of British Columbia, 1992).

Goldberg, Louise: '*Les Troyens* of Hector Berlioz; a Century of Productions and Critical Reviews' (unpublished PhD dissertation, Eastman School of Music, University of Rochester, 1973).

Goubault, Christian: *La Critique musicale dans la presse française de 1870 à 1914* (Geneva, 1984).
'Frédéric Chopin et la critique musicale française', *Sur les traces de Chopin*, ed. Danièle Pistone (Paris, 1984), 149–68.
Gourret, Jean: *Encyclopédie des cantatrices de l'Opéra de Paris* (Paris, 1981).
Dictionnaire des chanteurs de l'Opéra de Paris (Paris, 1982).
Grate, Pontus: 'Art, idéologie et politique dans la critique d'art', *Romantisme* no. 71 (1991), 31–8.
Grégoir, Edouard G. J.: *Recherches historiques concernant les journaux de musique depuis les temps les plus reculés à nos jours* (Antwerp, 1872).
Grempler, Ingeborg: 'Das Musikschrifttum von Hector Berlioz' (unpublished PhD dissertation, Göttingen, 1950).
Grey, Thomas S.: 'Wagner, the Overture, and the Aesthetics of Musical Form', *Nineteenth-Century Music* XII/1 (Summer 1988), 3–22.
'Metaphorical Modes in Nineteenth-Century Music Criticism: Image, Narrative, and Idea', *Music and Text: Critical Inquiries*, ed. Steven Paul Scher (Cambridge, 1992), 93–117.
Gubernatis, A. de: *Dictionnaire des écrivains du jour* (Paris, 1888).
Guichard, Léon: 'Autour des contes d'Hoffmann', *Revue de littérature comparée* XXVII (1953), 136–47.
La Musique et les lettres au temps du romantisme (Paris, 1955).
'Liszt et la littérature française', *Revue de musicologie* LVI (1970/71), 3–34.
Gut, Serge: *Franz Liszt. Les Eléments du langage musical* (Paris, 1975).
Haas, James: 'Berlioz and the "First Opera"', *Nineteenth-Century Music* III/1 (Jul. 1979), 32–41.
Hagan, Dorothy Veinus: 'French Musical Criticism between the Revolutions (1830–48)' (unpublished PhD dissertation, University of Illinois, 1965).
Félicien David, 1810–1876: A Composer and a Cause (Syracuse, 1985).
Haine, Malou: 'Concerts historiques dans la seconde moitié du 19e siècle', *Musique et société. Hommages à Robert Wangermée*, ed. Henri Vanhulst and Malou Haine (Brussels, 1988), 121–42.
Hallays, André: 'Hector Berlioz, critique musical', introductory essay to Berlioz, *Les musiciens et la musique* (Paris, [1903]).
Hallé, Charles and Marie: *Life and Letters of Charles Hallé. Being an Autobiography (1819–1860) with Correspondence and Diaries* (London, 1896).
Hanslick, Eduard: *Vom Musikalisch-Schönen. Ein Beitrag zur Revision der Aesthetik der Tonkunst* (Leipzig, 1854).
On the Musically Beautiful, trans. Geoffrey Payzant (Indianapolis, 1986).
Haraszti, Emile: 'Franz Liszt – Author Despite Himself. The History of a Mystification', *Musical Quarterly* (Oct. 1947), 490–516.
Hatin, Louis: *Histoire politique et littéraire de la presse en France, avec un introduction sur les origines du journal, et la bibliographie générale des journaux depuis leur origine.* 8 vols. (Paris, 1859–61).
Bibliographie historique et critique de la presse périodique française (Paris, 1866).
Hegel, G. W. F.: *Vorlesungen über die Ästhetik*, ed. Rüdiger Bubner (Stuttgart, 1971).

Aesthetics. Lectures on Fine Art, trans. T. M. Knox (Oxford, 1975).

Heller, Stephen: *Lettres d'un musicien romantique à Paris, 1830 – 1880*, ed. J.-J. Eigeldinger (Paris, 1981).

Hoffmann, E. T. A.: *Œuvres complètes de E. T. A. Hoffmann, trad. M. Théodore Toussenel et l'auteur des romans de Veit-Wéber.* 12 vols. (Paris, 1830).

Œuvres complètes. 19 vols., trans. Loève-Veimars (Paris, 1830–2).

Schriften zur Musik (Munich, 1963).

E. T. A. Hoffmann's Musical Writings: Kreisleriana, The Poet and the Composer, *Music Criticism*, trans. Martyn Clarke, ed. David Charlton (Cambridge, 1989).

Huebner, Steven: *The Operas of Charles Gounod* (Oxford, 1990).

Huré, Pierre-Antoine; Knepper, Claude: *Liszt en son temps. Documents choisis, présentés et annotés précédés de Dionysos ou le Crucifié?* (Paris, 1987).

Johnson, James H.: 'Beethoven and the Birth of Romantic Musical Experience in France', *Nineteenth-Century Music* XV/1 (Summer 1991), 23–35.

Josephson, Nors S: 'F.-J. Fétis and Richard Wagner', *Revue belge de musicologie* XXVI–XXVII (1972–3), 84–9.

Jullien, Adolphe: *Mozart et Richard Wagner à l'égard des français* (Brussels, 1881).

Musique, mélanges d'histoire et de critique musicale et dramatique. 2nd edn (Paris, [1900]).

Kemp, Ian: '*Romeo and Juliet* and *Roméo et Juliette*', *Berlioz Studies*, ed. Peter Bloom (Cambridge, 1992), 37–79.

Kerman, Joseph: 'A Few Canonic Variations', *Critical Inquiry* 10 (September 1983), 107–25.

Kitchin, Joanne, *Un journal philosophique: 'La Décade' (1794–1807)* (Paris, 1965).

Klein, John. W.: 'Jacques Fromental Halévy (1799–1862)', *Music Review* XXIII (1962), 13–19.

Kraus, Beate Angelika: 'Beethoven and the Revolution: The View of the French Musical Press', *Music and the French Revolution*, ed. Malcolm Boyd (Cambridge, 1992), 302–14.

Kropfinger, Klaus: *Wagner and Beethoven. Richard Wagner's Reception of Beethoven*, trans. Peter Palmer (Cambridge, 1991).

Large, David; Weber, William: *Wagnerism in European Culture and Politics* (Ithaca, 1984).

Lavignac, Albert: *Le Voyage artistique à Bayreuth.* 1897. 5th edn (Paris, 1903).

Lavignac, A.; De la Laurencie, L.: *L'Encyclopédie de la musique et dictionnaire du Conservatoire.* 11 vols. (Paris, 1920–31).

L'Écuyer-Lacroix, Sylvia: 'Joseph d'Ortigue et la linguistique de la musique', *Etudes littéraires* XV/1 (Apr. 1982), 11–31.

Le Huray, Peter; Day, James: *Music and Aesthetics in the Eighteenth and Early-Nineteenth Centuries* (Cambridge, 1981).

Leroy, Maxime: *Les Premiers amis français de Wagner* (Paris, 1925).

Leduc-Adine, Jean-Pierre: 'Des règles d'un genre: la critique d'art', *Romantisme* no. 71 (1991), 93–100.

Lippman, Edward: *A History of Western Musical Aesthetics* (Lincoln and London, 1992).

Locke, Ralph P.: *Music, Musicians and the Saint-Simonians* (Chicago, 1986).
Loesser, Arthur: *Men, Women and Pianos. A Social History* (London, 1955).
Lough, John: *Writer and Public in France. From the Middle Ages to the Present Day* (Oxford, 1978).
Mahaim, Ivan: *Beethoven. Naissance et renaissance des derniers quatuors* (Paris, 1964).
Maniates, Maria Rika: '"Sonate que me veux-tu?" The Enigma of French Musical Aesthetics in the Eighteenth Century', *Current Musicology* 9 (1969), 117–40.
Marix-Spire, Thérèse: *Les Romantiques et la musique. Le cas George Sand 1804–1838* (Paris, 1954).
Marmontel, A.: *Virtuoses contemporains* (Paris, 1882).
Marx, A. B.: *Ludwig van Beethoven. Leben und Schaffen* (Berlin, 1859).
Merrick, Paul: *Revolution and Religion in the Music of Liszt* (Cambridge, 1987).
Mila, Massino: 'Fétis e Verdi, ovvero gli infortuni della critica', *Atti del IIIo congresso internazionale di studi Verdiani, Milano, Piccola Scala, 1972* (Parma, 1974), 12–17.
Mongrédien, Jean: 'La théorie de l'imitation en musique au début du romantisme', *Romantisme* no. 8 (1974), 86–91.
   'Les Mystères d'Isis (1801) and Reflections on Mozart from the Parisian Press at the Beginning of the Nineteenth Century', *Music in the Classic Period. Essays in Honor of Barry S. Brook*, ed. Allan W. Atlas (New York, 1985), 195–211.
   La Musique en France des Lumières au Romantisme (1789–1830) (Paris, 1986).
Morrow, Mary Sue: 'Of Unity and Passion: The Aesthetics of Concert Criticism in Early Nineteenth-Century Vienna', *Nineteenth-Century Music* XIII/3 (Spring 1990), 193–206.
Murphy, Kerry: 'Attribution of some unsigned articles of Berlioz in the *Revue et Gazette musicale* (1834–1837)', *Musicology Australia* VIII (1985), 39–49.
   Hector Berlioz and the Development of French Music Criticism (Ann Arbor, 1988).
   'Joseph Mainzer's "Sacred and Beautiful Mission": an Aspect of Parisian Musical Life of the 1830s', *Music & Letters* 75/1 (Feb. 1994), 33–46.
Nettement, Alfred: *Histoire politique, anecdotique et littéraire du* Journal des débats. 2 vols. (Paris, 1838).
Nichols, Robert: 'Fétis' Theories of *Tonalité* and the Aesthetics of Music', *Revue belge de musicologie* XXVI–XXVII (1972–3), 116–29.
Ollivier, Daniel: *Correspondance de Liszt et de la Comtesse d'Agoult 1833–1840*. 2 vols. (Paris, 1933–4).
Oulibicheff, Alexander: *Beethoven, ses critiques, ses glossateurs* (Leipzig, 1857).
Parent-Lardeur, Françoise: *Lire à Paris au temps de Balzac. Les cabinets de lecture à Paris. 1815–1830.* (Paris, 1981).
Pendle, Karin: *Eugène Scribe and French Opera of the Nineteenth Century* (Ann Arbor, 1979).
Perrier, Henri: *Les Rendez-vous wagnériens* (Lausanne, 1981).
Peyser, Joan (ed.): *The Orchestra: Origins and Transformations* (New York, 1986).
Pickering, Mary: 'Auguste Comte and the Saint-Simonians', *French Historical Studies* 18/1 (Spring 1993), 211–36.

Pisarenko, Olgierd: 'Chopin and his Contemporaries. Paris 1832–1860', *Studies in Chopin*, ed. D. Zebrowski (Warsaw, 1973), 30–48.

Pistone, Danièle: *La Symphonie dans l'Europe du XIXe siècle* (Paris, 1977).

La Musique en France de la Révolution à 1900 (Paris, 1979).

'Dossier: Wagner à Paris (1839–1900)', *Revue internationale de musique française* VI/17 (Feb. 1980), 7–84.

'Reflexions sur l'évolution du public musical parisien', *Romantisme* no. 38 (1982), 19–23.

Heugel et ses musiciens. Lettres à un éditeur parisien (Paris, 1984).

Pistone, Danièle; Gut, Serge: *La Musique de chambre en France de 1870 à 1918* (Paris, 1978).

Plantinga, Leon B.: *Schumann as Critic* (New Haven, 1967).

Pougin, Arthur: 'Notes sur la presse musicale en France', *L'Encyclopédie de la Musique et Dictionnaire du Conservatoire*, ed. Lavignac and De la Laurencie (Paris, 1920–31) pt II vol. 6, 3841–3859.

Prod'homme, J.-G.: 'Essai de bibliographie des périodiques musicaux de langue française', *Bulletin de la Société française de musicologie* II (1918), 76–90.

Randier-Glenisson, Anne: 'Maurice Schlesinger, éditeur de musique et fondateur de la "Gazette musicale de Paris", 1834–1846', *Fontes artis musicae* 38/1 (Jan.–Mar. 1991), 37–48.

Reeve, Katherine Kolb: 'The Poetics of the Orchestra in the Writings of Hector Berlioz' (unpublished PhD dissertation, Yale University, 1978).

'Hector Berlioz', *European Writers* VI (New York, 1985), 771–812.

'Rhetoric and Reason in French Music Criticism of the 1830s', *Music in Paris in the Eighteen-Thirties*, ed. P. Bloom (New York, 1987), 537–51.

Regard, Maurice: 'Balzac est-il l'auteur de "Gambara"?', *Revue d'histoire littéraire de la France* LIII (1953), 496–507.

Répertoire international de la presse musicale. A Retrospective Index Series (Ann Arbor, 1988–).

Reynaud, L.: *L'Influence allemande en France au XVIIe et au XIXe siècle* (Paris, 1922).

Ribeyre, F.; Brisson, J.: *Les Grands journaux de France* (Paris, 1863).

Rosen, David; Porter, Andrew (eds.): *Verdi's Macbeth. A Sourcebook* (Cambridge, 1984).

Roth, Nancy Ann: ' "L'Artiste" and "L'Art pour l'Art": The New Cultural Journalism in the July Monarchy', *Art Journal* 48/1 (Spring 1989), 35–9.

Rousseau, J.-J.: *Lettre sur la musique française* (Paris, 1753).

Les Rêveries du promeneur solitaire, ed. Henri Roddier (Paris, 1960).

Rushton, Julian: *Berlioz: Roméo et Juliette* (Cambridge, 1994).

Saint-Lambert, Michel de: *Les Principes du clavecin, contenant une explication exacte de tout ce qui concerne la tablature et le clavier* (Paris, 1702).

Schafer, R. Murray: *E.T.A. Hoffmann and Music* (Toronto and Buffalo, 1975).

Schellhous, Rosalie: 'Fétis's *Tonality* as a Metaphysical Principle: Hypothesis for a New Science', *Music Theory Spectrum* XIII/2 (Fall 1991), 219–40.

Schelling, F. W.: *Schellings Werke*, ed. Manfred Schröter. 12 vols. (Munich, 1927–54).

Schenk, H. G.: *The Mind of the European Romantics* (London, 1966).

Scher, Steven Paul (ed.): *Music and Text: Critical Inquiries* (Cambridge, 1992).

Schrade, Leo: *Beethoven in France: The Growth of an Idea* (New Haven and London, 1942).

Schumann, Robert: *The Musical World of Robert Schumann*, ed. Henry Pleasants (London, 1965).

Schwarz, Boris: *French Instrumental Music between the Revolutions (1789–1830)* (New York, 1987).

Servières, Georges: *Richard Wagner jugé en France* (Paris, 1887).

Shulman, Laurie C.: 'Music Criticism of the Paris Opéra in the 1830s' (unpublished PhD dissertation, Cornell, 1985).

Siegel, Linda: 'Wagner and the Romanticism of E. T. A. Hoffmann', *Musical Quarterly* LI/4 (1965), 597–613.

Simms, Bryan Randolph: 'Alexandre Choron (1771–1834) as a Historian and Theorist of Music' (unpublished PhD dissertation, Yale, 1971).

Sonneck, O.: *Beethoven: Impressions by his Contemporaries* (New York, 1967).

Spitzer, Alan B.: *The French Generation of 1820* (Princeton, 1987).

Standley, A. R.: *Auguste Comte 1798–1857* (Boston, 1981).

Teichmann, Elizabeth: *La Fortune d'Hoffmann en France* (Geneva and Paris, 1961).

Texier, Edmond: *Biographie des journalistes. Histoire des journaux* (Paris, 1950).

Thoumin, Jean-Adrien: *Bibliographie rétrospective des périodiques français de littérature musicale 1870–1954* (Paris, 1957).

Timbrell, Charles: *French Pianism. An Historical Perspective* (New York and London, 1992).

Ulibishev, see Oulibicheff.

Vapereau, G: *Dictionnaire des contemporains*, 6th edn, 6 vols. (Paris, 1893).

Vernaelde, Albert: 'La Société des concerts et les Grandes Associations symphoniques', *L'Encyclopédie de la musique et Dictionnaire du Conservatoire*, ed. Lavignac and De la Laurencie (Paris, 1921–33) pt II vol. 6, 3684–714.

Wagner, Richard: *Gesammelte Schriften und Dichtungen* (Leipzig, 1871–83).
  Richard Wagner's Prose Works, trans. W. A. Ellis (London, 1895–9).
  Lettres françaises de Richard Wagner, ed. J. Tiersot (Paris, 1935).
  Wagner Writes from Paris, trans. and ed. R. Jacobs and G. Skelton (London, 1973).
  My Life, trans. Andrew Gray, ed. Mary Whittall (Cambridge, 1983).
  Un musicien étranger à Paris, ed. Renée Cariven-Galharret (Paris, 1989).

Walker, Alan: *Liszt: The Virtuoso Years, 1811–1847* (London, 1983).
  Liszt: The Weimar Years, 1848–1861 (London, 1989).

Wallace, Robin: *Beethoven's Critics. Aesthetic Dilemmas and Resolutions during the Composer's Lifetime* (Cambridge, 1986).

Walsh, Thomas Joseph: *Second Empire Opera: The Théâtre Lyrique, Paris. 1851–1870* (London, 1981).

Wangermée, Robert: *F.-J. Fétis, musicologue et compositeur. Contribution à l'étude du goût musical au XIXe siècle*. Académie Royale de Belgique. Classe des Beaux-arts. Mémoires, t. VI, fasc. 4 (Brussels, 1951).
  'Les Techniques de la virtuosité pianistique selon Fétis' *Revue belge de musicologie* XXVI–XXVII (1972–3), 90–105.

Weber, C. M. von: *Carl Maria von Weber: Writings on Music*, trans. Martin Cooper, ed. John Warrack (Cambridge, 1981).

Weber, William: *Music and the Middle Class. The Social Structure of Concert Life in London, Paris and Vienna, 1830–48* (New York, 1975).

'La Musique Ancienne in the Waning of the Ancien Régime', *Journal of Modern History* LVI/1 (March 1984), 58–88.

'The Rise of the Classical Repertory in Nineteenth-Century Orchestral Concerts', *The Orchestra: Origins and Transformations*, ed. Joan Peyser (New York, 1986), 361–86.

'The Eighteenth-Century Origins of the Musical Canon', *Journal of the Royal Musical Association* 114/1 (1989), 6–17.

Weinberg, B.: *French Realism – The Critical Reaction (1830–1870)* (New York, 1937).

Wild, Nicole: *Dictionnaire des théâtres parisiens au XIXᵉ siècle* (Paris, 1989).

Will, Frederic: *Flumen Historicum. Victor Cousin's Aesthetic and its Sources* (Chapel Hill, 1965).

Williams, Adrian: *Portrait of Liszt by Himself and His Contemporaries* (Oxford, 1990).

Zebrowski, D. (ed.): *Studies in Chopin* (Warsaw, 1973).

Index of musical works cited

References to Fétis are to F.-J. Fétis, unless otherwise indicated. Attributed articles give the name of their presumed author.

Alkan, Charles-Valentin: *Souvenir des concerts du Conservatoire*: 83
Allegri, Gregorio: *Miserere*: 65, 67

Bach, J. S.: Orchestral Suite no. 3 in D major BWV1068: 66
'Air' from Orchestral Suite no. 3 in D major BWV1068 (arr. cello and piano): and Davidov, 72
St Matthew Passion: 6, 70–1, 236
Beethoven Ludwig van: *Christ on the Mount of Olives* Op. 85: Castil-Blaze on, 30, 102; Berlioz on, 111–12
Piano Concerto no. 1 in C major Op. 15: Blanchard on, 113
Piano Concerto no. 3 in C minor Op. 37: 95
Piano Concerto no. 4 in G major Op. 58: 96, 168
Piano Concerto no. 5 in E-flat major Op. 73 'Emperor': 164
Violin Concerto in D major Op. 61: compared with Mendelssohn, 140
Fidelio: 119, 121–2
String Quartet in F minor Op. 95: Botte on, 117
String Quartet in E-flat major Op. 127: Blanchard on, 115; Damcke on, 116; Bannelier on, 125
String Quartet in B-flat major Op. 130: Blanchard on, 114–16; Botte on, 117
String Quartet in C-sharp minor Op. 131: 105n; Fétis on, 112; Blanchard on, 115–16
String Quartet in A minor Op. 132: Blanchard on, 113; Botte on, 117
String Quartet in F major Op. 135: Blanchard on, 113–14
Septet in E-flat Op. 20: 92

Violin Sonata in F major Op. 24 'Spring': Blanchard on, 113
Violin Sonatas Op. 30: 20; *CAM* on Op. 30/1, 21
Violin Sonata in A minor Op. 47 'Kreutzer': 98; Botte on, 117
Symphony no. 1 in C major Op. 21: Berlioz on, 86, 106–7; neglect of, 105
Symphony no. 2 in D major Op. 36: Berlioz on, 106–7
Symphony no. 3 in E-flat major Op. 55 'Eroica': Castil-Blaze on, 31–2; Berlioz on, 109–10; Heller on, 126
Symphony no. 4 in B-flat major Op. 60: 40; Berlioz on, 107; Bannelier on, 124
Symphony no. 5 in C minor Op. 67: 43n; Berlioz on, 84, 107–8, 110–11; Stoepel on, 102; Bannelier on interpretation, 123
Symphony no. 6 in F major Op. 68 'Pastoral': 43; Berlioz on 109–10, 176; Bannelier on interpretation, 123
Symphony no. 7 in A major Op. 92; Berlioz on, 18, 109; compared with Schubert, 134
Symphony no. 8 in F major Op. 93: 162; Berlioz on, 107–8
Symphony no. 9 in D minor Op. 125 'Choral': Berlioz on, 84, 108, 110–12; Marx on, 104; public reception, 105; Fétis on, 112; later reception, 119–21; Bannelier on Wagner's revisions, 122, 124–5; Bannelier on interpretation, 123
Piano Trio in B-flat major Op. 97 'Archduke': 105n
De Bériot, Charles-Auguste: Violin Concerto no. 7 Op. 76: 166
Berlioz, Louis-Hector: *Benvenuto Cellini*: failure played down, 221
Béatrice et Bénédit: 221, 226, 232

285

UNIDENTIFIED WORKS

General index

References to Fétis are to F.-J. Fétis, unless otherwise indicated. Attributed articles are indexed under the name of their presumed author. Main entries are in bold.

'A.M.': on Méhul, 22, 26; on Mozart, 24–5
L'Abeille musicale: 45
Abendzeitung (Dresden): 130, 193
Abraham, Emile: 203–4
Adam, Adolphe: as reorchestrator of Grétry, 69–70
Adam de la Halle: 62
Administration de l'Enregistrement et des Domaines, 1n
D'Agoult, Marie: 145n, 149–51
Aitken, Shelagh: 9n 19n
Alard, Delphin: 95n, 116, 132
Alard/Franchomme Quartet: 116
Alkan, Charles-Valentin: 83, 145, 157
Allegri, Gregorio: 65, 67
Allgemeine musikalische Zeitung (Leipzig): 107n, 122n
'archéologie musicale': 57, 62; used sarcastically, 66
Arlin, Mary I.: 37
Armingaud/Jacquard Quartet: 116
L'Art musical: 235
artwork (integrity of): 240; *Don Juan*, 19–20, 128; *Figaro*, 23–4; Haydn symphony, 26; and operatic adaptations, 67, 69–70, 128–9; in Schumann, 71, 170; and performer's licence, 96–7; and editorial practice, 124–5
Atlas, Allan W.: 11n
Auber, Daniel: 143–4, 202, 206
Aulagnier, Antonin: 70
autonomous music: 4; Cambini on, 15–16; 'P.P.' on, 17–18; Hoffmann on, 42–3, 229; Cousin on, 43; as one-dimensional, 221; and Berlioz, 228–9

Bach, C. P. E.: 61
Bach, J. S.: 34, 66, 94–5, 138–9, 202, 236; performance practice, 70–3, 98

Bach, W. F.: 61
Baillot, Pierre: 89
Balzac, Honoré de: 49; 'Gambara' 51, 211, 241–2
Bannelier, Charles: 60, 64, 78, 116, 130, 156, 160, 205, 238; on integrity of composer's thought, 67; on Baroque choral revival, 70–1; on performance practice, 72–3, 77, 240; on editing, 74; on Haydn reception, 92; on Mozart reception, 93; on Beethoven, 101, 120, 122–6; on Schumann, 122, 167, 169–70; on Deldevez, 122–3; as formalist on Liszt, 153–4, 176, 206n, 239; as formalist on Heller, 157, 175; on Chopin, 158–9; on conservative symphonic writing, 161; on contemporary concertos, 166; on Brahms, 171–2; as formalist on Saint-Saëns, 174–7, 180–1; and Hanslick, 175; on materialism, 175–6, 178; on D'Indy, 177; on Cui, 177–8; as formalist on Rimsky-Korsakov, 178; as formalist on Tchaikovsky, 178–9; on French autonomous works, 180–3; on Lalo, 181; on Fauré, 181–2; on Gounod, 200–2; on Bizet, 202; on Offenbach, 205, 234, 240; on Wagner, 211–14; on Massenet, 217; on Verdi, 217; on Berlioz, 222, 226, 232–3
Barbereau, Auguste: 59, 63n
Barricelli, Jean-Pierre: 51n
Barzun, Jacques: 229n
Batta, Alexandre: 24n, 105n, 151
Baudelaire, Charles: 206, 213n
Bayreuth: 179, 213–15
Beaulieu, Marie-Désiré: 67
beauty, historical: 64–5, 69–70, 240
beauty, ideal: Fétis and, 43–4, 207–8
Becker, Gudrun: 187n